The Pilgrimage of Philosophy

Other Books of Interest from St. Augustine's Press

Gerard V. Bradley, *Unquiet Americans*

Christopher Kaczor (editor), *O Rare Ralph McInerny:*
Stories and Reflection on a Legendary Notre Dame Professor

Christopher Kaczor, *The Gospel of Happiness:*
How Secular Psychology Points to the Wisdom of Christian Practice

James V. Schall, *At a Breezy Time of Day:*
Selected Schall Interviews on Just about Everything

James V. Schall, *The Praise of 'Sons of Bitches':*
On the Worship of God by Fallen Men

James V. Schall, *The Regensburg Lecture*

Gary M. Bouchard, *Southwell's Sphere:*
The Influence of England's Secret Poet

Charles R. Embry and Glenn Hughes (editors), *Timelessness of Proust:*
Reflections on In Search of Lost Time

Frederic Raphael and Joseph Epstein, *Where Were We?*

Étienne Gilson, *Theology and the Cartesian Doctrine of Freedom*

Josef Kleutgen, S.J., *Pre-Modern Philosophy Defended*

Charles Cardinal Journet, *The Mass:*
The Presence of the Sacrifice of the Cross

Edward Feser, *The Last Superstition: A Refutation of the New Atheism*

Ernest A. Fortin, A.A., *Christianity and Philosophical Culture in the Fifth*
Century: The Controversy about the Human Soul in the West

Peter Kreeft, *Ecumenical Jihad*

Peter Kreeft, *Socrates' Children: The 100 Greatest Philosophers*

Josef Pieper, *The Christian Idea of Man*

Josef Pieper and Heinz Raskop, *What Catholics Believe*

Karl Rahner, *Encounters with Silence*

The Pilgrimage of Philosophy

A Festschrift for Charles E. Butterworth

Edited by
René M. Paddags
Waseem El-Rayes
Gregory A. McBrayer

St. Augustine's Press
South Bend, Indiana

Manufactured in the United States of America.

1 2 3 4 5 6   25 24 23 22 21 20 19

Library of Congress Control Number: 2019950014

∞ The paper used in this publication meets the minimum requirements of the American National Standard for Information Sciences - Permanence of Paper for Printed Materials, ANSI Z39.48-1984.

St. Augustine's Press
www.staugustine.net

Contents

Introduction

Life

Charles E. Butterworth was born and raised in Detroit, Michigan. He attended Samuel C. Mumford High School, graduating with the school's first class of seniors in 1955. Butterworth caddied at the Detroit Golf Club during his high-school years and competed successfully for a scholarship from the Evans Scholars Foundation. Named for the renowned amateur golfer, Charles "Chick" Evans, the scholarship covered room and tuition, enabling Butterworth to pursue undergraduate studies in the Honors College at Michigan State University. To this day, Butterworth is quick to acknowledge his gratitude for the scholarship that started his academic career. At Michigan State, Butterworth studied sociology with A. O. Haller and John Useem and political philosophy with Robert Horwitz; he also benefitted greatly from the guidance and prodding of Stanley J. Idzerda, founder and director of the Honors College at MSU. He took a leave of absence from MSU for the Spring and Fall quarters of 1958 to serve as a guide representing the State of Michigan at the 1958 Bruxelles World's Fair. After graduating Magna cum Laude from MSU in 1959, he received a Fulbright scholarship to study at the University of Bordeaux for 1959–1960 and a renewal of it to complete a doctoral thesis at the University of Nancy on Jean-Jacques Rousseau under the supervision of Robert Derathé.

While Butterworth was an undergraduate at Michigan State, Robert Horwitz encouraged him to pursue graduate study with Leo Strauss at the University of Chicago; in Bordeaux, Professor François Bourricaud did the same and then introduced him to Allan Bloom, who also insisted that there was only one person with whom to study political philosophy seriously and one place to do so: Leo Strauss at the University of Chicago. Following this advice, Butterworth began graduate studies in the Department of Political Science there in Fall 1961. In addition to his study with Strauss, Butterworth took courses from Herbert J. Storing and Joseph Cropsey. Then, as his interest in Arabic and Islamic philosophy developed, he began to study intensely with Muhsin Mahdi in the Oriental Institute, eventually writing his PhD dissertation on Averroes's Middle Commentary on Aristotle's *Rhetoric* under Mahdi's direction.

Upon completion of his doctoral degree, Butterworth taught for one quarter at the University of Chicago, then entered the US Army to fulfill his military obligation as an ROTC commissioned officer. He taught for one year at Federal City College in Washington, D.C. (now University of the District of Columbia), opened in 1968 as the first land-grant college in the nation's capital and accepted a position in the Department of Government and Politics at the University of Maryland, College Park in 1969, where he remained until his retirement in 2007. Always a prolific scholar, Butterworth also mentored countless undergraduates at UMD (many of whom went on to pursue doctoral work elsewhere), won teaching awards, and directed numerous dissertations. Along the way, he has held visiting positions at Georgetown University, Harvard University, St. John's College, University of Paris Nanterre, and the Institut für Politische Wissenschaft, Friedrich-Alexander Universität. He has also taught in Ramallah and Gaza, Palestine in 1988 and 1990. Those of us who are fortunate enough to have studied with him during his tenure at Maryland will remember with fondness the seminars he taught on Plato, Alfarabi, Maimonides, Ibn Khaldun, and Tocqueville among others.

Scholarship

Butterworth is a rare kind of scholar, one whose work combines an intense focus on intellectual pursuits with an equally intense commitment to sharing the fruits of these pursuits to a wider community of scholars and humanity at large. He is well known for his expertise on medieval Arabic and Islamic political philosophy, primarily as an interpreter, editor, and translator of medieval works by Alfarabi (d. 950) and Averroes (Ibn Rushd, d. 1198). In more than four decades of research and writing, Butterworth has produced some twenty book-length studies, including critical editions of medieval Arabic manuscripts and translations of works by Alfarabi, Averroes, and Jean-Jacques Rousseau. He has two monographs and well over a hundred articles that examine not only medieval, ancient, and modern philosophy but also contemporary politics in the Arab world. He has authored more than thirty review essays and research notes as well as over a hundred and thirty reviews of books, ranging from translations of ancient Greek and medieval Arabic to studies of colonialism and political Islam. In addition, Butterworth has been and continues to be a dedicated member of his scholarly community. As an active participant in many learned societies, he has taken on key leadership roles over the years as well as serving as editor, associate editor, and consulting editor for some fifteen scholarly journals and as a peer referee for countless others.

Butterworth's expansive intellect and love of medieval Arabic and Islamic political philosophy cement the link between his scholarly work and disciplinary and public service. His focus on medieval Arabic and Islamic political philosophy goes beyond what might be erroneously characterized as an antiquarian interest in the minutiae of the medieval text. It instead should be understood as part of a larger philosophical project to plumb the relationship between the past and the present in order to discover how the intellectual past informs our experience of the present. In the study of political philosophy, medieval texts receive scant attention in comparison to ancient Greek and modern European works. When scholarship does focus on medieval works, Latin and Christian texts are more visible than those of Arab and Muslim thinkers. Apart from a few key scholars, the discipline has thus sidelined medieval Arab and Muslim texts in the effort to understand the relationship between past and present. Butterworth's teacher and friend, Muhsin Mahdi (1926–2007), pioneered the recovery and study of medieval Arabic and Islamic political philosophy by seeking to construct a more complete picture of medieval intellectual history and understand more comprehensively the medieval period as a bridge between ancient and modern. Butterworth is the best of a generation of scholars who have carried on this task by recovering medieval teachings through the publication of critical editions, translations, and interpretations and by examining how that knowledge informs contemporary thought. He has pursued this invaluable mission with the consummate professionalism of a master scholar, all the while serving as a tireless advocate for his discipline and a kind and committed mentor to junior scholars and students.

As noted, within Butterworth's wide body of scholarship, Alfarabi and Averroes have a special place. He began his career with a focus on Averroes, dedicating most of his time to the translation and analysis of works by the philosopher between 1972 and 2000. During this period, he produced six critical Arabic editions of Averroes's middle commentaries on Aristotle's *Topics, Categories, De Interpretatione, Posterior Analytics, Prior Analytics*, and *Poetics*. In addition, he produced two full translations of Averroes's middle commentaries on the *Poetics, Categories, and De Interpretatione;* an edition and translation of Averroes's short commentaries on *Topics, Rhetoric*, and *Poetics;* and a translation of one of Averroes's most famous political treatises, *The Book of the Decisive Treatise: Determining the Connection Between the Law and Wisdom.*

The Smithsonian Institution, through its PL 480 program, supported the recovery of many of the manuscripts of the middle commentaries on Aristotle's *Logic* by Averroes once Butterworth was able to persuade its grants committee that medieval manuscripts are valuable artifacts worth recovering and preserving for posterity. A National Endowment for the Humanities grant further supported the publication of English translations of these works, making Averroes's thought accessible in both Arabic and English to a new generation of scholars.

Butterworth additionally published over twenty articles that explore the relationship between Aristotelian logic, Averroes's interpretation, and the roots of the Enlightenment as well as contemporary Arab secularism, nationalism, and political Islam. The latter works are deeply informed by his work on the medieval past as well as a profound and nuanced understanding of the political present.

In the last two decades, Butterworth has shifted his scholarly focus from Averroes to Alfarabi without abandoning his first body of work. For example, he continues to be a leading expert on Averroes, which is evidenced by recently published articles and book reviews as well as a forthcoming translation of Averroes's *Short Commentaries on Aristotle's Organon*. Nevertheless, his most central publications from 2000 onward focus on the works of Alfarabi, including *Alfarabi, The Political Writings, Volume I: "Selected Aphorisms" and Other Texts*; *Alfarabi, The Political Writings, Volume II: "Political Regime" and "Summary of Plato's Laws"*; and the soon to be published *Alfarabi, The Book of Letters*. These works provide English-speaking scholars with a far more complete picture of Alfarabi's political writings. In addition, Volume II of *The Political Writings* contains two important interpretive essays that encapsulate over forty years of intellectual engagement with medieval political philosophy in general and the thought of Alfarabi in particular.

Butterworth's scholarship on Alfarabi treats the texts with great respect by giving a detailed examination of their paradoxes and complexity of thought. Accordingly, his interpretations of Alfarabi's works follow what Alfarabi himself teaches in his preface to the *Summary of Plato's Laws* when he cautions his readers not to assume to know more about the thought of a philosopher than what that philosopher precisely teaches. This is a lesson that unfortunately goes unheeded by many scholars today, perhaps because Alfarabi's warning requires scholars to moderate the love of recognition and forego cleverness for respect for the truth in all its nuances and frustrating complexity. Butterworth's vast body of work clearly positions him as a scholar who takes Alfarabi's lesson to heart by spending immense time and energy recovering, editing, and translating medieval Arabic and Islamic texts before finally providing thoughtful and thought-provoking interpretations of those works.

Summary of Contributions

The contributions to this Festschrift exhibit the range of Charles Butterworth's philosophic interests as well as his wide-ranging academic influence. The contributors hail from all corners of the United States and the world, they study and work at all types of institutions, from small liberal arts colleges to large research centers, and they are connected to Butterworth as former students, as fellow academics, and, above all, as friends.

Butterworth's main interests have been in the awakening of philosophy in the early Muslim world, and consequently most essays in the Festschrift take up this thread and discuss the key figures of these events, such as Alfarabi and Averroes. Furthermore, the contributors examine the relationship between philosophy and religion and compare the Islamic and Christian worlds. The essays are divided into four sections, loosely arranged in chronological order according to the text they address.

The essays by Janet Holl Madigan and Steven Ealy, in the first section, discuss the Bible and the Quran. In her essay, Madigan suggests in her essay that the separation between reason and faith, and therefore between philosophy and theology, should be abandoned. Using the examples from the story of the fall from Paradise and the story of Abraham, Madigan shows that both Biblical stories correspond to the view later expounded by Thomas Aquinas and Pope John Paul II, who claim that reason and faith are compatible and even complementary approaches to the truth. In an essay on the story of Cain and Abel, Steven Ealy compares the differing accounts in the Torah and Quran. Ealy concludes that the Torah emphasizes human freedom in various forms, but especially in man's detachment from tradition, while the Quran emphasizes the experience of freedom within Islamic history.

The second group of essays focuses on Alfarabi. Steven Harvey asks how Leo Strauss came to attribute to Alfarabi a key role in the history of political philosophy. In doing so, Harvey traces the development of Strauss's writings on Alfarabi to show how Strauss refined his views on Alfarabi over time. He did so partly through the discovery of new texts and partly through seeing Alfarabi's manner of proceeding more clearly. Furthermore, Harvey expresses his concern that among those who have not studied with Strauss and Mahdi a different view of Alfarabi has become dominant, threatening to make his work irrelevant to political philosophy. Joshua Parens's essay takes up the topic of Alfarabi's alleged Neoplatonism. Parens looks primarily at Alfarabi's *Virtuous City* and argues that Alfarabi cannot be considered a Neoplatonist because he does not share the Neoplatonists' key assumption of a strict hierarchical ordering of the universe. Alfarabi's deviation on this assumption points to the fundamental importance of political philosophy for Alfarabi. Parens further suggests that the study of Alfarabi or Platonic political philosophy remains important as long as revealed religions are effective truths.

Christopher Colmo looks at a related aspect in the same writing, the

Virtuous City. While not explicitly raising the issue of Neoplatonism, Colmo investigates Alfarabi's explication of the first being or first cause. He concludes that the first cause is either completely unlike human beings or that a connection between the first cause and man exists, e.g., the pleasure experienced in thinking. However, this connection implies that the first cause is not qualitatively but only quantitatively different from human beings, indicating that Alfarabi comes down on the side of philosophy in the debate between philosophy and religion. Colmo concludes with a note of caution: In order to decide ultimately which side Alfarabi takes, it is necessary to investigate his understanding of religion.

In her essay, Miriam Galston compares Alfarabi's claims about the origins of knowledge, or primary principles as she calls them, across six of Alfarabi's writings. As Galston reminds us, the question about the origin of knowledge is connected to the question, also raised by Parens, of whether the universe is hierarchical and whether human beings are capable of knowledge of God. She concludes that Alfarabi does not present a consistent account of the origin of knowledge in all six works. Instead, some remarks could support the view of Neoplatonist readers while others support the reading of Alfarabi as a Platonic political philosopher. In order to reveal Alfarabi's own opinion on the matter, Galston offers an account of why we ought to turn toward the more political works.

Terence Kleven turns to Alfarabi's seemingly apolitical and technical works, *A Treatise on the Canons of the Art of Poetry* and *The Book of Poetry*, in his essay. Alfarabi, however, focuses more on the political uses of poetry rather than the technical aspects in these works. Kleven aims to dispel the modern notion, advocated by twentieth-century scholars, that Alfarabi had a poor understanding of Aristotle and poetry due to his lack of technical discussions and his inclusion of poetry among the logical arts. Thus, Kleven's essay rightly points to poetry in an answer to Galston's question about the first principles of knowledge. In both writings, Alfarabi divides the syllogistic arts, which are said to lead to knowledge, by the degree of certainty with which they lead to truth. Poetry is here the complete opposite of a demonstrative syllogism, the latter of which Alfarabi claims leads to certain knowledge. Yet poetry, which Alfarabi claims makes completely false statements, is a part of the logical arts. This raises the question of why poetry, which is only capable of making absolutely false statements, is still capable of revealing knowledge.

An answer to the question of poetry is provided by Shawn Welnak in his discussion of Alfarabi's comparison between Plato's Allegory of the Cave and Aristotle's Organon, which Welnak has translated from a Latin manuscript and included in his essay. In this text, Alfarabi suggests that Plato's Allegory of the Cave resembles the order of Aristotle's Logic. Welnak then spells out the meaning of this surprising remark by Alfarabi. This provides a clue to the answer raised by Kleven's essay. The art of poetry takes up the beginning point of the people in Plato's cave as well as the endpoint when the philosopher returns to the cave. Therefore, a poetry which is part of logic would be capable of revealing the limits of one's knowledge and thereby serve as the ground for philosophy. As Welnak shows, the allegory of the cave as well as the ordering of logic suffer from the defect that their peak, either the wisdom attained by the philosopher or the definitely true statements attained by demonstrative syllogisms, is unavailable. It consequently leaves the art of poetry as the foundation for philosophy, pursued dialectically.

David DiPasquale's contribution opens the third section, which includes three essays dedicated to debates surrounding al-Ghazali and Averroes. DiPasquale elaborates how Averroes attempts to counter the charges made by al-Ghazali against the philosophers. Averroes argues that the explication of the Quran, called for in the Quran itself, should be placed in the hands of philosophers. If one were to respond that this would make theologians out of philosophers, DiPasquale shows that Averroes places almost no limits on the philosophers' freedom of interpretation and says nothing specific about the philosophers' beliefs. Instead, the only limit placed on philosophers is their duty to maintain political stability by refusing to divulge any teachings of the Quran that would be beyond the grasp of the non-philosophers. The reason for this restriction is strictly political.

Carmela Baffioni and Monica Scotti present the dissenting view of the Ismaili theologian Ali ibn Muhammad ibn al-Walid. In the text supplied by Baffioni and Scotti, al-Walid discusses Quran 3:7 in order to show what he views as common misunderstandings of the text. Among those he opposes are the philosophers, and presumably Averroes. While al-Walid agrees with Averroes that the Quran has multiple levels of meaning, al-Walid suggests that contrary to Averroes's turn toward philosophers and reason, the most exemplary readers of the Quran are the Prophet's descendants. Furthermore, those who have received correct instructions, the imams, are also privy to the Quran's esoteric meaning. As Baffioni points out in her commentary, al-Walid further argues that knowledge leads to faith and not the reverse.

Even if al-Walid's argument against Averroes is only valid for Ismaili thought, its apparent effectiveness in suppressing philosophy seems to be validated by the ensuing history of philosophy in the Muslim world. John Pottenger shows in his essay how Western philosophy benefited from its discovery of Averroes. For Pottenger, the arguments of the so-called Latin Averroists forced Thomas Aquinas to incorporate Aristotelian philosophy into Roman Catholic theology. Put differently, Aquinas elevated practical science over theoretical science. Moreover, Averroes's scientific logic would be adopted, albeit in modified form, by Francis Bacon and lead to modern science. Even Martin Luther seems to have read Averroes and used him to attack the Thomistic position of the Roman Catholic Church, promoting inadvertently religious pluralism and freedom.

In his essay, David Burrell calls Pottenger's account of the diverging history of philosophy in the West and the East, "The Standard Story"— a story that Burrell rejects. In that story, al-Ghazali is arguably the crucial political thinker responsible for this divergence. Burrell suggests instead that al-Ghazali is the turning point towards an Islamic philosophical theology. For Burrell, al-Ghazali strengthened the role of reason in Islam in order to strengthen Muslims' understandings of their religion's mysteries. In addition to evidence taken directly from al-Ghazali, Burrell relies on the writings of Suhrawardi, Ibn al-Arabi, and Mulla Sadra with regard to the problem of essence and existence and their insistence that there are different modes of inquiry beyond rational arguments. In these writings, Burrell finds a continuous pursuit of wisdom rather than the break proclaimed by the narrators of the "Standard Story." Gary Kelly, in his recounting of Etienne Gilson's works on Averroes, proposes a further clarification of the story and suggests that Averroes, contrary to the charges brought against him by some his opponents, was a pious Muslim as well as a philosopher. Burrell's and Kelly's essays thus address the issues raised at the beginning of the Festschrift, namely questions regarding the relation between reason and revelation, freedom in Islam, and the Neoplatonist reading of Islamic philosophy.

In the Festschrift's final section, the essays by Melissa Matthes and Joshua Bandoch investigate what the question of reason and revelation and freedom in Islam means in the modern context. Joshua Bandoch looks at Montesquieu's observations on Islam. He concludes that Montesquieu criticizes Islam's limits on freedom, particularly with regard to politics, women, and international relations. Melissa Matthes discusses the relations of American Christian churches towards Germany during the Nazis' rule in the 1930s and early 1940s. Matthes establishes that the mainstream Protestant churches in the United States were opposed to Nazism and goes on to investigate why they failed to be more effective advocates for Jews and against the Nazi regime. She concludes that the American Protestant churches, despite some anti-Semitism among their ranks, tried to influence Hitler and Nazi Germany, but they failed because their political theology did not propel them to take the radical measures necessary to convince the American people and to influence the American political system. Matthes suggests that Karl Barth's political theology, if adopted in the United States, might be sufficiently strong to propel action for a just cause.

The crisis of the West, most manifest in the rise of fascism and communism in the twentieth century, propelled the deliberation of the roots of Western civilization and the search for alternatives or modifications by, among others, Leo Strauss. Jürgen Gebhardt reminds us in his Festschrift contribution of another attempt to address the crisis of the West, namely the one by Eric Voegelin. Gebhardt sketches in his essay Voegelin's analysis of the crisis of the West, beginning with the corruption of the social sciences and its subsequent misunderstanding of religion. In particular, Gebhardt suggests with Voegelin that religion is a central part of human experience which then manifests itself in different political forms. Moreover, Gebhardt asserts with Karl Jaspers that the different religious experiences can be the foundation of a comprehensive conversation about truth. Gebhardt's essay thereby leads us to compare Voegelin's and Strauss's analyses of the crisis of the West, to reveal their fundamental principles, and to judge the answers they have suggested, hopefully guiding us to a deeper understanding of ourselves.

In sum, the essays in this Festschrift take up four distinct themes, which all have been central in Butterworth's scholarship. Specifically, the authors question the predominant Neoplatonist reading of Alfarabi and muster many arguments to demonstrate the flaws of this position. Furthermore, and in part to buttress their argument, many contributors show the importance of rhetoric and esoteric writing for Muslim political philosophers. A third group of authors examine the status of reason within Islam. A final group of authors grapple with the uneasy balance between reason and revelation in the Modern world. The variety of positions taken in the Festschrift show the influence Butterworth and his scholarship have had on the study of religion and philosophy as well as the dialogue and friendship he has shared with his intellectual community. The editors of this work, together with those who contributed to this volume, and on behalf of Butterworth's colleagues, students, and friends, offer this *Festschrift* in honor of our beloved teacher. On, on.

Waseem El-Rayes
Gregory A. McBrayer
René Paddags

Revelation as the Marriage of Faith and Reason

Janet Madigan

Has the human mind been suffering from a tension headache since the dawn of Judeo-Christian revelation? Perhaps Leo Strauss thought so, for he taught that although reason and revelation, Athens and Jerusalem, were fundamentally united in their opposition to the project of modernity, there was nevertheless an irreconcilable tension between the two. This is because in the Biblical tradition man is not primarily "a knowing, contemplating being," but one who is "meant to live in childlike obedience," whereas the philosophic life places the highest value on "seeing with one's own eyes as distinguished from hearsay." Thus, one must choose between obedience and independence, for "no one can be both a philosopher and a theologian, or, for that matter, a third which is beyond the conflict between philosophy and theology, or a synthesis of both."[1] Is this really the case? Does one cease to be a philosopher the moment one accepts revelation as true, as if being a "seer" precludes one from being a "listener" as well? Put differently, does philosophy annihilate itself in crossing the threshold of belief? If so, perhaps the philosopher has a vested interest in remaining agnostic on the question of ultimate truth. But then philosophy is no longer the quest for truth but the ongoing attempt to preserve the philosophic way of life.

Strauss believed that philosophy as the "quest for knowledge" of an incomprehensible whole could only be the pursuit, and not the attainment, of wisdom; therefore, "the problems are always more evident than the solutions," which are all "questionable."[2] This uncertainty about the

---

1 Leo Strauss, "Progress or Return?" in *Introduction to Political Philosophy: Ten Essays by Leo Strauss*, ed. Hilail Gildin (Detroit: Wayne State University Press, 1989), 289–90.

2 Ibid., 297.

complete truth makes the philosophic life necessary, and appears to place it in opposition to a life informed by revelation. But as the philosopher Josef Pieper contends, "faith indeed implies precisely the *absence* of assured knowledge, in spite of all 'revelation.'" Because all things emanate from God, they are infinitely ordered; but because they are *infinitely* ordered, we cannot know them in their entirety. "Questioning means to be aware of the elusiveness of any final answer yet nevertheless to pursue such an answer and remain open to it."[3]

This essay explores the interplay of reason and revelation, as determined by the human capacity for relationship with another, in two stories from Genesis—that of Adam and Eve, and that of Abraham and Isaac. The first story speaks directly to the idea that human beings are creatures who must live according to truth in a community of understanding. The second explores the way in which human faith is, or should be, informed by reason, and how this is best accomplished in a climate of trust. From the very beginning, the Bible shows that the concepts of reason (that is, the power of the individual mind to comprehend truth) and relationship (understood as the need for each person to live in communion with the Other) are intrinsically connected, and that the breakdown of one inevitably injures both. This is significant because revelation is inherently relational—one knows the truth because one has been told by another, as opposed to sorting it all out for oneself. I then turn to the thought of Thomas Aquinas to suggest that if truth is one, and the philosopher and the believer are actually in pursuit of the whole truth (rather than self-interest, whether they are conscious of it or not), then reason and revelation cannot ultimately stand in contradiction. By referring to the "synthesis" of philosophy and theology in the context of the supposed conflict between them, Strauss would appear to be using the word in its Hegelian sense, to mean the reconciliation of clashing parts through a higher truth. But in fact, philosophy and theology—reason and faith— are part of the *essence* of human nature and therefore cannot naturally be in contention any more than the heart and lungs can conflict in a healthy human body. Aquinas notes that the contemplation of truth

---

3   Josef Pieper, *In Defense of Philosophy* (San Francisco: Ignatius, 1992), 114–15.

resides in the will as much as in the intellect, since the will "moves all other powers, even the intellect, to their actions." (II.II.*q*.180.*a*.1)[4] The integral connection between the intellect and the will means that faith properly understood is not blind obedience, but the result of free will informed by reason. Perfect knowledge is beyond the grasp of the human mind, but does our understanding move any nearer to truth by precluding other ways of knowing? Is reasoning *from* first principles necessarily less philosophical than reasoning *to* them?

Reason and Relationship in Genesis 2

Genesis 2, which provides a detailed account of the creation of human beings and their fall from grace, reveals much about the interconnectedness between revelation, reason, and relationship. In the beginning, the reader is told, God creates Adam and supplies his every apparent spiritual and material need. Adam is in union with God and has access to "every tree that is pleasant to the sight and good for food, the tree of life also in the midst of the garden, and the tree of the knowledge of good and evil."[5] (Gen. 2:9) God tells Adam, "You may freely eat of every tree of the garden; but of the tree of the knowledge of good and evil you shall not eat, for in the day that you eat of it shall die" (Gen. 2:15–17). But for all the gifts Adam has been given, he is not complete, for God notes, "It is not good that man should be alone." A fully human life, it would seem, calls for not only knowing the truth, but to know it in communion with another. Only Eve, "bone of my bones and flesh of my flesh," is a helper "fit" to receive the intellectual and physical gifts Adam can offer. Not through the power of reason alone, then, does man achieve the highest human life, but through his capacity for relationship as well.[6]

4   All references to Aquinas are taken from: *Summa Theologica*. Translated by Fathers of the English Dominican Province (New York: Benziger, 1948).

5   Genesis, 2:9. All Scripture quotes taken from the Book of Genesis, Revised Standard Version.

6   Leon Kass points out that this corporeal description of Eve indicates that Adam's desire for her is grounded first of all in carnal desire. "To him she is fleshy and bony, not brainy or soulful." *The Beginning of Wisdom: Reading Genesis* (Chicago: University of Chicago Press, 2006), 102. This

So Adam and Eve possessed truth (i.e., they knew God) and freedom from material need. How could things have possibly gone wrong? If communion with another human person was important to the fullness of Adam's spiritual development, could it be that neglecting the relationship in some way led to losing sight of God? Note that God forbade Adam to eat from the tree of knowledge of good and evil *before* the creation of Eve. It would seem probable that she received her knowledge of God's commands from her husband, but was the message properly conveyed? One may wonder, for when the serpent asks Eve whether any tree is forbidden, she answers, "God said, 'You shall not eat of the fruit of the tree which is in the midst of the garden, neither shall you touch it, lest you die'" (Gen. 3:3). As in a game of telephone, the message Eve repeats is not exactly the one that God had relayed to Adam.[7] The tree in the midst of the garden is identified as the tree of life, and not necessarily that of the knowledge of good and evil. Furthermore, God did not say "neither shall you touch it, lest you die." Had Adam explained *why* the tree of the knowledge of good and evil was off limits, or merely forbidden her to touch it? Indeed, does she even know the tree by its name, which possesses its own inner logic? For the forbidden fruit is not of the tree of knowledge simply, as if knowing were itself a bad thing. Rather, the name implies claiming the right to decide for oneself the *meaning* of good and evil as opposed to freely choosing between the two.

The serpent tells Eve, "You will not die." This indeed seems to accord more with her own sense of facts, for she sees that the attractive fruit is obviously not poisonous, for "the tree was good for food, and ... was a delight to the eyes and that the tree was to be desired to make one wise" (Gen. 3:6). The serpent, then, encourages Eve to believe not in what she has heard or to reflect on why it was said, but rather to rely on her own power of sight. His suggestions convince her that living by her own interpretation of truth is preferable to trusting in the word of

---

would imply that the most complete union possible between people is that which encompasses the bodily and spiritual dimensions of their being.

7   Kass makes this point, adding that whether the command Eve recites was miscommunication or a purposeful addition by Adam, "she converts the predicted dire consequences of disobedience ... into the reason for obedience," 85.

someone else (Adam or God). One might say he is exhorting Eve to be one who "sees," rather than one who "hears." And indeed, in relying on the powers of observation alone it seems reasonable to suppose that the fruit is a good thing. Ironically, though, Eve is no less a "hearer" for deciding for herself the value of that which is forbidden. She simply places her faith elsewhere—in the word of the serpent. She listens to a lie under the illusion that she is seeing things for herself. But seeing alone is not always enough to understand the full reality of what *is,* and the refusal to heed God means a separation from reality.

Faith sometimes calls for accepting as truth that which is not immediately apparent to the senses. Eve, however, trusts the devil's appeal to her own perception over Adam's word; Adam then trusts Eve rather than God, resulting in devastating rifts in the relationship between man and wife (Adam is quick to lay all the blame on Eve) and between mankind and God. Because humans are both material and spiritual entities, actions in one realm inevitably reverberate in the other (in other words, just as grace builds on nature and perfects it, destroying nature extinguishes grace). Perhaps Adam and Eve first sullied their relationship with each other, and this opened the door to a more significant injury — separation from God. And because man's relationship with God orders all others, the marital bond is further fractured as well, and is now marked by alienation and domination.

Ironically, pondering more over the reasoning behind the prohibition might have increased Eve's trust in Adam, since it would have called her to contemplate the possibility of something beyond her immediate impressions. Or conversely, placing more faith in Adam (and God) might have spurred her to employ her reason to better understanding the proscription. The story suggests that reason thrives best not in the soil of skepticism, but when grounded in trust, and that trust itself must be tethered to truth to endure. Adam is punished because he did not heed the word of God, but "listened to the voice" of his wife instead. Like Eve, Adam is a "hearer" who fills his ears with the wrong things. Proper reflection on the meaning of God's commands, as opposed to blind obedience, might have prevented this. The lesson seems to be that human beings are "hearers" by nature as well as "seers," and it requires reason cultivated in an atmosphere of trust to discern the proper voice to which one should listen.

Revelation and Relationship in the Story of Abraham and Isaac

1. Promises and Provisos: The Importance of Relationship

Reason and revelation might appear to be most at loggerheads in the Biblical account of the binding of Isaac. Specifically, how could God command Abraham to do something so obviously contrary to natural law? Does an act become right simply because God commands it? If so, then blind obedience is the highest human virtue. How does one square this with the power of human reason to know right from wrong? What kind of test is this command, anyway? If God does not desire the death of Isaac, is it not deceptive to allow Abraham to think that he does? In fact, a close examination of the story indicates that far from being an act of thoughtless obedience, Abraham's offering of Isaac is a shining example of faith informed by reason. Let us see how this is so.

The story begins when God speaks to Abram, saying, "'Go from your country and your kindred and your father's house to the land that I will show you. And I will make of you a great nation" (Gen. 12:1–2). Abram immediately does what he is asked; not necessarily out of a primal urge to obey God, but perhaps because the promise of greatness is very appealing.[8] He brings his wife, Sarai, and nephew, Lot. This is not technically in accordance with God's command, since Lot, as a blood relative, is "kindred"—who might serve as "perpetuation insurance" for founding a nation when one's elderly wife is childless.[9] In the land of Canaan, God brings further specificity to his promise, adding, "To your descendants I will give this land" (Gen. 12:7). Abram is seventy-five years old, but since he was born when his own father was seventy this promise of descendants perhaps does not sound absurd. Presumably, Abram's father had multiple wives since Abram and his brothers were all born in the same year, (Gen. 11:24)[10] so he might not even be considering the barren Sarai as an obstacle to the fulfillment of the promise or as in any way essential to it.

8 Kass, 257.
9 Ibid., 271.
10 We will also learn later that Sarai is in fact Abram's half-sister, sharing the same father; cf. Gen. 20:12.

Coming into the land of Egypt, Abram indeed fears more for his life and legacy than for Sarai, since he gives her to the Pharaoh of Egypt as his sister rather than face the possibility of being killed over her (she must have been beautiful indeed if at the age of sixty-six she is still deemed so desirable). But although Abram does not deem Sarai essential to God's promise, God evidently does, for he afflicts Pharaoh's house on account of her, and she is forthwith returned to Abram. Contrary to Abram's assumptions, then, God does not view his safety as more important than his marriage. Now, the encounter with Pharaoh has left Abram greatly enriched with many material possessions thanks to his association with Sarai. But all of these added possessions mean less land to share, and growing tension between Abram and Lot. So they agree to separate, with Lot choosing to depart for the reprehensible Sodom and Gomorrah. After this, God again speaks to Abram, elaborating on his promise of descendants, who will be as numerous as the dust of the earth (Gen. 13:16). This should confirm to Abram that Lot has nothing to do with the fulfillment of God's promise, and that "perpetuation insurance" is superfluous.

Lot meets with trouble in his new land, and Abram must enter into battle to free him when he is captured as a result of war between nine kings. After this victory, God addresses Abram a fourth time, and only then does Abram question him: "Behold, thou hast given me no offspring; and a slave born in my house will be my heir." God assures him that "your own son shall be your heir" and that Abram's descendants will be as numerous as the stars in heaven (Gen. 15:3–5). He then elevates this promise to the form of a covenant.

Abram still believes it is up to him to help God's promises along, however, so at the urging of the barren Sarai, he, at the age of eighty-six, fathers a child, Ishmael, by Sarai's maidservant Hagar. Here Abram "listens" to his wife, as Adam "listened" to Eve, to similar effect—namely much domestic tension and discord. Sarai and Hagar treat each other with resentment and retaliation, and we are told that Ishmael will be a "wild ass of a man" which can only give one pause as to what kind of a child he is. Abram in this period (lasting 13 years) might have pondered much on whether the fulfillment of God's promise requires such tension in the house when God shows him very clearly that this is not to be so.

When Abram is ninety-nine, God speaks to him again, saying "I am

God Almighty; walk before me and be blameless. And I will make my covenant between me and you, and will multiply you exceedingly" (Gen. 17:1-2). Abram shall now be Abraham—meaning father of a multitude. God asks Abraham to "walk before me," meaning, "in my presence, as if conscious of my inspection and solicitous of my approval; not behind me as if sensible of shortcomings and desirous to elude observation."[11] Furthermore, Abraham is instructed to be "blameless," which in the Jewish Bible is translated as "wholehearted." In other words, God is asking him to be wholeheartedly devoted to God's plan, rather than his own. It is here that God first asks Abraham to do something specific to fulfill his part of the covenant—to circumcise himself, all members of his household and all further generations. Significantly, it is here that God tells Abraham that it is through Sarah, now ninety years old and well past child-bearing age, that the covenant will be fulfilled. In asking Abraham to consecrate his sexual organ to God while reiterating that Sarah (not Hagar) will bear the chosen heir, God seems to be making the point that a true marriage is the essential first step for receiving his intended promises. True to his nature, Abraham immediately carries out the word of God, submitting himself and all members of his household to a painful procedure right where it hurts most "that very day" (Gen. 17:23).

Amazingly, even after this, Abraham, once again in fear for his life in a strange land, attempts to pass Sarah off as his sister (and we also learn here that she is actually his half-sister, by a different mother) to King Abimelech, a righteous man who is stopped by God before he ever approaches Sarah. He reprimands Abraham for doing such a thing. Leon Kass points out that in the three trials concerning "woman" or "wife" (with Pharaoh in Egypt, in the struggle between Sarah and Hagar, and here with Abimelech in Gerar) only direct intervention by God can make things right. Abraham himself was incapable of solving these problems and probably clueless as to his role in bringing them about. "Whatever his beginning virtues, Abraham seems, to say the least, clearly inept in the matter of women, wives and marriage." Indeed, "before he can become a proper founder, and even a proper father, he must become a

---

11 Pulpit Commentary of Genesis 17 accessed at http://biblehub.com/commentaries/pulpit/genesis/17.htm.

proper husband and appreciate Sarah as a wife."[12] It is only at this point that Sarah finally conceives a child. Just as a severed marital relationship leads to alienation from God in the second chapter of Genesis, in Chapter 17 understanding the true nature of marriage will open the doors to a restoration of God's relationship with mankind. God's revelation is needed for proper human relationships, and the attitude of trust that is proper to human relationships in turn further opens man to God's revelation, as we shall see in the story of the binding of Isaac.

2. Reason and Faith (or "I think, therefore I hope")

Genesis 21 opens with the conception and birth of Isaac and then recounts the subsequent banishment of Ishmael and Hagar. It ends with Abraham swearing an oath with Abimelech that he will never "deal falsely" with him, his offspring or his posterity, and a mutual peace covenant made between the two at Beersheba. In Genesis 22, "After these things"—that is, after God fulfills his promise to Abraham with the birth of Isaac, and confirms his will that Sarah be an essential part of the covenant by condoning the banishment of Ishmael; and after Abraham demonstrates through his dealings with Abimelech that he understands the meaning of being true to one's word and the solemnity of a covenant—*after these things*—"God tested Abraham":

> Take your son, your only son Isaac, whom you love, and go to the land of Moriah, and offer him there as a burnt offering upon one of the mountains of which I shall tell you (Gen. 22:1–2).

So Abraham arises early the next morning and, taking Isaac and two servants, he sets out for Moriah, a three-day journey away. It is significant that even if it has been in Abraham's nature to follow God reflexively, as seen by his readiness to pick up and leave the land of his father and his rapid execution of the circumcision command, there is no way Abraham can carry out this command immediately. Indeed, God seems to intend that he reflect long and hard before offering Isaac.

---

12 Kass, *The Beginning of Wisdom*, 265–66.

And what might Abraham have reflected upon? To begin with, God had for the first time here summoned Abraham "by his new name and *only* by name: 'Avraham!'—'Father of Multitudes!'"[13] Perhaps, this was an assurance that God's covenant was in no way revoked by this strange command and that what God was asking of Abraham would not damage it.[14]

Then there was the fact that although Abraham could not fully comprehend the meaning of God's command, there were two things he did know: 1. God can act in ways that exceed the law of nature; thus, the miraculous birth of Isaac to the post-menopausal Sarah. 2. God has promised over and again that he will grant Abraham many descendants through Isaac. Based on this, Abraham apparently chooses to believe that God will keep his promises (which is not unreasonable, especially given point one). Furthermore, God did not destroy Lot when executing judgment on Sodom and Gomorrah due to Abraham's plea to spare the innocent, and Lot is far less innocent than Isaac. Moreover, there has been no evidence that God has ever been deceptive with Abraham—to the contrary, God has fulfilled the most seemingly impossible promise he made.

Abraham certainly does not give any indication that he expects to lose Isaac. When the time comes for Abraham and Isaac to ascend the mountain, he tells his servants, "I and the lad will go yonder and worship, and come again to you" (Gen. 22:5). While Abraham has been guilty of half-truths thus far (passing Sarah off to foreign kings as his sister when she is more importantly his wife), he has not been deceptive in any other way. Telling his servants so directly that he and Isaac would return indicates that Abraham is *hoping* to come back with Isaac, as does

13 Ibid., 335.
14 See Kass, 336: Referring to the Robert Sacks translation of Genesis, Kass notes that God does not exactly *command* Abraham to sacrifice Isaac, He requests it of him ... God says "please." (Nearly all translators fail to translate the Hebrew particle *na'*, which accompanies the imperative verb, "take.") One might reply here that, as basic grammar rules teach, an imperative sentence does not change its nature by the addition of the word "please." Thus, "sit down, please" is still a command, however sweetly issued.

his response to his son when he explains that "God will provide himself the lamb for a burnt offering" (Gen. 17:8).

So he and Isaac go up the mountain, Isaac carrying the wood and Abraham carrying the fire and the knife. We read that Abraham then built an altar, laid the wood in order, bound Isaac and placed him on the altar:

> Then Abraham put forth his hand and took the knife to slay his son. But the angel of the Lord called to him from heaven, and said, "Abraham, Abraham!" And he said, "Here am I." He said, "Do not lay your hand on the lad or do anything to him; for now I know that you fear God, seeing you have not withheld your son, your only son from me" (Gen. 22:10–12).

It is interesting to consider how this scene is nearly universally depicted in art.[15] Abraham is shown with one hand on the head of Isaac as if to keep him steady while wielding a knife in the other, as an angel intervenes. These images certainly reinforce the notion that God is ordering something contrary to the natural law, suggesting that something is right not because it conforms to reason, but because God commands it.

But is this necessarily the way the scene played out? Remember that although Abraham went up the mountain carrying the knife, he would have had to lay it down in order to build the altar and bind Isaac. The moment Abraham "took" the knife, the angel called out to him. Thus, Abraham might not even have been anywhere near Isaac at the time of the intervention, depending on where the knife had previously been laid. Furthermore, the angel does not say "take your hand off the lad," but rather, "Do not lay your hand" on him. This indicates that Abraham is not really at the point of wielding the knife at Isaac in a threatening way and it is fully possible that God never even allowed Isaac to actually feel endangered. Furthermore, it is conceivable that when God initially told Abraham to offer his son "*as* a burnt offering," (emphasis added) he

15 Works by Rembrandt, Caravaggio, and Titian spring immediately to mind; countless more can be found, from famous masterpieces to the more pedestrian offerings of religion textbooks.

meant "*in the manner*" of a burnt offering. This would not entail commanding Abraham to do anything against the natural law. After the angel comes, Abraham spies a ram in a thicket and offers it up instead. But in fact God never told him to do so. Perhaps God did not require the blood of a ram here because the blood sacrifice—the circumcision—had already been completed, and what was now needed was a symbolic gesture and evidence of total trust in God.

The test for Abraham, then, is not about blind obedience to irrational commands, but rather, as Leon Kass puts it,

> The depth of Abraham's awe-fear-reverence before God: Later, perhaps, men can learn to love God, but it is the fear of the Lord that is the beginning of wisdom … it is the primary religious passion, experienced in recognition of a form of being beyond our comprehension, of a power beyond our control, of a force before which we feel small and toward which we look up. Curiously, awe in acknowledging the gap thereby partly overcomes it: awe or reverence establishes a relationship across the unbridgeable divide.[16]

The test, then, is about whether man trusts God over his own instincts. Man approaches wisdom, not in the supposition that he is the highest thing, but in the recognition that he is not. While it is possible that at other times in the story, Abraham acted out of a natural fear of losing the thing he hoped for (namely, Isaac), he now acts from what Aquinas would call "filial fear"—that is, the dread of separation from God, never presuming equality with God, and reverently approaching him as the "unfathomable and supreme good" (II-II.*q*.7.*a*.1). In short, Abraham seems to have recovered what Adam and Eve had lost, thus paving the way for renewal of mankind.

Abraham ascends the mountain in hope—a hope grounded not so much in the wish that God is only joking, lying, or capable of changing his mind, but rather in the acknowledgement that God's ways are so far above our own that sometimes the only response is to trust for the time

16 Kass, 344–45.

being. Abraham's hope foreshadows that of Peter, who is also confronted with the choice of whether or not to trust God in the face of a mystery beyond one's comprehension. In John 6, Jesus teaches about the future sacrifice of the Mass. This occurs right after he multiplies the loaves and fishes and walks across the water during a storm. Buoyed by the miracle of the loaves, people ask Jesus what they need to do to accomplish the works of God. He gives a two-part answer. To do the work of God requires first "that you believe in him whom he has sent" (Jn. 6:29). This might not sound too difficult, but Jesus follows this with a directive that is perhaps less easy to digest:

> I am the living bread which came down from heaven; if any one eats of this bread, he will live forever; and the bread which I shall give for the life of the world is my flesh ... Truly, truly, I say to you, unless you eat the flesh of the Son of man and drink his blood, you have no life in you; he who eats my flesh and drinks my blood has eternal life, and I will raise him up at the last day. For my flesh is food indeed, and my blood is drink indeed. He who eats my flesh and drinks my blood abides in me, and I in him. As the living Father has sent me and I live because of the Father, so he who eats me will live because of me (Jn. 6:51–57).

Now, just as it seemed Abraham was asked to do something in contradiction to the natural law—namely, homicide—the words here, taken in their plain sense, would seem to be advocating not only murder, but cannibalism as well. Three times Jesus refers to himself as the "living bread" or "bread of life," but lest there be any misunderstanding about exactly what he means, he explicitly states five times that this living bread is his own flesh and blood.

Many in the crowd respond, "This is a hard saying; who can listen to it?" (Jn. 5:60). But Jesus does not assuage their doubts by explaining that he is speaking symbolically or has been misunderstood. Instead, he simply wonders, if people take offense at this, what they might think if they were to "see the Son of man ascending where he was before?" (Jn. 6:62). Followers left in droves after this, indicating that that there was little doubt among the crowd as to the meaning of Jesus's words. Christ then turns to the twelve, asking if they also will leave. Peter responds:

> Lord, to whom shall we go? You have the words of eternal life; and we have believed, and have come to know, that you are the Holy One of God (Jn. 6:68–69).

Peter's response is perhaps not unlike the interior movement of Abraham's heart and mind, and a magnificent testament to the interplay of faith and reason. Because they have *believed*, they have come to *know* that Jesus is God. As evidence, Peter does not cite the numerous miracles that Christ performed, but rather, his *words*—and everything Jesus has said, as well as what he has done, points to the fullness of truth. If the teachings of Christ had been in any way in conflict with the natural law, then perhaps after this Peter would decide that it is high time to part ways. But in admitting that there is indeed nowhere left to go, Peter is acknowledging that even if the full meaning is not yet clear to him, either Jesus is the truth or *nothing* is.

Given the limits of the human mind, Peter, like Abraham, knows it is better to first trust the Promisor and hope that the meaning of difficult words will later become clear. And in the Catholic tradition, the words of Jesus *do* become clear, for Christ's presence in the Eucharist is seen as being not symbolically, but actually true. The doctrine of transubstantiation holds that ordinary bread and wine, while retaining their appearance, actually do become a different substance altogether—the body and blood of Christ—through a process that is beyond human comprehension; mysterious, to be sure, but not, for that reason, absurd. For Catholics, the Eucharist speaks to the need of humans, who are embodied souls, to receive spiritual sustenance through physical channels. Just as Adam, even while knowing God, was "alone" without Eve, Catholicism holds that believers, in order to fully know God, must do so in a physical as well as in a spiritual sense.

Returning to Abraham, we see that following the offering of Isaac, God renews all his promises of blessings to Abraham "because you have obeyed my voice" (Gen. 22:17). Thus, notes Kass, "Abraham's supreme virtue resides in his hearing and hearkening, born of awe-fear-reverence, yet not without hope."[17] To approach God in awe is to acknowledge that he is the source of all good, and therefore will provide. It is to be a hearer—that is, to listen and trust in the ways of God even when it is difficult to square with what we may know through our senses. Thus, we cannot gain wisdom until we accept that our understanding is limited. But is it true that we cannot have wisdom if we admit knowledge gained through hearing rather than seeing? Hearing is also a way of knowing. It is the beginning of wisdom, if not perhaps the end point of it. Had Abraham not trusted in God but, like Eve, trusted more to his own sense of the matter, God's promise could not have been fulfilled. Although Isaac would have survived nonetheless, the relationship between Abraham and his posterity and God would have been severed.

Abraham reaches the true starting point of wisdom when he values the relationship with God for its own sake apart from any promised rewards. Prior to this, although he had indeed listened to the voice of God, he also tried at various stages to help the promise along—in bringing Lot to Canaan as a safeguard of posterity, in offering Sarah to foreign princes in the interest of protecting his own life and progeny, and in fathering Ishmael to provide himself the promised heir. But none of these things moved the plan along any farther and in fact stood as hindrances: The inclusion of Lot led to his troubles in Sodom and Gomorrah as well as his eventual rape by his daughters, the households of two foreign kings were ravaged through the contact with Sarah, and the birth of Ishmael obviously did nothing to promote domestic peace in Abraham's house. Through each of these, God shows Abraham that His ways are above human ways. God has taught him that the fulfillment of the promise requires nurturing the relationship with Sarah and this perhaps helps Abraham to train his focus from reward to relationship. So if at the start he obeys in the hopes of gaining the promised goods, by the end he has reached the summit of virtue—a wholehearted focus on the promisor, rather than just the promise—for "only if Abraham is willing to do without the covenant ... out of awe-reverence for the Covenantor, can he demonstrate that he *merits* the covenant and its promised blessings."[18]

17   Ibid., 347.
18   Ibid., 337.

Abraham has learned to trust God first of all when reasoning his way toward how to achieve the good. Hearing—which by nature requires Other—is reasoning from the standpoint of relationship: I believe because I trust, and I trust because my reason tells me it makes sense to do so. In this way, reason and faith exist in a symbiotic relationship. By hearkening to the voice of God, Abraham shows that he will allow this relationship to order all the others—that he is "wholehearted" enough to love and obey God, simply for his own sake.

Abraham seems to have trodden a different path to the wisdom of the ancient philosophers, who taught that the highest good, truth, is that which is loved for its own sake. But if there is truth, then it must be one; if revelation is true, then there cannot be a contradiction between the God of Abraham and the truth that orders the philosophical life; there cannot even be a tension—just simply two ways of knowing the same truth. And if this is so, revelation is *not* revelation unless it is reasonable.

Revelation, Reason, Relationship, Resolution

If revelation must be reasonable, then God could not in fact have actually commanded Abraham to violate the natural law, even if that is what, at first blush, the words seem to suggest. But one can only discern the reasonableness of revelation in a climate of trust. Without trusting that God's command was beyond his immediate comprehension, Abraham would have had to suppose that God, in commanding the death of Isaac, was breaking his promise. Can God break a promise? Let us consider this question in view of Thomas's teaching on the essence of God.

1. God's Nature

Thomas notes that because God is the first efficient cause of all things, "to act belongs to Him primarily and essentially" (I.*q*.3.*a*.8). God is pure *subject,* upon whom all else is predicated. His essence, though, is not action but existence—"I am Who Am." "God Himself is His own nature ... [and] ... comprehends in Himself the whole perfection of being" (I.*q*.11.*a*.3). Perfect being requires singularity, for if there were many gods, they would necessarily be different from one another and possess different qualities. If the difference were one of privation, then one god would lack perfection; if the difference were a perfection, all would necessarily have it. "Hence also the ancient philosophers, constrained as they were by truth when they asserted an infinite principle, asserted likewise that there was only one such principle" (I.q.11.a.3).

As the first cause, God is "pure act, without the admixture of any potentiality." Potentiality refers to what can be changed, but "it is impossible for God to be in any way changeable." Because God is perfectly complete, "he cannot acquire anything new, nor extend himself to anything whereto He was not extended previously. Hence movement in no way belongs to Him" (I.q.9.a1).

From this, we learn that God simply is "what is." He is eternal and he is one, supremely undivided. His primary nature is reason rather than will, for his mode of being is *to be*, rather than to move toward something.

2. God's Will

Where does will fit into this? For human beings, the will is a movement toward an object of the intellect. It resides in our appetitive nature insofar as it seeks what it lacks, but also exists in "the loving and delighting in what it does possess." Movement does not belong to God, who is complete, so insofar as God possesses will, it is in the second respect, which is in the delighting in goodness. In this way, God's will is "not distinct from His essence" (I.q.19.a.2). And God's essence is the fullness of being—that is, *what* is. So since God's essence is goodness, his will, which is a part of that, must also be goodness. Thus, we follow God's will, not primarily because it is God's will, but because it is good; and for human beings, reason properly employed is always a movement toward the good.

God's will is not in an appetitive nature because he is complete and in need of nothing; but it does have two dimensions: that which is necessary and that which is not. Thomas explains that something can be absolutely necessary from the relation of terms, such as when the predicate defines the subject ("it is absolutely necessary that man is an animal"), or is part of the concepts attaching to it (it is "absolutely necessary that a number must be odd or even"). (I.q.19.a.3). In this way, God necessarily wills his own goodness just as man necessarily wills his own happiness. God, as pure being, necessarily wills his goodness because he *is* goodness, just as man is animal.

God can have also have a will regarding non-necessary things, like the creation of the universe, but once he wills something to be, he cannot change it, for, as Aquinas stresses, "God, although He has infinite power, cannot make a thing to be not made (for this would imply that two contradictories are true at the same time)" (I.*q.*7.*a.*2). God too, is beholden to the laws of reason because he is truth itself.

So God can also will things apart from himself, and does so "insofar as they are ordered to His own goodness as their end," but it is not necessary that God wills the various things that lead to that end, unless it is unattainable without them, such as nourishment to sustain life (I.*q.*19.*a.*3). But whatever God does will into existence, he orders to his own goodness, although there can be different paths to achieving this end.

If God is the source of all goodness and human beings necessarily will their own good, human happiness requires a movement toward God. But although man necessarily seeks happiness, he has free will with regard to how he seeks it and where. Thus, men are free to perfect their nature or deny it. But while various movements may present equal paths to God, the one condition that is strictly necessary to all of them is that of hearing and hearkening. For our reason (i.e., what we can see for ourselves) can tell us what God is *not*, but only revelation (that is, what we are told) can enable us to know what God *is*.[19]

In this sense, the core of the sin of Adam and Eve is not so much disobedience to the will of God (although that is part of it), but rejection of reality; refusal of what *is*. In disobeying God in Eden, our first parents separated themselves from the reality by which they were sustained. It was sin against the *essence* of God, of which his will is a part.

3. Promises

Where does promising fit into this? For human beings, promises are an act of the will—on the part of the promisor, who pledges to perform

19 See John Paul II, *Fides et Ratio*: *On the Relationship between Faith and Reason* (Boston: Pauline, 1998), and *Summa Theologica*, I.*q.*11.*a.*3.

an action at some future time, and on the part of the promisee, who must choose whether or not to believe in the promisor. While promises pertain to future actions for human beings, this cannot be the case for God, who "sees all things in one (thing) which is Himself." Since God sees all things together, and not successively" the future does not pertain to him (I.q.14.a.8). In human relationships, promises require faithfulness—on the part of the promisor to be true to his or her word (that is, unchanging with regard to the thing promised), and on the part of the promisee, who must trust enough to give the other the freedom to fulfill the pledge.

It was not necessary for God to make a promise to Abraham, but having done so, it could not be revoked because God's will is unchangeable. As Thomas notes, God cannot make a thing to be not made, as this would entail two contradictories being simultaneously true (I.q.7.a.3). Without trusting that God's command was beyond human comprehension, Abraham would have had to suppose that God was breaking his promise about Isaac. But logic dictates that this is not in the nature of God. So it made sense for Abraham to obey—not simply because it was God's will, and certainly not, as Kierkegaard would have it, because it was absurd, but precisely because it was the most reasonable thing to do.

Furthermore, it would not be logical to presume that although God intended to keep his promise about Isaac, he also meant to deceive Abraham just to see what would happen. If God necessarily wills his own goodness and orders all things in creation to it, then he cannot will to move anyone away from truth, which is his very existence.

So God could not have expected the extermination of Isaac because this would be to break a promise, which contradicts the unchangeable will of God. Neither could he have been intending to deceive Abraham, because this would contradict his nature as Truth. Finally, he could not have commanded Abraham to actually violate the natural law because this would contradict God's essence as the fullness of good. Truth is what "is." The being of God is truth. The "good" is the fullness of being—how closely something approaches what *is*. The good cannot be achieved, then, if one is cut off from what *is*. The true is prior to the good because "it is more closely related to being than is good. For the true regards being itself simply and immediately, while the nature of good follows being in so far as being is in some way perfect; for thus it is desirable" (I.*q.*16.*a.* 4). So if the primary dictate of natural law is, as Thomas says, "good is to be done, evil is to be avoided," then willing that Abraham kill the innocent Isaac would be to wish to move him away from the fullness of being.

What about God's omnipotence? Could we not presume that God has power over the natural law and the ability to change it? In fact, as Thomas notes, God's omnipotence dictates not that he can do all things, but that he can do "all things that are possible:"

> The divine existence ... possesses within itself the perfection of all being ... nothing is opposed to the idea of being except non-being. Therefore, that which implies being and non-being at the same time is repugnant to the idea of an absolutely possible thing ... Therefore, everything that does not imply a contradiction in terms is numbered amongst those possible things, in respect of which God is omnipotent (I.*q.*25.*a.*3).

God's supernatural power exceeds natural powers (thus, he can bring someone back from the dead because death was not part of the original condition of man—what man was intended to be in the will of God), but his omnipotence cannot displace reason, because God is reason itself. To obey the command of God, then—to obey his voice—is to obey the command of reason, wherever it may lead. To obey simply because God *says* so, or to fail to obey simply because *God* says so, is to thwart the exercise of reason and thus hinder oneself from reaching the fullness of being.

Revelation: The Marriage of Faith and Reason

On the surface, the story of Abraham and Isaac might seem relatively easy to place in the service of the idea that faith, as blind obedience, is in conflict with reason. But a closer examination has shown that faith properly understood is inseparable from reason. To say that human beings possess *logos* — reasoned speech — is to affirm that they are reasonable beings meant to live in society with others. Faith, encompassing the dimensions of reason, will, and relationship, is a fuller expression of human being than the faculty of reason alone. Let us see why this is so.

As John Paul II, notes, everyone has a natural desire to know, and "truth is the proper object of this desire."[20] Because we are capable of knowing, and can know that we know, we are necessarily concerned with "the real truth" of our perceptions. This entails questions on the meaning of life and a search for the absolute, ultimate ground of all things, "which refers to nothing beyond itself and which puts an end to all questioning."[21] Human beings are truth-seekers by nature, but the reality of human life is inextricably marked by faith. As John Paul II further explains:

> There are in the life of a human being many more truths which are simply believed than truths which are acquired by way of personal verification. Who, for instance, could assess critically the countless scientific findings upon which modern life is based? Who could personally examine the flow of information which comes day after day from all parts of the world and which is generally accepted as true? Who in the end could forge anew the paths of human experience and thought which have yielded the treasures of human wisdom and religion? This means that the human being—the one who seeks truth—is also the one who lives by belief.[22]

While the knowledge we gain from belief may seem less perfect than what we can learn on our own, John Paul II points out that "belief is often humanly richer than mere evidence" because it occurs through relationship, which "brings into play not only a person's capacity to know but also the deeper capacity to entrust oneself to others."[23] Thus,

---

20 John Paul II, 40.
21 Ibid.
22 Ibid., 44.
23 Ibid., 44.

the perfection of human being—the movement toward the fulfillment of human nature—lies not simply in the quest for "abstract knowledge of truth," but in seeking truth "in a dynamic relationship of faithful self-giving with others" in which the person can find "a fullness of certainty and security"; indeed, "the capacity to entrust oneself and one's life to another person and the decision to do so are among the most significant and expressive human acts" and this is why the ancient philosophers upheld friendship as the best context for philosophizing.[24]

The reality of human existence, then, points to the need to rely on faith in our pursuit of truth. Aquinas shows that even the discernment of truth is an act of faith insofar as it pertains to the will. He explains that "faith implies assent of the intellect to that which is believed." The intellect can be moved to assent "by its very object," such as with first principles or scientific proofs. But the intellect can also assent to something "through an act of choice, whereby it turns voluntarily to one side rather than to the other" (II–II.q.1.a.4).[25] The human will is at rest and unchangeable only when it at last possesses the beatific vision. At that point, we might say it moves from being an appetitive force to more completely reflecting the divine will, which delights in what "is." Analogously, we might say that philosophy, once in possession of the full truth, would no longer be the pursuit of wisdom, although it would still delight in it. We "see" those things which of themselves can be known by the intellect or senses. But neither faith nor opinion can belong to this category and in this sense, one cannot simultaneously be a knower and a believer. And yet, a philosopher is not a knower. He is rather one who loves and pursues wisdom—not necessarily one who possesses it.

As Josef Pieper explains, philosophy itself "is primarily really a negative term, explicitly expressing the *absence* of wisdom";[26] nevertheless, the true philosopher is one who relentlessly and lovingly pursues the search for all that is worth knowing, even if the "ultimate, finally satisfying

---

24 Ibid., 44–46.
25 Thomas adds here a useful teaching on how to discern the authenticity of one's faith when he notes that if this voluntary choosing is "accompanied by doubt and fear of the opposite side, there will be opinion, while if there be certainty and no fear of the other side, there will be faith" (II–II.q.1.a.4).
26 Pieper, 72.

answer remains ever elusive."[27] But to say the object of philosophy is "unknowable" does not necessarily mean that it cannot be known, but that the proper conditions don't exist for its being fully known. Thus, while the stars may be "invisible" by day, this is not because they are invisible as such but are merely invisible to the human eye under the conditions of daylight.[28] We may realize that a final answer is elusive, but the important thing is to remain open to its possibility rather than demand its exclusion out of a fixation on the "purity of questioning."[29]

Does the possession of both faith and reason mean that man holds within himself an irreconcilable tension? This could only be if both faith and reason truly are opposites which necessarily lead the human mind, not only in different directions, but to different destinations as well. And outside of the beatific vision, neither faith nor reason can enable one to grasp the complete understanding of truth. Perhaps tension arrives when we assume reason and faith must be mutually exclusive. But this was not the case for the ancient philosophers, for as Pieper points out, Plato and Aristotle were not so much concerned with the philosophical method but rather "the search for answers" regardless of whether they were incomplete, and especially, "no matter what quarter they came from."[30] Socrates in particular "was never embarrassed to admit that the ultimate, the ontologically decisive truths were known to him not by his own accomplishments but ... 'because he heard them.'"[31] In the honest pursuit of truth, the question is not so much of whence truth comes, but how well it squares with what we already know from observation. As Pieper says:

> A believer neither "knows" nor "sees" with his own eyes; he accepts the testimony of someone else. Much of this testimony, indeed, regards the same universe that his own eyes behold, and that he, as a scientist or philosopher, investigates

27 Ibid., 72.
28 Ibid., 72–73.
29 Ibid., 115.
30 Ibid., 116.
31 Ibid., 116.

using his own faculties. Such testimony may even guide his attention or sharpen his perception so that he suddenly sees with his own eyes what otherwise would have remained hidden, had he not heeded and pondered the message reaching him from elsewhere ... Why should I be compelled to choose in favor of "hearing" and against the use of my own eyes, and vice versa? What could prevent me from accepting both: seeing and hearing, philosophy and faith? ... A philosophy truly embracing all attainable information is superior, not because it would be able to offer smoother answers but because it will bring out more clearly the dimension of mystery that pervades all reality.[32]

Does accepting revelation mean that reason has been relegated to handmaiden status, as is sometimes suggested? Perhaps the most fitting analogy is not that of master-servant, but husband-wife. Philosophy, the love of wisdom, is ever seeking to possess it more fully. Revelation teaches that the highest truth to be known is that of a personal God. Once having glimpsed the truth of revelation, the work of philosophy is not so much to complete the deposit of faith, but to protect it by making it more understandable. John Paul II quotes Clement of Alexandria to drive this point home:

The teaching of the Savior is perfect in itself and has no need of support, because it is the strength and the wisdom of God. Greek philosophy, with its contribution does not strengthen truth, but, in rendering the attack of sophistry impotent and in disarming those who betray truth and wage war upon it, Greek philosophy is rightly called the hedge and the protective wall around the vineyard.[33]

In the marriage of faith and reason, philosophy goes from being the pursuer of wisdom to its protector. But just as in a marriage, where the

32 Ibid., 118–19.
33 John Paul II, 52–53.

mystery of the "other" can never be fully penetrated, even in the course of a lifetime, a union of reason and faith does not presume that all the answers are now understood; for while to "know" something is to perceive it in itself, as with sight, to "understand" means to grasp the reasonableness of the thing—to see it in context, so to speak. As Aristotle defines it, wisdom is the understanding of causes; that is, knowing *why* things are a certain way, and not just *that* they are a certain way. But given human limitations, the perfection of this kind of understanding can never be achieved in this life, even if revelation enables us to "know" that God is truth. As St. Anselm says, "whoever investigates something incomprehensible should be satisfied if, by way of reasoning, he reaches a quite certain perception of its reality even if his intellect cannot penetrate its mode of being."[34]

Within the search for knowledge itself, one might say that seeing is the masculine, active principle—the pursuing of what can be known with one's own eyes. Hearing is a passive, feminine principle. Just as "it is not good for man to be alone" physically or spiritually, neither is the human mind operating at the fullness of its existence if it is guided by only one of these faculties. As John Paul II notes, "it is necessary not to abandon the passion for ultimate truth, the eagerness to search for it or the audacity to forge new paths in the search. It is faith which stirs reason to move beyond all isolation and willingly to run risks so that it may attain whatever is beautiful, good and true. Faith thus becomes the convinced and convincing advocate of reason."[35] As with the evolution of eros into agape, faith moves reason beyond its preoccupation with itself and its own processes to the search for something "other." If philosophy rejects the possibilities and challenges posed by faith, it risks degenerating from the pursuit of "what is" into omphaloskepsis. (It is not good for man to be alone indeed!)

So perhaps one is not absolutely, simultaneously a philosopher and a believer—a seer and a hearer—but instead holds the two faculties within himself in equal measure—not as a tension, but rather, a dance in which complementary halves engage in a single motion. The marriage

34 Quoted in ibid., 57.
35 Ibid., 75–76.

of faith and reason is not then a synthesis, but a partnership in the most human sense of the word. Just as male and female are not *naturally* in conflict, but in their complementary natures supply what is lacking in the other, philosophy, in admitting the truths of revelation, does not annihilate itself, but merely changes its orientation from pursuer to protector, enabling the human mind to reach more complete forms of knowledge. As John Paul II notes, without revelation, reason can be easily sidetracked from its ultimate purpose. And without reason, faith degenerates into the emphasis on "feeling and experience, and so runs the risk of no longer being a universal proposition."[36] There can be no ultimate conflict between faith and reason, because each requires the other to remain true to its own nature: "Faith asks that its object be understood with the help of reason, and at the summit of its searching reason acknowledges that it cannot do without what faith presents."[37]

Faith and reason may be different ways of knowing, but difference need not entail opposition, and all lovers of wisdom should honestly ask themselves what purpose is to be served in making this assumption. We may realize that presuming a conflict where none exists is not a recipe for intellectual sophistication, but cognitive dissonance—and a tension headache to boot.

36 Ibid., 64.
37 Ibid., 57.

The Story of Adam's Sons Cain and Abel in Torah and Quran

Steven D. Ealy

My concern in this paper is what one can learn from the structure and action of the story of Cain and Abel as it is related in the Hebrew Scriptures (Genesis 4: 1–16) and in the Quran (Q 5: 27–32).[1] Although Heribert Busse maintains that "the qur'anic account of Cain and Abel closely follows the narrative in the Bible,"[2] a comparison of the action and dialogue of the two shows this not to be the case. My working hypothesis is that identifying the important structural and dynamic differences of these texts will provide a foundation for a comparative understanding of their visions of the nature of man and of God, and of the relationship between man and God, and the modes of human and divine interaction and instruction. Understanding the dynamic of the sacred text places one on the threshold of understanding man's relation to the divine as enacted in that text.

In addition to my reflection on these sacred texts, I examine one contemporary interpretation of each. Yoram Hazony's *The Philosophy of the Hebrew Scriptures* offers a comprehensive understanding of the

---

1   Unless otherwise noted, all Genesis quotations are from Adele Berlin and Marc Zvi Brettler, eds., *The Jewish Study Bible* (Oxford University Press, 2004), 18–19, and all Quran quotations are from M. A. S. Abdel Haleem, trans., *The Qur'an* (Oxford: Oxford University Press, "Oxford World's Classics," 2005), 70–71. This paper is a further exploration of the question of whether the Bible and the Quran offer, in the terms of Eric Voegelin, an equivalence of experience and symbolization, which I began in Steven D. Ealy, "The Quran's Guidance to Readers," *Society* (2013) 50: 506–16.

2   Heribert Busse, "Cain and Abel," in Jane Dammen McAuliffe, ed., *Encyclopedia of the Qur'an*, Vol. 1 (Leiden: Brill, 2001), 270.

role of reason in the Hebrew Scriptures, and he uses the story of Cain and Abel to focus his argument. Ali Shari'ati's "The Philosophy of History: Cain and Abel" offers a close theological, sociological, and historical reading of the story as presented in the Quran. I selected these examples of scriptural exegesis as representative, rather than authoritative, analyses. Each is forceful and provocative, and therefore a good vehicle for promoting a serious consideration of the claims of their sacred text.

I

In Genesis 4 the story of Cain and Abel consists of three divisions: the birth and occupations of Cain and Abel, the murder, and the murderer's sentence.[3] I begin by noting a number of details that pose questions or puzzles. The introduction to the story of Cain and Abel opens with a mention of Adam ("the man") and his wife Eve, and thus offers a backward glance to what has transpired earlier in Genesis. Genesis 3 provides an account of Adam and Eve breaking the one prohibition God had set down for them: do not eat the fruit of the tree of knowledge of good and evil. The failure of Adam and Eve to abide by this restriction resulted in their expulsion from the relative plenty and ease of the Garden of Eden and their entry into a world in which pain and toil would be their lot.

After the expulsion from Eden, Eve gives birth to Cain. Abel is born sometime later. As an influence on his sons, Adam is nonexistent in the text, for he disappears after his role in siring Cain, and reenters Genesis only after the events involving Cain and Abel have played themselves out. Eve commemorates the birth of her first child with a comment: "I have gained a male child with the help of the LORD" (Gen 4:1). When Abel is born Eve offers no commentary. Is this an example of the human tendency to lavish attention on one's firstborn and show less interest in

---

3   I am following the division of the story as outlined by Umberto Cassuto, *A Commentary on the Book of Genesis, Vol. I: From Adam to Noah*, Israel Abrahams, trans. (Jerusalem: The Magnes Press, The Hebrew University, 1961), 196–227. Cassuto adds a fourth division, the descendants of Cain, which will not concern me in this paper (228–38).

additional children? What should be made of the fact that Eve speaks at the birth of Cain and that Adam is silent? Is this a comment on a mother's natural instinct to nurture and a father's natural distancing of himself from the responsibilities of child-rearing?[4] After the birth of Abel, Eve too disappears from this account of her first sons.

No family life is depicted in this story of Cain and Abel. Any education Cain and Abel may have received remains unclear, and the next we hear of them they seem to be functioning on their own as adults. In any event, they are operating independently of their parents and are identified by their respective occupations. Cain is a "tiller of the soil," a farmer, while Abel is "a keeper of sheep." Both appear to be productive and pious men, for both bring an offering to God, an offering representative of their productive labor. Cain brings some of "the fruit of the soil" he has harvested, and Abel offers "the choicest of the firstlings of his flock." This account offers no insights into the motivations of the brothers in making their offerings to God, but it does emphasize that God's response to each was distinct. God "paid heed to Abel and his offering, but to Cain and his offering He paid no heed" (Gen 4:4–5). Genesis explains neither why God took note of Abel's offering but not Cain's, nor what God's "heed" entailed. What is clear is that God's responses were known to the brothers, or at least known to Cain, because Cain was "much distressed" (Gen 4:3) (in Cassuto's translation Cain was "very vexed").[5] What does God's decision to accept one offering and reject the other tell us about God? What does Cain's reaction tell us about Cain? What exactly was Cain's reaction—anger, confusion, depression?[6] If Cain is angry, who is the object of his anger? Is he angry with God, and therefore motivated by

---

4   In this connection note that at the end of Genesis 4 when Eve gives birth to a third son, Seth, she again speaks: "And again Adam knew his wife, and she bore a son and called his name Seth: 'For God has appointed for me another child [she said] instead of Abel, for Cain slew him'" (Cassuto, 245).

5   Cassuto, *A Commentary on the Book of Genesis*, 205, 207.

6   Nahum M. Sarna comments, "Cain's mood is depression, not anger. Hebrew *harah l-* expresses despondency or distress, as opposed to *harah 'af*, *which means* 'to be angry'." *The JPS Torah Commentary: Genesis* (Philadelphia: The Jewish Publication Society, 1989), 33.

hubris? Is his anger at God legitimate—did God do Cain an injustice? Is he motivated by envy, and therefore angry with Abel? Or is it possible that Cain is angry with himself?

Cain did not mask his disappointment, and his distress was immediately obvious because his "face fell" (Gen 4:5). Cain's reaction led God to talk with him, and God's opening question to Cain seems to eliminate any simple reading of this story. God asks Cain, "Why are you distressed, and why is your face fallen?" (Gen 4:6). While God is the creator of mankind, one might wonder how well He understands the human creatures that He created. Was God surprised by Adam and Eve's inability to abide by His only stricture? Was God surprised by Cain's distress after He rejected Cain's offering? One possible understanding of God's refusal to "pay heed" to Cain's offering—perhaps the natural first reaction to such an occurrence—is that God's response was not just a rejection of Cain's offering but was a rejection of Cain himself. God's question to Cain, however, suggests that He is surprised by Cain's distress, and His subsequent comment—"Surely, if you do right, There is uplift" (Gen 4:7)—appears to be an effort to raise Cain's spirits and encourage him to persist in pursuing the good. God warns Cain that sin is waiting for an opportunity to overtake him, but emphasizes that, rather than being mastered by this sin, "You can be its master" (Gen 4:7). This is the first appearance of the word "sin" in the Hebrew Scriptures.

Having been presented with these alternatives, Cain chose his course of action. He spoke to Abel, although we do not know what he said.[7] The Hebrew word translated as "said to" usually prefaces a direct quotation, but the text gives no hint of what Cain said to Abel. Some translations provide a conjectural statement to cover this gap—the New Revised Standard Revision, for example, inserts "Let us go out to the field." Perhaps Cain intentionally arranged to meet Abel in order to do

---

7   See Cassuto, 213–15. After examining all of the examples of the Hebrew word ("spoke") in the Bible, Kenneth M, Craig, Jr. writes, "We conclude that the author has created a sense of mystery, wittingly or unwittingly, by not rendering the speech itself. Cain spoke, but what did he say?" ("Questions Outside Eden [Genesis 4:1–16]: Yahweh, Cain and Their Rhetorical Interchange," *Journal for the Study of the Old Testament* 89 [1999], 119).

him harm, or perhaps a confused Cain simply wanted to talk over with his brother the implications of his recent conversation with God. (Nahum Sarna's view that Cain is depressed rather than angry suggests that this is a reasonable possibility.)[8] Perhaps when they met, Abel said something that set Cain against him and thus deflected Cain's vexation from God, or from himself, to Abel.[9] In any case, when the opportunity presented itself, Cain killed his brother. Soon God approached Cain with another question, "Where is your brother?" (Gen 4:9) Cain offers a two-fold response. First, he lies by saying that he does not know where Abel is. Second, he tries to divert God's attention by raising a question of his own, "Am I my brother's keeper?" (Gen 4:9). This question, which hangs in the air through the ages, is one of the reasons we find the story of Cain and Abel so intriguing. While the flow of the narrative perhaps encourages the reader to a kneejerk affirmative response, God does not answer Cain's question.[10] God was not sidetracked by Cain's diversionary tactics, and his next question is the preface for Cain's condemnation. "What have you done?" is not a call for Cain to come clean but a rebuke for his crime, which is attested to by Abel's blood, which is still soaking into the ground. In Genesis 3:17, in response to Adam and Eve's disobedience, God said to Adam, "Cursed be the ground because of you." He now tells Cain, "You shall be more cursed than the ground" (4:11). Adam would have to toil in order to make the soil yield crops, but Cain is told, "If you till the soil, it shall no longer yield its strength to you" (Gen 4:12). Rather than continue his stationary life as a farmer working

---

8   The JPS Torah Commentary: Genesis, 33.

9   According to James L. Kugel, Targum Neophyti "imagines that Cain did not simply up and kill his brother, but was provoked to do so by an argument that developed as the two were strolling along in the field." Jamies L. Kugel, "Cain and Abel in Fact and Fable: Genesis 4:1–16," in Roger Brooks and John J. Collins, eds., *Hebrew Bible or Old Testament? Studying the Bible in Judaism and Christianity* (Notre Dame, IN: University of Notre Dame Press, 1990), 178. See 177 for Kugel's translation of the pertinent passage from Targum Neophyti.

10   Sarna comments on Cain's question, "The Sevenfold stress in this chapter on the obvious fraternal relationship of Cain and Abel emphatically teaches that man is indeed his brother's keeper and that all homicide is fratricide." (*The JPS Torah Commentary: Genesis*, 34.)

the soil, Cain is destined to "become a ceaseless wanderer on earth" (Gen 4:12).

Cain laments his dual banishment—banished from the soil and from the presence of God—and bemoans the possibility that, as an outcast, "anyone who meets me may kill me!" (Gen 4:14). God then places a mark on Cain, not as a punishment, but as a protection designed to warn away potential executioners.

Following the order of the biblical narrative, here are some of the questions suggested but left unanswered by the text.

1. Does Eve's comment on the birth of Cain and lack of comment concerning Abel indicate that she paid heed to Cain but not to Abel?
2. How did Cain and Abel come to their respective occupations and is there any significance as to their respective choices?
3. Why did Cain and then Abel bring an offering to God?
4. Why did God accept Abel's offering but not Cain's?
5. Did God's rejection of Cain's offering constitute a rejection of Cain?
6. Is God's first question to Cain ("Why are you distressed …?") serious or rhetorical?
7. Does God's advice to Cain suggest support? Or does it suggest derision?
8. God tells Cain that "sin crouches at the door" (Gen 4:7). Does this suggest that sin is somehow an external force that can work on man? Or, is sin an internal component of man's nature?
9. What does God mean when he tells Cain that he can be the master of that crouching sin?
10. Did Cain have anything to say to or ask of God?
11. What did Cain say to Abel? Was the killing of Abel intentional and planned in advance—first degree murder? Was the killing spontaneous and unplanned—second degree murder?
12. Why did God ask Cain where Abel was if He already knew?
13. God does not answer Cain's question, "Am I my brother's keeper?" What would God's answer be to that question?
14. God tells Cain that Abel's blood cries out to Him. What is the significance of this statement? Does it suggest that there is a natural order of justice?

15. God tells Cain he will be "more cursed than the ground"—what does this mean?
16. Is being deprived of his livelihood and home Cain's real punishment?
17. Cain says that he must avoid God's presence—did God require this of Cain? Or is this evidence that Cain felt shame for his action (or for being found out?)?
18. When Cain expresses his fear that he may be killed as he wanders the earth, God places a mark on him to warn off potential killers. Why? Is this part of Cain's punishment or is God for some reason protecting Cain? Does the "mark of Cain" hold any general lesson for us?

II

The story of Cain and Abel is now incorporated into the fabric of world literature.[11] Perhaps one of the reasons that it has been so widely embraced and used is that it is an empty vessel that can be filled with a wide variety of interpretations.[12] Given its dynamic of brothers in conflict, the story perhaps lends itself to any dualism in need of a human face. One way of engaging the story of Cain and Abel at least since Augustine's *The City of God* is to treat the brothers as archetypes of humanity. Augustine argues that mankind is "distributed into two parts, the one consisting of those who live according to man, the other of those who live according to God."[13] Cain was the first citizen of the city of man, while

11 Sol Liptzin, *Biblical Themes in World Literature* (Hoboken: Ktav Publishing House, 1985), "Defiant Cain," 13–24; Richard J. Quinones, *The Changes of Cain: Violence and the Lost Brother in Cain and Abel Literature* (Princeton: Princeton University Press, 1991).

12 Consider the implications of this exchange from Samuel Beckett's *Waiting for Godot* (New York: Grove Press, 1954), 95–96: "Vladimir: I tell you his name is Pozzo. Estragon: We'll soon see. *(He Reflects.)* Abel! Abel! Pozzo: Help! Estragon: Got it in one! Vladimir: I begin to weary of this motif. Estragon: Perhaps the other is called Cain. Cain! Cain! Pozzo: Help! Estragon: He's all humanity. *(Silence.)*"

13 Saint Augustine, *The City of God*, Marcus Dods, trans. (New York: The Modern Library, 1950), 478.

Abel belonged to the city of God. Abel's status as a citizen of the city of God is not a matter of his actions or free choices, however, but because he was "predestined by grace, elected by grace, [to be] a stranger below [in the city of man], and ... a citizen above [in the city of God]."[14]

One potential pitfall in the typological approach is that our constructed types may lead us into predictable and oversimplified categories that miss the paradoxes and tensions contained in the original biblical story. Yoram Hazony's *The Philosophy of Hebrew Scripture* treats Cain and Abel as types but attempts to avoid this danger.[15]

In many discussions of Genesis 4 the focus is almost entirely on Cain, and any discussion of Abel is merely an afterthought. This is certainly the case when we come to the literary treatments of the biblical story as presented in Lord Byron's *Cain: A Mystery* and John Steinbeck's monumental *East of Eden*. For both of these writers, Cain is the crucial figure. In Byron, he is treated as a Prometheus-like figure who establishes human freedom through his refusal to obey God. In Steinbeck's novel, Cain is also central to establishing the principle of human freedom, which is built around Cain's discussion with God and the meaning of the Hebrew word "timshel," which is translated by the house-servant Lee as "mayest." Lee argues that God's use of the word "may," as opposed to "must," contains the kernel of contingency and openness found at the heart of human freedom.[16] For both Byron and Steinbeck, it is not

14 Augustine, 479.
15 While Hazony makes an important contribution to understanding the dynamic of the biblical story of Cain and Abel, his argument is important not just for understanding Genesis 4 but as a radical critique of the generally accepted understanding of the entire Hebrew Bible. Hazony's major focus in this regard, of which his treatment of Cain and Abel is but a small piece, is to dismantle the popular view that the Hebrew Bible cannot be treated as a serious intellectual document because it is based on revelation and not on reason. He seeks to establish the role of reason in the Hebrew Bible through a discussion of its structure and by highlighting and illustrating the array of techniques it uses to make arguments of a general nature that can be judged by reason. Here I set Hazony's overall project aside to concentrate on his discussion of Cain and Abel.
16 John Steinbeck, *East of Eden* (New York: Penguin Books, "John Steinbeck Centennial Edition," 2002), 301–02.

unfair to say that Abel is just a stage prop, while the real action of the story swirls around Cain. This neglect of Abel is perhaps not surprising, and is even suggested in Genesis by Abel's very name, which is related to the Hebrew word for "vapor" and "puff of air"[17] and signifies "something transitory."[18]

Hazony's work runs counter to the general treatment of the story, which emphasizes the relative importance of Cain and unimportance of Abel. In contrast to this traditional emphasis, Hazony's first mention of this story refers only to Abel. In an overview of his book, Hazony writes, "The Bible is often said to advocate an ethics of obedience. But … this view involves a serious misreading of Hebrew Scripture."[19] The figures most celebrated in the Hebrew Bible, Hazony argues, "are esteemed for their dissent and disobedience—a trait the biblical authors associate with the free life of the shepherd, as opposed to the life of the pious submission represented by the figure of the farmer."[20] In effect, Hazony sets out to turn the tables on Byron's understanding; for Hazony, Abel (as the type of the shepherd) will represent dissidence and disobedience, while Cain (as the type of the farmer) will represent conformity and submission.

The shepherd's dissidence manifests itself in opposition to corrupt institutions, but it goes beyond this. Hazony writes, "Abel, Abraham, Jacob, Moses, Aaron, and other biblical figures are at times portrayed as resisting not only man, but God *himself*."[21] Hazony signifies the importance to Abel by placing him first in this list of biblical heroes. He concludes, "The biblical narrative endorses … an *outsider's ethics*, which encourages a critique even of things that appear to be decreed by God in the name of what is genuinely beneficial to man."[22] From this biblical perspective, Hazony continues, "what is genuinely beneficial to

---

17 Robert Alter, *Genesis: Translation and Commentary* (New York: W. W. Norton, 1996), 16 n.2.

18 *The Five Books of Moses*, Everett Fox, trans. (Dallas: Word Publishing, 1995), 25 note.

19 Yoram Hazony, *The Philosophy of Hebrew Scripture* (Cambridge: Cambridge University Press, 2012), 23.

20 Hazony, 24.

21 Ibid.

22 Ibid.

man is that which will ultimately find favor in God's eyes,"[23] even if the idea did not originate with God and even if it was in opposition to God's original plan.

Perhaps as surprising as Hazony's emphasis on Abel is his characterization of Cain, which is also at odds with the popular treatment of the story. Hazony's introduction of Cain occurs when he places Cain's story within the broader sweep of biblical history, and he argues that it "is very uncertain ... that we can really understand the story of Cain, a farmer, murdering his brother Abel, who is a shepherd, if we do not recognize that this first act of violence between farmers and shepherds is a premonition of the violence between farmers and shepherds that appears in the later story of Abraham, and then again in the story of Moses, and yet again in the story of David."[24]

Cain is a farmer "who represents tradition-bound and idolatrous societies such as Egypt and Babylonia" and "whose highest value is obedience."[25] Abel is a shepherd "who stands for the spirit of freedom in search of that which is the true good." Abel represents the individual and the society "that is willing to forsake the might and riches of the great civilizations for the sake of personal freedom and the hope of something higher."[26]

Hazony notes that Cain and Abel are born to Eve after she and Adam have sinned and been expelled from the Garden of Eden, with Adam destined "to work the ground from which he had been taken."[27] This passage emphasizes the "bitterness of the farming life" and is made even stronger by the words used to describe Adam's fate. According to Hazony, the Hebrew term usually translated "till" or "work" the soil also means "serve." Thus, "God has in fact punished man by sending him 'to serve the ground'—to become the servant and slave of the earth itself."[28]

Hazony's discussion of Genesis 4 emphasizes two points concerning Cain that diverge from the popular understanding. First, "The text emphasizes

23 Ibid.
24 Hazony, 45.
25 Hazony, 60.
26 Ibid.
27 Quoted at Hazony, 106.
28 Hazony, 107.

that the idea of making a sacrifice to God is Cain's. It is Cain who inclines toward piety, and thinks to take some of his meager supply of food, which he has scraped from the soil, and sacrifice it to God in gratitude."[29] Second, as a tiller of the soil, Cain is following the instructions God had given to Adam. Hazony writes, "He works the ground just as God had told his father to do. He submits to God's will, and, even amid the curse and the hardship, finds it in his heart to be grateful to God for what he has."[30]

Hazony's account of Abel is also different from the standard view. First, Abel merely follows Cain's example in making a sacrifice. There is no suggestion that his offering is superior to his brother's. Second, while Cain has followed in his father's career and tilled the soil in accordance with God's instructions, in becoming a shepherd, "Abel has ... found a way to escape the curse upon the soil."[31] Hazony maintains that the biblical text emphasizes "the fact that this is about what Abel wants, first and foremost, rather than about what God wants."[32] So the pious and hard-working Cain's sacrifice is rejected while the sacrifice of the self-indulgent Abel is accepted. How can this be brought into an understandable framework?

Hazony argues that the story is constructed so as to present readers with a stark choice concerning the best way of life: "Each archetype represents a way of life and an approach to living as a human being, to ethics."[33] First is the life of the farmer as portrayed in Cain. "Cain has piously accepted the curse of the soil ... as unchallengeable. His response is to *submit*, as had his father before him ... In the eyes of the biblical author, Cain represents the life of the farmer, a life of pious submission, obeying in gratitude the custom that has been handed down, which alone provides bread so that man may live."[34]

Next is the life of the shepherd.

> Abel takes the curse of the soil as a fact, but not as one that
> possesses any intrinsic merit, so that it should command his

29 Ibid.
30 Ibid.
31 Ibid.
32 Ibid.
33 Hazony, 108.
34 Ibid.

allegiance. The fact that God decreed it, and that his father had submitted to it, does not make it good. His response is the opposite of submission: He resists with ingenuity and daring, risking the anger of man and God to secure improvement for himself and for his children. Abel represents the life of the shepherd, which is a life of dissent and initiative, whose aim is to find the good life for man, which is presumed to be God's true will.[35]

While God did not have shepherding in mind when he ejected Adam and Eve from Eden, it develops that shepherding does fit within God's plans. What God really wants, according to Hazony, is "an improvement in man's station, a greater goodness which comes of man's own unsolicited efforts."[36] He concludes, "God accepts the offering of a man who seeks to improve things, to make them good of himself and his own initiative. This is what God finds in Abel, and the reason he accepts his sacrifice."[37]

For both John Steinbeck and Yoram Hazony the significance of the Cain and Abel story is found in its emphasis on freedom. The difference between the two is that Steinbeck finds the locus of human freedom in God's discussion of the ability to master sin directed to Cain, while Hazony locates human freedom in Abel's ability to step outside of tradition and act on his own initiative to promote his well-being. This raises the possibility that human freedom is not univocal and perhaps should be understood in terms of process rather than content. Does God's charge to Cain offer a model of negative freedom ("freedom from") while Abel's innovative activity is an example of positive freedom ("freedom to")?[38]

35 Ibid.
36 Ibid.
37 Ibid. I note in passing a point that Hazony does not make—this discussion of man's improvement of his situation sounds much like Locke's account of the divine origins of property in his chapter on property in the *Second Treatise.*
38 See Isaiah Berlin, "Two Concepts of Liberty," in *Four Essays on Liberty* (Oxford: Oxford University Press, 1969), 118–72.

III

The Quran's account is even briefer than Genesis, and concludes with God issuing a universal judgment: "We have decreed to the Children of Israel that if anyone kills a person—unless in retribution for murder or spreading corruption in the land—it is as if he kills all mankind, while if any saves a life it is as if he saves the lives of all mankind."[39] The Sura continues with a detailed discussion of the punishments appropriate—including death and crucifixion—for "those who wage war against God and His Messenger and strive to spread corruption in the land."[40] Because this discussion of appropriate punishments is so strongly worded and forcefully stated, it is possible that the effect of what began as a statement limiting the taking of human life might actually be to encourage the execution and maiming of those thought to spread corruption.

There are a number of differences in the accounts from Genesis and the Quran that should be noted. In Genesis Adam is never mentioned by name but Eve is (and has some dialogue), while in the Quran Eve is omitted and the brothers are identified only as Adam's sons. The occupations of the sons are not mentioned in the Quran. After his sacrifice is rejected, one brother threatens to kill the other. The reason for God's rejection of one offering is unclear in Genesis, but in the Quran the brother whose offering was accepted explains that God accepts only the sacrifices of those who are mindful of Him. This same brother, who is silent in Genesis, is quite talkative in the Quran, for he then tells the other that he fears God more than man, and he will not raise his hand to harm his brother, and further forecasts eternal punishment in the fire for his brother if he follows through on his threat. After the killing, the murderer learns by watching a raven that he could have buried his brother's body. He is remorseful, but it is not clear whether this remorse is because of the murder he committed or because he did not hide the body. There is no indication in the Quran that God marked Cain in order

---

39 M. A. S. Abdel Haleem, trans., *The Qur'an* (Oxford: Oxford University Press, "Oxford World's Classics," 2005), Q 5: 27–32, 70–71. Hereafter cited by Sura and verse and page number to this edition.
40 The Qur'an, 6:33, 71.

to protect his life. A final difference is the universal principle that God announces.[41]

While God does not enter into dialogue with Cain in the Quran, there is an exchange between the two brothers. It is important to keep in mind that God Himself is the source of this entire passage, and He is instructing Muhammad to relate the story to those to whom he is preaching, thus the story as presented is in God's own words. In the Quran's account of this story, all of the ambiguities found in Genesis 4 are eliminated.

First, God's account accepts at face value, and thus tacitly endorses, the righteous brother's understanding of God's action: "God only accepts the sacrifice of those who are mindful of him" (Q 5:27, 70). In the Quranic account there appears to be no possibility of separating the sacrifice from the one making the sacrifice, thus eliminating the possibility that the rejected brother was blameless, or at least salvageable.

Second, it is clear that the target of the rejected brother's anger is his brother, and his immediate intention is clear from the beginning: "I will kill you." When he carries through on his intention, he becomes one of the losers.

Third, the Quran appears to offer a universal principle in contrast to the very event-specific nature of the resolution in Genesis. However, the apparent prohibition of killing and affirmation of saving lives does not condemn killing "in retribution for murder or spreading corruption in the land."

IV

In "The Philosophy of History: Cain and Abel," Ali Shari'ati argues that from the Islamic perspective, "the philosophy of history is based on a certain kind of historical determinism."[42] Both history and man himself are "dominated by a dialectical contradiction, a constant warfare

---

41   Abraham Geiger, *Judaism and Islam* (Madras: MDCSPCK Press, 1898), 80–82, suggests that various rabbinic writings were the source of details in the Quran account not found in Genesis.

42   Ali Shari'ati, *On the Sociology of Islam*, Hamid Algar, trans. (Berkeley: Mizan Press, 1979), 97.

between two hostile and contradictory elements that began with the creation of humanity and has been waged at all places and at all times." Simultaneously, however, Shari'ati maintains that "the human species itself is a microcosm, representing the most perfect expression of being, the most evident manifestation of creation." Shari'ati argues that "man is a manifestation of God's will, the absolute will and consciousness of all being,"[43] God's own representative on earth (Q 2: 30).

The contradiction within man begins with the creation of Adam by God, for "man is a compound of clay and divine spirit."[44] The subjective struggle within Adam "between spirit and clay, God and Satan" is foundational for man and is reflected in the inner turmoil of each individual. While this "inner war" may mark the beginning of biography, history begins with the "objective [war] that took place in outer life" between the sons of Adam. In Shari'ati's words, "One killed the other, and the history of humanity began."[45]

For Shari'ati, as for Augustine and for Hazony, Cain and Abel are types. Abel "represents the age of a pasture-based economy" and "the primitive socialism that preceded ownership." Cain "represents the system of agriculture, and individual or monopoly ownership." Shari'ati maintains that before the emergence of the agricultural system, "the individual had not existed in human society; the tribe itself was the individual."[46] The groups that later became "opposing classes used to live in a uniform society, animated by a single spirit, a single sentiment, a single concept of honor and dignity—that of the tribe."[47]

"With the coming of agriculture," however, "that unitary society, where all men were like the brothers in a single household, was divided." While this may sound like a Marxist analysis, Shari'ati maintains that it is not—at the "crucial point in history, the exact opposite of Marx's theory applies; it is not ownership that is a factor in the acquisition of power, but the converse. Power and coercion were the

---

43   Ibid., 97.
44   Shari'ati, 98. Cf. Q 15: 26–29, 163.
45   Shari'ati, 98.
46   Shari'ati, 100.
47   Shari'ati, 101–02.

factors that first bestowed ownership on the individual. Power brought about private ownership, and then in turn, private ownership bestowed permanence on power and strengthened it by making it something legal and natural."[48]

We live in a world in which "the death of Abel and the survival of Cain are objective, historical realities," which in turn point to "the fact that henceforth religion, life, economy, government and the fate of men were all in the hands of Cain." Today the world is dominated by "the heirs of Cain."[49]

But this is not the end of the historical story. Because "man is a manifestation of God's will ... the history of man ... cannot therefore be accidental, something fashioned by events, the plaything of adventurers, banal, vain, aimless, purposeless and meaningless." Rather, "History ... began at a certain point, and must inevitably end at a certain point. It must have an aim and a direction."[50]

Cain and Abel play a role in this trajectory of history, according to Shari'ati, for the war between them has been fought in every generation. In this war "the weapon of Cain has been religion, and the weapon of Abel has also been religion," and therefore religious wars are one of the constants of history.

> On the one hand is the religion of *shirk*, of assigning partners to God, a religion that furnishes the justification for *shirk* in society and class discrimination. On the other hand is the religion of *tauhid*, of the oneness of God, which furnishes the justification for the unity of all classes and races. The transhistorical struggle between Abel and Cain is also the struggle between *tauhid* and *shirk*, between justice and human unity on the one hand, and social and racial discrimination on the other.[51]

48 Shari'ati, 100.
49 Shari'ati, 104. In a footnote he clarifies, "heirs in a typological sense, not a genealogical one."
50 Shari'ati, 97.
51 Shari'ati, 108–09.

The "inevitable direction of history" is toward a revolution that will occur when Cain dies and "the system of Abel" is established. This "inevitable revolution" will mean that "equality will be realized throughout the world, and human unity and brotherhood will be established, through equity and justice."[52] "The glad tidings of God will be realized," but they will not be glad tidings for all, for in the revolution "the oppressed classes of history will take their revenge."[53] In this regard it is worth reading in its entirety the passage in the Quran's discussion of the sons of Adam that deals with punishment.

> Those who wage war against God and his Messenger and strive to spread corruption in the land should be punished by death, crucifixion, the amputation of an alternate hand and foot, or banishment from the land: a disgrace for them in this world, and then a terrible punishment in the Hereafter, unless they repent before you overpower them—in that case bear in mind that God is forgiving and merciful.[54]

In the great final battle between the forces of Cain and the forces of Abel, is the possibility of forgiveness and mercy foreclosed when the final triumph of Abel occurs, as it inevitably will? Consideration of one final issue may help answer this question.

I noted the centrality of human freedom in my discussion of Yoram Hazony's analysis of Cain and Abel. Shari'ati also addresses the question of freedom, and is particularly concerned with reconciling the possibility of freedom with the reality of historical determinism. Shari'ati begins this discussion with a strong affirmation of individual responsibility: "It is the responsibility of every individual in every age to determine his stance in the constant struggle between the two wings we have described, and not to remain a spectator." How can individual responsibility be combined with the historical determinism that Shari'ati has outlined in his essay? He maintains that "the freedom of the individual

---

52   Shari'ati, 109.
53   Ibid., 109.
54   Quran, Q 5:33–34, 71.

and his human responsibility … lie at the very heart of the process of historical determinism."

Shari'ati denies that there is a contradiction between individual freedom and historical determinism. He has already laid the foundation for their reconciliation in his earlier contrast of Adam's "subjective, inner" war and the "objective [war] that took place in outer life" between Cain and Abel. At the objective level, "history advances on the basis of a universal and scientifically demonstrable process of determinism." At the subjective level, however, "'I' as an individual human being must choose whether to move forward with history and accelerate its determined course with the force of knowledge and science, or to stand with ignorance, egoism, opportunism in the face of history, and be crushed."[55] Thus for Shari'ati, freedom consists in choosing one of two options: embrace the historically inevitable, and thus become a winner, or fight a rearguard action against progress, and thereby condemn oneself to "disgrace … in this world, and then a terrible punishment in the Hereafter."

V

The world depicted in Genesis is one of ambiguity and contingency, a world in which much of the action takes the form of speech, with an emphasis on dialogue or conversation. Even God, earlier portrayed as the Creator of the world and mankind, does not appear to be in total control of the flow of events, and His plans may be thwarted by human decision and action. In some of the episodes presented in Genesis, God's intentions and actions appear to be as hard to fathom as those of the humans that He interacts with and that He chooses to carry out His will. And God's plans appear to be as subject to the contingencies of the world as do the plans made by his creations. As Yoram Hazony states, "God is found to be vulnerable before man's rebelliousness and depravity."[56] This certainly seems to be the case in the story of Cain and Abel.

The text does not explain why Cain brings an offering to God, or why Abel follows his example. The text does not explain why God ac-

55 Shari'ati, 109–10.
56 Hazony, 97.

cepts Abel's offering and rejects Cain's. When God talks with an obviously upset Cain after His rejection of Cain's offering, He does not explain the reason for the rejection and seems surprised by Cain's reaction to this rejection. His counseling session with Cain offers an early example of the limits of therapeutic intervention in modifying a patient's perceptions and actions. At their next meeting, after Cain has killed his brother, God confronts Cain with his deed and sets forth his punishment. In response to Cain's expressed fear that he too will be slain, however, God extends His protection to Cain by marking him in a way that will warn off any potential executioners. While at other points in the Hebrew Scriptures the principle of justice is "an eye for an eye, and a tooth for a tooth," God does not demand—or take—Cain's life as punishment for his killing of his brother.

Hazony notes that "the Hebrew Scriptures purposely provide us with multiple perspectives on a great many issues."[57] This allows for a layering and for the development of a textured and more complete picture than could be achieved from any single source—perhaps even if that single source is divine. The multiple perspectives are often provided through the dialogue of primary figures during the course of the narrative. As an instructional method, the presentation of multiple perspectives forces the student (reader/listener) to ask questions of him or herself concerning the veracity and reliability of the actors in the narrative. Perhaps this approach is pushed even further in the Cain and Abel story by the intentional omission of the dialogue between the brothers just before the murder occurs,[58] forcing the reader to construct the encounter imaginatively.

This presentation of multiple perspectives and layered understanding opens up the possibility that the Hebrew Scriptures point to what Carol Newsom calls "dialogic truth," as opposed to monologic truth. "Dialogic truth" is characterized by a plurality of consciousness (as opposed to a

---

57 Hazony, 45.
58 See note 6 above. W. Gunter Plaut suggests that "the omission of what Cain said may be a purposeful ellipsis." *The Torah: A Modern Commentary I: Genesis* (New York: Union of American Hebrew Congregations, 1974), 42 note.

single perspective), a personal embodied understanding (as opposed to a universal abstractionism), an emphasis on concrete events (as opposed to development of a system), and openness to additional evidence.[59]

Perhaps dialogic truth ties closely into the importance of human freedom in the Hebrew Scriptures, including in the story of Cain and Abel. I have already outlined Yoram Hazony's argument concerning freedom in Genesis 4, so will conclude this discussion of the structure and dynamic of Cain and Abel with his overview of the place of freedom in Tanakh. When God creates man "in our image" this entails the freedom to act on his own, and "man's freedom to choose appears to be a delight to God."[60] This evaluation remains even when man violates God's restrictions and goes his own way.

> Even once this freedom leads man to evil, God does not repent having given man this freedom. On the contrary, it is man's freedom to act against mankind's evildoing, and even against God, that is presented in the narrative as man's greatest glory, with those whom God loves best—Abel, Abraham, Jacob, Moses—being those who presume to challenge God, to wrestle with him, and even to defeat him for the sake of what is good. No, there is no hint that the biblical authors would have found virtue in a man denuded of his freedom, an automaton.[61]

In comparing the general features of the Quranic story of the sons of Adam with the account of Cain and Abel in Genesis 4, perhaps the most important difference to note is that the Quran contains no confusion of perspective—the vision and the words are God's alone.

God's pedagogy in the Quran appears to eschew most of the elements that seem to characterize the Hebrew Scriptures—an underlying emphasis on the contingency of events, and the portrayal of both characters (including God Himself) and actions in subtle and at times

---

59   Carol A. Newsom, "Bakhtin, the Bible, and Dialogic Truth," *The Journal of Religion* 76 (1996): 290–306, at 293–94.
60   Hazony, 97.
61   Ibid., 97.

ambiguous terms. While both texts may have moral lessons to teach, they take different approaches to this end. Genesis apparently instructs by goading the reader into an engagement with the questions raised by the narrative in the hope that students will articulate the lessons for themselves, while the Quran often prefaces its account with a straight-forward statement of the story's moral lesson. Where the reason for God's rejection of Cain's sacrifice is left open in Genesis, in the Quran it is clear that Cain is rejected because "God only accepts the sacrifice of those who are mindful of Him" (Q 5:27, 70). In Genesis, Abel appears as an object of sympathy because of his murder but is otherwise un-known. In the Quran it is clear that he is a devout follower of God, for he tells his brother, "If you raise your hand to kill me, I will not raise mine to kill you. I fear God, the Lord of all worlds, and I would rather you were burdened with my sins as well as yours and become an inhab-itant of the Fire: such is the evildoers' reward" (Q 5: 28, 70). In Genesis, while God metes out punishment to Cain, His initial stern approach is perhaps undermined when He acts to protect Cain after Cain expresses his fear of being killed. In the discussion of punishments appended to the tale of the sons of Adam, the Quran leaves no room for the tempering of justice by the application of mercy, for mercy applies only to those who have repented before they have been caught.

I conclude with a word about human freedom in the Hebrew Scrip-tures and the Quran. Yoram Hazony argues that the Hebrew Scriptures do not advocate a simple "ethics of obedience." Can the same be said of the Quran? Does it offer a foundation for what Hazony calls the "outsider's ethics" aimed at what is truly beneficial to man, or does it advocate an ethics bounded by the detailed commands of authority—of God? This out-sider ethic seems to be at the heart of the freedom and creativity found in the Hebrew Scriptures and celebrated in God's continuing embrace of those He has chosen even when they challenge Him and argue with Him.

An early example of man's freedom in Genesis is Adam's naming of the animals,[62] while in the Quran God teaches Adam the names of the animals.[63] Is the kind of creative capacity represented by naming the

---

62 Genesis 2:19.
63 The Quran, Q 2:31, 7.

animals a necessary foundation for the development of an ethical perspective that goes beyond mere obedience? Assuming the answer to this question is yes, we can then ask whether man in the Quran has this capacity.

Are there any heroes of the faith in the Quran, as there are in the Tanakh, who challenge God? Or would such a challenge immediately place one in the category of wrongdoer or loser? The Quran says that the response of the faithful to God and to His messengers is, "We hear, and we obey."[64] If this represents man's greatest capacity, it does not mean that man has no freedom. It does however, suggest that the freedom of man in the world of the Quran is constrained, contrasted to the freedom of man in the Hebrew Scriptures. Perhaps Ali Shari'ati captures the spirit of human freedom in the Quran when he articulates freedom as a binary choice: either move forward with history (and with God) and be a winner, or stand with ignorance and be crushed.

---

64   The Quran, Q 2:285, 33; Q 24: 51, 224.

Leo Strauss's Developing Interest in Alfarabi and Its Reverberations in the Study of Medieval Islamic Philosophy

Steven Harvey

Alfarabi is dying a slow and agonizing death, and few scholars of Islamic Philosophy today are even aware of it. Most of those who have noticed couldn't care less. In the present paper, I will give an account of the rise and gradual fall in our times of this fascinating philosopher, the inaugurator of the tradition of Aristotelian philosophy in Islam, who emphasized the importance of rooting one's studies in Aristotelian formal logic, of studying the sciences in the proper order, and of turning to Plato in matters concerning the city and its governance. Curiously, Alfarabi's downfall comes at a time when his most important followers, Avicenna and Averroes, have been receiving unprecedented scholarly attention. This significant phenomenon may be appreciated by rehearsing the role of Leo Strauss in the modern study of medieval Islamic philosophy. My paper will thus recount Strauss's contribution to the modern reading of Alfarabi and the *falāsifa* and the impact of that contribution.

My statement that "Alfarabi is dying a slow and agonizing death" needs some explanation. Alfarabi died around the year 950, slightly more than a millennium before the publication of Strauss's eye-opening study, "Fārābī's *Plato*,"[1] so he can hardly be said to be dying now. Nor may it be

*   My thanks to Dr. Thomas Meyer for his very helpful comments on an earlier draft of this paper. I look forward to his forthcoming detailed intellectual biography of Strauss. An early version of this paper was presented at the workshop, "Leo Strauss, Islamic Philosophy, and the End of Pre-modernity," The University of Chicago, May 2013.

1   Leo Strauss, "Fārābī's *Plato*," in *Louis Ginzberg Jubilee Volume* (New York: The American Academy for Jewish Research, 1945), 357–93.

said that the memory of him is currently fading from the consciousness of scholars of Islamic Philosophy. In the past few years, a number of new editions and translations into several languages of his works have appeared. Moreover, according to Thérèse-Anne Druart's annual on-line bibliographies of medieval Islamic philosophy, some fifteen to twenty studies on Alfarabi in various European languages have appeared annually for the past several years.[2] Although this is only a fraction of the number of annual studies on Avicenna and Averroes, it still bespeaks continued interest in Alfarabi. The point of my statement is not that Alfarabi is disappearing from the study of Islamic philosophy, but rather that his revolutionary importance for the study of Islamic philosophy, in particular, and medieval philosophy, in general, is less and less understood and barely appreciated any more. A sign of this is that while the past decade has seen many important conferences on Avicenna and Averroes, a Google search of "Alfarabi conference" (or congress or colloquium) uncovers almost exclusively conferences in modern science held at Al-Farabi University in Kazakhstan, at which, it seems, no one spoke about the views of Alfarabi.[3] Alfarabi continues to be studied, but the picture of the profound thinker uncovered by Leo Strauss— and the distinguished scholars who followed his lead in the second half of the twentieth century, such as the scholar to whom this volume is dedicated—is less and less known and rarely appreciated.

I will begin by sketching the picture of Alfarabi that emerged first through the studies of Strauss, and by pointing to certain significant elements of this picture. In order to appreciate fully Strauss's contribution, it will be useful to recall in some detail the fact that studying Alfarabi some ninety years ago was far more difficult than it is today.

I begin with a biographical supposition that in 1930–1931 when Strauss wrote the third and last essay of *Philosophie und Gesetz*, his knowledge of Arabic was elementary and his reading in Alfarabi was

---

2   See most recently: https://philosophy.catholic.edu/faculty-and-research/publications/dr.-druarts-bibliographic-guide.html. More studies on Alfarabi than usual are listed in the 2012–2013 and 2015–2016 bibliographies.

3   One exception was the video workshop on Alfarabi held in June 2014 at Marquette University. The opening speaker was Charles Butterworth. See: http://academic.mu.edu/taylorr/The_Abrahamic_Traditions/2014_Summer_Conference_Milwaukee.html. On this workshop, see below, n.58.

basically limited to the *Virtuous City* (through Dieterici's edition and German translation, *Der Musterstaat*),[4] to certain other texts edited and translated by Dieterici,[5] and to Steinschneider's *Alpharabius*.[6] He certainly knew enough Arabic at the time to compare Arabic editions and manuscripts with printed translations, but did he read any untranslated texts?[7] And he certainly knew enough about Alfarabi to state near the end of the third and last essay of *Philosophie und Gesetz* that "the originator of this view of prophecy" that he had been discussing in Avicenna and Maimonides "appears to be Alfarabi,"[8] but how familiar was he with Alfarabi at the time? The discussion in that book of Alfarabi's prophetology is based almost exclusively on the *Virtuous City*, but then again Strauss considered that book to contain the "most comprehensive and detailed presentation of Alfarabi's prophetology."[9] In any event, Strauss's focus in

---

4   *Alfārābī's Abhandlung der Musterstaat*, ed. Friedrich Dieterici (Leiden: E. J. Brill, 1895); German trans. Friedrich Dieterici, *Der Musterstaat von Alfārābī* (Leiden: E. J. Brill, 1900).

5   *Alfārābī's philosophische Abhandlungen*, ed. Friedrich Dieterici (Leiden: E. J. Brill, 1890), German trans. Friedrich Dieterici, *Alfārābī's philosophische Abhandlungen* (Leiden: E. J. Brill, 1892).

6   Moritz Steinschneider, *Al-Farabi (Alpharabius) des arabischen philosophen Leben und Schriften mit besonderer Rücksicht auf die Geschichte der griechischen Wissenschaft unter den Arabern* (St.-Petersbourg: Commissionnaires de l'Académie Impériale des sciences, 1869).

7   One possibility is Avicenna's short treatise *Fī ithbāt al-nubuwwāt* (On the Proofs of Prophecies), which he cited from *Tis' rasā'il* (Istanbul, 1881), 82–90, in *Philosophie und Gesetz* (Berlin: Schocken Verlag, 1935), 103 n.5; English trans. Eve Adler, *Philosophy and Law: Contributions to the Understanding of Maimonides and His Predecessors* (Albany: State University of New York Press, 1995), 149 n.41. On Strauss's early knowledge of Arabic, see my "The Story of a Twentieth-Century Jewish Scholar's Discovery of Plato's Political Philosophy in Tenth-Century Islam: Leo Strauss' Early Interest in the Islamic *Falāsifa*," in *Modern Jewish Scholarship on Islam in Context: Rationality, European Borders, and the Search for Belonging*, ed. Ottfried Fraisse (Berlin: De Gruyter, 2018), 219–43, esp. 224–26.

8   *Philosophie und Gesetz*, 114; trans., 125.

9   Ibid., 99: "*Die zusammenhängendste und ausführlichste Darstellung der Prophetologie Alfarâbis*"; trans., 113.

describing the prophetology of the Islamic *falāsifa* in this final part was, for various reasons, Avicenna more than Alfarabi. But it is clear that he already had an interest in both Alfarabi and Avicenna as keys to understanding the puzzles of Maimonides' *Guide of the Perplexed*. His study of their prophetology led him to understand the nature and unappreciated importance of the Platonic character of the Islamic Aristotelians and hence to view the *Guide* as a decisively political book.

If *Philosophie und Gesetz* was a flash of lightening in the interpretation of the *falāsifa*, "Fārābī's *Plato*," which appeared ten years later, provided the full prophecy. Yet already in 1935, Strauss was interested in Alfarabi's *Philosophy of Plato* as well as another at the time unedited work by Alfarabi, his *Summary of Plato's Laws*, which two decades later would also be the focus of a suggestive study on Alfarabi by Strauss.

Regarding the *Philosophy of Plato*, Strauss would later state that Alfarabi "expressed his thought most clearly" in this short treatise.[10] Back in the mid-1930s, once Strauss had begun to appreciate the importance of Alfarabi's Platonism, in itself and for understanding his philosophy, he no doubt became very interested in Alfarabi's *Philosophy of Plato*. The problem was at the time there was no edition of the Arabic text. Strauss knew something about this work from Steinschneider's *Alpharabius*, wherein Steinschneider suggested a connection of this book and of Alfarabi's *Philosophy of Aristotle* to the third section of Shem-Tov ibn Falaquera's *Reshit Hokhmah*, a thirteenth-century Hebrew text edited in 1902.[11] Little more could be said at the time as both Arabic texts were presumed lost. But Strauss was becoming more and more interested in Falaquera. In *Philosophie und Gesetz*, he cites Falaquera's commentary on Maimonides' *Guide of the Perplexed* twice. In the first instance, Falaquera cites Maimonides' discussion in *Guide* II, 40 that "man is political by nature and that it is his nature to live in society," that the human species needs a ruler-

---

10 Leo Strauss, *Persecution and the Art of Writing* (Glencoe, Ill.: The Free Press, 1952), 11; cf. Strauss, "Fārābī's *Plato*," 359–60.

11 Steinschneider, *Alpharabius*, 176–78. See Shem-Tov ben Joseph ibn Falaquera, *Reshit Hokhmah*, ed. Moritz David (Berlin: M. Poppelauer, 1902). The section that parallels the *Philosophy of Plato* was printed and translated in Steinschneider, *Alpharabius*, 224–30 (text), 179–85 (German trans.), and edited in Falaquera, *Reshit Hokhmah*, 72–78.

legislator "so that the community becomes well ordered," that it is "a part of the wisdom of the deity" that there be individuals who "have the faculty of ruling," and that such among them is "the prophet or the bringer of the nomos."[12] Several lines later Falaquera cites a lengthy parallel quotation from Avicenna, which Strauss correctly identified as from his Metaphysics of the *Shifā'*. This passage also speaks of man's need to live in society, his need for a ruler-legislator, and that this ruler-legislator, provided by God, is the prophet. Falaquera was perhaps the first to point to Avicenna's influence upon Maimonides' discussions of prophecy, and Strauss likely saw him as a kindred soul.[13] The second instance refers to the Avicennian-Maimonidean imagery of lightning flashes where the vulgar do not see the light, the few see the flashes in different degrees of frequency and clarity, and the great prophets are in unceasing light. Strauss observes that Falaquera relates the passage to the parable of the sultan's palace in *Guide* III, 51, where in his commentary Falaquera cites from Ibn Bājja's *Epistle on Conjunction of the Intellect with Man*, where Ibn Bājja discusses the ranks of men using the light imagery as well as Plato's cave. This reference by Falaquera, for Strauss, confirmed the relation (*bestätigte Verwandtschaft*) between Plato's parable of the cave and Maimonides' image of the very dark night illumined by lightning flashes. He concluded:

> [J]ust as, according to Plato, the perfect state can be actualized only by the philosopher who has ascended out of the cave into the light, and has beheld the idea of the good, so, according to Maimonides and the Falasifa, the perfect state can be actualized only by the prophet, for whom the night in which the human race is stumbling about is illuminated by lightning flashes from on high, by direct knowledge of the upper world.[14]

12 *Guide of the Perplexed*, trans. Shlomo Pines (Chicago: University of Chicago Press, 1963), II, 40, 381–82.

13 *Philosophie und Gesetz*, 110–11; trans., 122–23; Shem-Ṭov ben Joseph ibn Falaquera, *Moreh ha-Moreh*, ed. Yair Shiffman (Jerusalem: World Union of Jewish Studies, 2001), 288–340 (on *Guide* II, 40).

14 *Philosophie und Gesetz*, 116 (and 54 n.3); trans., 126–27 (and 140 n.16); cf. Falaquera, *Moreh ha-Moreh*, 121–22 (on *Guide*, I, intro.) and 318 (on

Now Strauss at the time was interested in Falaquera's *Reshit Ḥokhmah* for another reason. As Steinschneider had surmised in *Alpharabius* in 1869, there seemed to be some relationship between the second part of this book and Alfarabi's *Enumeration of the Sciences (Iḥṣā' al-'ulūm)*, and Steinschneider regretted that he was not able to make a careful comparison of this section of the *Reshit Ḥokhmah* with Alfarabi's book.[15] Part of the problem was that there was no edition of the Arabic text, although Steinschneider cited a few pages of the text in Arabic on the parts of logic from the biographer Ibn Abī Uṣaybi'a's entry on Alfarabi, along with the corresponding passage from a Munich manuscript of the medieval Hebrew translation of the *Enumeration* by Qalonimos ben Qalonimos.[16] At the time, certainly in 1931 when Strauss wrote the third essay of *Philosophie und Gesetz*, I don't think he knew very much about Alfarabi's *Enumeration*. He had, however, read Avicenna's *On the Divisions of the Rational Sciences*, and refers to a passage in it at length in this third essay, where he writes that "according to Avicenna's view, the science that deals thematically with prophecy is politics." In other words, "the aim [*der Zweck*] of prophecy is political, the supreme practical role of the prophet is ... political governance." Strauss cites Avicenna's statement here that whatever has to do with prophecy and religious law (*sharī'a*) is contained in both books by Plato and Aristotle about the laws.[17] Strauss returns to this passage in the introduction to

Guide III, 51). The 1837 Pressburg edition of Falaquera's commentary, following copyist errors in certain manuscripts, attributed this citation from Ibn Bājja (Abū Bakr) to Alfarabi (Abū Naṣr). As a result of this error, Strauss thought the citation from Ibn Bājja was from an unknown work by Alfarabi.

15 Steinschneider, *Alpharabius*, 177.

16 Ibid., 208–11. Qalonimos's translation was edited by Mauro Zonta over 120 years later, *La "Classificazione delle scienze" di Al-Fārābī nella tradizione ebraica* (Torino: Silvio Zamorani Editore, 1992). The passage cited by Steinschneider is on 12–14,

17 *Philosophie und Gesetz*, 110–11; trans., 122 (with minor changes). On the great importance of this statement by Avicenna for Strauss, see further, Georges Tamer, *Islamische Philosophie und die Krise der Moderne: Das Verhältnis von Leo Strauss zu Alfarabi, Avicenna und Averroes* (Leiden: Brill, 2001), esp. 60–62. It may be noted that Tamer disagrees with

Persecution and the Art of Writing, where he sums it up succinctly: "According to Avicenna, the philosophic discipline which deals with prophecy is political philosophy or political science, and the standard work on prophecy is Plato's *Laws*." Strauss explains, "For the specific function of the prophet, as Averroes says, or of the greatest of all the prophets, as Maimonides suggests, is legislation of the highest type."[18] Strauss, near the end of his life, reflected on the importance of this text for him.

> One day when reading in a Latin translation Avicenna's treatise, *On the Divisions of the Sciences*, I came across this sentence (I quote from memory): the standard work on prophecy and revelation is Plato's *Laws*. Then I began to understand Maimonides' prophetology and eventually, as I believe, the whole *Guide of the Perplexed*.[19]

Strauss's reading of this passage, and questions whether Avicenna was even referring to Plato's *Laws* (ibid., chap. 2, 58–86, esp. 60–66).

18 *Persecution and the Art of Writing*, 10.
19 "A Giving of Accounts: Jacob Klein and Leo Strauss," *The College* (April, 1970), 3. Strauss made this comment on January 30, 1970 at St. John's College, Annapolis, Maryland, where at the time he was distinguished scholar in residence and teaching a course on Xenophon's *Oeconomicus*. I was a senior at St. John's and had just completed sending out the last of my applications for graduate school. It was Strauss (and two other people, one of whom was Charles Butterworth) who advised me several months before where to apply for my studies. I had told Strauss I was most interested in Plato and Aristotle and that when I had learned that medieval Jews were in part responsible for transferring their teachings to the West, I decided I wanted to study their writings. Strauss seemed pleased, but emphasized that medieval Jewish philosophy could not be understood properly without first studying the Islamic philosophers and for that reason I would do well to try to study at a university that has a learned scholar of Islamic philosophy. The leading such scholar, he said, was Muhsin Mahdi. He then went on to mention the names of other professors of Islamic and Jewish studies. Although I heeded his advice and thought I understood his point, it was not until I heard his reflection regarding this passage in Avicenna that I realized what he meant and eagerly began to look forward to my graduate studies.

In *Philosophie und Gesetz*, Strauss noted that he compared Avicenna's passage in the printed edition with an Arabic manuscript, the medieval Latin translation of Alpagus, and an abridged Hebrew version in Falaquera's *Reshit Ḥokhmah*.[20] He clearly wanted to make sure he understood Avicenna correctly. Now in 1935, the same year that *Philosophie und Gesetz* appeared, Israel Efros, a Hebraist and scholar of medieval Jewish philosophy, who had already written several important works in the field, published an article in the *Jewish Quarterly Review*, perhaps the most respected journal in Jewish studies at the time, entitled "Palquera's *Reshit Hokhmah* and Alfarabi's *Iḥṣa al 'Ulum.*" This article, I imagine, must have very much interested Strauss. He knew Falaquera's *Reshit Ḥokhmah* well and, I suspect, following Steinschneider's lead, probably knew of the connection between this book and Alfarabi's *Enumeration*, for the Arabic text of it with medieval Latin and Castilian translation had appeared in Madrid in 1932,[21] and we know that this edition and a Cairo one from the previous year were being read at that time in Paris, where Strauss then resided. Efros began his article by stating that it is his goal to show that the second part of *Reshit Ḥokhmah* is "a literal translation of Alfarabi's important work known as the 'Encyclopedia' or by its Arabic title *Iḥṣa al 'ulum.*"[22] He based his claim on two comparisons: one of the Arabic passage of the *Enumeration*, cited by Steinschneider from Ibn Abī Uṣaybiʿa, which he compared with the corresponding passage in the Hebrew translation cited by Steinschneider, and a corresponding passage from *Reshit Ḥokhmah*; and second, two passages from the *Enumeration*—one of which included the contents of the book—which appeared in German translation from the medieval Latin translation in a 1907 study by Eilhard Wiedermann, which he also

20 This footnote from *Philosophie und Gesetz*, 111 n. 2 (trans., 152 n.57), appears as well in the earlier version of this third essay, written in 1931, "Maimunis Lehre von der Prophetie und ihre Quellen," *Le monde oriental* 28 (1934), 125 n.3.
21 *Alfarabi catálogo de las ciencias*, ed. and trans. Angel González Palencia (Madrid: Imprenta de Estanislao Maestre, 1932).
22 Israel Efros, "Palquera's *Reshit Hokhmah* and Alfarabi's *Iḥṣa al 'Ulum.*" *Jewish Quarterly Review* 25 (1935): 227–35, on 227.

compared with corresponding passages from *Reshit Ḥokhmah*. Efros concluded:

> Thus we see that all that has been published of the *Iḥṣa al 'Ulum*—Steinschneider's fragment and the longer excerpt in a German translation of a Latin translation, as well as the outline of the entire work—agrees word for word with our Hebrew work. We cannot therefore escape the conclusion that the second part of Palquera's *Reshit Hokhmah* is a complete and literal translation of Alfarabi's *Iḥṣa al 'Ulum*.[23]

To state that Strauss was disappointed with this study and the rashness of its conclusion is probably an understatement. That Efros did not know Strauss's study that first appeared a few years earlier is understandable, but how could Efros not have heard a word about González Palencia's 1932 Arabic edition and translations of the *Enumeration*? or Amin's edition that appeared in Cairo a year earlier?[24] And how could one reach such a grand conclusion on the basis of several random pages, some of which were from a German translation of a medieval Latin translation of Alfarabi's Arabic text? Strauss must have responded almost immediately, as his article, "Eine vermißte Schrift Farābīs," appeared in the *Monatsschrift* the following year.[25]

If Strauss had indeed been disappointed with Efros's scholarship, he did not show it. His concern was not to point to Efros's overhasty claims, but to establish clearly and methodically the precise relation between the second part of *Reshit Ḥokhmah* and Alfarabi's *Enumeration*. To this end, he stated at the outset of his article that Efros's assertion needed to be significantly qualified. He gently added that Efros's problems were evidently because he did not have access to the editions of

---

23 Ibid., 235.
24 In fact, there was even an earlier edition published in Syria in 1921, and listed along with the other two editions in the bibliography of Ibrahim Madkour, *La Place d'al Fārābī dans l'école philosophique Musulmane* (Paris: Librairie d'Amérique et d'Orient, 1934), 224; see also, 3 n.4.
25 Leo Strauss, "Eine vermißte Schrift Farābīs," *Monatsschrift für Geschichte und Wissenschaft des Judentums* 80 (1936): 96–106.

Alfarabi's *Enumeration*.[26] Others would not have been so kind, but Strauss was simply interested in straightening out the relation between the two books. Strauss—who, as we have seen, did have access to the editions—clarifies the correspondence and precise relationship between the chapters of the two books, shows that two chapters of the second part of *Reshit Ḥokhmah* are not taken from the *Enumeration*, and more interestingly that sections of Avicenna's *Divisions of the Rational Sciences*—including the passage discussed above that places prophecy in the province of political philosophy—were woven into the last three chapters of this part of Falaquera's book.

Strauss next makes a point—whose importance cannot be overestimated—about a significant difference between the two books:

> Falaquera's book is a decisively Jewish book, while the work after which it was modeled is not similarly an Islamic book. Thus to the biblical quotations in *Reshit Ḥokhmah* do not correspond any quotations from the Quran or other Islamic sources in the work of Alfarabi. The same difference manifests itself perhaps most clearly in Falaquera's adding to the benefits of an encyclopedia of science enumerated by Alfarabi the following two benefits, concerning which he explicitly notes that both these are of greater importance than the prior (i.e., those derived from Alfarabi) benefits: (1) a Hebrew encyclopedia of sciences is necessary so that the wisdom of our Sages, lost in the Exile, can be reclaimed; (2) from this book it will become clear whether we are entitled to study these sciences, or not, or whether they contradict anything that is mentioned in our Torah.[27]

---

26 Ibid., 96–97. Thomas Meyer suggested to me another explanation for the gentleness of Strauss's critique. Because of the political situation of the time, Jewish academic journals, such as the *Monatsschrift*, decided not to publish harsh critiques of Jewish scholars, and this would have been particularly true for this volume of the *Monatsschrift*, which was a Festschrift for Isaak Heinemann.

27 Ibid., 98–99.

Strauss then observes that as interesting as these facts concerning the sources of the second part of *Reshit Ḥokhmah* may be, they are of no particular importance, for we have editions of the Arabic texts and Latin translations of them, more complete than Falaquera's Hebrew versions. In contrast, for him, quite different was the matter of the third part of *Reshit Ḥokhmah* and its connection with other texts by Alfarabi, a connection not even mentioned by Efros, although as Strauss points out, already, to some extent, presumed by Steinschneider.[28] Strauss discovered and showed that the first part of this third part of *Reshit Ḥokhmah* was an abridged version of Alfarabi's *Attainment of Happiness*, which had just been printed for the first time in Hyderabad ten years earlier. He then explained that the *Attainment of Happiness* was "an introduction to a work that was a presentation devoted to the philosophy of Plato and Aristotle."[29] On the basis of the *Attainment* and the biographer al-Qifṭî's account of this book, Strauss was able to argue that the second and third parts of the trilogy, the *Philosophy of Plato*, and the *Philosophy of Aristotle*, hitherto unprinted and unstudied, were available in Falaquera's Hebrew version. The case for the *Philosophy of Aristotle* was strengthened by Strauss's citation of Averroes's quotation from the end of the *Philosophy of Aristotle* which matched Falaquera's translation in *Reshit Ḥokhmah*.[30] The discovery was momentous, and at once made available for the first time to the scholarly world a view of Alfarabi's trilogy on the Philosophy of Plato and Aristotle, arguably the most important work of Alfarabi known at the time. Strauss pointed out that while, in general, one may say—on the basis of the comparison of the *Enumeration* and the *Attainment* with the corresponding passages in *Reshit Ḥokhmah*— that Falaquera translates very literally, he omits considerable parts of the original, and at times deviates from it.[31] In other words, Strauss recognized that while his discovery pointed to a new understanding of

28 Ibid., 99–100. Cf. Steinschneider, *Alpharabius*, 177.
29 Strauss, "Eine vermißte Schrift," 100–01.
30 Ibid., 103–04. See Averroes, *Ibn Rushd's Metaphysics: A Translation with Introduction of Ibn Rushd's Commentary on Aristotle's Metaphysics, Book Lam*, trans. Charles Genequand (Leiden: E. J. Brill, 1986), 109 with n.91. Cf. Tamer, *Islamische Philosophie* (above, n.17), 107 n.59.
31 Strauss, "Eine vermißte Schrift," 104–05.

Alfarabi, which should be viewed in light of other of his edited texts, a full and reliable study of the teachings of Alfarabi's Plato and Aristotle would have to await the publication of the original Arabic texts. Seven years later in 1943, Richard Walzer and Franz Rosenthal published an Arabic edition of the *Philosophy of Plato*, based on a unique Constantinople manuscript and Falaquera's Hebrew version. Within two years, Strauss's "Fārābī's Plato" appeared. The modern study of Alfarabi should never have been the same.

Already in 1936—after *Philosophie und Gesetz*—with Alfarabi's *Enumeration* in the Arabic and Latin texts now available to him, along with Falaquera's Hebrew version, Alfarabi had replaced Avicenna for Strauss as the most interesting Islamic philosopher and the one whose political teachings most influenced Maimonides. The more texts of Alfarabi that became available, the better he understood him, and the more convinced he became of his greatness and, in particular, of his profound political teachings. This is evident from his 1936 French study, "Quelques remarques sur la science politique de Maïmonide et de Fārābī."[32]

In this study, Strauss begins with a brief sketch of his conclusions in *Philosophie und Gesetz*. In particular, he mentions the political science of Maimonides and the *falāsifa*, the need for the city, a ruler, indeed a philosopher-ruler-prophet, who could transmit the divine Law, and thereby guide its adherents to the highest happiness and perfection of which they are capable. Strauss then raises the question why did these Islamic and Jewish philosophers contaminate their Aristotelian science with obtrusive Neoplatonic elements? For Strauss, the key to understanding—not simply noticing or stating—this Neoplatonic influence is to grasp the impact of Plato's political teachings on Alfarabi and his followers. This, of course, was the main theme of *Philosophie und Gesetz*. But here, as I have mentioned, the emphasis has moved from Avicenna to Alfarabi. He now writes that "to understand Maimonides, Alfarabi's opinion is much more important than that of Avicenna."[33] But why does he make

32 Leo Strauss, "Quelques remarques sur la science politique de Maïmonide et de Fārābī," *Revue des études juives* 100 (1936), 1–37.
33 Ibid., 16.

this claim when he maintains that for Avicenna, like Alfarabi, Averroes and other *falāsifa*, there is agreement on the "essentially political character of prophecy?"[34] It seems the answer is that during those few years in Paris between sending *Philosophie und Gesetz* off to press and writing the present article, a number of works by Alfarabi had suddenly become available to Strauss, and he began to appreciate that his political teachings were much more developed than he had originally thought on the basis of the *Virtuous City*. While Strauss relied almost exclusively on the *Virtuous City* in presenting Alfarabi's teachings in his book, here he cites freely from the *Political Regime*—which is now counted along with the *Virtuous City* as Alfarabi's most important political works—the *Enumeration of Sciences*, which he cites from the 1931 edition, the *Attainment of Happiness*, the *Philosophy of Plato* from Falaquera's book, *Showing the Way to Happiness* (*Al-Tanbīh 'alā sabīl al-sa'āda*), and even a citation from Falaquera's book, which he correctly presumed to be from a lost book of Alfarabi's, which would later be identified as the *Book of Letters* (*Kitāb al-ḥurūf*).[35] Through these books he learned of Alfarabi's identification of the philosopher-ruler-prophet and of his art of framing the divine Law, of the need to distinguish true happiness from what is presumed or imagined to be happiness, of the need for esoteric writing, and of the need for propounding a metaphysics upon

---

34 Ibid.
35 Ibid., 30 n.3. For the identification of the *Book of Letters* as the source for certain passages in *Reshit Ḥokhmah*, see Muhsin Mahdi's edition of the *Book of Letters* (Beirut: Dar El-Mashreq Publishers, 1969), xii (and Mahdi's Arabic intro., 40), and Lawrence V. Berman, "Maimonides, the Disciple of Alfārābī," *Israel Oriental Studies* 4 (1974), 167 n.43. What Strauss, nor anyone else at the time, could not have known is that Falaquera, whether out of reasons of piety or propriety, was not prepared to follow Alfarabi in his discussion of the relation of philosophy and religion. Thus where Alfarabi gives us an account of the origin of philosophic religion in the *Book of Letters*, Falaquera, through his slightly abridged translation of selected passages from this book, gives us instead an account of the origin of perhaps the virtuous city. See Steven Harvey, "Falaquera's Alfarabi: An Example of the Judaization of the Islamic *Falâsifah*," *Trumah: Zeitschrift der Hochschule für Jüdische Studien Heidelberg* 12 (2002), 97–112.

which the political teachings could be based. While some of this could be found in Avicenna, it was fully articulated in Alfarabi's newly accessible writings. Strauss's article for the first time touches on all these matters in Alfarabi, and suggests their impact on the thought of Maimonides.

Over the next decade, with this rather clear picture of the political teachings of the *falāsifa*, and particularly Alfarabi in mind, Strauss would write a number of studies on Maimonides and other medieval Jewish thinkers in light of the political teachings of the *falāsifa*, but it was not until the Arabic edition of the *Philosophy of Plato* appeared in 1943 that Strauss would write again on Alfarabi. We can only imagine the excitement and curiosity he felt when this edition first appeared. Within two years his "Fārābī's *Plato*" was published in a Festschrift in honor of the distinguished scholar of rabbinic literature, Louis Ginzberg. The appearance of this article in a volume that would be read by scholars of Jewish thought and culture is not without interest. Strauss framed his lengthy article on Alfarabi with statements at the beginning and very end that suggest that only through understanding Alfarabi's philosophy, a main component of Maimonides' philosophical background, can we hope to understand properly his *Guide of the Perplexed* and "fathom its unexplored depths."[36] But what could this study add to his previous studies? One aspect to the answer is suggested in the opening paragraph where Strauss expresses the need to make sense of the seemingly accurate description of the writings of the *falāsifa* as a "heterogeneous" "blend of genuine Aristotelianism with Neo-Platonism and, of course, Islamic tenets."[37] Harmonizing philosophy with religion is difficult enough, but why would a serious Aristotelian contaminate his philosophy with Neoplatonic imagery? Moreover, why did Alfarabi in his two parallel works—one of which was singled out for praise by Maimonides—present his entire philosophy in a political framework? In the course of these opening pages, Strauss makes another interesting

36 Strauss, "Fārābī's *Plato*," 357–60 and 393.
37 Strauss, "Fārābī's *Plato*," 357. For support of the position that Alfarabi knew that the *Theology of Aristotle* was not by Aristotle, see Miriam Galston, "A Re-examination of al-Fārābī's Neoplatonism," *Journal of the History of Philosophy* 15 (1977): 13–32, esp. 15–16.

observation. Alfarabi's *Harmonization of the Two Opinions of the Two Sages, Plato the Divine and Aristotle* is most likely an "exoteric treatise," and thus it would not be wise "to attach great importance to its explicit argument." Strauss further intimates that the so-called *Theology of Aristotle*, the Neoplatonic work on which Alfarabi relies in several passages of his book, was put forward by him as a genuine Aristotelian work only in order to facilitate his attempts to harmonize the opinions of Plato and Aristotle.[38] But Strauss's paper does not concern this work—which he saw of little use for understanding Alfarabi's philosophy—and indeed he would have nothing more to say about it. Rather, it would focus on a close reading of the newly-edited *Philosophy of Plato*, about which he wrote that by studying it, "one is enabled to grasp fully the character of Fārābī's Platonism and therewith of Fārābī's own philosophy.[39]

Strauss's first conclusion after a brief consideration of the *Philosophy of Plato* is that Alfarabi's apparent view of Plato's philosophy as essentially political "cannot be traced to Neoplatonism."[40] This is a rather strange—although certainly true—conclusion, but it leads the reader to wonder about that part of Alfarabi's philosophy that is traceable to Neoplatonism, and what appealed to Alfarabi about it, as well as Alfarabi's true view of Plato's philosophy. A closer examination of the book, based on Alfarabi's Plato's definition of philosophy as the "theoretical art that supplies 'the science of the essence of all beings,'" seems rather to exclude "the study of political and moral subjects from the domain of philosophy proper."[41] Strauss's effort to uncover Alfarabi's true views—as

---

38   Strauss, "Fārābī's *Plato*," 359. On the exoteric character of the *Harmonization*, see further, Muhsin Mahdi, "Introduction, 1962 Edition," in *Alfarabi's Philosophy of Plato and Aristotle*, trans. Muhsin Mahdi (rev. ed.; Ithaca, New York: Cornell University Press, 1969), 3–6; Miriam Galston, *Politics and Excellence* (Princeton: Princeton University Press, 1990), 9–10; and Charles E. Butterworth, *Alfarabi, The Political Writings: "Selected Aphorisms" and Other Texts*, (Ithaca: Cornell University Press, 2001), 119–24.

39   Strauss, "Fārābī's Plato," 359–60.

40   Ibid., 362.

41   Ibid., 364. See Alfarabi, *Philosophy of Plato*, in *Alfarabi's Philosophy of Plato and Aristotle* (above, n.38), sec. 3, 54, and sec. 19, 59–60.

opposed to his apparent or exoteric ones—is rooted in his claim that when Alfarabi does not speak in his own name, but in that of someone else—in this case Plato—he is more likely to reveal his true opinions than when he speaks in his own name. Thus, for Strauss, Alfarabi's failure to mention Plato's doctrine of the immortality of the soul in a work that promises to deal with all parts of his philosophy, may be read as an indication of Alfarabi's own silent rejection of this teaching, so fundamental to his own religion, which he explicitly accepts in some of his writings where he speaks in his own name. In this sense, it may be seen that his *Philosophy of Plato* is not a historical work, intent above all to present accurately all of Plato's teachings. Alfarabi is interested here in philosophical truth far more than historical truth.[42] For Alfarabi and his Plato, a central concern of political philosophy is happiness, but if happiness consists in perfecting one's knowledge of theoretical science, which consists in knowledge of the essence of beings, it excludes the "very prospect of happiness" from most men. Strauss tells us that Alfarabi, for reasons of philanthropy, if for no other reason, needed to hold out the possibility of happiness for all men.[43] For Strauss, his true opinion that happiness is only possible for the philosophers, even in an imperfect city, through their theoretical activity can only be hinted at for the few. The reason for this is that the philosopher, who necessarily lives in political society, is – as Alfarabi's Plato teaches us—in "grave danger," and must therefore—as Alfarabi's Plato learned from Socrates' fate—express himself with great caution, taking into consideration the different ranks of human beings.[44]

Strauss's next and last study devoted to Alfarabi appeared in 1957. As mentioned earlier, the subject of this study, Alfarabi's *Summary of Plato's Laws*, had caught his attention in the early 1930s when he saw it referred to by Steinschneider.[45] Mahdi notes that Paul Kraus dictated to Strauss a German translation of parts of the *Summary* in 1930–1931.

---

42   Strauss, "Fārābī's Plato," 371–77.
43   Ibid., 378.
44   Ibid., 382–83. See Alfarabi, *Philosophy of Plato*, sec. 38, 67.
45   Steinschneider, *Alpharabius*, 61. See *Philosophie und Gesetz*, 114 and n.3; trans., 125 and 153 n.66.

In 1937 Strauss notes in his study on Isaac Abravanel that Kraus was preparing an edition of the text, and in 1938 Strauss asked Kraus to send him his edition and translation of the text.[46] The occasion for Strauss's own study was the appearance in 1952 of the first Arabic edition, along with Latin translation, of the work. Strauss apparently waited until he had the full edition of the text before he discussed it. Readers of Strauss's study, "How Fārābī Read Plato's *Laws*," learn how to read Alfarabi, and not just his *Summary of the Laws*. Indeed Alfarabi's *Summary*, with its instructive and vivid introduction, invites us to apply the lessons we learn regarding how to read Plato toward reading Alfarabi's own writings. The problem with the *Summary* as a whole is that it just does not seem very helpful, and this has dissuaded some modern readers from spending much time on it. As Strauss himself notes, a quick reading of the *Summary* presents the work as "a pedantic, pedestrian and wooden writing which abounds in trivial or insipid remarks and which reveals an amazing lack of comprehension of Plato."[47] On the other hand, his study shows that the work is "much less monotonous than it appears to be at first sight."[48] One lesson he

46 See Leo Strauss, "On Abravanel's Philosophical Tendency and Political Teaching," in *Isaac Abravanel: Six Lectures*, ed. J. B. Trend and H. Loewe (Cambridge: Cambridge University Press, 1937), 96 n.3. See further, Muhsin Mahdi, "The *Editio Princeps* of Fārābī's *Compendium Legum Platonis*," *Journal of Near Eastern Studies* 20 (1961), 15, along with n.55. Mahdi reported on Strauss's request of Kraus. Thomas Meyer suggested to me that it seems, based on correspondence from that period, that it was more a cooperative effort than a simple dictation. See further, Joel L Kraemer, "The Death of an Orientalist: Paul Kraus from Prague to Cairo," in *The Jewish Discovery of Islam: Studies in Honor of Bernard Lewis*, ed. Martin Kramer (Tel Aviv: The Moshe Dayan Center for Middle Eastern and African Studies, Tel Aviv University, 1999), 209; and Harvey, "A Twentieth-Century Jewish Scholar's Discovery" (above, n.7), 226 n.22.

47 Leo Strauss, "How Fārābī Read Plato's *Laws*," in *Mélanges Louis Massignon*, vol. 3 (Damascus, 1957), 319–44; reprinted and cited from Leo Strauss, *What is Political Philosophy?* (Glencoe, Ill.: The Free Press, 1959), 134–54, on 140.

48 Ibid., 141. Strauss's statement is certainly correct. One problem, however, with the arguments of those, like Strauss, who argue *e silentio* from Plato's teachings or statements that Alfarabi ignores is that it is not at all certain

learns from his careful reading of the *Summary*—alluded to in Alfarabi's introduction—is that not all of Plato's statements should be read in the same way. Indeed Alfarabi, both in his introduction and at the end of the *Summary*, says his goal is to extract certain notions to which Plato alludes in the *Laws* and intended to explain, but apparently did not.[49] At the end of his essay, Strauss turns to the statement regarding the *Laws* in the *Philosophy of Plato*, but more importantly to the distinction made near the end of that work between the method of Socrates, who did not possess the ability to instruct the multitude, and the method of Thrasymachus, who did. Alfarabi writes: "The philosopher, the prince, and the legislator ought to be able to use both methods: the Socratic method with the elect, and Thrasymachus' method with the youth and the multitude." For Strauss, Plato learned this lesson from the fate of Socrates. Plato's own method is a correction of Socrates' method and combines both methods. It demands inter alia "judicious conformity with the accepted opinions."[50]

Although not an Arabist, Strauss was at the cutting edge of Alfarabi studies.[51] His discovery of the medieval Hebrew version of Alfarabi's trilogy, the *Philosophy of Plato and Aristotle*—at the time the only known version of the last two treatises of the trilogy—and his pointing to its importance for understanding Alfarabi's own teachings, was a groundbreaking contribution to our reading of Alfarabi. He was the one who emphasized that Alfarabi – like Plato or, for that matter, Maimonides—wrote with

that there were complete Arabic translations of any of Plato's dialogues, but only of summaries of some of them. On this problem, see Harvey, "Falaquera's Alfarabi" (above, n.35), 98–101, and idem, Steven Harvey, "Did Alfarabi Read Plato's *Laws*?" *Medioevo, Rivista di storia della filosofia medievale* 28 (2003): 51–68.

49   See ibid., 137.

50   Ibid., 153; cf. idem, *The Rebirth of Classical Political Rationalism: An Introduction to the Thought of Leo Strauss*, ed. Thomas L. Pangle (Chicago: The University of Chicago Press, 1989), 159. See Alfarabi, *Philosophy of Plato*, sec. 36, 66–67. On the importance of this statement for Strauss, see Tamer, *Islamische Philosophie* (above, n.17), 114, 172, 215, and 237.

51   See also Harvey, "A Twentieth-Century Jewish Scholar's Discovery" (above, n.7).

extreme care, and that tedious study of his writings beyond their apparent or literal meanings was needed to understand them properly. His studies on Alfarabi guided the next generation of scholars—foremost among them, Muhsin Mahdi—to present a fuller and more detailed picture of Alfarabi's thought, and that of the *falāsifa* who followed in his wake.

We have seen that Strauss uncovered the impact of Plato's political teachings on Alfarabi and the *falāsifa*. This included, inter alia, attention to the rulership of the philosopher-ruler-prophet, the place and relevance of prophecy and divine Law in political philosophy, the importance of distinguishing between true and presumed happiness, the adoption of an esoteric/exoteric style of writing, the consequent role of Neoplatonic elements and imagery, the connection between metaphysics and cosmology and political thought, and the distinction between speaking in one's own name or as a commentator or interpreter of someone else. Strauss was the first modern scholar to teach us how to read and understand Alfarabi and the *falāsifa*. Steinschneider set the stage in 1869 with his *Alpharabius*; Dieterici put out the props with his editions and translations of various works of Alfarabi; and Ibrahim Madkour gave us the first philosophical presentation of Alfarabi in 1934; but it was Strauss who showed us an unknown side of Alfarabi's thought and thereby presented the key to understanding his philosophical writings and those of his greatest followers.

How was this different from the Alfarabi known in the mid-1930s when Strauss began to write on Alfarabi? Ibrahim Madkour began his study of Alfarabi by pointing out that "among the great Islamic philosophers, Alfarabi is the least known … and his [many] writings … remain, for the most part, unknown."[52] His study sought to remedy this situation and, to his credit, the young Madkour compiled a detailed list of editions and translations of Alfarabi's works available in 1934, which served as the basis of his study. He was particularly interested in what he called, Alfarabi's "philosophical syncretism," or bold view that all great philosophers must surely agree with each other given that their common goal is the search for truth.[53] To this end, Madkour spent much time on Alfarabi's

---

52 Madkour, *La Place d'al Fārābī* (above, n.24), 1.
53 Ibid., 11. His first chapter is called "Le syncrétisme philosophique d'al Fārābī."

Harmonization, and like previous scholars, such as T. J. De Boer, considered this work central to understanding Alfarabi, and believed that the *Theology of Aristotle* was hence certainly considered by Alfarabi as genuine.[54] Madkour's work was an impressive study, but he did not seem able to distinguish Alfarabi's popular writings from his more philosophical ones, and thus could not distinguish falsely-attributed books from genuine ones. Works such as the *Enumeration* and the *Attainment*, which Madkour had before him, are barely touched upon. The Alfarabi known in the 1930s and Strauss's Alfarabi were two very different philosophers.

As a graduate student in the 1970s, Strauss' reading of Alfarabi, particularly as it was refined, expanded, and developed by Mahdi and others—in part, on the basis of important texts of Alfarabi, which were published for the first time by Mahdi in the 1960s—made very good sense to me. In fact, seeing how highly Mahdi was respected by his colleagues, it was hard to imagine that there were many scholars who viewed Alfarabi otherwise. Over the following decades, I learned that this assessment was not quite accurate. Some could not fathom how one could claim that Alfarabi, in truth, rejected Neoplatonic metaphysics when this philosophy is so manifest in his writings. Others rejected the very existence of Farabian political philosophy. In 2001 Mahdi's magisterial book on Alfarabi, *Alfarabi and the Foundation of Islamic Political Philosophy*, appeared and made such a compelling case for his lifelong reading and interpretation of Alfarabi—rooted in Strauss's earlier studies—that it seemed to me in my naïveté that every reasonable scholar could not but agree. I was sorely mistaken.[55] The following year

---

54 Ibid., 18–43. Cf. T. J. De Boer, *The History of Philosophy in Islam*, trans. Edward R. Jones (London: Luzac & Co., 1903), 109. Cf. above, n.37.

55 Muhsin Mahdi, *Alfarabi and the Foundation of Islamic Political Philosophy* (Chicago: University of Chicago Press, 2001). See my review in *Journal of the American Oriental Society* 123 (2003): 443–46. This, of course, does not mean that Mahdi (or Strauss) was always correct in interpreting Alfarabi (cf. above, n.48). No one is, but it does mean that anyone seeking to understand Alfarabi's philosophy ought not ignore their studies or dismiss them out of hand, but should read them with great care and reflection. Cf. Dimitri Gutas's dismissive and sarcastic review of Mahdi's book in *International Journal of Middle East Studies* 35 (2003): 145–47. Gutas ac-

Majid Fakhry's book, *Al-Fārābī: Founder of Neoplatonism*, appeared. Fakhry, far from agreeing with Mahdi, ignored his studies completely, as well as those of Strauss. Fakhry portrays an Alfarabi who "never questioned the claim that the *Theology* was a genuine work of Aristotle," and thus believed that his own Neoplatonic scheme was thoroughly reconcilable with Aristotelianism.[56] Perhaps even more disappointing to me were the entry on Alfarabi by the learned Avicennian scholar, David Reisman, in the 2004 *Cambridge Companion to Arabic Philosophy*, and the 2007 popular sourcebook by Reisman and Jon McGinnis, *Classical Arabic Philosophy*, where not a single study may be found on any of the *falāsifa* by Mahdi or Strauss or, for that matter, Charles Butterworth, Miriam Galston, or others who followed their lead.[57] There is for them no interpretation or argument by any of these latter scholars that ought to be taken seriously or even rebutted; they are simply not mentioned. Since Mahdi's death in 2007, the situation seems to be only deteriorating, and there has been a general reversion to a pre-Strauss reading of Alfarabi. As an example of this, consider the current debate over whether Alfarabi indeed wrote the *Harmonization*. Strauss, Mahdi, Galston, Butterworth, and others have explained that he did and what his purpose was in doing so. Today, learned scholars argue that he could not have written it because it parts from views he holds elsewhere. Other leading scholars claim he did write it, but while he was a youth, or that he wrote it and that his views may be harmonized with his teachings elsewhere.[58]

cuses Mahdi of things one might well accuse Gutas of in this review (being tendentious and "speaking ex cathedra in authoritarian voice"). Gutas concludes in typical Gutasian language that Mahdi's book is "an antiquated curio, of interest only to historians of American intellectual currents in the middle of the 20th century" (147).

56 Majid Fakhry, *Al-Fārābī: Founder of Islamic Neoplatonism* (Oxford: Oneworld, 2002), 152.

57 David C. Reisman, "Al-Fārābī and the Philosophical Curriculum," in *The Cambridge Companion to Arabic Philosophy*, ed. Peter Adamson and Richard Taylor (Cambridge: Cambridge University Press, 2005), 52–71; and Jon McGinnis and David C. Reisman, *Classical Arabic Philosophy: An Anthology of Sources* (Indianapolis: Hackett Publishing Co., 2007).

58 Much has been written over the past decade on the question of Alfarabi's authorship of the *Harmonization*. In general, the various critiques of pre-

Others simply assume he did write it and are hardly aware of any problem. Rarely do these scholars even mention in passing the position of

vious views are much more persuasive than the new views and hypotheses that are offered. See, e.g., Marwan Rashed, "On the Authorship of the Treatise *On the Harmonization of the Opinions of the Two Sages* Attributed to al-Fārābī," *Arabic Sciences and Philosophy* 19 (2009): 43–82. Unlike some of the participants in this debate, Rashed values Alfarabi as a "rigorous and thoughtful" philosopher (78). Rashed argues that "some features of the text make it impossible to consider al-Fārābī as its author" (43–44). In this conclusion he agrees with Joep Lameer, but wishes to put forward "much more cogent arguments" that show that the *Harmonization* "contradicts crucial aspects of al-Fārābī's [philosophical] doctrine" (44). Significantly, such contradictions, in part, are precisely what moved Strauss to suggest that Alfarabi likely considered his book an "exoteric treatise" (above, n.38). Rashed's article is of interest not only for the case he makes, but also for his reference to the views of other scholars on this question (see 44 n.1, and his replies to Gerhard Endress and Cecelia Martini Bonadeo in appendix 2, 75–82). For a more complete and updated list of the scholarly literature on this debate, see Cecelia Martini Bonadeo's, bibliography at: http://academic.mu.edu/taylorr/Abrahamic_Workshop_Presenters/Cecilia_Martini_Bonadeo.html. See also Cecelia Martini Bonadeo's lecture, "The Debated Question of al-Fārābī's Authorship of the *Harmony of Plato and Aristotle* (*Kitāb al-Ğam' bayna ra'yay al-Ḥakīmayn Aflāṭūn al-ilāhī wa Arisṭūṭālīs*): A question of method," June 11, 2014, along with the ensuing discussion with Charles E. Butterworth, Philippe Vallat, Richard C. Taylor and others at: http://academic.mu.edu/taylorr/The_Abrahamic_Traditions/2014_Summer_Conference_Milwaukee_2.html. See further, Cecelia Martini Bonadeo's critical review of Damien Janos' 2012 book, *Method, Structure, and Development in al-Fārābī's Cosmology, Studia graeco-arabica* 4 (2014): 357–64, esp. 361–63. She reports that Janos (1) rejects what he terms the "comparative" method, according to which Alfarabi's authorship of the *Harmonization* may be rejected solely on the basis of the conflict of its teachings (such as those concerning the creation or eternity of the world) with those presented by Alfarabi in other works, and (2) instead puts forward a "developmentalist" reading of Alfarabi that explains the different positions in different texts as a result of the periods in which they were written and the changes in Alfarabi's views. For Martini Bonadeo, "although the developmentalist hypothesis is fascinating, it should not be taken to extremes. There is still room for a more nuanced hypothesis: a progressive evolution of thought" (363). She concludes her critique on a

Strauss, Mahdi, Butterworth, Galston, and their followers.[59] The problem is that today, with all the recent editions and studies, such a position is no longer defensible. Indeed the Straussian reading of the *Harmonization* as an authentic, but popular writing of Alfarabi, has now been further strengthened through the recent publication of newly-discovered fragments from Alfarabi's lost *Commentary on the Nicomachean Ethics* by Chaim Neria.[60]

Strauss was the one who recognized Alfarabi as the founder of the school of Islamic Aristotelianism (which made possible medieval Western Aristotelianism) and as an insightful and influential political thinker.[61] He was not the first non-Muslim to interpret Alfarabi in this

positive note that Janos's book "shows that al-Fārābī has important things to say, and that he is a figure with whom we should engage intellectually in the present" (364). That these things still need to be shown to scholars of Islamic philosophy—things understood and emphasized by Strauss over eighty years ago—brings to the fore the relatively low estimation of Alfarabi that the present article bemoans.

59 Among recent exceptions are Martini Bonadeo and Janos.

60 Chaim Meir Neria, "Al-Fārābī's Lost *Commentary on the Ethics:* New Textual Evidence," *Arabic Sciences and Philosophy* 23 (2013): 69–99. Yet even before Neria's article, one could wonder about the suggested early dating of the *Harmonization* by the developmentalists, given the fact that it explicitly refers to Alfarabi's *Commentary [sharh] on the Ethics* (unless one wishes to argue that this reference is a later addition to the text), a commentary that should perhaps be considered late, given its radical and unexpected teachings.

61 See Rémi Brague, "Athens, Jerusalem, Mecca: Leo Strauss's 'Muslim' Understanding of Greek Philosophy," *Poetics Today* 19 (1998): 235–59. Brague writes: "Strauss invites the reader to reconsider the history of medieval philosophy as a whole by giving Farabi the place that becomes him: the place of primacy" (240). But for Brague, the importance of Alfarabi for Strauss was even greater than this. Strauss read the ancients "with medieval eyes, ... although he seldom acknowledged it explicitly." Brague continues: "Thus, the thesis I should like to defend ... is that the pattern of reading Strauss applied to the Greeks is neither ancient nor modern, but medieval—to be precise, Islamic—in origin. ... [T]he most important source of Strauss's hermeneutics is probably Farabi. Especially important is the view of Plato that is to be found in the writings of this tenth-century thinker. ... Strauss's Plato is basically the same as Farabi's" (239–40).

light. This was explicitly how Maimonides understood him, and also later medieval Jewish philosophers, particularly Falaquera. Sadly, the Alfarabi of today is no longer viewed by most scholars of Islamic philosophy as of great philosophical stature, and his brilliance has lost its luster. He can no longer even distinguish Aristotle's teachings from those of the Neoplatonists. He is dying a slow and agonizing death.

Vipers, Weeds, and Disorder in the Whole[1]
Joshua Parens

Alfarabi revived ancient, especially Platonic, political philosophy. Two obvious things seem to confirm this: That Alfarabi devoted more attention to politics than perhaps any other medieval philosopher—indeed, placing a majority of the non-logical works that have come down to us in a political frame. And that at the end of the *Attainment of Happiness,* Alfarabi underlines that he had learned from Plato and Aristotle how to revive philosophy when it had ceased to be actively pursued. The more widely received view among scholars, however, is that Alfarabi is a Neoplatonist of some kind. Of course, Neoplatonism is hardly known for its interest in politics. Indeed, Neoplatonists prefer to focus on things that transcend earthly existence. In doing so, they highlight the way in which one thing proceeds from another in an ineluctable descent from the mysterious One or Good which is beyond Being—putatively following Book VI of the *Republic*. Now, even though Alfarabi never speaks of a One or Good beyond Being—but rather of a First Cause—he does frequently describe a hierarchy of being and of ascents and descents through such hierarchies. Indeed, many of his non-logical works contain some form of this ascending, descending process (*Political Regime, Virtuous City, Book of Religion, Attainment of Happiness*). As a result, Alfarabi appears to fit a premodern mold made most famous by the Neoplatonists and captured by Lovejoy's phrase, the Great Chain of Being. The Great Chain of Being is often invoked to explain why

---

1   An earlier version of parts of this chapter were first delivered as "How Alfarabi, Following Plato and Aristotle, Gives the Lie to the 'Great Chain of Being,'" at the Classical Greek Political Thought conference, hosted by the Center for Teaching of America's Western Foundations, Mercer University, March 24–26, 2010.

premodern thinkers were so enamored of hierarchy in politics as well as a corollary claim: theology or metaphysics as higher than politics must be its ground. The main purpose of this paper is to show that Alfarabi, following Plato and Aristotle, highlights failures within the apparently hierarchical ordering of things, and these failures are in turn linked to and support his denial that theoretical science provides the ground of practical science.

Before turning to the evidence in Alfarabi, let us outline the parallels to the challenging of hierarchy that we find in Plato and Aristotle. We do not begin in chronological order because Aristotle's subversion of hierarchy is in some ways more obvious—even though Aristotle is often cited as maintaining that metaphysics grounds politics.

Aristotle

We have in mind both the openings of Aristotle's *Nicomachean Ethics* (EN) and *Metaphysics*, on the one hand, and EN bk. 6, on the other. We begin with the latter because it is the more explicit and comprehensive case, EN bk. 6. At the end of bk. 6, Aristotle has been battling his way through the most challenging inquiry of that book, his inquiry into intellectual virtue, especially the difference between prudence (the intellectual virtue of practical affairs) and wisdom (the intellectual virtue of theoretical matters). He concludes by announcing that prudence does not have authority over wisdom; rather, it has authority for the sake of wisdom (1145a7–12). Why this should be the case was established back in EN 6.7, when in the heart of the EN, politics or prudence was put in its rightful subordinate position, vis-à-vis wisdom. The object of wisdom, the divinely ordered cosmos, is higher than the merely human. This arrangement at the end of EN 6, rule by the lower for the sake of the higher, is hardly the most stable of arrangements. Must not the higher simply rule over the lower? Certainly, a Neoplatonist would uphold such a view.

Leaving aside EN 6, we turn back to the opening of EN and of the *Metaphysics*, which both anticipate this problem. Near the opening of EN, Aristotle highlights the uneasy relation between politics and science and the closely related tension between practical and theoretical science.

In EN 1.2, he is inquiring into what art or science would specify the end of human actions, and he states the following:

> [O]ne must try to grasp, in outline at least, whatever it [the end of human actions] is and to which of the sciences or capacities it belongs. But it might be held to belong to the most authoritative and most architectonic one, and such appears to be the political [art]. For it ordains what sciences there must be in the cities and what kinds each person must in turn learn and up to what point. We also see that even the most honored capacities—for example, generalship, household management, rhetoric—fall under the political [art]. Because it makes use of the remaining [political?] sciences and, further, because it legislates what ought one to do and what to abstain from, its end would encompass those of the others, with the result that this would be the human good (1094a25–b8).[2]

The material from EN 6 that we have already considered helps explain some of the ambiguities and controversies surrounding this passage. It is ambiguous about whether what is architectonic is an art, a science, or the capacity of a ruler. In effect, might there be a political capacity of a ruler that should dictate the fate of the sciences? Or must science control the fate of the sciences? And it is somewhat ambiguous about the extent of that rule. Does it extend to all sciences or only political ones? The third sentence makes this political thing sound like the ultimate architectonic science—as if it is supposed to rule over all sciences studied in the city. The ambiguities here even lead one to wonder whether Aristotle envisions a political science that politicizes all of the sciences.[3] We will return to this last concern later.

2   As Bartlett and Collins, whose translation (*Nicomachean Ethics*, trans. Robert Bartlett and Susan Collins, [Chicago: University of Chicago Press, 2011]) is here quoted with minor changes, indicate that they have adopted Ingram Bywater's emendation in *Aristotelis Ethica Nicomachea* (Oxford: Oxford University Press, 1894), which drops "political" from the readings of the MSS (3 n.0).

3   Those who are troubled about this last issue are most emphatic that "political" referred to in note 2 must be restored—contrary to Bywater's emen-

In the second chapter of the *Metaphysics*, Aristotle reviews six reasons that wise men are considered wise. The last of the six poses challenges highly reminiscent of those we have run into in EN. The wise man's knowledge is (1) most universal, (2) concerns the most difficult things, (3) concerns things about which one can be most precise (about which there are the fewest principles); he (4) can teach the causes about them, (5) their objects are known for their own sake, and (6) their knowledge concerns what is *archikōtatē* (supreme or highest, 982b5)[4]—and knows the end for which each thing is done (*prakteon*), the good of each, and the best in the whole.[5] Whether our translator is the more adventuresome and challenging Sachs or the traditional Ross-Barnes no one can avoid the oddity regarding things "done." Here, in the opening of the *Metaphysics* we're somewhat unexpectedly taken back to the beginning of the *Ethics* where the relation between doing and the end(s) at which all things aim were underlined. It is unexpected here both because the present inquiry would seem to have little if anything to do with "doing" and because one would have thought that the link between the many senses of being, underlined in EN 1.6, and the search for the highest good should have been severed prior to the *Metaphysics*. This odd dalliance with "doing" in the *Metaphysics* reminds us of the uneasy

dation. I thank Edward Macierowski for insisting upon the importance of contravening Bywater's emendation at an NEH Summer Institute that Douglas Kries, Joseph C. Macfarland, and I co-directed at Gonzaga University in the summer of 2014. Yet the third sentence seems to argue against dropping Bywater's emendation.

4   Sachs has "most ruling" (cf. *-krate*) (*Nicomachean Ethics*, trans. Joe Sachs [Newburyport, MA: Focus Publishing, 2002]) and Ross-Barnes has "most authoritative" (cf. *kurios*) (*The Complete Works of Aristotle*, eds. W. D. Ross and Jonathan Barnes [Princeton: Princeton University Press, 1984].). Cf. *architektonikē* with *archikōtatē*: The former term denotes a master craft; the later though there might be some connotation of the rule of the *archon* does not refer unambiguously to rule. It's the superlative of what is first in rank.

5   We leave aside here the formidable problem of reconciling this apparent reversion to some universal good or best being, which has already been repudiated in EN 1.6. This moment in the *Metaphysics* after all is a survey of *endoxa*.

relation between high and low at the end of EN 6. Desirable though it might be that the high should possess unchallenged rule over the low—there is a tendency in the order of things, especially in human things, toward the inverse, the rule of the low.

Plato

Let us turn now to Plato. To some extent, Plato made this problem a, or even the, centerpiece of his corpus. There are two deeply interrelated emblems of this problem: the death of Socrates and the improbable or impossible character of philosopher-kingship. As Leo Strauss says, regarding the accusations against Socrates where there is smoke there is fire (where the smoke is the public accusations against Socrates, and the fire is inquiring in a subversive fashion into the gods and the afterlife, what is above and what is below). Even if one does not take Strauss's view, everyone who has read the *Apology* senses the topsy-turvy character of the lowly Athenian *demos* putting to death that divine man, Socrates. Similarly, the ultimate source of the impossibility of the philosopher-king is the injustice of the notion that the philosopher as inquirer into the order of all things should be put in service of a band of mere human beings. That is improbable or impossible because it demands that the higher be put in the service of (that is, rule over!) the lower, which can only occur if the higher, that is, the philosophers compel *themselves* to rule! Contrary to the Neoplatonists, Plato and Aristotle argue that there is nothing necessary or even probable about the Neoplatonic expectation that the high (whether it be human wisdom or the divine itself) should rule over the low (whether it be human prudence or the city itself).

Although Neoplatonists in general are well aware of the defectiveness of humanity, their greatest departure from Plato or at least from Alfarabi's Plato is to emphasize the role of what is lowest in us (namely, matter) as causing disorder in the whole. This led eventually to an underlying tendency to what for lack of a better word we might call Manicheanism or what Nietzsche has referred to as Platonism for the people, that is, it led to a tendency to denigrate this world of materiality in favor of all that is immaterial. Of course, there are moments in the

Platonic oeuvre that have seemed to sanction this view: most notably the Pythagorean drift of the *Phaedo*. One ought, however, pay sufficient attention to the general trend of Socrates' argument (his call to remain on earth rather than to flee this putative prison of the body) and the imagery of Plato (having Socrates remark on the odd pleasure of removing the shackles and send away his wife, with a small child recently born in Socrates' old age!) to put to rest the idea that Socrates or Plato intend to support the animus against the body of his Pythagorean interlocutors, Simmias and Cebes. The radical opposition between body and mind in the *Phaedo* is surely not Socrates' last word on the relation between body and soul—as even the most casual glance at the *Republic* and *Phaedrus*, to name the obvious, would indicate. On the contrary, Plato, Aristotle, and Alfarabi all locate the most interesting and perplexing disorders not in materiality but in the strange leavening of human reason itself. For example, in the *Nicomachean Ethics*, Aristotle underscores how that indispensable power prudence in its original form, cleverness, is just as ready to serve vice as virtue. Although he implies this near the end of bk. 6 (1144b1–25), he shows by example in bk. 7 the chilling meaning of this fact: Human beings are potentially ten thousand times more harmful than are the brutes (1150a9) because reason or intellect has not become fully what it can become.

Alfarabi

Alfarabi, unlike the Neoplatonic tradition that came before him, lacked the confidence of the Neoplatonists that a neat hierarchy exists between low and high, and especially between the theological or metaphysical, on the one hand, and politics, on the other. Although he, as all or nearly all philosophers do, assents to the superiority of the theological or metaphysical, Alfarabi is just as uneasy about the confidence the Neoplatonists had in the Great Chain of Being. In the *Virtuous City*, whose full title is *The Principles of the Opinions of the Inhabitants of the Virtuous City*, he offers such hierarchy without much obvious questioning—in a manner that seems in keeping with the title of that work. That is, this work explains the opinions or the principles of the opinions of those who live in virtuous cities, which are not necessarily the opinions of the philosophers. Only when describing these opinions or their principles does Alfarabi sound like a confirmed Neoplatonist.[6] In contrast, in the *Political Regime*, he offers a far more sober account. It is not by chance that this work contains his most extended discussion of non-virtuous political regimes—in obvious debt to *Republic* bk. 8. As in the *Virtuous City*, the first half offers that Lovejoy-like account of the theological and natural order; the second half is devoted to a far more philosophical inquiry into the human things. But the insinuation that the first half somehow grounds the second half is the most widely accepted reading of both *Virtuous City* and *Political Regime*. But we are most interested in a striking parallel in the first half and the second half of the *Political Regime*: Near the end of the first half as he descends toward the bottom of the natural realm, Alfarabi highlights that there are vipers that destroy things higher than they, without any apparent purpose. Similarly, near the end of the second half, after having descended to the worst kinds of regimes, he concludes with a discussion of "the weeds within virtuous cities"— n.b., the reappearance of the term "virtuous city"—and in a most unexpected place, at the end of a descent through increasingly bad regimes. By locating these weeds in the virtuous cities, he veils their status. As misfits within the virtuous cities, they appear at first to be simply bad. Closer inspection, however, reveals that along with those enamored of falsifying things (sophists) are to be found those who are looking for the "right path" and "the truth," whose instruction is then outlined. These inquirers are nothing if not potential philosophers. At first reading, they don't appear as such because they appear in opposition to the lawgiver in the virtuous city, whom we might reflexively assume must be the philosopher-king.[7]

We could work through other interesting details in Alfarabi's account of the weeds—but we arrived here with the intention of clarifying Alfarabi's credentials as a Neoplatonic proponent of the Great Chain of

---

6   It should also be noted, however, that Alfarabi includes a relatively extensive discussion of vicious regimes in *Virtuous City*.

7   "Weeds" become a leitmotif of subsequent Islamic medieval political philosophy, especially that of Ibn Bajja and Ibn Tufayl—though the meaning of "weed" is not always identical to Alfarabi's sense.

Being. Several things stand out in Alfarabi's account that give the lie to that portrait: First (1) and most importantly, the chain of being is interrupted. Second (2), in addition to the chain, another key principle, teleology, is challenged by the existence of the viper—whether that description of vipers is correct is unimportant, here we are most interested merely in parsing what Alfarabi is trying cryptically to convey. Having acknowledged that Alfarabi here challenges teleology, I want to underline that I do not hold that Alfarabi is wholly abandoning teleology.[8] Third (3), another central theme, if not principle, is raised by these bizarre cases, the viper and the philosopher: namely, the character of evil or disorder in the whole, which, of course, is closely related to the principle of teleology. (Cf. Maimonides, *Guide* 3.12 and 3.13.) Fourth (4) and back to the central point, the locus of the interruption of the chain of being is nearly identical in all three authors, Plato, Aristotle, and Alfarabi. The philosopher, the emblem of what is best in man, stands at the center of the failure of the chain. In other words, although the viper is an odd, quirky, and largely inconsequential example of the failure of the chain of being—obviously a mere hint—one could hardly choose a more salient case of its failure than the fate of the philosopher. Not only does the Great Chain of Being not hold in bizarre cases such as the viper, it fails in the most important instance for human affairs. Indeed, it would seem to give the lie to the most naïve reading of Alfarabi, namely, that Alfarabi is naively confident that the human order mimics a hierarchical divine order and that the former is grounded in the latter. Neoplatonism can avow such a view because it has such disdain for the human and the material that it expects little but evil in this vale of tears—in other words, it fobs off on materiality any departures from the right ordering of things, high over low. Alfarabi is not so unearthly.

8   Though I have my doubts that he adheres to anything like the teleology Aristotle offers in *Politics* 1.8 (what I take Seth Benardete to mean when he speaks of "teleological physics," in contrast to Socrates' forms," in his preface to *Socrates' Second Sailing* [Chicago: University of Chicago Press, 1989]), where all living things are said to find their fulfillment in subordination to the human. Indeed, I doubt that even Aristotle means this seriously as a theoretical claim. After all, the claim is made in his most political or practical work.

Although in a number of Alfarabi's works he outlines the character of the virtuous city, or regime, or religion, and although, at times, he leads his reader to expect that such virtue is not only achievable but that the philosopher-king-legislator's rule promises to bring it about; here, in the *Political Regime*, he leaves the reader crestfallen. This should lead complacent Neoplatonic readers of Alfarabi to reassess how they read Alfarabi. When Alfarabi describes such ascents and descents, one must ask oneself whether he is attempting to capture the way things really are—or is merely conveying the opinions or principles of the opinions of the inhabitants of virtuous cities. Rather, he is capturing the "world-view" or opinions of his community about how the world should be or "ultimately" is. One must resist the temptation to read such descriptions as expressing either Alfarabi's own preference or what Alfarabi takes to be an accurate description of the reality of things.

We ought to consider why Alfarabi would question his own community's view but in such a roundabout way. Why would he not be concerned that he is inspiring devotion to a misguided ideal? For the same reasons that Plato had little reason to be concerned about portraying the *kallipolis* in the *Republic* (than Alfarabi was about insinuating the possibility of the rule of philosopher-king-prophets over large swaths of, if not the whole, Earth), though it might inspire the imprudent to strive to establish castles in the sky. Neither Plato nor Alfarabi were terribly concerned about this risk for two reasons: Because they knew that at least some human beings will always harbor a desire to have all things, and if not all then at least the human things conform to their own desires (*Laws* 687c), *pace* Nietzsche's worries about last men. And because they knew that the best way to purge men's souls of such desires is to dramatize or perform or enact and explore them.[9]

Why the Primacy of Political Philosophy Does Not Entail the Politicization of Philosophy

Let us turn back to whether Aristotle envisions a political science that politicizes all of the sciences! When students of medieval Christian

---

9   See Parens, *Islamic Philosophy of Virtuous Religions.*

thought hear tell that political philosophy has greater primacy in medieval Jewish and Islamic philosophy than in medieval Christian thought, they often begin to suspect such an architectonic political philosophy of falling prey to a thorough politicization of science.[10] Henceforth, I will reference not only Alfarabi but also Maimonides because I believe that Maimonides followed Alfarabi in viewing political philosophy more comprehensively than was the case in the medieval Christian tradition.

No one doubts that Christian metaphysics is somehow Christianized, but that rightly does not raise the same kind of hackles that the suggestion that metaphysics should be politicized raises. After all, Christianity claims to have uncovered the key truth regarding the whole. Why then should not that truth color metaphysics? That political philosophy should be the architectonic science, however, raises more serious questions because politics seems to be ineradicably partisan. If politics is ineradicably partisan, then the modifier "politics" in political philosophy seems to guarantee that any metaphysics developed under its auspices would be partisan. I will leave aside, at least for now, whether all politics is so deeply partisan, and instead question whether "political philosophy" is "political" in this sense or some other.

In fact, Alfarabi and Maimonides rarely use the phrase "political philosophy." Far more frequently, they speak of "political science," but by this phrase they, of course, do not mean political science as we might think of it today. That being said, why do we use this term today? Strauss is famous or infamous, depending upon whom you speak to, for reviving this inquiry—and crucial for the revival of the study of medieval Jewish and Islamic political philosophy. What he meant to indicate by "political philosophy" is often indicated by the addition of the modifier "Platonic" to the phrase: Platonic political philosophy. Platonic political philosophy is distinguished by having preceded Aristotle's division of the sciences—and in particular his distinction between theoretical and practical science. Although it is true that there are anticipations of such a division in Platonic works such as the *Sophist* and the *Statesman*, those divisions are championed by Plato's Eleatic Stranger rather than his Socrates. What

10 See note 3, above.

does all of this have to do with Alfarabi and Maimonides? After all, isn't Alfarabi referred to in the Muslim tradition as "the second teacher," that is, the second teacher after Aristotle? And aren't both of these authors, perhaps especially in the *Enumeration of the Sciences* and in the *Treatise on the Art of Logic* under the influence of Aristotle in the divisions of the sciences they discuss?

Let us broach these questions about Alfarabi and Maimonides' view of Aristotle's division of the sciences by revisiting the striking process of reversion to Plato highlighted already in one of Alfarabi's most introductory writings, the *Enumeration of the Sciences*. In chapter 5, Alfarabi moves from an initial account of political science that sounds quite a bit like Aristotle's in the *Nicomachean Ethics* and *Politics* back to an account that sounds strikingly like Plato's approach. That is, he moves from a political science that at least appears to have little or no connection to theoretical philosophy to one that requires that the ruler possesses both theoretical and practical philosophy. In other words, Alfarabi announces that in his setting, in a community ruled by divine law, political science (or political philosophy) will take its lead from the philosopher-king conceit of the *Republic* (and to some extent the *Laws*) rather than the lead of the prudent political actor with little or no interest in theoretical knowledge of Aristotle's political writings. That the philosopher-king conceit is central to the thought of Alfarabi and Maimonides is difficult to gainsay. What needs to be added is that the philosopher-king appears variously also as prophet or legislator, depending upon which work of theirs one considers. In brief, divine law somehow necessitates the reversion to Plato's philosopher-king.

Broadly speaking, it isn't difficult to say what about the divine law necessitates the reversion to Plato: The divine law is itself a theoretico-practical phenomenon, or to speak with greater precision it is a theologico-political phenomenon. One cannot speak of politics and law in the Islamic and Jewish settings without also somehow talking of theology. Does this not then still imply that all theoretical inquiry (in which the truth is of paramount concern) is somehow tainted, in these traditions, by the merely useful, which plays such an important role in practical inquiry? Such a concern might be valid if it were the case that the true and the good have no bearing upon one another. That they must have bearing on one another is evident from the fact that in the medieval Christian tradition the true and the good are thought to be in harmony. If anything Alfarabi and Maimonides are freer of the taint of the true by the useful, insofar as they do not presuppose the harmony of the good and the true. Rather the relation of these and the relation of politics and theology is central and always in play and under scrutiny in their thought.

Let us return then to the original question about the meaning of "political philosophy" in the medieval Islamic and Jewish traditions. We're now able to see that what is meant by "political philosophy" has less to do with partisan politics than it has to do with the relation of the highest themes of theology and politics. That theology should have political implications and that politics should have theological meaning would come as no surprise to any medieval thinker. More importantly, though, our digression on what Strauss dubbed "the theologico-political problem" offers us another avenue to deepen our understanding of why political philosophy, in the broadly Platonic sense of the term, should be the architectonic science. Once we add to the mix of "the true" and "the good" the even more obviously political concept or idea, "the just," we begin to gain a better sense for why Alfarabi and Maimonides treat political philosophy as the architectonic science. Is the just a merely human concern or does it transcend the political by means of considerations of providence? That Christian theology (or metaphysics) bears on providence is undeniable. Indeed, providence is a very high theme of the theoretical portion of sacred doctrine. The same, however, is not true of the thought of Alfarabi and Maimonides. Matters specifically of particular providence, in Alfarabi and Maimonides, are treated not as part of a purely theoretical inquiry into providence. Rather they are considered under the aegis of political science! Does this then mean that their inquiry into particular providence is less philosophic or scientific and more partisan than the inquiry in the Christian setting? Ultimately, I believe that the reverse is the case. Particular providence is considered under the aegis of political science in Alfarabi and Maimonides because the very notion of particular providence is itself partisan. In other words, the very conception of particular providence presupposes that the whole could take its lead from the part.

Putting the shoe on the other foot, as it were, the question could reasonably be asked whether when Christian thinkers treat matters of particular providence as part of a theoretical science, they do not presuppose the possibility of demonstrating the truth of God's particular providence for the Christian. Be that as it may, we have tried here to allay some of the concerns of those who suspect that if political philosophy is first philosophy, philosophy will be tainted by a form of political partisanship. The qualifier "political" in Strauss's notion of political philosophy as first philosophy refers not to political partisanship but to the comprehensiveness of the inquiry—that the highest inquiry is not limited to that which transcends the human because, as it happens, the theologico-political surface of things contains the core of things.

God's Perfection and Negative Theology in Alfarabi

Christopher Colmo

Charles Butterworth has trained a generation of Alfarabi scholars. Through his meticulous translations of Alfarabi and Averroes he has given scholars in fields far beyond Arabic studies access to the philosophic treasures of the *falāsifa*.[1] His introductions and other essays are themselves a rich source of insight into this heritage. We cannot be too grateful for this extraordinary labor of love. It is a pleasure to honor him.

By God's perfection, I mean his infinite richness and abundance. Following a suggestion of Ibn Bājja, we might say that anything added to God would diminish him, as a sixth finger would diminish the hand.[2] By negative theology, I mean the body of argument concluding that we can say only what God is not. We cannot articulate the positive attributes of God in a way that is both true and intelligible.[3] God's perfection

---

1 An example of Butterworth's fruitful collaboration with others may be seen in the "Foreword," written jointly with Thomas Pangle, to Alfarabi, *The Philosophy of Plato and Aristotle*, Mahdi trans. (Ithaca, NY: Cornell University Press, 2001).

2 See Joshua Parens and Joseph C. Macfarland, *Medieval Political Philosophy: A Sourcebook* (Ithaca, NY: Cornell University Press), 99.

3 See David B. Burrell, C.S.C., *Knowing the Unknowable God: Ibn-Sina, Maimonides, Aquinas* (Notre Dame, Indiana: University of Notre Dame Press, 1986); Christopher Hughes, *On a Complex Theory of a Simple God: An Investigation in Aquinas' Philosophical Theology* (Ithaca, NY: Cornell University Press, 1989); Ian Richard Netton, *Allah Transcendent: Studies in the Structure and Semiotics of Islamic Philosophy, Theology and Cosmology* (London: Routledge, 1989). See also the discussion of Meister Eckhart in Richard J. Woods, O.P., *Eckhart's Way* (Dublin: Veritas Publications, 2009).

clashes with the requirement of negative theology. If God is the fullness of being, then it would seem that there is much we could say about him. Only an infinite speech could exhaust his attributes or sing his praises. In this short essay, I will argue that Alfarabi brings these two conflicting thoughts together at the beginning of the *Principles of the Opinions of the People of the Virtuous City*, and I will try to explain how the two thoughts might belong together.[4]

I

There seem to be certain perennial questions in philosophy to which men turn whether in Baghdad or Florence, Königsberg or Copenhagen. Alfarabi raises one of these questions in the first sentence of the *Virtuous City*. Is the first being or cause a perfect being without any deficiency (*naqs*), or can any being be without deficiency? To ask the same question in different words, can anything be simply good? Is this question somehow related to the question, can anything be simply one? In the first sentence of the *Virtuous City*, Alfarabi states that the first being is without any deficiency, but being a philosopher, he proceeds to explore this claim in the pages immediately following.

Before we pursue Alfarabi's argument, we might consider the provenance of his assertion and his question. Does the assertion that the first existent has no deficiency come to Alfarabi from Islam? In reflecting on this assertion, in probing its consequences, is Alfarabi working within the confines of Islam? Is he spelling out the implications of the faith? Or has he brought to Islam a question that comes from outside of Islam? Is the assumption that the first existent has no deficiency one that Islam embraces, or is it an assumption that Alfarabi arrives at through rational

---

4   I have worked from the text and translation provided by Richard Walzer in Alfarabi, *On the Perfect State* (Oxford: Oxford University Press, 1985; Great Books of the Islamic World, 1998) and from the text and French translation by J. Youssef Karam and A. Jaussen Chlala in Alfarabi, *Idées des Habitants de la Cité Vertueuse* (Beyrouth: Librairie Orientale, 1986). In referring to the *Principles of the Opinions of the People of the Virtuous City,* I have sometimes used the short title *Virtuous City*. All citations are to pages and lines of Walzer's edition.

reflection, so that everything that follows from that assumption, including its consequences and difficulties, comes ultimately from reason and not from Islam? Has Alfarabi started from common ground that the philosopher shares with the believer? The question is important, perhaps even decisive. If Islam is not implicated in the assumptions that Alfarabi examines, then it is not implicated in the logical consequences of those assumptions. Alfarabi does not mention Islam; he does not cite the Quran as the authority for his assertion about God. One could cite the passages of the Quran that talk about the riches of God, but Alfarabi does not.[5] He does say, in his Summary of the *Virtuous City* (Walzer, p. 39), that what he has said about the first is what should be believed about God. Even then he does not mention Islam. Is Alfarabi's argument intended to be persuasive only to the Mutazilites, who recognize the authority of reason? Is it simply irrelevant to those who ground themselves on revelation alone?

The point made in the preceding paragraph can be stated even more forcefully if we introduce Alfarabi's own logical distinction between dialectical argument and demonstration.[6] A dialectical argument is one that begins with the premises assumed by one's interlocutor. If one refutes the interlocutor, the force of the argument derives from the fact that the interlocutor shares the assumptions on which the argument is based. The argument, however, has the limitation that it is based on premises that are not necessarily true, even though shared by the interlocutor. The dialectical argument confirms or refutes the opinion of the interlocutor; it is in no way a demonstration of the truth. A demonstration starts from premises that are true, not merely agreed upon. A demonstration from true premises always leads to true conclusions. Demonstration thus understood is unqualifiedly superior to dialectical argument assuming that one can begin from true premises. But how is one to know the truth of

5   See Harry Austryn Wolfson, *The Philosophy of the Kalam* (Cambridge: Harvard University Press, 1976), 76, and Quran, 27:40, 64:6.

6   See Miriam Galston, *Politics and Excellence: The Political Philosophy of Alfarabi* (Princeton, NJ: Princeton University Press, 1990) and David Michael DiPasquale, *Alfarabi and the Starting Point of Islamic Philosophy: A Study of the Kitab al-Jadal (Book of Dialectic)* PhD dissertation, Harvard University, 2002.

a premise? From a logically prior demonstration? Obviously the recourse to a prior demonstration cannot go on forever. Finding a true premise from which to begin proves difficult. Alfarabi has written a short book called the *Conditions of Certainty*. If I am right, the title of this book is both informative and humorous. The opening phrase of the book is "absolute certainty." Absolute certainty cannot have conditions. All human reasoning does have conditions, and its certainty can be only conditional. This, to say the least, raises the status of dialectical argument, particularly in disputes involving religious issues. The dialectical argument can, indeed, begin from the very premises that might eventually be questioned. Since a philosopher is always his own interlocutor, since he is always talking to himself, he cannot simply begin from the prejudices of reason.[7] Such an argument would be a meaningless exercise in digging up what you yourself have buried. A dialectical argument may be more binding than a demonstration in the sense that it begins from the very premises that one wishes to interrogate.

Let us return to Alfarabi's assertion, at the beginning of the *Virtuous City*, that the first existent has no deficiency or defect. Such a claim immediately raises the question whether or not an existent with no defect is possible. Machiavelli reasons that among the human things every good thing comes into being with some attendant evil. This union of good and evil obstructs our wish to bring a thing to its perfection. The perfection we wish for is not possible. In the first sentence of the *Foundations of the Metaphysics of Morals*, Kant is more emphatic. Nothing, he says, is or can be perfect and without defect, the only exception being the good will, which is a human thing. Both Kant and Machiavelli rule out the perfection of God, which would seem to rule out the existence of God.[8]

---

7   On thinking as talking to oneself see *Theaetetus* 189e and *Sophist* 263e, as well as Christopher Colmo, "Socrates Talking to Himself: On the *Greater Hippias*," in Christopher Dustin and Denise Schaeffer, eds., *Socratic Philosophy and Its Other* (Lanham, Maryland: Lexington Books, 2013), 75–89.

8   In his commentary on the Book of Job, Carl Jung posits a dark side to God. See Clodagh Weldon, "God on the Couch: Teaching Jung's *Answer to Job*," in Kelly Buckeley and Clodagh Weldon, *Teaching Jung* (Oxford: Oxford University Press, 2011), 111–25. Perhaps such a God escapes Machiavelli's

Kant's sentence is the perfect expression of an atheistic humanism, though I cannot reconcile with reason a human perfection that is premised on the notion that nothing can be perfect.

There is no reason to think that Alfarabi entertained in Baghdad the thoughts of Machiavelli or Kant. Of course, as soon as one says this, one is brought up short recalling Alfarabi's very surprising account of justice as a kind of rivalry among mutually exclusive qualities. Justice is presented as if it is itself the flux of things.[9] No one state of affairs ever achieves the whole of justice.

II

The opening pages of the *Principles of the Opinions of the People of the Virtuous City* are dense, but identifying and reasoning about some of the highlights of these pages may show their philosophic importance. The first existent is the first cause of the existence of all of the other existents. The first cause is not the immediate or proximate cause of our knowledge that there is a first cause. Our knowledge of the first cause is presented as a product of our reasoning about the many things that exist in the world of our experience. In other parts of the book that deal with prophecy Alfarabi does suggest that there might be a kind of immediate experience of the divine, but not here. In these opening pages, the first and the highest is known to us by reasoning.

argument. In his commentary on *Discourses* III 37, Mansfield says that Machiavelli means to retract the claim that everything has its own evil or defect, at least with respect to man. Such a retraction would undercut Machiavelli's argument against the existence of God, if, in fact, he makes such an argument. Harvey Mansfield, Jr., *Machiavelli's New Modes and Orders* (Cornell: Ithaca, 1979), 417.

9   Christopher A. Colmo, *Breaking with Athens: Alfarabi as Founder* (Lanham, MD: Lexington Books, 2005), 33. Does this non-hierarchical account of justice have democratic political implications? Does it help to explain why, in the *Political Regime*, sec. 114, Alfarabi calls the democratic regime the most "admirable and happy" of the ignorant regimes? Moreover, are there democratic or, at any rate, non-hierarchical, implications to Alfarabi's reflections on the difficulties of conceiving a first cause that has no cause?

What can reason tell us about the first existent? One of the most important arguments that Alfarabi makes here is that the first existent is one and unique. How do we reach this conclusion? It is possible to say that in making this argument, Alfarabi is merely accommodating the monotheism of his coreligionists, but he also gives reasons. The first existent must be the first cause and an absolutely first cause cannot itself have a cause. The first existent has no cause. It is uncaused. We cannot help but notice that Alfarabi does not go as far as Spinoza does in claiming that the first cause is the cause of itself.[10] Can one, in fact, hold these two ideas apart? Can we say of the first—or of the whole or of nature—that it has no cause without meaning by this that the first is the cause of itself? Perhaps the contradiction involved in saying that X is the cause of itself seemed to Alfarabi too obvious to go down that road. Surely the one thing that would prove, from a rational point of view, that the first existent cannot exist would be a necessary contradiction in the idea of a first existent. For Alfarabi, there are three kinds of causes: by which, from which, and for which.[11] Parenthetically, one might notice that Alfarabi does not simply follow Aristotle in identifying four causes. Whatever the significance of this fact might be, in the present context the important point is that the first existent being also the first cause cannot have a cause. Hence it cannot be a form instantiate in a matter, for then matter and form would be two causes of the first cause, which is a contradiction. It is important that the first existent has no matter, because two existents with the same form might be distinguished by their matter. The first existent cannot be distinguished from another first existent by having a different matter. Curiously enough, Alfarabi does not explicitly say this. Nor does he explicitly say that one first existent could not be

10 *Ethics*, I, First Definition and Prop. 7. In commenting on Heidegger, Leo Strauss raises the possibility that "causality cannot be explained causally." See Thomas Pangle, ed., *The Rebirth of Classical Political Rationalism* (Chicago: University of Chicago Press, 1989), 44. This passage is cited in Richard L. Velkley, *Heidegger, Strauss, and the Premises of Philosophy* (Chicago: University of Chicago Press, 2011), 190 n.19.

11 Compare Walzer's translation of 561 n.15 ("through which, out of which, and for the sake of which") with Mahdi's translation of *Attainment of Happiness* sec. 6. The Arabic phrase is the same in both texts.

distinguished from another by its form since form can exist only in matter (Walzer, 59). Alfarabi proceeds on the hypothetical assumption that one first might differ from another and reflects on this difference. Each first might have something different from the other or one might have something the other did not have. In either case, the first would be divisible, at least in thought. It would have parts, and the parts would be causes of the first existent. But this is a contradiction. The first can have no cause.

Reflection on the case in which one first existent has some distinguishing feature that the other does not helps to shed light on the notion that the first has no defect. All the attributes that might distinguish one first existent from another are perfections. If this is the case, then the first existent that lacked an attribute possessed by another first existent would reveal by its defect that the other was not simple but divisible and, if divisible, then it would have parts and the parts would be causes of the first.[12]

The preceding argument leads to the familiar conclusion—familiar in monotheistic religions—that there can be only one first existent or first cause. But this conclusion is based on another conclusion that is not quite so explicitly announced. There can be only one first existent because the first existent can have no features that might distinguish it from another first existent. As we have seen, two distinguishable features must have a cause which unites them, but the first has no cause. So the first cannot have two distinguishable features. The argument is too simple to be burdened with examples of distinguishable features, and Alfarabi does not give any examples. He has already told us that the first cannot have matter and form. He does not say that the first cannot be subject to the distinction between existence and essence. This example fits well with Alfarabi's subsequent argument that two first existents could not be distinguished by something added to one of them because that one would then have two parts. For example, one first existent could

12 Avicenna's version of this argument is spelled out in Parviz Morewedge, "A Third Version of the Ontological Argument in the Ibn Sīnian Metaphysics," in Parviz Morewedge, ed., *Islamic Philosophical Theology* (Albany, NY: State University of New York Press, 1979), 188–222, at 219 n.36.

not differ from another first existent by having existence added to one of them. Existence cannot be added to the first because the first would then have two parts or two distinguishable features. This illustration of Alfarabi's argument against the possibility of two first existents or two first causes leads to the very interesting conclusion that the first existent cannot have existence as something added to its essence. Existence cannot be added to the essence of the first. The essence of the first must be its existence.

That the essence of the first must be its existence is a conclusion that Alfarabi states in so many words in other places,[13] but in those places Alfarabi does not give an argument. We see that the argument is supplied at the beginning of the *Virtuous City*, though Alfarabi leaves it to the reader to spell out the conclusion in that place. At this point, two lines of reflection are available to the reader. One line of reflection is traced by the following questions. Is it possible to make sense of a first whose essence is its existence? Is it simply nonsense to conflate essence and existence? Is the notion of existence as the essence of anything unintelligible? Is Alfarabi deconstructing the idea of a first existent or a first cause? Did Alfarabi, in fact, conceive of a world in which every cause is also an effect of some cause distinct from itself? Is such a non-hierarchical view of causation inconceivable, since it would present us with a circle of causation rather than a hierarchy?[14]

The second line of reflection follows up on a corollary of the former. Assuming that the essence of the first is its existence, it is utterly unique

---

13 Netton, *Allah Transcendent*, 111.
14 Avicenna apparently saw the need to refute the idea of a "circular regress." See Herbert A. Davidson, "Avicenna's Proof of the Existence of God as a Necessarily Existent Being," in Parviz Morewedge, *Islamic Philosophical Theology* (Albany, NY: State University of New York Press, 1979), 165–87, at 186 n.113. See also *Alfarabi's Philosophy of Plato and Aristotle*, trans. Muhsin Mahdi (Cornell: Cornell University Press, 2001). In the *Philosophy of Aristotle*, Alfarabi considers the question of whether there must be a hierarchy. How is it possible that of two things, each should be the end of the other? The question seems intended to imply that this is impossible, but in the previous sentence Alfarabi had suggested that each of two things might be "for the sake of the other in a circular way" (64:6–7).

in this respect. The collapse of the distinction between existence and essence follows from the uncaused character of the first existent. There cannot be two things of this character, as Alfarabi shows. Every other existent has a cause and in everything having a cause we may distinguish existence and essence. Existence is always something added to essence. What is the significance of this corollary? Is it not simply trivial? Is it not obvious that existence is something added to essence? The problem here is that only essence has a logical structure that makes one thing follow necessarily from another. If essence and existence are always distinguishable, then no essence *exists* necessarily.

Charles Butterworth has translated what he calls the Introductory Sections to the *Virtuous City*, and in this short document, Alfarabi makes the following assertions about the consequences of the existence of a first existent or a first cause. I will quote at some length a section which reads in part like a table of contents.

How the governance of God, may He be exalted and his praise magnified, reaches out beyond the highest heavens until it returns to the center of the earth and what surrounds it. How the material bodies are linked and what their rankings are. How they were formerly brought into being with respect to rulership. How some govern others and all of them are subdued. Whatever may have been, it necessarily follows that nature exists as it does now and that nothing else is possible. There is no perfection other than the existence it has now, nor is it at all possible for it to have another existence other than this existence; and whatever existence a human being fancies it to have other than the one it has now is a deficiency and delusion, not an existence, and it is something that cannot be from God's action, may he be exalted; nor is it seemly of Him.[15]

---

15 Charles E. Butterworth, "Al-Farabi's Introductory Sections to the *Virtuous City*" in Y. Tzvi Langermann and Josef Stern, eds., *Adaptations and Innovations: Studies on the Interaction between Jewish and Islamic Thought and Literature from the Early Middle Ages to the Late Twentieth Century* (Leuven: Peeters, 2007), 27–49, at 46.

Alfarabi's claim here—if it is a claim—that "nature exists as it does now and that nothing else is possible" seems to be a way of articulating Aristotle's thesis of the eternity of the visible world or of articulating the consequence of that thesis for the permanence of nature as it is.[16] In the essay that accompanies his translation, Butterworth points out that Alfarabi does not explicitly claim any of these things in his own name, however salutary he may regard it to make such claims. I agree with the point Butterworth makes, and I think it is equally true that in the passage we have quoted above Alfarabi supports the conception of the necessity of nature as it is now on a foundation that Aristotle might have found less than helpful. Alfarabi makes it clear—does he not?—that the necessity of the natural world as it is follows from the causality of a first existent or a first cause. Alfarabi presents the thesis of the necessity of nature as it is or the eternity of the visible world as dependent on a metaphysical or theistic assumption about the first existent or the first cause while at the same time, at the very beginning of the *Principles of the Opinions of the People of the Virtuous City*, forcing us to consider how difficult it is to coherently articulate the meaning of such a first. I am suggesting that Alfarabi is providing a critique of the Aristotelian notion of the eternity of the visible world by exposing—in the above quoted passage—what he regards as the necessarily theistic basis of such a conception of nature, a conception which, in Alfarabi's view, Aristotle did not sufficiently explore.[17]

Alfarabi goes on to present the perfect as that which stands alone in its species (Walzer, 60). The perfect is the sum of all of the virtues of the members of its species. One might, of course, assume that the perfections of a species could only exist as distributed among the members of the species. But Alfarabi asserts the opposite, that there could only be one exemplar of all of the good qualities of a species. The perfect is that apart from which no other member of its species can be perfect. The

---

16   See *Breaking with Athens*, 24, for references to Aristotle. Would one consequence of the eternity of the world as it is now be the impossibility of another world after this one?

17   David Rapport Lachterman, *The Ethics of Geometry: A Genealogy of Modernity* (London: Routledge, 1989), 106.

perfect is the thing apart from which no other member of its species can exist (Walzer, 60, 15–16). The imperfect cannot exist without the perfect.[18] Does Alfarabi mean to imply that the perfect is the cause of the existence of all of the imperfect members of its species? The perfect is the cause of the imperfect. Alfarabi does not explicitly raise the question whether being the cause of something imperfect is a kind of imperfection. Nor does he suggest that this imperfection might pertain to the first.

The first is presented as having no cause and as being a cause. We can distinguish in speech and in thought these two different aspects of the first. But do these two aspects of the first violate the simplicity of the first without which Alfarabi says the first cannot be uncaused?

Alfarabi's proof that there can be only one first existent leads him to conclude that the first does not share its existence with the existence of any other thing (Walzer, 58, 10–11). His first proof or argument or reasoning is based on the assumption that the first must be completely uncaused and therefore completely simple and indivisible. We cannot even follow Spinoza in thinking of the first as the cause of itself, since this would give it two different aspects—as cause and thing caused—a division that violates its simplicity. His second proof is based on the assumption that the first has no defect or that it has every perfection belonging to a thing of its kind. We have seen with respect to the human things, for example justice, how, at least on the face of it, one perfection sometimes (always?) precludes another. But the first is radically different from the human things. Indeed, the assumption that the first is uncaused and perfect leads Alfarabi to the conclusion that the existence of the first is not shared by anything else that might be called the first. In fact, the existence belonging to the first is not shared by anything else at all.[19] We can see this in a way from the thought that the existence of the first does not have a cause whereas the existence of every other thing does have a cause. When we say that the first exists, we cannot mean the same thing that we mean when we say that we exist or that a body in the world

18 Is this not a way of saying that the actual must always be somehow prior to the possible and the potential?
19 See Maimonides, *Guide of the Perplexed* I 56.

exists. In saying this, we are already at the threshold of negative theology.

We have seen that in the case of the first, the difference between essence and existence must collapse.[20] For the first its essence is its existence. How does Alfarabi arrive at this idea? We are told that the first has no contrary. The contrary of a thing is that which would destroy that thing. Alfarabi gives no example. Perhaps knowledge and ignorance are contraries, since the existence of the one precludes the existence of the other. At any rate, the contrary of the first would destroy the first. But what can be destroyed is not eternal, and its coming-into-being must have a cause (Walzer, 63–65). Before we accept the idea that the first has no contrary and move on, we should pause long enough to ask what the contrary of the first might be. If the essence of the first is existence, then its contrary is non-existence. We have arrived at the Parmenidean idea that non-existence cannot exist. But one can look at the question of the contrary of the first in another way. The first is uncaused and the contrary of uncaused would seem to be that which has a cause. But the first existent is also in Alfarabi's scenario the first cause from which all else emanates. Assuming that the first is itself the cause of all that has a cause and that the uncaused is the contrary of the caused, it follows that the first is the cause of its own contrary. The first and perfect existent would be the cause of its own contrary and hence the cause of its own destruction. No doubt Alfarabi escapes this dilemma by claiming that the first is of a different rank than everything else. Indeed, it is because Alfarabi asserts that contraries are of the same rank (Walzer, 67) that the first can have no contrary; the first can have nothing of the same rank. Against Alfarabi's abstract argument that the first has no contrary, it seems possible to actually name and describe that contrary. The contrary of the uncaused first is the effect emanating from it. The first that has no cause can have no contrary of the same rank only if it is not itself a cause of anything. It would be hasty to conclude that Alfarabi is consciously deconstructing his own idea of a first existent that is also a first cause.

---

20 We are reminded of Spinoza's claim that the essence of substance involves existence (note 10 above). Also Netton, *Allah Transcendent*, 110.

Alfarabi argues that the first is one, but the argument confuses two kinds of oneness. The one is indivisible. It cannot have matter and form since these would be divisible, at least in thought. It cannot have an essence other than its existence since again these would be divisible in thought. The first is one simply and without division. Alfarabi seamlessly transitions to the meaning of one whereby oneness characterizes a particular existing thing. The wine glass on the table next to me is one thing distinct from the other things in the room by virtue of its own particular matter, its form, its function. It is the perfect glass for red wine, although for white wine another shape is perfect. This meaning—the oneness of a particular thing—goes necessarily with its existence (Walzer, 68, 12).[21] The first is one in the sense of a particular one, yet Alfarabi has described as clearly as is possible the indivisible oneness of the first as being not at all like the oneness of the wine glass.[22]

We have said enough at this point to see that the first existent is both utterly simple and utterly unlike anything else. It lacks any kind of division or multiplicity that might give rise to a search for the cause of that multiplicity. Likewise, while one first existent can in no way be different from another first existent, it must be very different from other things. In one of his more humorous turns of phrase, Alfarabi says that he does not mean to deny that the first existent is different from some other things (Walzer, 67). Indeed, as we have seen, it must be very different from all other things since it does not consist of matter and form. To be is to be something, but can something be without a form?[23] It is utterly simple and one. Alfarabi speaks of the first existent and other existents, using the same word for existent in both cases. Does he mean by this that the first existent is a thing in the way that other things are? Is there

21 The necessity here is not the necessity of that which cannot not be but rather the necessity that all that exists can also cease to be.

22 Compare the two meanings of oneness in Plato, *Protagoras* 349c.

23 Leo Strauss, *Natural Right and History* (Chicago: University of Chicago Press, 1953), 122, says that to be is to be something, but the paragraph in which this claim is articulated seems to qualify it. Heidegger's *The Question of Being* (New York: Twayne, 1958) argues that Being is not a thing only by separating Being from logos and intelligibility. In contrast, Alfarabi's first existent seems to be or to be intended as fully intelligible being.

any significance to the fact that Alfarabi sometimes drops the word existent, calling the first existent simply the first? It seems reasonable to ask whether the first is a thing at all given that it cannot be a form in matter.

We are now utterly astounded when Alfarabi goes on to tell us that the first is a thinking thing. How can something utterly simple or indivisible carry on an activity, much less an activity like thinking? If thinking is, as Plato suggested, a kind of conversation with oneself, how can it be an activity of the one?[24] Alfarabi sets out to explain this paradox. Alfarabi must explain the intellectual activity of the first in a way that accommodates its role as the first cause of the multiplicity of existing things. We are reminded, of course, that Aristotle explained the highest as thought thinking itself, but we are at the same time reminded that he also said that thought of itself moves nothing.[25] Alfarabi's task is not made simpler by the fact that whereas Aristotle aims to account for a final cause of motion, Alfarabi wants to account not only for the motion of things but for their existence as well.

The indivisible first is then a thinking thing or an intellect. Since the first has no matter, it is form alone. How form can be separate from matter we are not told. Alfarabi indicates that if form—any form— were separate from matter, it would be thought. Thinking and the thing thought—the participle and the noun—are one and the same. Does this mean that form which is not separate from matter cannot be identical with thought? This would place a severe limit on human understanding of things consisting of matter and form. The indivisible first is form alone—a form stripped of its matter?—and hence a thinking thing or an intellect. It thinks always in actuality, or it is always the active intellect. When the first thinks, it thinks itself. This observation leads Alfarabi to divide the indivisible into two parts. When the first thinks, it is both that which thinks and that which is thought. Alfarabi distinguishes subject from object within the activity of thinking. He gives a

24 Leo Strauss, *The City and Man* (Chicago: Rand McNally, 1964), 119, asserts that for Plato, the highest is not a thinking thing.
25 Aristotle *Metaphysics* 1072b19 and 1074b34; *Nicomachean Ethics* 1139a35.

list: Thought, the thing thought, and the union of the two in the activity of thinking. We now have a threefold division, but these three are one.[26] Even or especially on Alfarabi's account it is necessary to say that intellect is caused by the union of that which intellects and that which is intellected. Precisely such a cause is unthinkable for the first that has no cause.

Alfarabi explicitly distinguishes, in the *Virtuous City*, between the thinking of the first and human thinking.[27] The first thinks only itself. Thought thinking only itself would itself be empty of every specific thought. The first thinks only itself. It does not think man. Man does think man, but only potentially, not always or from the outset. Actually thinking the essence of man is something that is lacking prior to man's thought and that the thinking man adds to the universe. But in the Aristotelian scheme of things, actuality must always be prior to mere potentiality. Merely human thought cannot actualize that which does not already exist in actuality. Man cannot be thought of as completing a somehow imperfect world. Alfarabi avoids this consequence by separating the active intellect understood as being the first from the active intellect understood as emanating from the first. The active intellect emanating from the first does think man in actuality prior to this thought occurring to the mind of any man. But Alfarabi has made it perfectly clear that this solution is not without its difficulties.

III

We have seen that the first has no parts, that it is utterly simple, that it exists with an existence unlike any other thing. How then are we to speak about a first that is not a thing like any other thing? We can have some confidence that Alfarabi also posed this question, because he provides an answer. In speaking of the unlikeness of the first, we can say only

---

26   Alfarabi does not explicitly count to three, but the three items in his list must have been obvious to both Christian and Muslim readers and affected each quite differently.

27   As regards the threefold aspect of thought, Maimonides does not clearly distinguish between human and divine in *Guide of the Perplexed* I 68.

what it is not.[28] This is what I mean by Alfarabi's negative theology. It seems to lead to the problem that when we speak of the existence of the first, we simply cannot know what we are talking about because we have discovered in the uncaused first existent characteristics that make the first radically unlike anything else whatsoever.[29] The poet and critic Paul Valéry in our time characterized existence by the formula, "Anything that resembles nothing else does not exist."[30] To be is to be like something else. Alfarabi treats the first as a cause, but must a cause not be somehow like its effect? Does this make the absolutely first cause impossible? The central problem of the first part of the *Principles of the Opinions of the People of the Virtuous City* is that the first is said to exist with an existence unlike anything else, and yet it is also described as thinking and living. The issue comes to a head when Alfarabi describes the first as taking pleasure in its existence (Walzer, 85). At this point, Alfarabi says that the pleasure the first takes in itself is completely unlike the pleasure a human being takes in thinking and knowing or if it is at all similar the similarity is trifling or insignificant. We see that Alfarabi has backed himself into a corner—or is it perhaps better to say that he has led the reader into a dead end? On the one hand, there must be some analogy (*qiyās*) between the first and the world of our experience, for if this were not the case then we simply would not know what we are talking about when we talk about the first. On the other hand, if there is an

---

28 See. F. W. Zimmermann, *Al-Farabi's Commentary and Short Treatise on Aristotle's De Interpretatione* (Oxford: Oxford University Press, 1987), 120 and Colmo, *Breaking with Athens*, 125–27.

29 Leo Strauss discusses the problem in relation to Maimonides in *Liberalism Ancient and Modern* (New York: Basic Books, 1968), 175–76. Christopher Hughes' *Complex Theory of a Simple God* discusses it in relation to Thomas Aquinas. Alfarabi never uses the expression "absolutely other" to describe the first, perhaps because "other" is an essentially relative term. What is other than another cannot be absolute. Unlike the first, which is one and unique, it would seem that the absolutely other can only come in pairs. For example, if God is the absolutely other of man, then with respect to God man too must be the absolutely other! Confusion reigns when we observe that at least in this the two must be alike.

30 Quoted in Nathan Leites, *The Rules of the Game in Paris* (Chicago: University of Chicago Press, 1969), 4.

analogy between the first and man, then we begin to suspect that our notion of the first is merely a projection of our own good qualities raised to perfection. Alfarabi says as much when he says that the thinking of the first is a pleasure of the same kind that a human being experiences in thinking and understanding, though in the case of the first—of God—it is an infinitely greater pleasure.

I have tried to follow Alfarabi as he leads us from the notion of a perfect being, a being with no defects, into the silence of a being about which we can say nothing meaningful because it is radically unlike us and unlike everything in our experience. In a spirit of compromise, Alfarabi introduces the notion of an analogy between the first and man. But the compromise turns out to be somewhat shocking, since it leads to the suggestion that the pleasure of the first differs only in degree from the pleasures of man. Otherwise no analogy would be possible. In conclusion we are reminded of a question we raised at the beginning of our essay. Do arguments such as these presuppose the validity, the binding character, of reason? If so, do they affect only the Mutazilites and other rationalist theologians? We must return to Alfarabi in search of answers to these questions. In particular, we must ask what Alfarabi really understood by religion and the intention of religion. Does the intention of religion differ from the intention of philosophy and, if so, how?[31]

---

31 Charles Butterworth has frequently dealt with the relation of religion and philosophy for Alfarabi, most recently in the Introduction to his *Alfarabi: The Political Writings, II, "Political Regime" and "Summary of Plato's Laws"* (Ithaca: Cornell University Press, 2015), 18. It is my pleasure to thank Professor Steven Harvey for his helpful comment on the draft of this essay.

The Origin of Primary Principles:
The Role of Nature and Experience
Miriam Galston

In 2005 Deborah Black observed that some of Alfarabi's works portray the genesis of intelligibles, including first or primary principles, as empirically based, while in others he appears to depict their origin differently.[1] This assessment is not surprising: Alfarabi's theories are notoriously difficult to summarize or even to describe in detail because he wrote so many books, commentaries, and treatises of various types, and the teachings of these works are not always consistent with one another. Perhaps the goal of isolating a "theory" or "teaching" is ill-advised to begin with. It may be more fruitful to see his various works as providing sometimes competing, sometimes complementary explorations of important philosophical topics that encourage the reader to reflect on the difficulties inherent in adopting any of the perspectives as definitive. It is in this spirit that the following essay about the role of experience and nature in the genesis of primary (first) premises in several of Alfarabi's works has been written.[2]

---

[1] Deborah L. Black, "The Nature of Intellect," in *The Cambridge History of Medieval Philosophy*, ed. Robert Pasnau (Cambridge: Cambridge University Press, 2010), vol. I, 323 (she identifies the non-empirical path with "first principles … received by the material intellect directly from the agent intellect"). For Black's articles elaborating the alternatives, see note 2.

[2] Because it is not possible to analyze all of Alfarabi's writings bearing on this topic given space limitations, I hope to supplement this essay with an analysis that examines Alfarabi's political treatises and other works not discussed here. For additional commentary on the topic of this essay, see Thérèse-Anne Druart, "Al-Fârâbî (870–950), "Une éthique universelle fondée sur les intelligibles premiers," in Louis-Leon Christians et al., dir., *Droit naturel: relancer l'histoire?* (Brussels: Bruylant, 2008), 215, 220–24; Deborah L. Black, "Al-Fārābī on Meno's Paradox," in Peter Adamson,

Nature as the Source of Primary Principles

Alfarabi's *Selected Aphorisms* gives a clear statement of the natural origin of primary principles.[3] In this work Alfarabi divides the rational faculty into a theoretical (*naẓarī*) and a reflective (*fikrī*) part (*Aphorisms*, no. 33). He attributes certain knowledge of the universal and necessary premises that are the principles of the sciences to a faculty of the theoretical part called "theoretical intellect" (*al-'aql al-naẓarī*) and stipulates that such principles arise naturally (*bi-l-ṭab'*), not through inquiry (*baḥth*) or syllogism (*qiyās*) (*Aphorisms, no. 34*).[4] Alfarabi then repeats this point in the passage elaborating the meaning of the term "knowledge" or "science" (*'ilm*), where he states that knowledge comes from demonstrations ultimately derived from primary premises that become

ed., *In the Age of al-Fārābī: Arabic Philosophy in the Fourth/Tenth Century* (London: The Warburg Institute, 2008), 15–34; Black, "Knowledge (*'ilm*) and Certitude (*yaqīn*) in al-Fārābī's Epistemology," *Arabic Sciences and Philosophy* 16 (2006), 11–46; Druart, "Al-Fārābī, Ethics, and First Intelligibles," *Documenti e studi sulla tradizione filosofica medievale* 8 (1997), 403–23; Herbert L. Davidson, *Alfarabi, Avicenna, and Averroes, On Intellect: Their Cosmologies, Theories of the Active Intellect, and Theories of Human Intellect* (New York & Oxford: Oxford University Press, 1992), 44–73.

3   *Fuṣūl Muntaza'ah*, edited with an introduction and notes by Fauzi M. Najjar as *Alfarabi's Selected Aphorisms* (Beirut: Dar el-Mashreq, 1971) (hereafter *Selected Aphorisms*), nos. 33–34. This work was translated into English with an introduction by Charles Butterworth in *Alfarabi The Political Writings: Selected Aphorisms and Other Texts* (Ithaca & London: Cornell University Press, 2001) (hereafter *Political Writings I*), 11–67. The English translation has the pages of Najjar's edition in brackets and follows that edition's paragraph numbering. For an earlier edition and translation, based upon two incomplete manuscripts, see *Al-Fārābī: Fuṣūl al-Madanī, Aphorisms of the Statesman*, edited with an English translation, introduction and notes, by D. M. Dunlop (Cambridge: Cambridge University Press, 1961). For an analysis of the book, see Dunlop's introduction and notes; Charles E. Butterworth, *Ethical and political philosophy*, in Peter Adamson & Richard C. Taylor, eds., *The Cambridge Companion to Arabic Philosophy* (Cambridge: Cambridge University Press, 2005), 276–80.

4   *Qiyās* means syllogism, reasoning, analogy, or comparison. In the passages referred to in this essay, it seems to refer to deductive reasoning.

known to the intellect naturally (*Aphorisms, no. 35*). When theoretical intellect possesses such foundational knowledge, it is transformed from potential intellect into intellect in actuality (*Aphorisms, no. 34*).

The *Letter on the Intellect*,[5] perhaps Alfarabi's most systematic treatment of the nature of the human intellect, largely agrees with the account presented in *Selected Aphorisms*. In this work, Alfarabi elaborates the different meanings given to the term *'aql*, or intellect, in six different contexts. He begins by explaining the meaning given to the term by the public (*al-jumhūr*) and the theologians (*al-mutakallimūn*) (*Intellect*, 4:4–8:4). He then further distinguishes the meanings given to the term by Aristotle in the *Posterior Analytics*, the *Ethics*, and the *De Anima*. Alfarabi says that in the *Posterior Analytics* Aristotle means by intellect the faculty of the soul that is the locus of certainty about necessary, true, and universal premises that do not emerge based upon syllogistic reasoning (*qiyās*) at all or reflection (*fikr*). Rather, such premises emerge innately (*bi-l-fiṭra*), naturally (*bi-l-ṭab'*), while growing up, or otherwise without one being aware of where or how they arose (*Intellect*, 8:7–9).[6] These premises are the principles of the theoretical sciences (*Intellect*, 9:2–3).[7]

---

5   *Risālah fī'l-'aql*, edited by Maurice Bouyges, S.J., as *Alfarabi Risalat fī'l-'aql* (Beirut: Imprimerie Catholique, 1938), 8:5–7. The work was translated into French by Dyala Hamzah as *Abû Nasr AL-FÂRÂBÎ L'Épître sur l'intellect al-Risâla fī-l-'aql* (Paris: L'Harmattan, 2001). There is an English translation in Jon McGinnis & David C. Reisman, *Classical Arabic Philosophy: An Anthology of Sources* (Indianapolis/Cambridge: Hackett Publishing Company, 2007), 68–78. Alfarabi reiterates the point summarized in the text at the end of the same paragraph in *Letter on the Intellect*, where he says that primary knowledge (*al-ma'rifa al-ūlā*) emerges in this faculty neither by reflection nor contemplation (*lā bi-fikr wa-lā bi-ta'ammul*) at all (*Intellect*, 8:9–9:2).

6   There are alternative readings of this sentence among the manuscripts that would change the meaning somewhat. See *Intellect* 8, nn.12–14.

7   See also Alfarabi, *Conditions of Certitude* (*sharā'iṭ al-yaqīn*), in *Al-Fārābī. Kitāb al-Burhān wa Kitāb Šarā'iṭ al-Yaqīn*, edition and introduction by Majid Fakhry (Beirut: Dar el-Mashreq, 1987), 101, which divides certainty into what does not emerge from syllogistic reasoning at all and what does come from syllogism. The former, described as certainty in itself (*yaqīn bi-nafsih*), is equated with the principles of the theoretical sciences.

This description in the *Letter on the Intellect* appears to preclude other sources of the first or primary premises of the theoretical sciences, since Alfarabi claims that in the *Book of Demonstration*, Aristotle meant by intellect *only* the certainty in the soul that emerges without syllogism or reflection (*Intellect,* 8:6–8).[8] The passage appears to be at odds with what Alfarabi himself attributes to Aristotle in his commentary on Aristotle's *Posterior Analytics*, where he presents experience as a source of primary premises, since experience is defined there in a manner that suggests intentional pursuit of and, possibly, reflection on knowledge.[9]

Alfarabi's commentary on Aristotle's *Topics*, known as the *Book of Dialectic*,[10] describes the principles of philosophy as primary premises that are certain, true, and universal (*Dialectic,* 28:4–5) and explains that the principles of the theoretical sciences are the universal premises that correspond to things as they exist outside the soul (*Dialectic,* 18:8–10). In this work, Alfarabi characterizes such knowledge as the product of one's own insight (*baṣīra*), which results from a syllogism composed out of premises that have been known since the beginning (*mundhu awwal al-amr*), rather than from a syllogism (*qiyās*) or proof (*dalīl*) (*Dialectic,* 30:17–19). The *Book of Dialectic* thus appears to be in agreement with the *Letter on the Intellect* and *Selected Aphorisms* in attributing primary knowledge to what is known naturally, assuming that premises known "since the beginning" implies premises known "naturally," and it adds that certainty about the principles of the sciences entails knowing that the cognitions cannot be

---

8   *Selected Aphorisms* does not say "only"; rather, it states that there is no inquiry or syllogistic reasoning. This might exclude attaining primary premises through experience to the extent that experience presupposes intentionally seeking instances of sense-perception. See below, 121, 127–28, 131.

9   See below, 119–22.

10   Alfarabi, *Kitāb al-Jadal,* edited by Rafiq al-Ajam (Beirut: Dar el-Mashreq, 1985) (hereafter *Book of Dialectic*), 30. There is a partial French translation in Georges Vajda, "Autour de la connaissance chez Saadia," *Revue des études juives* 126 (1967): 135–89 and 375–97, reprinted in G. E. Weil, *Mélanges Georges Vajda* (Hildesheim, 1982), 71–149.

otherwise (*Dialectic,* 18:22–19:4). Yet the *Book of Dialectic* lacks re-strictive language (e.g., "only") that would preclude primary principles from originating other than "since the beginning," so the work does not necessarily conform to the account of primary premises in the *Letter on the Intellect.*

The *Book of Dialectic* clearly departs from the first two works in important ways. First, it states that certain and universal primary premises are all invariably generally accepted propositions (*mashhūrāt*) (*Dialectic,* 28:9–10, 31:14–16), i.e., they are recognized by all people as true independent of the strict standards required for certain knowledge.[11] Second, Alfarabi claims that these premises are adopted as true by people initially *because* they are generally accepted by other people (*Dialectic,* 28:10–11), i.e., on the authority of others rather than because of personal insight that the premises correspond to things as they are (*Dialectic,* 17:6–9, 18:14–16). In other words, according to this commentary, such premises may become known with certainty naturally, without the benefit of inquiry or reasoning, but they are not initially grasped as true, necessary, and certain. Rather, Alfarabi says, people start out with (*nashā'a 'alā*) and know at first (*awwalan*) opinions that are generally accepted at first glance, received from someone trusted, or based upon sense-perception (*Dialectic,* 30:13–15, see 17:9–18:7), and they may subsequently come to know some of these things with certainty in a rigorous way.

The latter two observations in the *Book of Dialectic* are either inconsistent with the accounts in *Selected Aphorisms* and the *Letter on the Intellect* or they can be seen as adding information about the origin of primary premises that is simply omitted in the other two works. In the latter case, *Selected Aphorisms* and the *Letter on the Intellect* could be viewed as supplementing the *Book of Dialectic,* although they give

---

11   The *Book of Dialectic* describes generally accepted opinions as opinions that all believe are true. However, in his commentary on Aristotle's *Posterior Analytics,* Alfarabi says "all or most or the like (*mā yajrī majrāhum*)." See Alfarabi, *Book of Demonstration,* in *Al-Fārābī. Kitāb al-Burhān wa Kitāb Šarā'iṭ al-Yaqīn,* 21:5. See also Aristotle, *Topics* 1.1 100b21–22 (generally accepted opinions are those held by all, most, or the wise—all the wise, most of them, or the most famous or generally known of them).

a very different impression about the origin of primary cognitions than is contained in the *Book of Dialectic* by failing to mention a period during which the content of some primary premises is recognized in a fashion best described as opinion rather than knowledge or certainty.[12]

Primary Principles in the Book of Demonstration

Alfarabi's commentary on Aristotle's *Posterior Analytics,* which is called the *Book of Demonstration,*[13] offers a more comprehensive account of the origin of the principles of reasoning than the works described so far. After dividing all cognition into conceptual understanding (*taṣawwur*) and assent (*taṣdīq*) (*Demonstration,* 19:7), Alfarabi states that there are two kinds of universal premises that admit of necessary certainty and also are not based on syllogistic reasoning, namely, those that emerge naturally and those that emerge through experience (*Demonstration,* 23:3–4).[14] As for those for which certainty emerges naturally, the *Book of Demonstration* observes that we do not know where or how the certainty emerges, we were not aware at any time that we were ignorant of or desired to have such knowledge, and we never considered

---

12 See Alfarabi, *Political Regime,* edited by Fauzi Najjar as *Al-Fārābī's The Political Regime (Al-Siyāsa al-Madaniyya also known as the treatise on the principles of beings)* (Beirut: Imprimerie Catholique, 1964), 72:5–9. A complete English translation of the work is in Charles E. Butterworth, *Political Writings II: "Political Regime" and "Summary of Plato's Laws"* (Ithaca, NY: Cornell University Press, 2015), 29–94. The text cited in this note is on pp. 62–63.

13 For the text and translation, see note 11. Usually when Alfarabi's text says *Kitāb al-Burhān,* I have translated it as *Posterior Analytics,* meaning the work of Aristotle. Since Alfarabi's own commentary on Aristotle's book is also called *Kitāb al-Burhān,* there is the possibility that he is referring to his own commentary, unless he specifies Aristotle. Sometimes, however, Alfarabi refers to *Anālūṭīqā al-Akhīra,* Arabic for *Posterior Analytics,* in which event he is clearly referring to Aristotle's work.

14 Alfarabi says that particular premises can be known with necessary certainty, but he declines to discuss them here, in part because universal premises are used in the sciences more (*Demonstration,* 22:14–15).

it a problem at all; rather, it seems to us as though we possessed it innately and instinctively from the beginning of our existence (*Demonstration*, 23:4–8).[15]

In his *Book of Demonstration*, Alfarabi observes that it appears[16] that the individual instances comprehended by most universal primary premises emerging naturally are grasped by sense-perception (*Demonstration*, 24:7–8)—a claim not made in the preceding works. Despite the fact that he then states emphatically that a book on logic is not the place to explore the genesis of necessary and universal primary premises emerging naturally (*Demonstration*, 23:9–10, 24:3–7),[17] Alfarabi nonetheless proceeds to make several observations about this very topic. First, he notes that sense-perception alone is insufficient to explain the existence of the primary premises in question because sense-perception is limited to particulars, not universals. Thus, sense-perception can only result in incomplete knowledge (*Demonstration*, 24:8–11). He therefore concludes that the human soul has an activity relating to things sensed that goes beyond the confines of sense-perception alone (*Demonstration*, 24:14). Although he declines to discuss the nature of that activity, Alfarabi calls the reader's attention to an even more subtle problem: he adds that among the subjects he will not entertain is whether the not-to-be-discussed activity of the soul presupposes prior sense-perception of particulars in every instance or is a form of perception (*idrāk*) peculiar to the soul that can operate in the absence of prior knowledge of individuals derived from sense-perception (*Demonstration*, 24:14–17). The topic alluded to is presumably whether human beings have the ability to obtain knowledge about

---

15 McGinnis and Reisman, *Classical Arabic Philosophy*, 63-68, contains a short excerpt from Alfarabi's *Demonstration* that includes the passage in question. They translate *tajriba* as "methodic experience" (66-67), which is an interpretation since the Arabic says only "experience."

16 The Arabic root *z-h-r* can connote superficial appearances or it can refer to what is obvious.

17 The origin of primary cognitions is "one of the problems of the sciences and philosophy" (*Demonstration*, 23:10–12), and ignorance about their origin does not diminish certainty about them nor prevent composing a syllogism out of them (*Demonstration*, 23:10–11). See also ibid., 23:14–24:2.

non-corporeal entities and subjects and, if so, the conditions under which such knowledge is possible.[18]

The *Book of Demonstration* explains that there is a second class of universal, necessary, and certain primary premises in addition to those arising naturally, namely, those that emerge from experience.[19] These premises, Alfarabi says, are obtained as a result of our intentionally using sense-perception (*ta'ammudun minnā li-l-iḥsās*) to perceive particulars (*Demonstration*, 24:17–19).[20] Experience, according to this passage, consists in our examining (*nataṣaffaḥ*) the particulars of universal premises to determine whether the predicate of the premise applies in each case and continuing this scrutiny in all or most of the particulars until necessary certainty emerges. The judgment (*ḥukm*) that results, then, is a judgment about all members of that species (*Demonstration*, 24:19–21).[21] As is the case with naturally emerging primary cognitions, for experience to occur, the soul needs to do more than intentionally examine particulars, because experience entails forming a general judgment (*ḥukm 'āmm*) that includes what has not been examined as well as what has (25:4-6). Here, too, Alfarabi announces that the way this process occurs is a topic for discussion in another place and he claims again that

18 See also *Demonstration*, 24:12–13 (the individual instances of most universals are objects of sense-perception), *Demonstration*, 105:7–13 (how to approach conceptualizing what is incorporeal).

19 These premises are primary in the sense that they are not a product of syllogistic reasoning. *Demonstration* 23:3–4.

20 The text says that this may involve sensing "a few or many" particulars (24:18–19).

21 So defined, experience resembles induction, leading many people to use the two terms interchangeably; induction, however, does not result in necessary certainty about a universal judgment, as is the case with experience (*Demonstration*, 24:21–25:3). That induction does not yield certainty is a position that Alfarabi advances elsewhere, for example, in his commentary of Aristotle's *Topics*. However, in that commentary he also asserts that there is a different kind of induction, which he calls "scientific induction," that can result in certainty. See *Dialectic* 101:16–102:18. In the passage in his *Book of Demonstration* summarized in the text, Alfarabi adds that it is "no concern of ours" how these two terms are interpreted by others (*Demonstration*, 25:4).

knowing how this occurs is not useful for attaining certainty about such premises nor will ignorance of the process destroy or decrease certainty about them or prevent us from using them (25:6-7). Alfarabi concludes, "Let's call these premises 'axioms of certainty'" (*awā'il al-yaqīn*) (25:9), apparently referring to both classes of primary premises, that is, the naturally emerging and those arising from experience intentionally undertaken.[22]

Two additional differences between the discussion in the *Book of Demonstration* and the *Letter on the Intellect* are noteworthy. The *Book of Demonstration* is more tentative in describing the naturally arising primary premises because Alfarabi says that we find the knowledge in ourselves "as though" it is innate from the beginning of our existence and "as if" it is instinctive (*ka-annahu gharīzī*) (*Demonstration*, 23:7–8). The *Letter on the Intellect*, in contrast, asserts their naturalness and innateness outright without any hedging (*Intellect*, 8:5–8), which is the same approach taken in the counterpart passage in *Selected Aphorisms* (*Aphorisms*, no. 34).

Second, it is curious that Alfarabi explains more about the genesis of naturally arising primary cognitions in this commentary on Aristotle's *Posterior Analytics*—a book on logic—than he does in the *Letter on the Intellect* when he describes what Aristotle means by the term intellect in the *Posterior Analytics*. In fact, the passage in the *Letter on the Intellect* does not even allude to the critical role of sense-perception in the

22 McGinnis and Reisman (67) translate *awā'il al-yaqīn* as "the first principles of certainty", which conveys the idea in the text, although the word "principles" does not appear in the Arabic. See also Druart, "Al-Fārābī, Ethics, and First Intelligibles," 413 ("first items of knowledge"). *Awā'il* is the plural of *awwal*, meaning first, so a literal translation would be "the firsts of certainty," which is not intelligible English. "Fundamentals of certainty" or "bases of certainty" are also possible translations. I chose "axioms" because the term connotes what is primary, true, and necessary. Like the primary premises Alfarabi is discussing, they are foundational and cannot be otherwise. On axioms in general, as opposed to axioms of certainty, see *Dialectic* 19:6 (there are four types of premises used as axioms: those that are received (*al-maqbūlāt*), those that are generally accepted (*al-mashhūrāt*), those that are perceived by the senses (*al-maḥsūsāt*), and those that are certain (*al-yaqīniyya*)).

formation of these cognitions, while the logical commentary not only raises the topic—it also calls the reader's attention to the fact that the distinction between what is particular and what is universal clearly implies that the soul has a role in the acquisition of primary knowledge that goes beyond its capacity to perceive what is grasped by sense-perception.

That sense-perception is a precondition for the emergence of naturally arising primary principles may not, however, be inconsistent with the statements made in the *Letter on the Intellect*. Perhaps Alfarabi has in mind this aspect of cognition toward the end of the *Letter on the Intellect*, after he describes the role of the agent intellect (*al-'aql al-fa''āl*) in transforming potential intellect into intellect in act (*Intellect*, 27:5–6). On that occasion, he characterizes the agent intellect as giving potential intellect the principle (*al-mabda'*) by means of which potential intelligibles become intelligibles in act (*Intellect*, 27:6–7).[23] He then contrasts the manner in which the agent intellect possesses intelligibles with the way the human intellect comes to possess them. In the human intellect, Alfarabi explains, often what is more base (*akhass*) is prior to what is more noble (*ashraf*) because often we (humans) progress to things more perfect (*akmal*) in existence from things more deficient in existence, as was explained in the *Posterior Analytics*. This, in turn, is because we proceed only from what is more known (*a'raf*) to us to what is unknown (*majhūl*) to us, and what is inherently more perfect in existence is more unknown to us (*Intellect*, 27:9–28:6).

The passage just sketched, which is the only other place in the *Letter on the Intellect* that mentions the *Posterior Analytics*, does not say

---

23 The sentence is ambiguous. The more obvious reading is that the very principle afforded by the agent intellect is what enables intelligibles to become actual. However, *bi-dhālika bi-'aynihi* could also refer to the process whereby the agent intellect is a catalyst for this transformation. The difference would be that the former reading may suggest that once the principle emerges, the potential intellect can use it to transform what is potentially intelligible into what is actually intelligible, while the alternative reading may suggest that the agent intellect is involved in the intellect's ability to transform what is potentially intelligible into what is actually intelligible on an ongoing basis.

anything explicit about sense-perception, but it may imply that sense-perception is the basis of some primary cognitions since what is grasped through sense-perception is usually what is "more known" to us. Aristotle makes this point in the *Posterior Analytics* (*Analytics*, I.2, 71b–72a), and it is repeated by Alfarabi in his commentary on that book (see *Demonstration*, 39:6–15). If we connect the two passages in the *Letter on the Intellect* concerning the *Posterior Analytics*, we are thus led to part of what Alfarabi discusses in his *Book of Demonstration*, i.e., that naturally emerging primary premises are grounded in sense-perception. However, the *Letter on the Intellect* fails to mention Alfarabi's further observation in the commentary, namely, that naturally emerging primary premises presuppose an activity of the soul above and beyond sense-perception—unless, of course, the bulk of the *Letter on the Intellect*, devoted to Aristotle's teaching in the *De Anima* about the four stages of intellect, can be viewed as the missing explanation.[24]

In sum, Alfarabi's *Book of Demonstration* provides a more fulsome account of primary cognitions that are true, universal, and necessary than do the first three works described, in particular, by detailing the role of sense-perception. In one critical respect, the commentary directly contradicts the *Letter on the Intellect*, namely, the *Book of Demonstration* identifies experience as a source of primary cognitions alongside of nature. This raises a question about the consistency among the works, especially since the *Letter on the Intellect* purports to describe the meaning of intellect for Aristotle in the *Posterior Analytics*, yet it omits reference to the possible origin of primary principles in experience that Alfarabi's commentary on that book discusses.

Primary Principles in the Great Book of Music

Alfarabi's *Great Book of Music*[25] has received relatively modest attention from scholars interested in Alfarabi's logic and political philosophy,

---

24 If a book on logic is not the place to discuss the genesis of primary premises that arise naturally, presumably a book devoted exclusively to the nature and activities of the human soul would be such a place.

25 Alfarabi, *Kitāb al-Mūsīqā al-Kabīr*, ed. Ghaṭṭās 'Abd al-Malik Khashaba

although it is well known and studied by students of the history and theory of music.[26] The reason is probably that it seems like an unlikely place to find important insights of the philosopher in areas other than music. Nothing could be further from the truth. The *Great Book of Music* contains several extended passages devoted to general discussions of the relationship between theoretical and practical arts. These discussions include some of Alfarabi's most detailed observations about the origin of foundational cognitions upon which the arts and sciences are erected.

The *Great Book of Music* introduces its discussion of the first principles of the theoretical art of music by discussing at some length the primary and certain principles of demonstrations in every art.[27] As is discussed in what follows, this work describes two types of primary, certain principles: those that emerge naturally and those that require intentional activity or experience to come into being.[28] Both accounts are consistent with, but in some respects more elaborate than, the counterpart descriptions in the *Book of Demonstration*.

and Mahmoud Ahmed El-Hefnī (Cairo: Dar al-Katib, 1967; reprinted 2009). There is a French translation, which is not very literal, by Baron Rudolphe D'Erlanger in *La musique arabe* (Paris: Librairie Orientaliste Paul Geuthner, 1930), Vols. I, II.

26 See, e.g., Saida Daukeyeva, *The Philosophy of Music by Abu Nasr Muhammad al-Farabi* (Almaty, 2002); Don M. Randel, "Al-Fārābī and the Role of Arabic Music Theory in the Latin Middle Ages," *Journal of the American Musicological Society* 29 (1976), 173–88.

27 Alfarabi states that every art is a rational disposition (*hay'a tanṭuq*) and that rational dispositions can be divided into those that are oriented toward action (*fā'ila*) and those that are oriented toward knowing (*'ālima*) (see *Music,* 82:4–6). Every theoretical art, he says, is rational and cognitive (*Music,* 82:7). The Arabic root *n-ṭ-q* has several sets of meanings. One has to do with speech, e.g., to speak, articulate, pronounce. Another set has to do with reason and rationality, e.g., *ḥayawān nāṭiq* means rational animal. The word for logic, *manṭiq*, also derives from this root.

28 In the *Great Book of Music*, Alfarabi does not cast the distinct paths to such primary premises as a "division," nor does he expressly divide the approaches into types or classes. He simply describes one path, followed by the other. He also refers to the cognitions at issue more consistently as principles (*mabādi'*) than occurs in his *Book of Demonstration*, which tends to speak of premises (*muqaddimāt).*

Referencing the text of Aristotle's *Posterior Analytics*, Alfarabi attributes the primary, certain principles of demonstrations to sense-perception of individual instances of the components of the principles (*'an iḥsās ashkhāṣ ajzā'ihā*), whether a few such instances or more are required (*Music,* 92:10–13).[29] He then explains the mind's progress from sense-perception to intellectual cognition as follows. A certain action specific to the intellect (*fi'lun mā li-l-'aql khāṣṣun*) occurs after things are grasped by the senses and by imagination (*maḥsūsa wa-mutakhayyala*), namely, it separates and combines some of each of the particulars retained in the mind (*Music,* 92:13–14).[30] In addition, the intellect has a natural faculty (*quwwa ṭabī'iyya*) for forming a judgment about these combinations and for attaining certainty about whatever admits of certainty (*Music,* 92:14–93:2). Sometimes the intellect can become certain about a thing the first time a particular instance of it is sensed, while sometimes becoming certain requires repeated sensations in connection with more subjects—all of which leads to considerable variation in the process (*Music,* 93:5–9).

As was described in Alfarabi's *Book of Demonstration*, grasping primary premises begins with what the senses can grasp but goes beyond sense-perception when the mind forms a judgment about what the senses convey to it, especially when the type of certain judgment defined in the *Posterior Analytics* is reached (*Music,* 93:3–5). The *Great Book of Music* also repeats what Alfarabi says elsewhere about some of these primary cognitions emerging when first a child or while growing up without the person being aware of their genesis (*Music,* 94:1–4, 96:8–9). However, he adds that, as a result, people suppose (*yaẓunn*) that these cognitions are innate and have been there since the beginning of their existence

---

29   The components or parts (*ajzā'*) of a premise are its subject and predicate (*Dialectic,* 23:9–10).

30   Walzer translates the second form of the Arabic root *kh-y-l* as "representation," reserving "imagination" for forms of Arabic *w-h-m*. Curiously, in the rest of the passage there are no references to imagination. The omission is curious because in other works of Alfarabi, it is the imaginative faculty that is said to retain the impressions (*rusūm*) left by sense-perception and to combine or separate them. See *Political Regime* 33:10–11 (*Political Writings II,* 31). On the retentive and compositive functions of imagination, see Davidson, above note 2, and sources cited.

(*Music*, 94: 4–8). By using the term "suppose" and by sketching the stages in the process whereby naturally emerging primary principles arise, the *Great Book of Music* makes clear the discrepancy between what is really occurring and what people think has occurred. This discrepancy is only alluded to in the *Book of Demonstration*, when it states that we find these cognitions "as if" innate in ourselves. The accounts of naturally emerging primary cognitions in *Selected Aphorisms* and the *Letter on the Intellect*, in contrast, may give the impression that the process is instantaneous as well as spontaneous.

In addition, Alfarabi observes in the *Great Book of Music* that the intellect cannot attain this kind of certainty at will, i.e., when it chooses (*bi-ikhtiyārihi*), because gaining certainty is up to the natural faculty that the intellect possesses (*Music*, 93:10–11), i.e., the faculty for forming a judgment about the combinations it makes out of the impressions that the senses and imagination bring to it (see *Music*, 92:13–93:2). Therefore, if this natural faculty fails to engage, people may be limited in their beliefs to mere supposition that something is true without obtaining certainty about it. This is a second sense in which such primary premises arise naturally: we lack the ability to initiate the process in addition to being unaware of the developments that crystallize in genuine certainty.[31]

In contrast to the situation with primary cognitions attributable to the intellect's natural faculty, to obtain certainty about some primary principles, a person needs to engage in sense-perception intentionally (*Music*, 94:9).[32] In some of these cases, Alfarabi says, the intellect's specific activity will be triggered by a single perception, while in some, the intellect will require the senses to perceive a thing numerous times, or

31 Alfarabi adds that because people may suddenly become aware that they possess this type of primary principle with certainty, they may suppose that the cognitions are like *ilhāmāt*, intuitions or inspirations, a term that can have a religious or divine connotation, although that possibility does not seem to be raised here. See below, 132.

32 The text says that this happens "after its completion" (*ba'da istikmālih*) (94:9). There is no clear antecedent to "its," which may refer to the certainty afforded by the natural faculty. The Arabic for "faculty" is feminine, so "its," which is in the masculine singular, cannot refer directly to the faculty.

even numerous different things numerous times, at which point the intellect will gain the certain premises (*Music*, 94:9–95:1). He concludes by stating that experience (*tajriba*) is the name for the process whereby certainty is obtained as a result of intentionally engaging in multiple acts of sense-perception so that the intellect may perform its specific activity in relation to what the senses convey to it (95:10–11, 96:2–4).[33]

In contrast to his other discussions of this subject, Alfarabi claims in the *Great Book of Music* that there are two types of certainty potentially available in connection with first principles, depending upon whether the matters about which certainty is sought themselves exist necessarily or exist for the most part (*al-umūr al-kā'ina 'alā al-akthar*) (*Music*, 94:12–95:1). If the matters are necessary, the intellect can obtain certainty that the predicate applies to all the subjects that fall under the universal, according to the rigorous conditions laid down in the *Posterior Analytics* (*Music*, 95:2). For matters that exist for the most part, but not always, certainty is defined in terms of the predicate applying in accordance with the way the matters exist (*Music*, 95:3–6).[34] Alfarabi is careful to distinguish certainty of the latter kind from judgment that is merely probable (*al-ẓann al-ghālib*), which is not a kind of certainty at all, since the judgment does not necessarily conform to things as they are (see *Music*, 95:4–9). Either way, Alfarabi terms "experience" the process whereby certainty is obtained as a result of intentionally engaging in multiple acts of sense-perception so that the intellect performs its specific activity vis a vis what the senses convey (*Music*, 95:10–11, 96:2–4).[35]

---

33 For a different description of the meaning of "experience," see Alfarabi, *Talkhīṣ Nawāmīs li- Aflāṭūn,* edited by Francesco Gabrieli as *Alfarabius, Compendium Legum Platonis* (London: Warburg Institute, 1952), 3:3–5. Alfarabi emphasizes in this work how easy it is to misinterpret experience by jumping to conclusions based upon insufficient observation (*Compendium Legum,* 3:7–8) a subject that is not broached in the passage under discussion in the *Great Book of Music.*

34 Contrast *Demonstration* 21:14–17, 20–21 (necessary certainty is possible only for what exists permanently).

35 Here, too, Alfarabi notes that experience can be mistaken for induction and emphasizes that experience can result in certainty, while induction cannot (*Music*, 96:1–5).

The *Great Book of Music* provides a succinct statement of the stakes involved in connection with first or primary principles: we cannot know what comes after the principles unless the principles are known first (*Music*, 44:5–6). Based upon the *Selected Aphorisms* and the *Letter on the Intellect*, where nature, not human initiative, appears to determine exclusively whether a person can grasp primary principles, the sciences and the arts would seem to depend for their success entirely upon forces outside the control of the individual seeker of knowledge. Thus, it should be somewhat reassuring to seekers of scientific knowledge that the *Great Book of Music*, like the *Book of Demonstration*, enlarges the sphere of foundational knowledge to include cognitions that we can seek through capacities within our control even if, ultimately, what determines the success of such efforts remains somewhat mysterious. Alternatively, it is possible that the *Great Book of Music* is suggesting that to attain sufficient foundational knowledge to ground most theoretical sciences, it is necessary to supplement primary knowledge attributable to the intellect's natural faculty with primary knowledge attributable to experience triggered by intentionally engaging in sense-perception (see *Music*, 96:2–4).

Harmonization of the Two Opinions of the Two Wise Ones, Plato, the Divine, and Aristotle

Alfarabi's *Harmonization of the Two Opinions of the Two Wise Ones, Plato, the Divine, and Aristotle* (hereafter *Harmonization*)[36] was composed, the author tells us, to quell controversy among his contemporaries attributable to the apparent differences in doctrines espoused by the two

36 Edited and translated into French by Fauzi Mitri Najjar and Dominique Mallet as *L'Harmonie entre les opinions de Platon et d'Aristote* (Damascus: Institut Francais de Damas, 1999). English translation by Charles Butterworth in *Political Writings I*, 125–67. On this work, see Majid Fakhry, "Al-Farabi and the Reconciliation of Plato and Aristotle," *Journal of the History of Ideas* 26 (1965), 469–78; Fauzi M. Najjar, "Al-Fārābī's Harmonization of Plato's and Aristotle's Philosophies," *The Muslim World* 94 (2004), 29–44; Butterworth, *Political Writings I*, 117–24; Black, "Al-Fārābī on Meno's Paradox," above note 2, at 15–23.

Greek philosophers.[37] Since, presumably, what is true cannot be both one thing and at the same time and in the same respect something different, demonstrating agreement between the two thinkers is necessary to preserve the good name of each as well as the integrity of the philosophic enterprise to which they devoted their lives.[38]

Alfarabi's effort in the *Harmonization*, then, is defensive in its origin. That does not, however, justify neglecting the text if for no other reason than that Alfarabi himself hints that the two philosophers had real differences in certain respects.[39] He notes repeatedly that they had the same purpose or intention, but at a certain level of generality that would be true regardless of substantive philosophic disagreements since both committed their lives to the pursuit of truth. As Charles Butterworth notes in the introduction to his translation, the very title of the *Harmonization*, which references "Plato the divine and Aristotle," announces rather openly that some differences between the two philosophers were significant.[40]

In the *Harmonization*, Alfarabi discusses the origin of primary or first principles in the context of the difference between Plato's and Aristotle's opinions about the relationship between learning and recollection. As is the case in two of the works discussed so far, the *Harmonization* states that the senses grasp only particulars and that universals emerge

---

37 *Harmonization* 55-57 (*Political Writings I*, 125–26). Najjar (above note 36, at 30) notes that Alfarabi's work also represents "a continuation of a syncretist tradition of philosophy that goes back to the late Hellenistic period."

38 See *Harmonization* 57–59 (*Political Writings I*, 126).

39 See Butterworth, *Political Writings I*, 120–24. Compare Muhsin Mahdi, *Alfarabi's Philosophy of Plato and Aristotle* (New York: The Free Press of Glencoe, 1962), 4; Miriam Galston, *Politics and Excellence: The Political Philosophy of Alfarabi* (Princeton: Princeton University Press, 1990), 9–10.

40 Butterworth, *Political Writings I*, 119. Butterworth concludes that "Alfarabi is more intent on showing that Aristotle agrees with Plato ... than on proving that Plato's teaching agrees with Aristotle." Ibid., at 124. He conjectures that this is because Plato's teachings are closer to the views considered acceptable in "the community," i.e., the Islamic community in which he lived.

based upon particulars (*Harmonization,* 121:13–14). However, in addition, the work contains several statements not made elsewhere.

First, Alfarabi asserts that "universals are true experiences" or "experiences in truth" (*al-tajārib 'alā al-ḥaqīqah*) (*Harmonization,* 121:14). This statement appears at odds with views he expresses about universals in the *Book of Demonstration* and the *Great Book of Music,* namely, that universal primary premises sometimes arise naturally and sometimes through experience. For, the view expressed in these two works implies that arising naturally and arising through experience are two distinct paths for universals that are primary principles to be grasped.[41] Second, the *Harmonization* divides experiences into those emerging as a result of intention (*yaḥṣul 'an qaṣd*) and those emerging unintentionally (or spontaneously) (*'an ghayr qaṣd*) (*Harmonization,* 121:14–15). The *Harmonization* is thus also at odds with the view suggested in the two other works that experience is necessarily intentional.[42] The implication of the *Harmonization,* in contrast, is that universals (just equated with experiences in truth) may be experiences emerging intentionally or not—but experiences either way. Third, the *Harmonization* states that universals attributable to unintentional or spontaneous experiences are called axioms (*al-awā'il*), cognitions (*al-ma'ārif*), first principles of demonstrations (*mabādi' al-barāhīn*), and similar names by those who are learned (*al-'ulamā'*) (*Harmonization,* 121:16–123:3).[43] The learned appear to have primary knowledge in mind when they use these names because

41 See *Demonstration* 23:3–4 (universal premises that admit of necessary certainty without syllogism (or reasoning, *qiyās*) can arise by nature or through experience; *Music* 94:1–95:1, 10–11 (distinguishing things grasped at birth or during childhood without a person being aware from things for which one must intentionally engage one's senses, the latter equated with what is called experience). Although the *Harmonization* does not say that "all" universals are true experiences, it seems implied by the structure of the sentence and by other things stated in the passage.

42 Both works describe experience is terms of intentionally undertaking acts of sense-perception. See above, 121, 128.

43 Alfarabi adds that the public (*al-jumhūr*) usually restricts the term "universals" to knowledge based upon experiences acquired intentionally, so it has no name for universals grasped unintentionally (*Harmonization,* 121:15–123:2).

the terms usually refer to primary knowledge[44] and because the context is universals emerging spontaneously.

If Alfarabi agrees with the terminology used by the learned ones,[45] then his subsequent comments about cognitions should be seen as referring to primary universal knowledge. Further, since universals were said to be grounded in particulars, and particulars, in turn, are the result of sense-perception (*Harmonization, 121:13–14*), it also follows that such primary universal cognitions are grounded in sense-perception. The *Harmonization* repeats what Alfarabi says elsewhere,[46] that because spontaneously emerging cognitions are grasped without people realizing that this is happening, most people fancy (*yatawahham*) that their souls always possessed these cognitions and, thus, that knowledge (*'ilm*) is possible without sense-perception (*Harmonization, 123:5–8*). Because Alfarabi just indicated that all knowledge[47] derives from sense-perception, he clearly believes that most people are wrong. But what is the harm caused by their misunderstanding, i.e., what is the harm from imagining that certain types of foundational knowledge are innate when they are not, or that they do not derive from sense-perception when they do? Is it only because this causes most people to believe that Plato and Aristotle disagree on an important problem of philosophy? That is certainly a concern of the *Harmonization*; however, as was just noted, Alfarabi refers to the same misunderstanding in other works not dedicated to reconciling the views of the two philosophers. The misunderstanding would presumably lead most people to side with Plato, who appears to have

---

44 "Axioms" typically refers to knowledge that is not derived from other, prior knowledge. "Cognitions" can refer to primary or derived knowledge, as can "principles of demonstrations." Considering that the knowledge in question is said to be unintentional or spontaneous, the context suggests primary or underived knowledge.

45 This is not to say that the learned folks would necessarily agree that the universals arising spontaneously are based in experience, as is asserted in the passage.

46 See above, 126–127.

47 *Harmonization* 121:13 says sense-perception only grasps particulars, but it seems to imply that particulars cannot be known without sense-perception.

believed that ideas exist in the soul prior to experience (see *Harmoniza-tion,* 117:6–119:10), and to disagree with Aristotle, for whom many, if not most, theoretical sciences presuppose empirical knowledge.[48] But what is the danger in that?

Plato's doctrine that all learning is recollection is connected with his belief in the immortality of the soul,[49] but it is unlikely that Alfarabi is subtly attacking that view, which he seems to adopt in his own name when he portrays the human soul as capable of surviving "when material perishes."[50] Perhaps Alfarabi is merely trying to reproduce faithfully Aristotle's emphasis on empirical knowledge as integral to theoretical inquiry. Alternatively, Alfarabi is worried that if the genesis of primary knowledge is thought to be innate, people will imagine that its origin is divine inspiration.[51] This could lead them to believe that the pursuit of knowledge is outside human control since the starting point depends upon divine intervention.

The *Harmonization*'s emphasis on the role of experience in the for-mation of primary premises is intensified when Alfarabi declares that once these experiences emerge in the soul, the soul becomes engaged in intellecting (*ṣārat al-nafsu 'āqila*), because "the intellect is nothing other than experiences" (*Harmonization,* 123:8–9). For readers who are more accustomed to Alfarabi suggesting that, when fully actualized, intellect encompasses intelligibles in actuality and may be described as some-thing like "thought thinking itself,"[52] the statement that intellect is noth-ing but experiences may come as a surprise. In short, the *Harmonization* presents the reader with the possibility that all primary cognitions de-pend at some point on experience of empirical reality, even if they

---

48   See above, 117, 124.
49   *Phaedo* 72e–78b; see *Harmonization* 119:11–13.
50   See *Political Regime* 81:10–13 (*Political Writings II*, p. 71). The translation is Butterworth's.
51   See above note 31; Black, "Al-Farabi on Meno's Paradox," at 31–32; Diana Lobel, *Between Mysticism and Philosophy: Sufi Language of Religious Ex-perience in Judah Ha-Levi's Kuzari* (Albany: State University of New York Press, 2000), 121–25.
52   See, for example, *Political Regime* 34:18–35:10 (*Political Writings II*, 32–33).

develop in ways that transcend experience. If so, this would be the case even for primary cognitions that appear to come into being naturally. In that event, what is natural about their origin would be that the experiential process responsible for their emergence arises independent of human intention.

Conclusion

These summaries of the views Alfarabi expresses in six of his works raise questions about his understanding of the genesis of primary knowledge. Some of these works emphasize the natural basis of primary knowledge, one asserts the empirical foundation of what appears to be all primary knowledge, and some depict primary knowledge as attributable sometimes to natural processes and sometimes to experience. They also appear to disagree about the role of volition or intention in prompting the acquisition of primary knowledge.

In addition to more traditional explanations of inconsistencies in Alfarabi's writings, such as the evolution of his thought over time, other explanations need to be explored to address these inconsistencies. It is always useful to consider the audience for which a particular work was written. However, only the *Harmonization* tells us what audience Alfarabi had in mind, and his statement may suggest that the work is less philosophic than the other writings surveyed. Yet it is unwise to dismiss the views expressed in that work if for no other reason than that in several instances they echo claims Alfarabi advances in the *Book of Demonstration* and the *Great Book of Music*—neither of which can be considered popular or defensive in purpose or execution. Further, some of the competing accounts can be seen as supplementing others that are simply more abbreviated, although a few points of irreconcilable contradiction have been noted. Finally, before a comprehensive account of Alfarabi's views about the origin of primary premises can be properly addressed, his political treatises must be consulted since they also discuss the genesis of primary knowledge, the agent intellect (*al-'aql al-fa''āl*) figures prominently in the emergence of primary premises in those works, and it seems to serve some of the functions explained in more prosaic ways in the works summarized here. Thus, a better understanding of Alfarabi's views on the character and origin of foundational knowledge must await an examination of the relationship between the ideas expressed in those works and those expressed in the works summarized here.

Alfarabi's Account of Poetry as a Logical Art in *A Treatise on the Canons of the Art of Poetry*[1]

Terence J. Kleven

I. Introduction

Alfarabi's two known commentaries on the art of poetry, *A Treatise on the Canons of the Art of Poetry* (abbreviated hereafter as *Canon*)[2] and *The Book of Poetry*,[3] present this art as one of the five syllogistic or logical arts. The other logical arts are rhetoric, sophistry, dialectic, and demonstration. That poetry is a logical art is stated explicitly in the *Canon*, as our examination in this essay indicates. Alfarabi's other

---

1   Charles Butterworth, more than any other teacher I have had, has taught me that philosophy entails rigorous yet gentle conversations and that the best conversations create friendships. I wish to thank him for the numerous conversations over the years. His publications have set the standard of meticulous Arabic editions, careful English translations and thoughtful, philosophic expositions of numerous primary texts of Alfarabi and Ibn Rushd. I can only hope that I understand and perpetuate to others a measure of their much-needed wisdom which Charles has made available to us.

2   Al-Fārābī, *A Treatise on the Canons of the Art of Poetry*, Arabic edition and translation by Arthur J. Arberry in a published essay entitled "Fārābī's Canons on Poetry," in *Rivista degli Studi Orientale,* Vol. XVII (Rome: Libreria di Scienze e Lettere, 1938), 266–78. Arberry's edition is based upon a single manuscript, the London Indian Office MS. 3832, folios 42v–45r. Arberry says that the manuscript is probably from India and was produced in the seventeenth century. Although Arberry's Arabic edition has an apparatus at the bottom of each page, it contains only his corrections to the text. The edition also lacks a thorough codicological description and does not have line numbers. We use Arberry's translations unless otherwise noted. He translates *risāla* in the title as "treatise."

3   Alfarabi, *Kitāb al-Shi'r*, edited by Muhsin Mahdi, *Shi'r,* 12 (1959), 90–95.

commentary on the art of poetry, *The Book of Poetry*, is included as part of a series of commentaries on the *Organon* of Aristotle and there, too, the art of poetry is designated as one of the five syllogistic arts.

It is perhaps unusual, especially in the modern context, to consider poetry a logical art. The poetry of prestige of our time is often identified and evaluated by its emotional intensity rather than its intellectual purpose or depth. T. S. Eliot, amongst others, provides an account of the reason for this:

> The poets of the seventeenth century, the successors of the dramatists of the sixteenth century, possessed a mechanism of sensibility which could devour any kind of experience. They are simple, artificial, difficult, or fantastic, as their predecessors were; no less nor more than Dante, Guido Cavalcanti, Guinizelli, or Cino. In the seventeenth century a dissociation of sensibility set in, from which we have never recovered; and this dissociation, as is natural, was aggravated by the influence of the two most powerful poets of the century, Milton and Dryden. Each of these men performed certain poetic functions so magnificently well that the magnitude of the effect concealed the absence of others. The language went on and in some respects improved; the best verse of Collins, Gray, Johnson, and even Goldsmith satisfies some of our fastidious demands better than that of Donne or Marvell or King. But while the language became more refined, the feeling became more crude. The feeling, the sensibility, expressed in the *Country Churchyard* (to say nothing of Tennyson and Browning) is cruder than that in the *Coy Mistress*.[4]

In the next paragraph, Eliot continues:

> The second effect of the influence of Milton and Dryden followed from the first, and was therefore slow in manifestation.

---

4   T. S. Eliot, *Selected Essays,* New Edition, (New York: Harcourt Brace Jovanovich, 1960), 247. The essay from which this quotation is taken is entitled "The Metaphysical Poets," which was first published in 1921.

> The sentimental age began early in the eighteenth century, and continued. The poets revolted against the ratiocinative, the descriptive; they thought and felt by fits, unbalanced; they reflected.[5]

After the seventeenth century the English poets, as Eliot says, "thought and felt by fits, unbalanced."[6] They did not think and feel their thoughts simultaneously; thought and feeling were not in harmony. Eliot says that this dissociation was one from which we have never recovered, and thus from the seventeenth century, we have seldom read nor have our poets written poetry for the rigorous intellectual discovery of a subject. Our poets, and the rest of us as a result, do not have a unified sensibility. The reason, however, that Eliot can make this argument is that there are poems and accounts of the art of poetry that do not support this dissociation. Eliot gives evidence in this essay of English poets who do not perpetuate this dissociation of sensibility. These metaphysical poets are William Shakespeare, Ben Jonson, and John Donne. Alfarabi's account of the art of poetry in his *Canon* is a medieval example of an argument in favor of the place of intellect in poetic art. Alfarabi not only predates this dissociation in English poetic sensibility, but he presents poetry as a rational art.

II. Poetry as one of the Five Syllogistic Arts of the Organon

There had been, to be sure, considerable attention given to poetry by the Greek and Arabic philosophers. One of the major inquiries amongst these philosophers concerned the question of whether the art of poetry, along with the art of rhetoric, belong to the logical arts, that is, whether commentaries on Aristotle's *Rhetoric* and *Poetics* were part of the *Organon*. The Arabic philosophic tradition included these two arts as parts of the *Organon* and this "longer" *Organon* was recognized by some, although not all, Latin Aristotelians. But the legitimacy of these arts as logical arts and as belonging to a sequence of logical treatises has

---

5   Ibid., 247–48.
6   Ibid., 248.

been regularly questioned. O. B. Hardison, for example, published an essay in 1970 in which he provides an examination of the place of Ibn Rushd's commentary on Aristotle's *Poetics* in medieval literary criticism.[7] Hardison gives a history of the *Poetics* from the time of Aristotle and says that, although the *Poetics* survived, it fell out of use shortly after Aristotle and was seldom used until the Renaissance. Hardison is aware, however, that the treatise was known and commented on amongst the Greek-, Syriac- and Arabic-speaking philosophers. In a brief account of the textual history of medieval translations, he says that the archetype of the Syriac, Arabic and Latin translations is the source of MS. Paris 1741. Hardison judges that the Arabic manuscript, which was translated from the Syriac in AD 920 by Abū Bishr Mattā ibn Yūnus al-Qunnā'ī, has "some significance" for a reconstruction of the Greek text, but on the whole the Arabic translation led to misunderstanding. Hardison says: "Its [the Arabic translation's] interest for the historian of criticism, however, is that its vocabulary departs widely from the Greek. It thus initiated the process of assimilating Aristotle by misinterpretation that continued throughout the Middle Ages."[8] His judgement is that although Aristotle's text survived, Arabic philosophy had a poor translation to work with from the beginning.

A poor translation, however, was not the only problem according to Hardison. He argues that when we examine the writings of the Arabic philosophers on the *Poetics,* we recognize that they did not understand Aristotle's treatise. Hardison's initial criticism is that they mistakenly included the book of the *Poetics* in the *Organon*. Hardison provides a summary of Dominicus Gundissalinus's (12th century) Latin translation of Alfarabi's *On the Division of the Sciences* in which Alfarabi explicates the five syllogistic arts and of which imaginative syllogism is one. Hardison quotes the following statement by Hermannus Alemannus who translated Ibn Rushd's middle commentary on the *Poetics* into Latin in

7   O. B. Hardison, "The Place of Averroes' Commentary on the *Poetics* in the History of Medieval Criticism," in *Medieval and Renaissance Studies: Proceedings of the South-eastern Institute of Medieval and Renaissance Studies, Summer, 1968,* ed. John L Lievszy, (Durham: Duke University Press, 1970), 57–81.

8   Ibid., 59.

AD 1256/AH 654 and who says that the *Poetics* should be included amongst the logical arts. Hermannus writes:

> That these two books [the *Rhetoric* and the *Poetics*] are part of logic no one will doubt who has read the books of Al-farabi, Avicenna and Averroes, and various others. Indeed this is quite obvious from this text itself. Nor can one be excused (as some may think) because of the *Rhetoric* of Marcus Tullius Cicero and the *Ars poetica* of Horace. Tully made rhetoric a part of "civil philosophy" and thoroughly treated it from this point of view. Horace, on the other hand treated poetry as a part of grammar.[9]

In this statement Alemannus supports the longer *Organon;* for Hardison, the inclusion of poetry as a logical art is an indication of the misunderstanding of the Arabic philosophers of Aristotle's treatise. Hardison makes specific criticisms of both Alfarabi and Averroes (Ibn Rushd).

Hardison makes four main criticisms of Alfarabi's account of the art of poetry. First, he writes: "To include the *Poetics* in the *Organon* is to assert that it is an essay on method, and that the method itself is a 'faculty' without 'content'."[10] In this context Hardison repeatedly calls logic and syllogisms "techniques" and these techniques are inappropriate to poetry. Second, he writes: "Furthermore, since each of the logical faculties was supposed to be distinguished from the others by its use of a unique logical device, the inclusion of the *Poetics* in the *Organon* shifted emphasis from 'imitation,' the key term in the Greek *Poetics*, to the 'device' which differentiates poetry from its sister faculties."[11] Third, he says: "This interpretation ignores imitation, plot, characterization, catharsis, and most of the other subjects stressed by Aristotle in favor of an element—the imaginative syllogism—for which the reader of the Greek text will search in vain."[12] Fourth, he says: "It also ignores the

---

9   Ibid., 65. Hardison quotes the passage in Latin from Lacombe's *Aristoteles Latines*, but he does not indicate who the English translator is.
10 Ibid., 60.
11 Ibid.
12 Ibid., 61.

moral 'purpose' usually attributed to poetry in the Middle Ages, because to bring in moral questions would be to assign a 'content' to poetry—in Aristotelian terms, to treat it as a subdivision of 'practical science' rather than of the *Organon*."[13] Thus, he concludes, Alfarabi misunderstood Aristotle's treatise.

When Hardison turns to Ibn Rushd's commentary, he gives three criticisms, all of which overlap with his criticism of Alfarabi. First, he says: "In fact, large sections of the *Poetics* were unintelligible to him [Averroes]. He had never read Homer, nor had he seen anything remotely resembling a Greek drama."[14] Second, Hardison repeats his criticism that the emphasis on logic in poetics in Ibn Rushd is foreign to Aristotle. Third, Ibn Rushd perpetuates the notion that poetry is about praise and blame. Hardison writes:

> This [idea which is foreign to Aristotle] is the idea that poetry can be defined as the art of praise and blame. Praise and blame are rhetorical techniques, explained at length in Books I and III of Aristotle's *Rhetoric*. They are brought into the *Poetics* in Chapter IV, where Aristotle asserts the first two forms of poetry were "lampooning verses" and "praises of famous men."[15]

These "techniques" of praise and blame are not moral evaluation, according to Hardison. His first criticism of Ibn Rushd here was not made of Alfarabi, although it would apply. The other two criticisms, namely, that poetry is a logical art and that the logical context diminishes the moral concern of the *Poetics*, were also made of Alfarabi. Thus, if we add one new criticism of these Arabic philosophers from his evaluation of Ibn Rushd, there are five criticisms made of these two Arabic philosophers. In summary, Hardison claims that Alfarabi and Ibn Rushd had no comprehension of what Aristotle intended in his *Poetics*. Hardison concurs with Jaroslav Tkatsch's evaluation of Ibn Rushd's commentary that

---

13 Ibid.
14 Ibid., 62.
15 Ibid., 63. The phrase is Hardison's translation of Tkatsch's German.

it is "a medley of monstrous misunderstandings and wild fantasies."[16] The most egregious errors of the Arabic philosophers were to include their commentaries on the art of poetry in the *Organon*.[17]

Can Hardison's criticisms of the Arabic philosophers' accounts of the *Poetics* be answered? Are Alfarabi and Ibn Rushd more careful readers of Aristotle's *Poetics* than Hardison claims? Or is Hardison correct that Aristotle's *Poetics* cannot be understood as a logical art? If Hardison's judgment is accurate, Aristotle could not be a source for the reconciliation of reason and feeling, poetry could not be a logical art. In Eliot's evaluation, the sentimental poets would have Aristotle on their side. Let us examine Alfarabi's *Canon*.

III. The Canon

Alfarabi begins the *Canon* with the statement that he does not attempt to describe in detail and in due order all that is necessary for the practice of the art of poetry.[18] He says his incomplete treatment is similar to Aristotle's incomplete treatments of certain arts inasmuch as Aristotle was not able to finish his accounts of either the arts of poetry or sophistry. Alfarabi reports that Aristotle himself admits at the end of the exposition of the art of sophistry that the examination of that art is incomplete. The reason Alfarabi gives for Aristotle's incomplete accounts of these two arts is that Aristotle found nothing in his predecessors that could function as a foundation for the formulation of the rules for the art. Nor will Alfarabi give a complete account here, even though he has an illustrious

---

16 Ibid.

17 Butterworth's Introduction and translation of Averroes's *Middle Commentary on Aristotle's* Poetics has made it possible for English readers to evaluate Ibn Rushd's understanding of Aristotle's *Poetics*. In the Introduction, Butterworth has made a number of appropriate challenges to Hardison's, Ernest Renan's, and Luis Borgès's inadequate criticisms of Ibn Rushd on the topic of poetry. See Averroes' (Ibn Rushd), *Middle Commentary on Aristotle's* Poetics, Introduction, translation, and notes by Charles E. Butterworth (South Bend, Indiana: St. Augustine's Press, 2000). This book was originally published in 1980 by Princeton University Press.

18 Alfarabi, *Canon*, Arabic, 267; English, 273.

predecessor in Aristotle; Alfarabi's *Canon* takes the form of a short commentary on the *Poetics*. In the nature of a short commentary, topics are summarized and certain aspects of the original text of Aristotle receive more complete elaboration while others do not. There are no actual quotations from Aristotle's text and Alfarabi never uses the verb "he said" as an indication of a direct quotation from Aristotle. The question for inquiry, therefore, is this: Are there sufficient indications in this short commentary that Alfarabi's account of the syllogistic art of poetry is an accurate exposition of Aristotle's *Poetics*? Without going into an extensive exposition of Aristotle's *Poetics,* we need to ask at the very least whether Hardison's judgments against the Arabic philosophers misrepresent their understanding of Aristotle. Alfarabi does say in the first sentence of the treatise that his intention is to give an account of Aristotle's art of poetry.

The next sequence in Alfarabi's treatise identifies how statements are made and what they are like.[19] Words are either significant or insignificant. If significant, some are compounded, that is, they are made into statements. These statements may be categorical or not categorical. Of the categorical, some are true and some are false. Of the false statements, some register in the mind of the hearer the object referred to and some register in the mind the imitation (*al-muḥākī*) of the object. The registering in the mind of the hearer a false statement by way of imitation is a poetical statement. With this stark comment he says that poetry consists of false statements, but they are no less imitations, and as imitations are useful for understanding. Of these poetical statements, some are perfect and some are imperfect.

In these introductory comments, Alfarabi identifies poetry with categorical statements made in words. Poetical statements are identified as one species of the genus of categorical statements. Poetical statements are not identified by emotional content or rhythm, however much these may also be present and however much the emotional content and the rhythm assist in the creation of the intellectual and emotional life of the poem. But what is first in the order of experience is not necessarily first in the order of rank, which means that feeling and rhythm may be what

19   Ibid.

a reader or listener immediately responds to in a poem but they are not what Alfarabi says constitute the essence of Aristotle's account of poetry. Alfarabi begins with the teaching that poetical statements are categorical statements, even if they are false categorical statements, and they are imitations or likenesses, however perfect or imperfect. Poetic syllogism is imitation; two terms are brought together by a resemblance, by the imaginative replacement of the middle term in a syllogism. Alfarabi's use of the term "syllogism" explains how the resemblance, how imitation, causes us to know and to recognize. All through this discussion, he proceeds in the same manner as he does with the other syllogistic arts; these arts simply represent different types of statements, and poetry, like the other arts, is composed of statements.

Notwithstanding the identification of poetical statements as false categorical statements, he distinguishes the poetic art from the art of sophistry.[20] Alfarabi says: "The sophist deludes his hearer into supposing that he is listening to a contrary proposition, so that he imagines that what is not, and what is not is; the imitator, however, causes his hearer to imagine, not a contrary, but a like proposition."[21] He uses several examples. Sophistry deceives the senses, as for example, when a standing person sees the stars in the sky behind fast moving clouds and it appears as if the stars are moving. What actually takes place is contrary to sense perception. In a second example, he says imitation, in contrast to sophistry, is seeing one's appearance in the mirror and what one sees is false inasmuch as it appears as a second entity, which it is not, but it is a likeness. The better the poet, the more perfect the likeness.

The division of statements into further species continues.[22] A statement must be categorical or the reverse. If categorical, it must be an analogy, a *qiyāsan* (accusative in the text), or not. The word "*qiyās*" is the very word that is used in Arabic philosophy for syllogism; a syllogism is an analogy, a linking or a relation between two terms. If it is an analogy, it is either potential or actual; if it is a potential analogy, it may either be induction or imitation. Poetry, thus, as imitation is potential

---

20 Ibid., Arabic, 267–68; English, 274.
21 Ibid.
22 Ibid., Arabic, 268; English, 274.

analogy. It is potential because it does not actually exist, it is false. But the connection it makes between two entities is like the connection of the two premises of a syllogism which forms the *qiyās*. Thus, in essence the imitation of poetical statement is what is basic to syllogism.

Alfarabi makes yet another set of divisions of statements, namely, the degree of truth or falsity in each one. He says: "Statements are either absolutely true, or absolutely false, or mainly true but partly false, or the reverse of this, or true and false in equal proportion."[23] With this division of statements he generates the distinctions between the five syllogistic arts. An absolutely true statement is demonstrative (*al-burhāniyya*). A mainly true statement is dialectical (*al-jadaliyya*). A statement that is equally true and false is rhetorical (*al-khaṭābiyya*). A statement that is mainly false is sophistical (*al-mughālaṭiyya*). A statement that is wholly false is poetical (*al-shi'riyya*). With these five degrees of the truth and falsity of a statement we have a complete account of the only possible rational arts. The syllogistic arts would be incomplete without the art of poetry. Alfarabi says that this division proves that a poetical statement is one that is different from the four other types of statements, yet it is a syllogistic art rather than belonging to some other species altogether. In a key passage, he says of the art of poetry: "And with this [, that is, the distinction from the other four arts], it reverts to one of the types of syllogisms or that which follows the syllogism, I mean in my statement, that which follows in the manner of induction, and simile, and insight, and what has resemblances with them, and has its power as the power of a syllogism."[24] The Arabic text is: *wa huwa ma'a dhālik yarji'u ilā nū' min anwā' al-sūlūjismūs aw mā yatba'u al-sūlūjismūs wa-a 'nī a'nī bi-qawlī mā yatba'uhu al-istiqrā' wa-l-mithāl wa-l-firāsa wa-mā ash-bahahā mimmā qawwatuhu quwwat qiyās.*[25] The verb *"tabi'a"*, used twice in the sentence, means "to follow" or "to be in consequence of" or "to comply with" or even "to imitate." The use of the word "induction" (*istiqrā'*) here provides an insight into Alfarabi's understanding of the art. In the art of dialectic, induction is a form of assent, alongside

---

23   Ibid.
24   Ibid., Arabic, 268; English, 274. The translation is mine.
25   Ibid., Arabic, 268. The translation here is mine.

syllogism, and although induction does not indicate as much certainty as a dialectical syllogism because it applies only to most of the particulars under a universal, it is still comparable to the syllogism.[26] Induction, simile, and insight[27] are like a syllogism or have the force of syllogism, and, thus, poetical statements have this capacity as well. In this key passage and also elsewhere in this treatise, Alfarabi uses *al-sūlūjismūs*, the transliteration of the Greek *sullogismós*, as a synonym for *al-qiyās*. The attainment of knowledge through the art of poetry is not inferior to what is attained through syllogism and therefore poetry is a type of syllogism.

In summary, this account of the syllogistic nature of poetical statements reveals what is at the heart of syllogism. Two words, the major and minor terms, are brought into relation in such a manner that knowledge is gained from the relation. In poetical statement the connection is made with imitation, and knowledge is gained from the relation. One term is brought into relation with another term, one entity with another, even if the one has no causal relation to the other. The imagined term or entity is individual or pertaining to a species, but it nevertheless, if there is a likeness, provides knowledge of the other individual or species.

In the next section of the treatise, Alfarabi says that poetical statements are analyzed either according to their rhythms (*awzān*) or according to their meanings (*ma'ānīya*).[28] He says: "The majority of poets of the past and present nations of whom we have any information make no distinction between rhythm and meaning and do not prescribe a special rhythm for each variety of poetical theme."[29] Most nations take no notice of the relation between rhythm and theme and mix rhythms and subject-matter indiscriminately. The only exception, he says, is the Greek nation. He then proceeds to enumerate at length the varieties of Greek poetry

---

26 For a definition of induction in Averroes, see Averroes, *Three Short Commentaries on Aristotle's "Topics," "Rhetoric," and "Poetics,"* edited and translated by Charles E. Butterworth, (Albany, NY: State University of New York Press, 1977), Arabic, 153, English, 48.

27 Following the translation from the entry on *firāsa* in E. W. Lane, *Arabic-English Lexicon,* revised edition (Cambridge, England: Islamic Texts Society, 1984).

28 Alfarabi, *Canon,* Arabic, 268-269; English, 274–75.

29 Ibid., Arabic, 269; English, 275. The translation is mine.

and he ignores the poetry of other nations. He even ignores the poetry of the Arabs and Persians because he says there are many experts in these nations on this poetry and their writings are not difficult to find. Without stating the reason he ignores the Arab and Persian experts directly, he moves on to the study of the Greeks because the Greeks have shown that rhythm must fit the subject-matter, or that there is a subject-matter that requires a certain rhythm. For poetry to be an art, rhythm and subject-matter need to be in harmony. Even as Alfarabi devotes his treatise to commenting on Aristotle's *Poetics*, he also devotes a significant portion of the treatise to the enumeration of Greek poetry. We do not know how much Greek poetry Alfarabi read; he lived in Constantinople for a number of years and, thus, would have had access to Greek poetry. It is certainly the case in this *Canon* that, according to Alfarabi, the Greeks know the most about the art.

Although there are many types of Greek poetry listed, two of the main genres addressed in the *Poetics*, tragedy and comedy, are also mentioned here.[30] According to Alfarabi, tragedy depicts good things and praises good actions and individuals. As in Aristotle, tragedy has to do with kings and those in authority, and either praises or laments their actions. In comedy, evil things are mentioned, personal actions are satirized, and blameworthy characteristics which are common to men and beasts are depicted.

After the enumeration of the varieties of Greek poetry, Alfarabi distinguishes between three types of poets; the primary criterion for the distinction is whether they are "syllogizing poets" (*al-shu'arā' al-musaljisin*) or "rationalizing poets."[31] There are poets who are possessed with a natural gift for composing and reciting poetry but who are not acquainted with the art of poetry. He says that they are not syllogizing poets. The second class are those who are fully familiar with the art of poetry, and they deserve the designation as a syllogizing poet. The third class consists in those who imitate the poets of the first two classes

---

30 Ibid., Arabic, 269–70; English, 275–76.
31 Ibid., Arabic, 271; English, 277. Alfarabi appears to be creating an Arabic participial neologism from the Greek noun *sullogeús*, "ratiocination or reasoning."

without truly having poetical dispositions or understanding the art of poetry. He says there are many errors in this poetry. Each class writes its poetry either out of natural gift or by compulsory invention. It may be that the poet, either one who has a natural gift or who knows the art of poetry, is forced to write in a genre of poetry he is unfamiliar with or with a part of the art with which he is untrained, and so writes under compulsion. He concludes, however, that the best poetry is written by natural gift, but it is a natural gift combined with excellent learning of the art, and it is this combination that makes the true syllogizing poet.

Poets differ in the degree of perfection of their verse; these differences arise for several reasons.[32] First, these differences are either due to a poet's idea (*khāṭir*) or his subject-matter (*amr*). Alfarabi claims the poet's idea may have different consequences at different times, but he defers this examination to books on virtue, types of psychological conditions and their effects on each person.[33] In regard to the subject-matter of the poem, the more perfect poems present better resemblances between two things. Although an occasional poet can produce some good verses, chance and coincidence do not make a syllogizing poet. Second, poets differ in the excellence of their use of similes; some poets are able to make resemblances which are not obvious. A poet will compare A with B and B with C and in doing so make a comparison between A and C. The comparison depends as much on difference as similarity because it is the distance (*ba'īda*) that illuminates the object.

Alfarabi concludes his short commentary with two statements.[34] First, he makes a comparison of the art of poetry and the art of painting. The medium is different, but the activities and the intentions are the same. They both produce likenesses and aim at impressing the imagination and senses with imitations. Second, he says that what he has written are "universal canons" which may be studied in acquiring the art of poetry. He says the canons may be elaborated in detail, and most poets specialize in one type of poetry and so use the canons in particular contexts.

---

32 Ibid., Arabic, 271–72; English, 277–78.
33 Ibid., Arabic, 271; English, 277. The translation is mine.
34 Ibid., Arabic, 272; English, 278.

IV. Conclusions

Alfarabi's account answers Hardison's criticisms. Hardison's first criticism is that Alfarabi's inclusion of the art of poetry in logic makes it a method and a technique, a "faculty without content." A syllogism for Alfarabi is based upon two coherent statements or premises that are brought into relation with one term, a middle term. The five arts constitute five different ways in which this middle term is connected to the other terms in the statements and this relation is one which either is or approximates cause and effect, that is, either is or approximates a rational relation. The poetic syllogism in particular establishes this relation between terms through a resemblance or imitation of two entities which have no direct causal connection; the entities may not share a common genus or species, but the imitation of one through another causes a recognition of an attribute which is similar in both. The strangeness or difference between the two may be essential to awaken us to the discovery of knowledge; Alfarabi says "in actual fact that resemblance is distant" (*wa inna kānat fī al-aṣli ba'īda*).[35] In Eliot's essay to which we referred earlier, he quotes Samuel Johnson's account of the way in which the imaginative resemblance works. Johnson says that in the resemblances "the most heterogeneous ideas are yoked by violence together."[36] Johnson, Eliot, and Alfarabi articulate precisely the same effect of imitation. Hardison's reduction of this account of poetic syllogism to a technique, device, or method does not do justice to the richness and precision of Alfarabi's notion of a rational art and of the forceful discovery of knowledge that is available through imaginative imitation. In Hardison's attempt to save Aristotle's *Poetics* for modern literary criticism, he trivializes Aristotle's account of logic and dissociates poetry from Aristotle's rational arts.

Hardison's second criticism, a variation on the first, is that the inclusion of the art of poetry amongst the syllogistic arts treats poetry as a "unique logical device" which distinguishes itself from its "sister" devices of the other logical arts and this removes the emphasis of poetry as an imitative art. According to Hardison, poetry is distinct from logic

35 Ibid.
36 Eliot, 243.

and is diminished if it is thought to be logic. As we have noted in Al-farabi's treatise, he gives a precise and extended account of imitation throughout the treatise, and it is nothing so trivial and irrational as to be a "device." Alfarabi's treatise concurs with Aristotle that the central principle of poetry is imitation, and there is no technique that will cause a poet to arrive at the astonishing resemblance that will bring about a discovery of knowledge. Moreover, in Alfarabi's account of imitation in Aristotle, the "unique logical device" is not "creativity"; the stress is not on "creativity" as understood or expected in contemporary accounts of poetry. If there is anything to call "creativity" in Alfarabi's account of imitation it is that of the selection of the right resemblance, the right imitation, for the poem. It is the faculty of the imagination, intelligently alive in the discovery of resemblances derived from sense perception and memories, that brings about the connection of two disparate things. For Alfarabi this imaginative capacity is nothing less than a rational or syllogizing art.

Hardison's third criticism is that the account of the Arabic philosophers ignored imitation, plot, characterization, and catharsis. In regard to plot, it is true that Alfarabi's treatise does not mention that word, but plot is a fairly modern term. Aristotle's word is *mûthos*, myth, because the story is untrue, even if forceful and illuminating through its imitation of life. Alfarabi is clear that poetic statements are untrue, though that is quite beside the point. The false stories still illustrate through their imitation.[37] In regard to characterization, Alfarabi's articulation of how tragedy and comedy praise and blame good and bad action and virtuous or unvirtuous characters shows that he does not ignore characterization. For Alfarabi, tragedy in particular is concerned with praiseworthy and blameworthy actions which pertain to the governance of a city. Catharsis is not mentioned in Alfarabi's treatise, as Hardison points out, but

---

37 Aristotle, *Aristotle's Poetics*, translated and with a commentary by George Whalley, edited by John Baxter and Patrick Atherton (Montreal & Kingston: McGill-Queen's University Press, 1997). See 1449b 1–7 on 61 and the commentary in footnote 24 on 70. Whalley's translation and interpretive essays, which are introduced and edited by John Baxter and Patrick Atherton, emphasize the significance of imitation, *mimēsis*, for Aristotelian tragedy.

Alfarabi does not claim to be exhaustive in this short commentary. We await the discovery of Alfarabi's long commentary on the *Poetics*.

Hardison's fourth criticism is that if the art of poetry is considered a logical art, the moral purpose of poetry is ignored. We have already addressed this in regard to character. It would be right to note, however, that Alfarabi's account of poetic syllogism is intellectualist in essence. The purpose of the poetic syllogism is to cause us to recognize our ignorance, and our ignorance is the cause of our moral failures. A "recognition" for Aristotle is a recognition of knowledge and an awareness that the main character acted in ignorance, even though the character was responsible for his or her ignorance. The ignorance led to irreparable damage in a tragedy, that is, death, moral catastrophes, the succession of tyrants, and so on, but the cause of moral failure is a failure of knowledge. Oedipus, not knowing who he was and being ignorant enough to think he can kill a common man on the road for a minor altercation and no one would notice, must learn of his own ruin and the ruin of those around him because the man he killed was the king, his father, though in disguise. Oedipus's mistake was not a fate that was inescapable, but rather a deliberate, reckless, and wanton lack of respect for a man of lower estate. King Lear does not know which daughter loves him best, and he gives his kingdom to the two who are greedy and treacherous manipulators. Lear's lack of self-knowledge manifests itself in his vulnerability to the wicked daughters' flattery. Alfarabi's exposition of the poetical syllogism is consistent with Aristotle's stress that the mistake, the *hamartía*, is ignorance, which the main character had an ability to change and did not.[38] Tragedy praises and blames the characters of the just and unjust. Although Alfarabi's account of tragedy is brief, he does not misunderstand Aristotle's view of tragedy.

Hardison's fifth and final criticism is that the Arabic philosophers could not have known Greek poetry and Greek drama. What is surprising, however, is how Alfarabi sidesteps his own traditions of Arabic and Persian poetry because, as he says, there are experts who have written about it which others can consult if they wish; his summary of poetry is that of the Greeks because they understood, amongst other things, the

---

38 Ibid., 26-27, in Whalley's essay "On Translating Aristotle's *Poetics*."

connection between rhythm and content, something other nations, including the Arabs and Persians, did not. As we noted earlier, rhythm is crucial in creating the immediate emotional content of the poem, but in the best poems, it is aligned with the intellectual content. And there was at least one Greek, Aristotle, who knew that the art of poetry required imaginative realization through imitation.

Eliot coined the phrase "dissociation of sensibility" to mark a change that took place in English poetry in the seventeenth century. That dissociation encouraged a separation between the head and heart, between knowledge and feeling. Although Alfarabi's treatise is not exhaustive, his account of the art of poetry would not contribute to such a dissociation because his emphasis throughout the treatise is that poetry is a logical or rational art. In poetry governed by the art, the sensual, the feeling, the rhythmic, and the imaginative are in harmony with the rational; they do not displace or oppose it but serve its fullest realization. There is no "revolt against the ratiocinative," to use Eliot's phrase. According to Alfarabi, one of the arts for that attainment of knowledge is missing if poetry is excluded. Thus, if all five of the rational arts are necessary for the flourishing of knowledge, the syllogizing art of poetry is necessary as well; philosophy and all of the sciences are diminished if the art is misunderstood or ignored. In contrast to Hardison's approval of Tkastch's statement that the medieval Arabic philosophers' apprehension of Aristotle's *Poetics* was "a medley of monstrous misunderstandings and wild fantasies," Alfarabi's account of the art of poetry is a sympathetic and accurate presentation of central themes of Aristotle's *Poetics*. Alfarabi's *Canon* is a short commentary on Aristotle's short and incomplete treatise, the *Poetics*. Alfarabi's inclusion of the art as one of the five rational or syllogistic arts is not a departure from Aristotle, and Alfarabi's placement of it within his commentaries on Aristotle's logical arts is a forceful account of how Alfarabi thought that reason, imagination, and feeling could and ought to be unified in the best poetry.

Alfarabi: The Cave Revisited[1]
Shawn Welnak

To prove to citizens that philosophy is permissible, desirable
or even necessary, the philosopher has to follow the example
of Odysseus and start from premises that are generally agreed
upon, or from generally accepted opinions: he has to argue
ad hominem or "dialectically."[2]

Introduction

In his *Didascalia in Rethoricam Aristotelis*,[3] Alfarabi draws a comparison between Plato's allegory of the cave from the *Republic*—what Alfarabi calls *On Politics* (*de Civilibus*)—and what has come to be known
as Aristotle's *Organon*. My goal here is to briefly elucidate some of the
interesting, if sometimes perplexing, aspects of this comparison. Besides
the initial surprise in learning that Plato intended, in the image of the

---

1   Fittingly, this article owes much to the numerous and extensive conversa-
    tions with Dr. Butterworth both during a wonderful semester studying with
    him at Georgetown University, as well as while completing my dissertation.
    From the first moment I reached out to Charles, as an unknown student in-
    terested in Alfarabi, to this very day, he has always been unsurpassingly
    generous with his time. I hope my future scholarship merely approaches
    the beautiful model he has provided.
2   Leo Strauss, *What is Political Philosophy?* (Chicago: University of Chi-
    cago Press, 1988), 93. For the most explicit instance of Odysseus's *ad ho-
    minem* speech, see *Iliad* 2. 188–332.
3   Alfarabi's commentary on Aristotle's *Rhetoric* survives only through the
    Didascalia, a single incomplete Latin translation. For an account of the
    history of the text, see William F. Boggess, "Hermannus Alemannus's Rhe-
    torical Translations," *Viator* 2, no. 1 (1971): 227–50.

cave, what Aristotle intended in his logic, we are also provoked to wonder at Alfarabi's adjustment of Plato. Rather than beginning as Plato had with human beings inside a cave, Alfarabi's human beings begin *outside,* though prior to the sun having arisen. In this way, Alfarabi discretely uncovers the fundamental change in the political philosophy of his time from Plato's and Aristotle's: the arrival of Revelation. A new competitor—if not *the* competitor—to the life of philosophy comes to light. Rather than starting within a dark cave artificially enlightened by poets—a cave from which one can, of one's own efforts, attempt to exit—one must wait for the natural light of the sun, God, to rise. For, as Heinrich Meier notes, "there is no more powerful objection to the philosophic life imaginable than the objection that appeals to faith in the omnipotent God and to his commandment or law."[4]

In addition, if we follow Alfarabi's thought, we are led to understand that just as the beautiful city of the *Republic*—epitomized in the allegory of the cave—is merely a city "rendered perfect in speech,"[5] so it seems Aristotle's account of the logical sciences may also have been rendered perfect merely in speech: demonstrative science is beyond human attainment, serving merely as a goal that would transform opinion into knowledge. The demonstrative science that completes wisdom by serving as the acme and theoretical ground of all the sciences recedes from human attainment. As Plato's *kalipolis* remains beyond reach existing largely according to prayer (cf. *Republic,* 540d1–6, and *Politics,* 1260b26–36, 1265a17–18), so remains Aristotelian demonstrative science. But concealing this fact from his audience, in the light of Revelation, seems essential to Alfarabi's rhetorical defense of philosophy in a way that it was not to his Greek predecessors.

Before turning to the *Didascalia,* we will first need to examine a few highly instructive passages from Alfarabi's *Short Treatise on the Syllogism* in order to understand Alfarabi's adjustments to Plato and

---

4   Heinrich Meier, *Leo Strauss and the Theologico-Political Problem* (New York: Cambridge University Press, 2006), xiii.

5   Cf. *Falsafah Aflāṭun* (*The Philosophy of Plato*), in *De Platonis Philosophia,* ed. Franz Rosenthal and Richard Walzer (London: The Warburg Institute, 1943), 20.15.

Aristotle as intentional, rather as the result of either confusion or dogmatic adherence to some tradition. Alfarabi here provides an account of why a philosopher *must* make such adjustments when living at different times and places in order to communicate the intentions of previous philosophers. Alfarabi thus finds it necessary to discard certain examples provided by Plato or Aristotle, since these are no longer within the customary experience of theoreticians of Alfarabi's time, and instead use things generally accepted by them (*STS*, 70.2–3).[6] With this account in mind, we will then be able to turn to Alfarabi's *Didascalia*.[7]

I. The Short Treatise on the Syllogism

Alfarabi holds that there is one *intention* common to Plato, Aristotle, and himself. For he tells his readers not only that his own description of philosophy provided in *The Attainment of Happiness* was conveyed to him from Plato and Aristotle, but also that their intentions were identical, namely, "to offer one and the same philosophy."[8] To entirely defend Alfarabi's interpretation of this matter would require a book-length study, however it is possible to at least make his position plausible in the face of the manifest differences among all three thinkers.

A possible misunderstanding must first be avoided. Alfarabi's position here in no way entails that the opinions of all three thinkers are

6   Alfarabi, *Kitāb al-qiyās al-ṣaghīr* (*Short Treatise on the Syllogism* [*STS*]), within *al-Manṭiq ʿind al-fārābī*, vol. 2. ed. Rafiq Ajam and Majid Fakhry (Beirut: Dar al-Mashreq, 1986). Translations from the *STS* are adapted from *Al-Farabi's Short Commentary on Aristotle's* Prior Analytics, trans. Nicholas Rescher (Pittsburgh: University of Pittsburgh Press, 1963). I'm reading *naṭṭār* based on Butterworth's suggested emendation, through personal correspondence, of the manuscript's *naṭārī*.

7   This essay is followed by two appendices: the first supplies Boggess's Latin text of the *Didascalia*, the second an accurate translation thereof, which—as far as I know—is not otherwise available.

8   Alfarabi, *Taḥṣīl al-saʿāda* (*The Attainment of Happiness*) (Hyderabad: Maṭbaʿat majlis dāʾirat al-maʿārif al-ʿuthmāniyya, 1926) 47.3–10. Translations are adapted from *Philosophy of Plato and Aristotle*, 2nd edition, trans. Muhsin Mahdi, foreword by Charles E. Butterworth and Thomas L. Pangle (Ithaca: Cornell Paperbacks, 2001).

identical, in spite of what Alfarabi's *Harmonization* might suggest.[9] Rather, it is merely their *fundamental* intention that is the same: to present the "way to philosophy," and the "way to reestablish [it] when it becomes confused or extinct."[10] How that intention is expressed is another matter entirely, and we must be open to significant differences.

Alfarabi clarifies his hermeneutic approach, and thus what his readers can expect from him, in his *Short Treatise on the Syllogism*. He announces there his aim to "see to it that the canons which [he] shall lay down are the very things which Aristotle contributed to the art of logic" (*STS*, 68.15–16).[11] A problem arises for his aim because the expressions and examples used by Aristotle, although generally accepted by the people of his time, are no longer generally accepted in Alfarabi's time. Aristotle's intention in his canons of the art of logic had thus become unclear to Alfarabi's generation, and hence not understood by it (*STS*, 69.3–4). And so it came to be believed that Aristotle's books on logic lacked value, and were accordingly discarded (*STS*, 69.4–5).

Alfarabi's reason for this unfortunate circumstance is that the theoreticians of his time had followed Aristotle too slavishly, thus failing to grasp his intention. Rather, Alfarabi argues that:

> To follow Aristotle's footsteps in explaining what he wrote about the canons does not consist in using his expression and his very examples as though one were a follower of his in accordance with the appearance of his deed. This would be the

---

9 As Galston says, "Al-Fārābī's purpose [in the *Harmonization*] is thus to restore philosophy's integrity and good name by showing that the two most distinguished thinkers of antiquity in fact agree on crucial issues. The *Harmonization*, then, is motivated by practical and not theoretical considerations," 19. Miriam Galston, "A Re-examination of Alfārābī's Neoplatonism," *Journal of the History of Philosophy* 15, No. 1 (Jan., 1977): 13–32.

10 *Taḥṣīl al-saʿādah*, 47.3–5.

11 The discussion here of the *Short Treatise on the Syllogism* is an abbreviated form of a larger argument presented in my "A Note on Alfarabi's Rhetoric: Following Deeds, not Words," *The Journal of Islamic Philosophy*, vol. 9, 2013.

deed of an ignoramus. Rather, to follow him is to follow suit in accordance with his intention in that deed. (*STS*, 69.6–9)

Theoreticians of Alfarabi's time followed the precise words on the surface of Aristotle's pages, leaving them lost owing to the differences in the generally accepted expressions and examples used in each time. Alfarabi saw that a new sort of "translation" of Aristotle had become necessary, one that penetrated to his core intention and presented it in an accessible manner. And such a method was also in agreement with Aristotle's intention: for he too intended that people grasp the topics of his books by means of what is better understood in their own time.

> Thus to follow [Aristotle] is not to express these matters to the people of our language by using expressions of the Greeks, even though he, when he composed them, expressed them in Greek. Rather, to follow him is to explain what is in his books to the people of any language by means of their customary expressions. Likewise in regard to examples, to follow him is not to limit ourselves only to what he provided, but to follow in his track in this regard is to explain the canons in his books to those adept in every art and to those adept in every science and language in every time by means of examples which are customary to them. For this reason, we have thought fit to discard certain examples which he provided that do not lie within the experience customary to theoreticians among the people of our time, and [instead] use [examples] generally accepted by them. (*STS*, 69.13–70.3)

Since what is customary and generally accepted changes, the expression of Aristotle's intention must change: one must always present the thought of previous philosophers by means of what is generally accepted in one's own time and place. One thus truly follows one's predecessors and makes their books accessible. Though Aristotle's deeds are universal, the words used to teach those deeds are particularly chosen to suit the time and place they were set down. Alfarabi's tremendous success with this method can be gleaned from the impact he had on no less than

Avicenna—who had otherwise given up trying to understand Aristotle's intention in his *Metaphysics*, until he discovered Alfarabi.[12]

II. Allegory and Organon

Turning to the *Didascalia*, Alfarabi begins his discussion of Plato's allegory thus: "And the allegory of Plato, which he set down in his book *On Politics,* about the cave—how a human being exits from it, and then returns to it—is greatly suited to the order that Aristotle set down for the parts of the art of logic" (*Didascalia*, 1–4).[13] Alfarabi divides the allegory into two fundamental parts: the human being's exit from the cave and consequent return into it. These two aspects must thus have corresponding parallels in the parts of Aristotle's art of logic: some parts must deal with the ascent of the human being out of the cave, and other parts with the return back into it. Alfarabi initially seems to suggest that Aristotle intended *certain people* to read *certain parts* of his art of logic. Those leaving the cave would read such and such, while those returning to it, after having exited, would read so and so. The public character of all books, however, should at least make us wary of this as an adequate understanding of Alfarabi's intention. Presumably, some parts are rather more useful for understanding the ascent, and others for understanding the descent, regardless of one's stage on the journey.

Alfarabi elucidates his analogy to the parts of the art of logic:

> For [Aristotle] begins from the lowest opinions, those that belong to the multitude, and then does not cease to proceed rank by rank and little by little, until he ascends to the most

---

12 See William E. Gohlman, *The Life of Ibn Sina: A Critical Edition and Annotated Translation* (Albany: State University of New York Press, 1974): 32–35.

13 All references from the *Didascalia* are to the Latin text of Boggess (1970), which has been provided below (appendix I) along with a complete translation (appendix II). Boggess, "Alfarabi and the 'Rhetoric': The Cave Revisited," *Phronesis*, 15, No. 1 (1970): 88–89. For the full text of the *Didascalia*, see *Deux Ouvrages Inédits sur la Réthorique*, eds. J. Langhade and M. Grignaschi (Beirut: Dar al-Mashreq, 1971): 148–252.

perfect of the sciences. And from this, he then starts to descend little by little until he ultimately arrives at the lowest, least, most subordinate of [the sciences]. (*Didascalia*, 4–8)

The initial starting point for the entire progression is the lowest opinions, those of the multitude. And from this starting point—which we will soon learn, quite to our surprise, is to be found in *On Categories*—Aristotle progresses upwards towards higher ranks of opinion until he ultimately reaches the highest rank of the sciences. At this point, mere opinions have presumably been transformed into perfect knowledge. The book that Alfarabi says corresponds to this highest level is *On Demonstration* (*Didascalia*, 8–9), though it is worth noting that his *Philosophy of Aristotle* accurately names it the "*Second Analytiká*" (*PA*, 78.6).[14] The *Didascalia* thus over-emphasizes the *demonstrative* character of both this text as well as the corresponding acme of the sciences. The ascent from the lowest opinions to the highest science is presented as culminating in demonstrative knowledge.

From this epistemic acme, Aristotle then begins his descent back into the cave. Little by little, he descends to lower and lower ranks of opinion until he returns to where he started, though transformed, now seemingly in possession of demonstrative science. And Alfarabi tells us that this lowest rank, which is "most opposed to the perfect science," belongs to what is in the book *On Poetry* (*Didascalia*, 10–11). If poetry brings us back to the place from which we started, then the initial lowest opinions of the multitude are *poetic* opinions. However, the multitude do not see them *as such*, but rather as knowledge. It is implied that poetry governs the opinions of the cave—we are compelled to recall that Socrates names those casting shadows on the wall of the cave "wonder-poets" (*Republic*, 514b5).[15] But by calling these opinions the "most subordinate," Alfarabi places their governance squarely under the perfect demonstrative knowledge allegedly attained outside the cave. And since

14 Citations refer to the *Falsafat Arisṭūṭālīs* (*Philosophy of Aristotle*), ed. Muhsin Mahdi (Beirut: Dār Majallat Shi'r, 1961). Translations from the *PA* are adapted from the *Philosophy of Plato and Aristotle*.
15 Plato, *Opera*, vol. 4, ed. John Burnet (New York: Oxford University Press, 1978). All translations from the Greek are my own.

the relationship between the sciences is such, so the relationship between the possessors of each science should be such: the poet whose poems shape the opinions of the multitude is a subordinate of the wise man who has returned from outside the cave. Aristotle's poet has become the hand-maid of his philosopher-king.[16]

Alfarabi turns back to his Platonic allegory:

> And what Plato set down in the allegory of the shadow in the cave is similar to the sciences. Surely a human being who lives in [the cave] recognizes neither himself, nor any of those who are with him, through his seeing them, but rather through his seeing their shadow. (*Didascalia*, 11–15)

Alfarabi tells us that the cave is similar to the ranks of the sciences as Aristotle presented them in the parts of the art of logic. But instead of focusing on the demonstrative knowledge of the whole, lacking in or possessed by various human beings, Alfarabi presents what is fundamentally an issue of human knowledge in general and *self*-knowledge in particular. Those in the cave recognize neither themselves nor those among them by direct sight: they are cognizant of themselves and others as mere shadows (cf. *Republic*, 515a5–8). Alfarabi thus suggests that not only the allegory of the cave, but also the parts of the art of logic are ultimately about *human* things, and one human thing in particular, following the Delphic Oracle's command: Know thyself.[17]

16   It is important to see that this categorization of poetry as the lowest, most subordinate of the sciences is based on poetry's imagistic status. Nevertheless, as a science (a knowledge), poetry is being treated eidetically and thus requires the poet to also be a wise man (a possessor of demonstrative knowledge). Thus conceived, poetry possesses the depth of demonstrative science; but since it presents an image of that science, it is subordinate to it: an image is always subordinate to the discursive understanding of which it is an image. Alfarabi's seeming depreciation of poetry is thus only os-tensibly at odds with the scholarly consensus that *On Poetics* reveals a high appreciate of poetry.

17   The meaning of the oracular utterance "*Gnōthi sauton*" is partially obscu-red when translated as "Know thyself": self-*cognizance*, not knowledge, is demanded by the god.

III. Farabian Interlude

At this point, there is an interesting development. Alfarabi turns away from Plato and Aristotle, thus following his own rule from the *Short Treatise on the Syllogism* not to limit himself only to what they provided:

> And if the cognizance of the multitude, by which they recognize themselves, were compared to the cognizance of the wise, it would be as follows. On the one hand, there would be someone who does not see himself or anyone of those with him in a dark place until after the sun were behind him. And then, from each of them, their shadow and phantom, which he perceives by sight, would appear forth. At this time he would be cognizant of himself and his companions with him through cognizance of their phantom and their shadow. On the other hand, that human being may be compared to someone who sees himself and those with him by proper vision, not through their shadow and their phantom.[18] (*Didascalia*, 15–23)

Alfarabi's comparison first divides ranks of cognizance into that of the multitude and that of the wise. But where we would expect to hear how the multitude are in a cave with a fire far above and behind them, thus casting their shadows (*Republic*, 514b2–3), we are instead told that these human beings are initially without light at all, "in a dark place," unable to see themselves or their companions. Alfarabi's natural darkness replaces Plato's cave artificially lit by a fire (*Republic*, 514b8–9): Alfarabi's human beings begin in total darkness.

It is not until the sun comes up behind these human beings, casting natural light upon them, that they are able to progress to the next rank and perceive their shadows and phantoms. The sun has risen, thus bringing humanity—through no action of its own—from total darkness, to at

---

18 Shadow (*umbra*) and phantom (*tenebra*) are surely meant to capture Plato's *skia* and *eidōlon* (*Republic*, 509e1–516a7). So although "phantom" most literally translates *tenebra*, "reflection" should be kept in mind as more truly capturing the meaning.

least looking at shadows and phantoms. Yet even with the sun up, having lit the previously dark place, these human beings still fail to look at themselves and their companions by means of the sun's light. Alfarabi replaces Plato's starting point *inside* the cave with his first level *outside*, without the sun having risen (cf. *Republic*, 515e6–516b2).

Lastly, the multitude, who have had the sun rise behind them, are compared to the wise man "who sees himself and those with him by proper vision, not through their shadow and phantom" (*Didascalia*, 21–23). The wise man—not the philosopher—gazes at the proper object in the lit place he shares with the multitude who gaze at shadows and phantoms.[19] And Alfarabi leaves the reader wondering whether it is reasonable to expect one to look directly at oneself without some reflective medium. We recall Aristotle's comment in the *Nicomachean Ethics*, on which Alfarabi commented, that "we are more able to look at (or contemplate [*theōrein*]) those near us than us ourselves, and their actions than our own" (*Ethics*, 1169b33–35). Is direct self-knowledge ultimately unavailable to humankind, with cognizance of oneself through others being the only available route?[20]

19 It is worth wondering how Alfarabi is using the term "wise man" here, for it could be taken either strictly—in which case it would suggest such direct vision may not be attainable—or analogously. For example, in the *Philosophy of Aristotle* Alfarabi claims that "every other art that follows the example of [the art of certainty] and emulates it in the exhaustiveness of its knowledge and actions is called 'wisdom' by comparison to it, just as a man is given the name of an angel or of a virtuous man in the hope that he emulate in his actions the actions of the virtuous man or the angel in question" (*PA*, 76.2–6).

20 Alfarabi consistently uses *scientia* generically (i.e., never standing for *scientia demonstrativa*), and carefully avoids the verb *scire*, instead preferring *noscere* and its derivative noun *noticia*. The translator of Alfarabi's Arabic text into Latin seems to be attempting to preserve the distinction between *'arafa* and *'alima*. In my translation of the Latin, I have followed Butterworth's model: "To distinguish *'arafa* and its derivatives from *'alima* and its derivatives, the former is translated as 'to be cognizant of' and so forth, while the latter is translated as 'to know' and *'ilm* as 'science' or 'knowledge.' The goal of such a distinction is to preserve the difference between *gignōskein* and *epistasthai*." *Alfarabi: The Political Writings, Vol. II, "Political Regime" and "Summary of Plato's Laws,"* 30 n.4. I have, ho-

But why should Alfarabi need to diverge from Plato's allegory such that everyone is initially outside the cave prior to the sun having risen? He seems to suggest that his time is essentially different from Plato's; for even with Plato's example ready to hand, Alfarabi intentionally turns away from it. The prisoners of Plato's cave had to attempt to ascend from and exit the artificially lit cave, either of their own accord (*Republic*, 515c4 ff.) or with the assistance of someone returned from the light. Now, a cave no longer exists to block the sun's light once it has risen— to say nothing of no one being in chains since childhood (*Republic*, 514a5). Humanity seems entirely dependent upon the natural rising of the sun.

It seems safe to assume that the fundamental difference between the times of the Greeks and Alfarabi is the receipt of Revelation from the Prophet. Alfarabi has adapted Plato's allegory in accordance with this new, generally accepted opinion. Prior to the sun having risen, humankind is without any recourse, natural or artificial, in a place of complete darkness, that is to say, either in irremediable ignorance *simpliciter*, or at least in ignorance of Islamic Law (*jāhilī*). With the receipt of Revelation, the sun, "the light of the heavens and the earth" (Quran, 24:35), is now presumably accessible to all, and Alfarabi adjusts things accordingly.

Many human beings, however, still look at the improper objects of cognizance, *i.e.*, the shadows and phantoms. Alfarabi's wise men are those who take advantage of this newly manifest natural lighting to look directly at others and perhaps at themselves, though there is no mention of any attempt to look at "the sun itself by itself in its own place" (*Republic*, 516b4–6). Further, we cannot help but notice that Alfarabi's human beings are looking westwards towards their shadows and phantoms precisely as the sun rises from the east: they might be said to be facing Athens, with their backs to Mecca.[21] So although Alfarabi sets his sights lower than Socrates, who would seem to have us stare directly at the sun, he nevertheless suggests the importance of Athens.

wever, allowed myself "self-knowledge" rather than the more accurate "self-cognizance" in a few places for fluency.

21 Many thanks are due to Dr. Alex Priou for this acute observation.

IV. The Search for the Certain Science

Having completed his brief survey of, and amendment to, the allegory of the cave, Alfarabi turns back to Aristotle. He tells us that Aristotle started with "the generally accepted and more universal cognitions" (*a noticiis notoriis et summatis*) in *On Categories* (*Didascalia*, 25–26). This text corresponds to being chained in the cave looking at shadows, i.e., we are among "the lowest opinions, those that belong to the multitude" (*Didascalia*, 4–5). In order to clarify Alfarabi's surprising implication here, we must briefly turn to the *Philosophy of Aristotle*, which contains an account of the *Categories*.[22]

Upon Aristotle's discovery that the science of certainty—and only this science—seems to supply the knowledge required by man to seek his proper end, he immediately saw that man must therefore "strive after the science of certainty in everything he investigates" (*PA*, 70.13–14).

> Therefore, he began first to investigate and enumerate the instances of being from which the first premises are compounded, that contain the questions to be investigated, and that are the primary significations of the expressions generally accepted by all. These [instances of being] are those whose being is attested by sense-perception and of which every intelligible is based on some sensible thing. He confined all of them to ten genera, called them categories, and set them down in a book called in Greek *Categories*…. (*PA*, 72.17–21)

Although Alfarabi's account sounds quite familiar to us, one aspect should be striking: the ten categories are the "primary significations of

22 The *Philosophy of Aristotle* presents the same ordering of the logical sciences as the *Didascalia*. The discussions of each can be found as follows: *Categories* 72.17–73.1 (cf. also, 85.21–90.5); *On Interpretation* 73.2–16; *Prior Analytics* 73.17–74.17, *Posterior Analytics* 74.18–78.6, *Topics* 78.7–79.19, *Sophistical Refutations* 79.20–84.2, *Rhetoric* 84.19–85.3; *Poetics* 85.4–95.12 (cf., also, 84.6–18 which introduces both rhetoric and poetics, in distinct contrast to dialectic and sophistry).

the expressions *generally accepted* by all." It seems that Alfarabi's Aristotle has given, in *On Categories*, something of a phenomenology of the opinions in Plato's cave. For the categories are "logical states with which we have designated the natural beings. But the natural beings are not beings only so far as they possess such states—which is how they were taken [*ukhidhat*] in logic" (*PA*, 86.8–10). Aristotle's *On Categories* radicalizes the beginning with generally accepted opinions to the most generally accepted opinions *simply*, and then ascends hypothetically from there.[23]

From these most generally accepted opinions merely assumed to be true, Aristotle then ascended in *On Interpretation* to a more authoritative cognizance than that found in *On Categories* (*Didascalia*, 27–28). From there, he ascended to the *Prior Analytics*, and ultimately arrived at the fourth book, which Alfarabi strikingly leaves unnamed (*Didascalia*, 29). So although the reader is momentarily left to wonder about not only the title of this fourth book (*On Demonstration* [or *Second Analytiká*]), but also, and more importantly, the status of its demonstrative science, he is ultimately led to accept that we have entirely left the cave of opinions and arrived at Aristotle's most complete science (*Didascalia*, 30–31). And no correction is made to the fact that this most authoritative rank of the sciences is, on the one hand, implicitly associated with human things and self-cognizance, or, on the other hand, merely hypothetical in character.

Nevertheless, once a human being has supposedly arrived at this most complete, most perfect, most authoritative science of the sciences, it is then time to descend— although Alfarabi gives us no indication of what motivates this descent other than what is implicit from the original allegory (*Didascalia*, 31; cf. *Republic*, 519c8–521b11). Have we come to possess complete demonstrative science of the whole (wisdom), or merely an understanding of the epistemic requirements of demonstrative science (self-knowledge)? If the former, the descent would appear to be

23 Throughout his discussion of Aristotle's categories, Alfarabi points to their fundamentally hypothetical character with numerous words derived from "assume" (*akhadha*), emphasized by the discussion's concluding remark: "Aristotle simply assumed these things ..." (*PA*, 89.11).

merely a part of the attempt to educate others. But would we not then run up against Glaucon's worry that we are doing the philosophers—or, to follow Alfarabi's language here, the wise men—an injustice? (*Republic*, 519d8–9) If the latter, does the descent increase one's self-knowledge? And if so, how? Or might there be a third option that puts these two together? Alfarabi leaves all these questions unanswered, inciting his readers to make the journey themselves.[24]

Again, Alfarabi's *Philosophy of Aristotle* can shed some light on our problems. The descent is there presented as having two distinct parts. With the first two logical arts on the descent, dialectic and sophistry, we have not yet left behind our concern with attaining the science of certainty. For after his discussion of them Alfarabi proclaims that they, along with the arts associated with the ascent, "are the methods by means of which Aristotle canvassed the science of certainty, gave an account of the way to it, and intercepted what stands in its way" (*PA*, 84.3–4). Dialectic provides us the way to the certain science, which is kept clear by sophistry. So we are forced to examine the roles of these two arts more closely. Regarding dialectic, Alfarabi provides the following synopsis:

> For [Aristotle] saw that it is extremely hard for man to hit upon the demonstration that leads him to certainty regarding the question before him, or for his mind to move immediately to inquire about the demonstration and consider it. Therefore, he required a training art and a faculty to be used as an instrument and servant or a preparation for the art of certainty.

---

24 Alfarabi leaves his readers no less perplexed about the role of Aristotle's demonstrative science as scholars today are. Jonathan Barnes aptly points out that "[t]he method which Aristotle follows in his scientific and philosophical treatises and the method which he prescribes for scientific and philosophical activity in the *Posterior Analytics* seem not to coincide. The task of explaining this apparent inconsistency is recognised as a classical problem of Aristotelian exegesis." "Aristotle's Theory of Demonstration," *Phronesis* 14, no. 2 (1969): 1. For a clear, brief articulation of the problem see Alfredo Ferrarin, *The Powers of Pure Reason: Kant and the Idea of Cosmic Philosophy* (Chicago: University of Chicago Press, 2015), 218.

He gave here an account of all the rules that can be employed by the man who investigates when he is investigating by himself and some for when he is investigating with others. He formulated this art primarily so that with it man will be equipped to show his power of finding a syllogism quickly when he is investigating with others; for when he is equipped with this art, it also substantially develops the faculty in him for using it when he is alone by himself, and makes him exceedingly cautious and more quick-witted. ... He called this training and investigating art, which is an equipment for training oneself and for becoming ready to approach science, the art of dialectic. He set it down in a book of his known as *Topiká*, which is the *Topics*. (*PA*, 78.13–79.4)[25]

Dialectic, which is "more proportionate to demonstrative science" (*Didascalia*, 23–24), appears to be a second sailing owing to the difficulty for man in attaining the science of certainty. So although we had already ascended to this science, we now descend to merely *preparing ourselves* for it, not having yet actually attained it. Dialectic, the preparation for the science of certainty, which one would expect to find *before* demonstrative science along the ascent, is placed after it along the descent. And its primary purpose is for "investigating with others." Is Alfarabi being generous in referring to the attainment of demonstrative science as merely "extremely difficult"? Has he provided a hint as to how the descent as education of others might be combined with the ascent as one's own education?

Alfarabi's account of dialectic within the *Philosophy of Aristotle* has a clear role for other human beings, making it much more fitting to his discussion of the cave. Dialectic provides us the tools to investigate with others for the sake of both attaining truth through their assistance, as well as honing one's skills for one's private investigations. For besides calling dialectic the "training art," Aristotle also called *it*, rather than the

25 Throughout Alfarabi, it is difficult to clearly distinguish between an "art" (*ṣinā'a*) and a "science" (*'ilm*); here, for instance, we see the "art of certainty" where we might expect the "science of certainty."

art or science of certainty, the "investigating art." So although dialectic still looks to demonstration as its ultimate, if unattainable goal, it remains essential to the search for the truth: it is both a training art *and* an investigative art.

This is clarified by the account of the second of the two logical arts along the descent within the *Philosophy of Aristotle:*

> [The art of sophistry's] purpose is to make the training art secure and prevent the preparation for truth from being dissipated. For this art of sophistry indeed contradicts the art of dialectic—that is, the training art—and obscures it from performing its functions, which are the way to truth and to certainty. It is in this manner that the art presented by Aristotle in this book of his [*On Sophisms*] is useful with reference to truth. It defends the instrument and servant of truth, for dialectic is the instrument and servant of the science of certainty. (*PA*, 83.16–84.2)

Alfarabi very clearly proclaims the functions of dialectic to be "the way to truth and to certainty," thus making it the instrument and servant of both truth and the science of certainty. For those on the way to truth without having attained "wisdom"—the name which Aristotle gave specifically to the art of certainty and *only* this art—dialectic is the proper instrument, with the art of sophistry serving to protect it. But the dialectical investigator must always keep an eye on the science of certainty as his goal, for his investigative art is merely proportionate to that science, it is the servant of that science, with demonstration serving as the rule by which dialectic and all the other sciences are judged (*Didascalia*, 23).

Having completed his account in the *Philosophy of Aristotle* of the first distinct part of our descent, Alfarabi turns to the second. As in the *Didascalia*, from *On Sophistry* Aristotle descends to *On Rhetoric* (*Didascalia*, 24–25) and ultimately to *On Poetry*, the lowest, most subordinate of the sciences, comparable to the rank of the opinions of the multitude (*Didascalia*, 31–33). These two arts of rhetoric and poetry are Aristotle's attempt to give "an account of the powers and the arts by which man comes to possess the faculty for instructing whoever is not to use the sciences of logic or to be given the science of certainty" (*PA*, 84.6–8).

On Rhetoric provides "an account of the art that enables man to *persuade* the multitude regarding all theoretical things and those practical things in which it is customary to confine oneself to using persuasive arguments based on particular examples drawn from men's activities when conducting their public business—that is, the activities through which they labor together toward the end for the sake of which man is made" (*PA*, 84.19–85.3, my emphasis). *On Poetry* descends further, providing the art that allows man "to *project images* of the things that became evident in the demonstrations possessing certitude within the theoretical arts, to *imitate* them by means of their similitudes, and to project images of and imitate all the other particular things in which it is customary to employ images and imitation through speech" (*PA*, 85.4–7, my emphasis). And poetry is particularly useful as a "way to instruct the multitude and the vulgar" (*PA*, 85.8). Just as in the *Didascalia*, here too poetry is both the lowest, most subordinate of the sciences, and explicitly subordinated to the art of demonstration, with rhetoric being only slightly less vulgar. The multitude gaze only at their shadows and phantoms: the similitudes and images of poetry perhaps corresponding to the shadows, with the persuasive arguments of rhetoric corresponding to the phantoms.[26] The wise, in contrast, having gazed directly at those with them and perhaps themselves, would possess the demonstrative science that serves as the theoretical ground of rhetoric's persuasions and poetry's images.

However, the subordination of rhetoric and poetry to the science of certainty requires that we are already in possession of that science; for one could not provide either the persuasive arguments or the images, both being based on the science of certainty, without first being in possession of that science. If human beings are not in possession of the science of certainty, Alfarabi's entire account would resemble something more to be prayed for than actually achieved.

---

26 This correspondence (shadows: poetry:: phantoms: rhetoric) is suggested by the fact that phantoms, as reflections in water (*Republic*, 516a7), are of a higher rank of cognizance than shadows.

V. Conclusion

In order to complete our discussion of the very brief synopsis of the logical sciences in the *Didascalia*, and show the idealistic quality of the role of the science of certainty, we must carefully examine the procedure of Aristotle in the *Philosophy of Aristotle* after having given his account of this science. Alfarabi makes utterly clear there that Aristotle's logical sciences are merely the formal conditions for demonstrative knowledge (and instruction in it) without *any* of its matter having been filled in. For it is only after precisely the same ascent to, and descent from, the science of certainty recounted in the *Didascalia* that Aristotle can even *begin* his investigations into the natural and voluntary sciences (*PA*, 90.6–97.15). And that investigation makes manifest use of the investigative art of dialectic. In fact, Alfarabi goes so far as to relate how Aristotle himself considered his work preparatory for "the investigators who will come after him" (*PA*, 91.18–19).

But ultimately, the most decisive evidence that the science of sciences and the wisdom of wisdoms is not in our possession is revealed at the very end of the *Philosophy of Aristotle*. For those familiar with Alfarabi's Aristotle are all too aware that—even after his Herculean efforts—"we do not possess metaphysical science" (*PA*, 133.1). We are still *on the way* to truth and certainty without having achieved either, for the possession of metaphysical science is a necessary condition to what is "unconditionally called wisdom and unconditionally called science" (*PA*, 77.2–3).

Alfarabi, Aristotle, and Plato seem to be at the dialectical stage of merely *seeking* the science of certainty, though we are now cognizant of what that science looks like. We possess a target by which to take our bearings; through an understanding of the character of demonstrative science, though we do not possess it itself, we have come to possess epistemic self-knowledge: we now know what would be required, strictly speaking, to truly *know* something, and we also now know that we have not met that requirement. And although surely containing many differences of style, the underlying dialectical character of the texts of these thinkers seems to vouchsafe this conclusion. They do not argue dialectically merely "[t]o prove to citizens that philosophy is permissible, desirable or even necessary," but also owing to the fact that

demonstrative science has not been achieved. The philosopher has neither ascended out of the cave (Plato), nor simply turned around (Alfarabi), in order to gaze at "the sun itself by itself in its own place," nor
satisfied the necessary conditions of demonstrative science (Aristotle),
and thus become unconditionally wise.[27]

Given Alfarabi's historical situation, however, a dialectical proof of
philosophy's permissibility, desirability, or necessity may have also entailed—and for novel reasons—his concealing the true state of philosophy. A philosophy that has not ascended to wisdom seems much less
able to respond to the claims of Revelation. If demonstrative science is
merely to be prayed for, while Revelation is at hand, philosophy seems
unnecessary and undesirable at best, and simply impermissible at worst.
Alfarabi's dialectical case for philosophy turns out to be largely rhetorical through its conflation of the love of wisdom with wisdom itself.
How philosophy might respond to Revelation on *truly* dialectical
grounds remains a question.

The brief comparison of the parts of the art of logic and the allegory
of the cave aptly concludes thus: "It's likely true, therefore, that Plato
intended, in the aforementioned *image*, this way by which Aristotle proceeded in the *education* of logic" (*Didascalia*, 33–34, my emphases).
Alfarabi thus uncovers the same intention in Plato's allegory as in Aristotle's logic. Plato intends to convey both the way to wisdom, as well as
the way of instruction by means of an image or allegory accessible even
to the multitude: Plato uses the science of poetics in order to communicate his intention. As Socrates says to Glaucon: "make an *image* (*apeika-
son*) of our nature in its education and lack of education" (*Republic*,
514a1–2, my emphasis).

---

27 Recall that Aristotle was careful to distance himself from the realization
of demonstrative science by means of a bold conditional claim: "Now *if*
[*ei*] science is such as we have set down (*ethemen*), it is necessary that demonstrative science be from things which are true, first, unmediated, and
better cognized than, prior to, and causes of, the conclusion. For only so
will the first principles be appropriate to what is to be brought to light. For
there will still be a syllogism without these, but there will not be a demonstration; for [such a syllogism] will not make science" (*Posterior Analytics*,
71b19–24, my emphasis).

But where Plato provides an image of our education, Aristotle seems to provide the education itself by means of generally accepted opinions, that is, by the art of dialectic; Aristotle has dialectically carried out Plato's intention in the poetic allegory of the cave. Alfarabi has thus given us an example of how the same intention—education in the human things, particularly self-knowledge—might be presented similarly *via* two different sciences. Alfarabi's Platonic poetics and Aristotelean dialectic, with an assured dose of rhetoric, provide us with both the way to and defense of philosophy.

Appendix I

Boggess's Latin text of Alfarabi's Allegory of the Cave

Et proverbium Platonis quod posuit in libro suo de Civilibus de   (1)
spelunca, qualiter egreditur homo ex ipsa deinde redit ad ipsam,
conveniens est valde ordini quem posuit Aristotiles partibus artis
logices. Incepit enim a sentenciis minimis, scilicet que pertinent
pluribus, deinde non cessavit gradatim procedere et paulatim   (5)
donec ascendit ad perfectissimam scientiarum, deinde cepit des-
cendere ab hac paulatim donec pervenit finaliter ad infimam et
minimam et vilissimam earum. Quod enim est in libro Demon-
strationis est completissimum scientiarum et altissimi gradus et
quod est in libro Poetrie est inperfectissimum et infimum earum   (10)
et <opponitur> maxime scientie perfecte. Et est simile scientiis
quod posuit Plato in proverbio umbre in spelunca. Homo nempe
in ea existens non novit se ipsum neque eos qui secum sunt per
casum visus sui super ipsos, sed per casus visus sui super umbram
cuiuslibet ipsorum. Et si comparetur noticia plurium qua no-   (15)
verunt se ipsos ad noticiam [ad noticiam] sapientium, erit sicut
compar<ati>o eius qui non videt se ipsum neque aliquem eorum
<qui> secum sunt in loco obscuro nisi postquam sol fuerit retro
ipsum et processerit a quolibet ipsorum umbra sua et tenebra
quam percipit visu et tunc noscit se ipsum et socios qui secum   (20)
sunt per noticiam tenebre et umbre ipsorum ad eum qui vidit

se ipsum et qui secum sunt visu proprio non per umbram et tene-
bram ipsorum. Et liber Topicorum magis proportionatus est
scientie demonstrative, post hunc librum Sophisticorum, et post
istum librum Rethorice. Aristotiles itaque incepit a libro Cathe-   (25)
goriarum a noticiis notoriis et summatis. Et postquam processit
ad librum Per Yarmenias. Posuit in eo ex noticiis quod erat ab-
solutioris ordinis quam id quod est in libro Predicamentorum.
Et similiter est de eo quod est in libro Priorum Analeticorum.
[posuit] Quartum vero librum posuit completissimum eius quod   (30)
est in scientiis, deinde descendit paulatim post hoc donec, ut dic-
tum est, provenit ad hoc quod vilissimum est in eis, scilicet
Poetria. Verisimile est igitur quod intenderit Plato in prelibato
exemplo hanc viam qua processit Aristotiles in traditione logices.

Appendix II

Translation of Alfarabi's Allegory of the Cave

And the allegory of Plato, which he set down in his book *On Politics,*
about the cave—how a human being exits from it, and then returns to
it—is greatly suited to the order that Aristotle set down for the parts of
the art of logic. For he begins from the lowest opinions, those that belong
to the multitude, and then he does not cease to proceed rank by rank and
little by little, until he ascends to the most perfect of the sciences. And
from this, he then starts to descend little by little until he ultimately arrives at the lowest, least, most subordinate of [the sciences]. For what is
in the book *On Demonstration* is the most complete of the sciences and
of the highest rank; and what is in the book *On Poetry* is the least perfect
and lowest of them, and most opposed to the perfect science.

And what Plato set down in the allegory of the shadow in the cave
is similar to the sciences. Surely a human being who lives in [the cave]
recognizes neither himself, nor any of those who are with him, through
his seeing them, but rather through his seeing their shadow. And if the
cognizance of the multitude, by which they recognize themselves, were
compared to the cognizance of the wise, it would be as follows. On the

one hand, there would be someone who does not see himself or anyone of those with him in a dark place until after the sun were behind him. And then, from each of them, their shadow and phantom, which he perceives by sight, would appear forth. At this time he would cognize himself and his companions with him, through cognizance of their phantom and their shadow. On the other hand, that human being may be compared to someone who sees himself and those with him by proper vision, not through their shadow and their phantom.

And the book *On Topics* is more completely proportionate to demonstrative science; after this book [is the book] *On Sophisms;* and after that book [is the book] *On Rhetoric.* Accordingly, Aristotle began in the book *On Categories* from the more generally accepted and more universal cognitions. Afterwards, he proceeded to the book *Peri Hermeneias.* He set down in it, from [the ranks of] cognizance, what is of a more authoritative order than what is in the book on predicables.[28] And similarly [is it so] from what he set down in the book *Prior Analytics.*[29] Indeed, he set down the fourth book [as being] the most complete of what is in the sciences; and then he descended, little by little, after this until, as has been said, he arrived at this which is the most subordinate among [the sciences], *Poetry.*

It is likely true, therefore, that Plato intended, in the aforementioned image, this way by which Aristotle proceeded in the education of logic.

28 I.e., the *Categories*
29 Reading, with Grignaschi (1971): *quod [est] in libro Priorum Analecticorum posuit.*

"On Averroes's Use of Logical Methods in Defense of Philosophy"

David M. DiPasquale

Philosophy (*falsafa*) was not a welcome addition to the community of Islam. The Qur'an was believed to have been divinely inspired, conveyed to Allah's chosen people by the Prophet Muhammad and meant to regulate both actions and beliefs. Early groups of theologians (*mutakallimūn*), such as the Mu'tazilites and Ash'arites, expounded upon and elaborated the sacred text for the sake of the majority of believers, for whom many of the passages and statements contained in the "noble book" were unclear and difficult to comprehend. Generally, these theologians accepted only the Qur'an itself and the Traditions (*aḥādīth*, or oral reports of the speech and deeds of the Prophet) as the means by which one may understand the Law. Independent reasoning (*qiyās*) was viewed suspiciously and, therefore, there existed little need to recognize or admit the challenge posed by philosophic activity.

This was true when, in the middle of the ninth century of the common calendar, Greek philosophy was introduced into the Arab world via Syriac-speaking intermediaries who, as Christians, were able to read the Greek texts and, as Syrians, were able to translate those texts into the Semitic family of languages. To be sure, philosophers did consider questions (such as the definition of justice or the creation of the world) that the Qur'an claimed to have answered decisively. Yet when a conflict arose between the two differing accounts of the just and moral life, the theologians dismissed the philosophers' ruminations as either pernicious or superfluous. As a result, theologians condemned the philosophical doctrines, and those who promoted them, as heretical. The most forceful attack against philosophy from the point of view of theology occurred in 1095, when the renowned Ash'arite theologian

Abū Ḥāmid Muḥammad ibn Muḥammad al-Ghazālī (d. 1111) issued his powerful *Tahāfut al-falāsifa* (*Destruction of the Philosophers*). This work attempted to illustrate that, from the standpoint of demonstrative reasoning itself, the Islamic philosophers failed to prove their un-Islamic theses regarding the origin of the world, God's knowledge of particulars, and bodily resurrection. His *Kitāb fayṣal al-tafrīqa bayn al-Islam wa-l-zandaqa* (*The Book of the Clear Criterion for Distinguishing between Islam and Heresy*) was composed after this, between 1096 and 1106, and considered the legal question of which type of allegorical interpretation (*taʾwīl*) in the Qurʾan should be classified as unbelief (*kufr*) and therefore expelled from the community of the faithful.

Nearly a century passed before this challenge was met. No philosopher answered al-Ghazali's potent attack until 1180, when Abū al-Walīd Muḥammad ibn Aḥmad ibn Muḥammad ibn Rushd (known more commonly in the West as Averroes) wrote his *Tahāfut al-tahāfut* (*Destruction of the Destruction*) and *Kitab faṣl al-maqāl wa taqrīr ma bayn al-sharīʾa wa al-ḥikma min al-ittiṣāl* (*The Book of the Decisive Treatise Determining the Connection between the Law and Wisdom; lit.: The Book of Decisively Judging the Statement and Determining the Connection between the Law and Wisdom*). The latter book offers a legal response to the charges presented in the *Kitab fayṣal al-tafrīqa* and is arguably the single greatest written "reconciliation" of philosophy and Islam written by a Muslim in the religion's almost fourteen-hundred-year history. The *Decisive Treatise* was composed in southern Spain during the Almohad rule of the twelfth century. Ibn Tumart (d. 1130), the founder of Almohadism, was of the opinion that a community defines itself through belief, and he created his movement to be a fusion of rational theology and practical philosophy. Although philosophy and philosophers were still viewed with either suspicion or contempt throughout this period (and even more so during the Almoravid rule that preceded it), the beginnings of a great change were effected when the Almohads (under the command of Abd al-Muʾmin) overthrew the kingdom of the Almoravids around the year 1151. Abd al-Muʾmin (d. 1163), the successor to Ibn Tumart who was the Mahdi (or leader) of the movement at the time of his death, began to express serious interest in both the various disciplines of the philosophical sciences as well as the patronage of those individuals who claimed to possess a competence in the teaching of these sciences to others eager to understand them.[1]

This interest was carried on and exaggerated by his son and successor Abu Ya'qub Yusuf, who exhibited sincere interest in literature and especially philosophy—so much so that he is said to have begun his councils with discussion of a learned question among theologians and philosophers.[2] Indeed, Yusuf allowed Ibn Ṭufayl (d. 1185), the great Islamic philosopher and author of *Ḥayy ibn Yaqẓān*, to become his chief physician and "stay in [his] palace ... for days, without emerging for nights and days on end."[3] Moreover, it was Ibn Ṭufayl who introduced his student Averroes to the ruler and told the young pupil of the prince's wish that someone write commentaries on the works of Aristotle. These events are narrated in *al-Muʿjib fī talkhīṣ akhbār al-Maghrib* by the Moroccan historian Abdelwahīd al-Marrakushi (d. ca. 1228) and are based on an account given by Averroes himself to one of his pupils:

> This Abu Bakr [Ibn Ṭufayl] continued to draw men of learning to the prince from every country, bringing them to his attention and inciting him to honor and praise them. It was he who brought to the Prince's attention Abul-Walīd Muḥammad ibn Ahmad Ibn Muḥammad Ibn Rushd; and from this time he became known and his ability became celebrated among men. Ibn Rushd's pupil, the lawyer and professor Abn Bakr Bundud Ibn Yahya al-Qurtubi, told me that he had heard the philosopher Abul-Walīd say on more than one occasion:

1 See Roger Le Tourneau, *The Almohad Movement in North Africa in the Twelfth and Thirteenth Centuries* (Princeton, N.J.: Princeton University Press, 1969).
2 Marrakushi, "Mu'jib," in *Averroes: On the Harmony of Religion and Philosophy*, by George F. Hourani (London: Luzak, 1961), 249.
3 Ibid. 172; in Hourani, 12.

When I entered into the presence of the Prince of the Believers, Abu Ya'qub, I found him with Abu Bakr Ibn Ṭufayl alone. Abu Bakr began praising me, mentioning my family and ancestors and generously including in the recital of things beyond my real merits. The first thing that the Prince of the Believers said to me, after asking me my name, my father's name and my genealogy was: "What is their opinion about the heavens?"—referring to the philosophers—"Are they eternal or created?" Confusion and fear took hold of me, and I began making excuses and denying that I had ever concerned myself with philosophic learning; for I did not know what Ibn Ṭufayl had told him on the subject. But the Prince of the Believers understood my fear and confusion, and turning to Ibn Ṭufayl began talking about the question of which he had asked me, mentioning what Aristotle, Plato and all the philosophers had said, and bringing in besides the objections of the Muslim thinkers against them; and I perceived in him such a copious memory as I did not think could be found [even] in any one of those who concerned themselves full time with the subject. Thus he continued to set me at ease until I spoke, and he learned what was my competence in that subject; and when I withdrew he ordered for me a donation in money, a magnificent robe of honor and a steed.

That same pupil of his also told me that Ibn Rushd had told him: "Abu Bakr Ibn Ṭufayl summoned me one day and told me, 'Today I heard the Prince of the Believers complain of the difficulty of expression in Aristotle and his translators, and mention the obscurity of his aims, saying 'If someone would tackle these books, summarize them and expound their aim, after understanding them thoroughly, it would be easier for people to grasp them.'" So if you have in you abundant strength for the task, perform it. I expect you will be equal to it, from what I know of the excellence of your mind, the purity of your nature, and the intensity of your application to science. I myself am only prevented from this undertaking by my age, as you see, my occupation with government service, and the devotion of my attention to matters which I hold more important. Abul-Walīd said: "This was what led me to summarize the books of the philosopher Aristotle."[4]

Averroes was born in Cordoba in 1126 and died at Marrakesh in 1198. He came from a distinguished family of Cordoban lawyers: his grandfather, Abul-Walīd the elder, was a chief justice in Cordoba and his father was a justice in that town also. His early schooling centered on an excellent legal education, and before he completed this schooling, he had already written three or four books on law. He also studied theology (or *kalām*) and Arabic literature but was most interested in, and persuaded by, the Greek sciences such as medicine (he wrote a text on "General Medicine" [*Kitāb al-Kullīyāt fī al-Ṭibb*] early in his career) and especially philosophy.[5]

He probably began to write his commentaries on Aristotle shortly after he was elected to the judgeship in Seville in 1169. In 1171 he returned to Cordoba and soon became chief justice. After Ibn Ṭufayl retired as the chief physician to Abu Ya'qub in 1182, Averroes was selected to take his place, a position he also held under Abu Yusuf Ya'qub who, to repeat, was the son and successor to his father. During this time, however, Averroes suffered a dramatic loss in popularity; his books were publicly burned and he was exiled to the small town of Lucena, which was located just south of Cordoba and the majority of whose inhabitants were Jews who associated Averroes with the despised Arab regime they believed was persecuting them. Consequently, his time there may have been mostly spent enduring the taunts and insults cast at him by the residents, some of whom were said to have called him a "false philosopher" or "mediocre heretic." A few distinguished members of Cordoba, upon hearing of his exile, soon petitioned for his release from Lucena. The

---

4   Ibid., 174–75; in Hourani, 12–13. See Averroes, *Decisive Treatise and Epistle Dedicatory*, trans. Charles E. Butterworth (Provo, UT: Brigham Young University Press, 2001), xiv.

5   Hourani, *Averroes: On the Harmony of Religion and Philosophy*, op. cit., 1–17.

Sultan responded and brought him back to his court in Marrakesh where he resided for the remainder of his life.[6]

By the time he began to write his commentaries on the works of Aristotle, Averroes's reputation was beginning to grow and he was already considered to be among the brightest of his generation. Between the period of the "middle" commentaries and the "great" (or more detailed and comprehensive) commentaries, Averroes turned to compose the three related treatises. These treatises were to become known as the "Trilogy": the *Ḍamīma* (or *Epistle Dedicatory*), the aforementioned *Kitāb Faṣl al-Maqāl* (*The Book of the Decisive Treatise*) and *Kashf 'an manāhij al-adilla fi 'aqā'id al-milla* (or *Uncovering the Methods of Proofs with Respect to the Beliefs of the Religious Community*). The Trilogy, and therefore the *Decisive Treatise,* which was most likely written around 1177, was composed to counter the growing hostility to philosophy on the part of the theologians as well as the multitudes who accepted the former's arguments to the effect that the philosophers were unbelievers and therefore dangerous to the continued health of the religious community, or *umma*. The *Decisive Treatise* itself was written during a very significant transitional period in Andalusian intellectual life and has the character of a doctrinal offensive. The work is a legal response to al-Ghazali's condemnation of philosophy that was, in 1177, being taken up in the Western, or *maghrebi,* portion of the Muslim empire by the Ash'arite theologians. Therefore, the *Decisive Treatise* is acutely aware of the explosive political circumstances under which it is written and to which it is responding.

Any reader of the *Decisive Treatise* must immediately be led to believe that the author will consider the nature of "the connection between the Law and wisdom" in a manner that is ostensibly decisive. However, even a cursory reading shows that, despite the fact that the work is said

6   For a somewhat more detailed biographical account, see David M. DiPasquale, "Averroes (Abu al-Walid Muḥammad ibn Ahmed ibn Muḥammad ibn Rushd)," in *The Encyclopedia of Political Thought*, ed. Michael Gibbons (Cambridgeshire: Wiley-Blackwell, 2015). For an illuminating discussion of the court case against Averroes, see: Josep Puig, "Materials on Averroes's Circle," *International Journal of Middle Eastern Studies* 51 (1992): 241–60.

to be a popular treatment of the issue, Averroes presents the solution in such a way as to seemingly call attention to both his method and the problematic character of the solution itself. In this work, he quickly concludes that the Law obliges a certain group of individuals to study the Qur'an in a manner that conforms to the demands of demonstrative reasoning. Any passage of the Qur'an whose apparent meaning conflicts with conclusions established by demonstration must be interpreted allegorically by this group, who will have been trained in this philosophic art.

Now, a host of questions arise in the minds of those readers who study this solution with any care at all. Surely, one of the most important concerns regards the nature of this type of allegorical interpretation (*ta 'wīl*) itself and what, if any, restrictions are placed on its use. Yet, because Averroes presents himself as intimately aware of the difficulties involved in presenting the true solution within his political environment and stresses how important it is to convey the solution differently to different types of people,[7] we too must be cognizant not only of his solution but the manner in which that solution is presented.

Before considering the nature and limits of allegorical interpretation as described in the *Decisive Treatise*, it is important first to sketch briefly the way in which Averroes prefaces this issue. The answer to the question posed at the beginning of the treatise is that the Qur'an commands the study of philosophy and does not prohibit the use of the ancient Greek texts for this purpose. Philosophy, as Averroes defines it, stands under the Law and must therefore answer to the Law because the Law has immediate priority. Yet, while it is subordinate to the Law, philosophy is also described as an activity that is commanded by the Law and whose intention is the same as the Law's: "it has become evident that reflection upon the books of the Ancients is obligatory according to the Law, for their aim and intention in their books is the very intention to which the Law urges us."[8] Averroes concludes, then, that it would be foolish to prevent the study of these texts. This formulation, however, is more complicated than it may first appear, as he later speaks of what the

---

7   For example, *Decisive Treatise*, op. cit., 20.18–19.
8   Ibid., 6.10–12.

Law "calls to" versus its "intention."[9] It also seems (as Muhsin Mahdi has suggested) that the manner in which the issue itself is presented is strange: instead of beginning the work by stating the intention of the Law and then inferring from this the legal status of human wisdom, Averroes begins the second part of the text by focusing on the Law's intention after he has already "established" the connection between the Law and human wisdom.[10]

Nevertheless, Averroes asserts that the truths known through demonstrative means do not contradict scriptural truths. A reason for this is given somewhat later: "for truth does not oppose truth; rather, it agrees with and bears witness to it."[11] For Averroes, philosophy is presented as a demonstrative science that provides knowledge about the world, and because the Law is a source for the same kind of truth, the two sources simply cannot contradict one another. Thus, we now know not only that the Law explicitly commands the study of philosophy, but also that there can be no conflict between them. The only problem, then, is to determine how the apparent contradictions can be explained by using methods that do not offend the Law. To resolve this discrepancy, Averroes determines that the Law must be interpreted figuratively.

Averroes defines allegorical interpretation as "drawing out the figurative significance of an utterance from its true significance without violating the custom of the Arabic language ...,"[12] which is comparable to the legal technique of inference.[13] We learned earlier that philosophy stands under the Law and must, at least in the beginning, answer to it. Yet what, if any, are the limitations the Law imposes on the ability to interpret the Qur'an allegorically? By the end of the first pages, it appears that there is one overriding limitation: passages that Muslims have unanimously agreed to take literally may not be interpreted allegorically.[14] Averroes appears to

9   See ibid., 24.1–13, 22.21, and 23.10 ff.
10 Muhsin Mahdi, "Remarks on Averroes' *Decisive Treatise*," in *Islamic Theology and Philosophy: Essays in Honor of George F. Hourani*, ed. Michael Marmura (Albany, N.Y.: SUNY Press, 1984), 190.
11 *Decisive Treatise*, op. cit., 9.1–2.
12 Ibid., 9.13–15.
13 For example ibid., 9.8.
14 See 10.21–12.2.

accept the judgment of the Islamic community and admits that philosophers must never violate Islamic consensus (*ijmā'*) when it is certain. However, because demonstrative certainty with regard to theoretical texts is impossible, one must conclude that this cannot be a binding limitation.

This leads to an inevitable problem. On the one hand, Averroes seems to emphasize that consensus of the Islamic community is the only legal source that has the potential for restraining the power of allegorical interpretation; yet, he also admits that it is virtually impossible to establish such a consensus on theoretical matters with demonstrative certainty. It seems, then, that those who interpret the Qur'an allegorically will not have much reason to accept an alternative interpretation. They appear to possess solid legal justification for their actions. However, as Mahdi says, if one must still determine the connection between the divine law and human wisdom even if the theoretical questions are not settled, "then the most reasonable course is to determine the matter on the basis of arguments that are legally permitted and theoretically possible."[15] The great danger of this procedure is that it provides few limits. That is, in recognizing that humans cannot achieve a certain consensus on theoretical questions, Averroes may be allowing the interpretation of the Law on theoretical concerns to proceed without controls or supervision.

As a result, philosophy seems to possess a large amount of freedom in interpreting the literal meaning of the divine law itself while not being bound by it. Averroes, however, recognizes the various dangers such a position might engender and ultimately admits that there is, in fact, a binding limit to the practice of allegorical interpretation beyond which the philosophers may not trespass: no interpretation may lead to unbelief (*kufr*), which is the denial of the truth of the Law. The one true limit to philosophic interpretation, then, is not arrived at philosophically; or as Leo Strauss put it: philosophy does not supply the decisive qualification of error that is "the qualification of error as unbelief. This qualification stems from the Law. In binding philosophy, it binds through an extraphilosophical, prephilosophical jurisdiction."[16] In other words, Averroes formulates the

15 Mahdi, "Remarks on Averroes' *Decisive Treatise*," op. cit., 194.
16 Leo Strauss, *Philosophy and Law*, trans. Fred Baumann (Philadelphia: The Jewish Publication Society, 1987), 67.

issue in such a way that the denial of rational truths is made to be analogous to the denial of the Law. To understand more thoroughly the reasons why the charge of unbelief is so binding for Averroes, it is necessary to understand allegorical interpretation itself and its relation to philosophy and the truths known through philosophic examination. Put differently, why are adequately trained philosophers the individuals who are said to possess the exclusive ability and obligation to reconcile the apparent contradictions between philosophy and the Law?

The fundamental reason why the philosophers are especially qualified for this activity (that is to say, why they may be legally excused for coming to certain conclusions, why they have a distinctive duty to interpret certain passages, and why they are bound by the charge of unbelief) has to do with the superiority of their natures. Earlier, we learned that there is an identity of purpose between the Law and philosophy. This could, of course, mean that the entire community of Muslims must engage in a serious inquiry into the nature of beings by means of the art of demonstration; it could mean, in other words, that all Muslims must become wise. Averroes does not accept this possibility. Only for some adherents of the Law is such theoretical study said to be obligatory, and this determination rests primarily on Averroes's understanding of how different types of humans require different kinds of proofs before they will assent to the truth of a proposition. For Averroes, those individuals who require a more demanding set of proofs must be allowed to engage in that activity which may satisfy their intellectual demands. That is, Averroes at bottom recognizes the distinctive human nature of the philosophers that separates them from other human beings.

Averroes's doctrine of the distinctive human classes is based on the text of the Qur'an that admits to containing two levels of meaning. He first speaks about this character of the Qur'an following his definition of allegorical interpretation: "the reason an apparent and an inner sense are set down in the Law is the difference in people's innate dispositions and the variance in their innate capacities for assent."[17] The next reference is found in the context of a discussion surrounding the inability to, with certainty, gain consensus with regard to theoretical texts. Certainty

17 *Decisive Treatise*, op. cit., 10.13–15.

can only be established if the following conditions are met: the period of time must be limited "by us," all of the scholars of that time must be known, and each of their opinions must have been handed down to us on an unassailable authority. Yet the decisive considerations appear to be the final two, which are that we must be sure that the scholars of this period were in agreement that "the Law has both an apparent and an inner sense and that it is not obligatory for someone to know about the inner sense if he is not capable of understanding it."[18] Due to the fact that this can never be the case (Averroes quotes here from al-Bukhari to support his argument), such unanimity can never be determined. The importance of these two considerations (and the emphasis on different natural abilities) can be observed when, in his restatement at 12.22–29, he only mentions the last two of the five reasons. Finally, the text at 19.8–11 reads: "this is the reason for the Law being divided into an apparent sense and an inner sense. For the apparent sense is those likenesses coined for those meanings, and the inner sense is those meanings that reveal themselves."[19] A little earlier in that same paragraph we learned that some need images coined for them "due to their innate dispositions, their habits, or their lack of facilities for education."[20]

We are also told here that there are both inner and surface teachings found in the Qur'an, which draw the attention of "those adept in demonstration" to the task of reconciling them. Due to natural differences, human beings, says Averroes, fall into three distinct classes. Because the methods available to humans for arriving at judgments are three (demonstrative, dialectical, and rhetorical) and because this can be derived from the "intention"[21] of the Law, he asserts also that the three classes of humans correspond to the three ways of assenting. The inability of certain types of individuals to grasp or pursue philosophy is a prominent reason why they are relegated to a lower class: "not all people have natures such as to accept demonstrations or dialectical arguments, let alone demonstrative arguments, given the difficulty in teaching demonstrative

18 Ibid., 11.14–17.
19 Ibid., 19.8–11.
20 Ibid., 19.3–4.
21 See ibid., 24.1.

arguments and the lengthy time needed by someone adept at learning them."[22]

Of course, Averroes understands that he must also show why the philosophers are the particularly competent "learned men" he claims they are. Therefore, one must examine what he views as the necessary qualifications for becoming a member of the elite demonstrative class. The three most important qualifications are: natural ability, organized study with a teacher knowledgeable in the field, and sound moral upbringing.[23] Throughout the rest of the work, however, Averroes seems to emphasize the overriding significance of the first qualification.[24] For example, he admits that only those who possess "superior natural intelligence" become acquainted with demonstrative books at all, and he later concedes that "not everyone has the ability to take in demonstrations."[25] At 17.11–29, he offers additional evidence: here he asserts that, even more than the jurists who have to draw inferences from the principles of the Law, it is vital that those who have to make judgments about beings (namely, the philosophers) are qualified because they must know "the primary intellectual notions and how to infer from them."[26] Interestingly, under this formulation the theologians are not considered to be qualified.

Averroes made note of the preeminent role of inference in the process of demonstrative reasoning earlier in the treatise when he stated that, because the Law commands reflection on beings by the intellect and "consideration is nothing more than inferring and drawing out the unknown from the known [which] is syllogistic reasoning ...,"[27] then it follows that "we" must study the beings by intellectual reasoning. "Reflect" is itself an interesting word, and Averroes's liberal use of it at the crucial opening passages underscores the importance he gives it. The word is derived from the Arabic root '-b-r and signifies passing over, on, by, beyond, or through. It also means to cross the borders of a land

22 Ibid., 24.7–10.
23 See ibid., 7.4–9.
24 See ibid. 22.18–20.
25 Ibid., 24.7.
26 Ibid., 17.28-29.
27 Ibid., 2.24–25.

or city and even to go beyond or violate those borders. As Mahdi states in his book on Ibn Khaldun, it is used in connection with the Law to signify the act of transgressing it by ignoring it, *or* of penetrating its inner meaning.[28] Various groups of theologians, mystics, or historians could and did employ the word in different ways to emphasize certain meanings that suited their purposes, but all seemed to use it to express the act of contemplating or penetrating the innermost significance of an object.[29] Indeed, Muslim philosophers found the word particularly helpful when communicating their writings to others:

> Muslim philosophers found the word, with its many conventional usages and its suggestion of what is beyond convention, of particular use when writing for the initiates. They employed it as a rhetorical tool to attract the potential philosopher to their "way": to lead him toward reflecting upon the external events of the universe of nature and the acts of man, and upon the equivocal expressions of the Quran, and to guide him to the knowledge of the rational principles beyond them.[30]

In the *Manāhij*, Averroes claims that the "whole of the Qur'an is nothing but a summons to theoretical study and reflection."[31] Here, he underscores the importance of the word (i.e., "reflect" or "reflection") by using it nine times in the first chapter alone.[32] As a result, one who would know God has at one's disposition "the most complete kind of syllogistic reasoning."[33] And because philosophy is, among other things, an art which calls for intellectual virtue, it is "useful in its nature and

---

28 Muhsin Mahdi, *Ibn Khaldun's Philosophy of History* (London: George Allen and Unwin, 1957), 65.
29 Ibid.
30 Ibid., 66.
31 Hourani, *Averroes: On the Harmony of Religion and Philosophy*, op. cit., 42.
32 See *Decisive Treatise*, op. cit., 1.5, 1.10, 2.7–8, 2.11, 2.23, 2.26, 2.27, 3.1, 3.16.
33 Ibid., 3.1–2.

essence"[34] and is a study that, when utilized by those who are qualified, leads to the "truest" knowledge of God Himself. Averroes decides that the rigors and demands of such reflection provide sufficient justification to call it "the most complete kind of reflection by means of the most complete kind of syllogistic reasoning"[35] that can only be properly utilized by the "best sort of people."[36] Thus, the philosophers are that special class of learned men who are obligated to interpret the Qur'an in certain instances; they have access to the true inner meaning of the Law that corresponds with philosophic truth. An important clarification occurs at 13.1–2: Averroes says here that the philosopher' superior kind of assent obliges them to a belief not found among the unlearned. It is this notion of assent that plays such an important role in his discussion of what kinds of errors the philosophers are excused from committing.

After he has shown how the philosophers are qualified in the field of interpretation, it seems proper to present an argument that exhibits both their freedom of interpretation within the Law and their respect for that Law which governs the society in which they must live. Averroes places the majority of his discussion of the excusableness of error in the very center of the *Treatise*. At 17.1, after he has treated the first two "questions"[37] and just before he begins to consider the difficult question of the afterlife, Averroes decides that it is appropriate to discuss this matter not on the basis of *ijmā'* per se but on the basis of the nature or qualifications of that individual who assents to a truth in a particular manner. He initially puts the matter in a religious framework: "it seems" that those who disagree on the interpretation of these difficult questions "either hit the mark and are to be rewarded or have erred and are to be excused."[38] One might expect Averroes to follow this with an appropriate quote from the Qur'an so that his position might be defended within a strictly scriptural framework. However, he next makes reference not to the Qur'an but to a position that appears to be inspired by the writings

34 Ibid., 7.12.
35 Ibid., 3.1–2.
36 Ibid., 22.22.
37 See ibid., 12.9–13.
38 Ibid., 17.2–3.

of Aristotle: "for assent to something due to an indication arising in the soul is compulsory, not voluntary—I mean that it is not up to us not to assent or to assent as it is up to us to stand up or not to stand up."[39] Only after this does he decide to set down a supporting quote from the Qur'an,[40] which might lead one to wonder whether Averroes himself is not here manipulating the Tradition (*hadīth*) so that it may more closely conform to the conclusions of demonstration. Indeed, he provides yet another Aristotelian source to justify his position before he concludes: "the one who assents to error because of vagueness occurring in it is excused if he is an adept of science."[41]

The important qualification, "if he is an adept of science," should compel us once again to consider the issue of human nature and its special place in Averroes's discussion of allegorical interpretation and its limits. Throughout his treatment of the issue of error and elsewhere, the learned are described as playing a special role when considering the correctness or incorrectness of judgments, and are usually excused if, in some cases, they make an error when interpreting. For example, when speaking about those Qur'anic passages about which there is doubt whether or not to interpret, Averroes admits that "one who commits an error with respect to this is to be excused—I mean, one of the learned."[42] Later, he speaks similarly when he addresses the difficult question of the afterlife and the problems of interpreting a topic of such gravity: "the learned person who commits an error with respect to this question is to be excused."[43] Here and elsewhere[44] the learned, and only the learned, are to be excused.

In fact, Averroes speaks not only of demands but also of duties. Because the correct allegorical interpretation, which is "the truth," can only be understood by demonstration, the learned have a "duty" to interpret. In contrast, the dialectical class, if an interpretation is more "persuasive" to them than the surface teaching, only possesses a "possible" duty to

39 Ibid., 17.3–6.
40 See ibid., 17.9–10.
41 Ibid., 17.6–8.
42 Ibid., 20.26–27.
43 Ibid., 21.9–10.
44 See, ibid., 6.19 and 13.6–10.

interpret. Meanwhile, the masses have the "duty" to take passages in their apparent meanings "for there is nothing more than that in their natures."[45] Averroes concludes that this makes the learned "specially chosen" judges of beings whose error is the only type of error that is "excused" with respect to the Law.[46] They are the only class, then, which can receive legal sanction for *ta'wīl*. This reminds one of Averroes's point at the beginning of the *Decisive Treatise*: that while philosophy, like all human activities, stands under the Law, it also, unlike all other human activities, is especially commanded by that Law and therefore occupies a privileged position. Error proceeding from any other class, however, is "sheer sin." In fact, the masses are not even permitted to know of the demonstrative interpretation, as he who makes judgments about beings without having the proper qualifications for such judgments is not excused but is "heretical" or "an unbeliever."[47] Therefore, it appears that through the discussion of human nature and the qualifications required for demonstrative study, one finally arrives at the only true binding limit to allegorical interpretation of the Qur'an, namely, the charge of unbelief.

Averroes begins his thorough discussion of the issue within the context of his treatment of the three kinds of text into which the Qur'an can be divided. He says that, "in general," there are two types of error with regard to the sacred text. One kind of error (which is excused) occurs to people, like doctors and judges, who are qualified in the subject that they are discussing and is not excused to those who are not qualified in that subject. The second kind of error is not excused to any individuals whatever and is called unbelief if it concerns the "principles of the Law," or heresy (*bid'a*) if it deals with those things which are subordinate to those principles.[48] It is therefore necessary to determine what these important "principles of religion" are. Later, Averroes lists three of them: acknowledgement of God, of the prophetic missions, and of happiness and misery in the next life. All such principles could be known by everyone

---

45 Ibid., 25.23-24; cf., ibid., 21.21.
46 See ibid., 18.1–6.
47 See ibid., 18.21–22.
48 Ibid., 18.7–10.

through all three methods of assent, so that no one can legitimately complain that they are beyond his or her own personal ability to understand them. As a result, anyone who interprets them allegorically is an unbeliever "because it is one of the roots of the Law and something to which assent comes about by the three methods."[49]

When he recounts his previous position, he only speaks as "if" that had been sufficiently established. From 19.1–14 he had mentioned those texts that "are known only by demonstration due to their being hidden" and those texts that are intended for the rest because they need images and likenesses of such things. Yet when he addresses the same issue again later he claims not only that these texts "have" to be interpreted by the demonstrative class, and that it is "unbelief or heresy" for the rest to interpret them allegorically, but he goes so far as to assert that it is "unbelief" for the learned to take them in their apparent meaning. It is also important to note that, while the two lower classes are threatened with both the charge of unbelief and heresy in this section, the elite are threatened only with the former charge. In fact, a heresy charge threatening the learned cannot be found in the text.[50] This should alert one to the way in which Averroes is presenting the learned person's relation to the charge of unbelief. Why, exactly, are they being threatened with this charge? Also, is it the same or a slightly revised version of the charge that is threatening the other classes?

The first place where we can find evidence of why the philosophers might be charged with unbelief is located at 21.21ff., following Averroes's conclusion that the question about the future life falls into the category of those texts that are uncertain. Here, he begins by mentioning that anyone who is not a "man of learning" is "obliged" to take such texts in their apparent meaning, since allegorical interpretation for them is unbelief "because it leads to unbelief."[51] As one learns later, these people whose "duty" it is to "believe" in the apparent meaning are the masses. Now, when speaking about the unbelief particular to the philosophers, Averroes puts the matter a bit differently: such an individual who

49 Ibid., 21.14–15.
50 A reason for this may be given at ibid., 4.5.
51 Ibid., 21.21–22.

"divulges" a demonstrative interpretation to someone not able to receive it is "calling him to unbelief; and the one who calls to unbelief is an unbeliever."[52] The difference between the two treatments can be observed more clearly when they are compared with a section of text later in the work that treats the same issue. Here he begins matters in virtually the same way as he did previously; when someone expresses allegorical interpretations to anyone who is unfit to receive them "both he who declares it and the one to whom it is declared are steered to unbelief."[53] However, now Averroes adds that "the reason for this [in the case of the latter] is" that allegorical interpretation comprises two things: rejection of the apparent meaning and the affirmation of the allegorical one, so that if the apparent meaning is rejected in the mind of someone who can only grasp apparent meanings (without the allegorical meaning being affirmed in his mind) "that leads him to unbelief if it is about the roots of the Law."[54] The individual who expresses allegories to unqualified people "is an unbeliever because of his calling people to unbelief."[55] Once again, the differing natures of individuals play the predominant role in such a classification; if one is not qualified one should not attempt things that take so much natural ability and study to learn.

However, there are slight and important differences with regard to the way Averroes presents the issue of unbelief. In his first treatment, he spoke of "obligation" and "duty"; here, there is not a single reference to either. In the first statement he says, "we hold that ..."; there is no reference to "we" in the second. While the second treatment specifically emphasizes the importance of the "principles of the Law" when trying to determine the correctness of an act, such principles do not play a specific role in the first formulation. Yet there is an even more important distinction to be made which does not concern the differences between the two treatments as much as it concerns an issue within each. That issue concerns the fact that the philosophers are said to be led into unbelief not because of the character of the truths they hold but because

52 Ibid., 21.22–23.
53 Ibid., 26.20–21.
54 Ibid., 26.25–26.
55 Ibid., 27.16.

their unpolitic promulgation of what they know may lead others to un-belief. That is, while the masses are called unbelievers as a result of their lack of "belief," the philosophers are never said to believe in the same things or even to "believe" in anything at all. The philosophers "know" and are called unbelievers if an unwise action of theirs "summons" oth-ers to unbelief. The fact that the imprudent manner in which philosophic truths have been publicized is a central concern of the *Decisive Treatise* helps to explain why Averroes pays such careful attention to the proper ways in which those truths should be expressed within a sensitive polit-ical environment.

At the end of the book, Averroes laments that "our soul is in utmost sorrow and pain due to the corrupt dissensions and distorted beliefs that have permeated this Law."[56] Much of the blame for this must be placed on the theologians: "because of the interpretations with respect to the Law—especially the corrupt ones—and the supposition that it is oblig-atory to declare them to everyone, factions emerged within Islam."[57] Thus, unlike Averroes himself, the theologians do not really understand the nature of truth or of men and how this understanding must alter the manner in which demonstrative truths are expressed to the public. In-deed, for Averroes, it is exceedingly important not only *what* gets put down in books as the certain truth, but *how* those truths are presented. For example, he says, "it is obligatory that [allegorical] interpretations be established only in books using demonstrations. For if they are in books using demonstrations, no one but those adept in demonstration will get at them";[58] later, he demands: "interpretations ought not to be declared to the multitude, nor established in rhetorical or dialectical books."[59] He even goes so far as to implore the imams of the Muslims to "ban those of his [sc. al-Ghazali's] books that contain science from all but those adept in science, just as it is obligatory upon them to ban demonstrative books from those not adept in them."[60] Al-Ghazali, he

56 Ibid., 32.20–21.
57 Ibid., 29.23–25.
58 Ibid., 21.24–27.
59 Ibid., 26.26–27.
60 Ibid., 22.14–16.

claims, not only misunderstood the manner in which demonstrative statements must be conveyed but also damaged the Muslim community by doing so.

The issue of the way in which demonstrative truths are divulged to the masses is so important to Averroes that he relates a parable near the end of the treatise which is said to show the relation between "these people's [who present allegorical interpretations, which may be false, to the masses] intention and the intention of the Lawgiver."[61] He associates the former with bad medical advisers, who tell the masses that the medicine prescribed by the physician is not appropriate and set out to discredit the physician and his medicine so that both are rejected by the people. Averroes then asks whether these men will now be able to use those things which they have discredited in helping to preserve the people's health or cure their disease. Following this, Averroes answers his own question: "he will not be able to practice these with them, nor will they be able to practice them; and perdition will encompass them all."[62] Averroes claims that the situation "is what happens with respect to the Law when anyone declares an interpretation to the multitude or to someone not adept for it."[63] The result is that he makes it appear false and therefore turns people away from it, and "the one who bars others from the Law is an unbeliever."[64]

There are also other clues in the text that arouse a reader's attention and compel him or her to believe that there is more to be learned from the story than what Averroes explicitly admits. The most immediate clue is provided by Averroes himself when, at the end of the parable, he proclaims that "this illustration is certain and not poetical, as someone might say."[65] This should compel one to go back and study the story more carefully once again in the hope of understanding why this particular comparison is so "certain." The parable (the Arabic word [*mithāl*] can also be translated as "symbol") describes an unskillful "physician" whose

---

61   Ibid., 27.27–28.
62   Ibid., 28.12–14.
63   Ibid., 28.21–23.
64   Ibid., 28.24.
65   Ibid., 28.25–26.

"primary" intention is to "preserve" the health of "all" the people by prescribing for them rules that can be "commonly" accepted. This reminds one also of the "primary" intention of the Law. In addition, earlier we were told that there are "common methods" of expression in religion which are the methods "by which the majority comes to form concepts and judgments." Averroes later explicitly calls these methods by which the majority are educated those which are "established in the precious Book alone ... and if the matter is examined with respect to them, it will become apparent that no better shared methods for teaching the multitude are to be encountered than the methods mentioned in it."[66]

It appears, then, that Averroes's emphasis on the different natures of human beings necessarily leads to a discussion not only of the way in which knowledge must be promulgated within a certain community, but of the philosophers' special, and indeed privileged, pedagogical role. Throughout the text, Averroes emphasizes that what separates philosophers from the other two classes is their superior ability to study and comprehend the truths that the Qur'an obliges them to understand. The only true limit to their use of allegorical interpretation in achieving this goal is the charge of unbelief (and, concomitantly, the careless promulgation of such truths that leads to unbelief). However, a question remains as to what precisely the philosophers believe and why this provides them with the authority to determine how one should convey scriptural truths.

Averroes specifically states that the belief among the learned is different than the belief that is found among the rest of the population because the philosophers have access to the truth known through "interpretation ... that is the truth."[67] Yet this belief which is based on the "science" of allegorical interpretation is, he claims, that very belief of which God Himself speaks: "So, if this faith by which God has described the learned is particular to them, then it is obligatory that it come about by means of demonstration."[68] Indeed, the Prophet appears to speak to people differently according to their natures and requirements

66 Ibid., 31.5–11.
67 Ibid., 13.7.
68 Ibid., 13.2–4.

for assent. As a result, Muhammad demanded that the black woman, who claimed that God was in the sky, be freed because (according to Averroes) "she was not one of those adept in demonstration"[69] and therefore could only believe in a thing that she could imagine. This, of course, is not what the philosopher "believes." Yet if the philosophers do not have the same sort of belief as the rest of the population, then one may also wonder if they don't have a different sort of unbelief. Averroes's position is that the philosophers are to be charged with unbelief if they take some texts in their apparent meaning or foolishly promulgate difficult truths and thereby confuse the unlearned. He hopes that, with a proper understanding of human nature and the special type of communication this necessitates, the philosophers (and especially the dialecticians) will not commit such harm.

Having addressed the charge of unbelief against philosophers like himself, Averroes places considerable emphasis on the importance of stability within the political community, or at least as much stability as will allow the philosophers to study that which God has commanded them to study. This is not, however, to imply that the philosophers in the society will be passive bystanders when questions regarding the preservation of the political community arise, since the fact that they have some power in this regard is made obvious by Averroes. Although he advises that the philosophers publicly "affirm" (not "prove" or "know certainly") the existence of an afterlife and the principles of religion,[70] they would be well advised to give a "certain sort" of allegorical interpretation that will not exhibit (or lead to) a denial of their existences.[71] The philosophers' presentation of the truth for the sake of political stability (and, of course, their own safety) can also be observed most conspicuously when one examines how they understand a passage of the Qur'an as opposed to how they teach the same passage to the unlearned. Averroes quotes one verse of the Qur'an not less than four times in the course of the treatise: at 10.18–20, 12.22–24, 20.15–16 and 27.12–14. The full verse is:

69   Ibid., 20.5.
70   Cf. ibid., 18.14, 21.11.
71   Ibid., 21.13–14.

> He it is who has sent down to you the Book, containing certain verses clear and definite—they are the essence of the Book—and others ambiguous. Now those in whose hearts is mischief go after the ambiguous passages, seeking discord and seeking to interpret them allegorically. But no one knows their interpretation except God. And those who are well grounded in science they say "we believe in it, it is all from our Lord; but only men of intelligence give heed." [3:7]

In his first reference, Averroes merely says: "This idea is pointed to in His Statement (may He be exalted), 'He it is who has sent down to you the Book; in it, there are fixed verses...' on to His statement, 'and those well grounded in science.'"[72] He next quotes the verse in the context of his discussion of the impossibility of a consensus against allegorical interpretation: "[this is so because] there are interpretations that it is not obligatory to expound except to those adept in interpretation. These are ''those well grounded in science.'"[73] Yet now Averroes boldly and with full confidence alters the punctuation of the quote to defend his philosophic position: "for we choose to place the stop [or period] after His statement (may He be exalted), 'and those well grounded in science.' [3:7] Now, if those adept in science did not know the interpretation, there would be nothing superior in their assent obliging them to a faith in Him not found among those not adept in science."[74] In the final two references, however, Averroes recommends the standard punctuation for the people. At 20.10, he claims that the proper answer "to these people [sc. the non-philosophers] about verses and Traditions like these is that they pertain to the verses that resemble one another and that the stop is at His saying (may he be exalted), 'None knows their interpretation but God' [3:7]."[75] And at 27.3–10:

> "For this kind [of people], it is obligatory to declare and to say, with respect to the apparent sense—when it is such that

72 Ibid., 10.17–20.
73 Ibid., 12.20–22.
74 Ibid., 12.22–26.
75 Ibid., 20.13–16.

the doubt as to whether it is an apparent sense is in itself apparent to everyone, without cognizance of its interpretation being possible for them—that is one of those [verses] that resemble one another [whose interpretation is] not known, except to God, and that it is obligatory for the stop in His saying (may He be exalted) to be placed here: 'None knows their interpretation but God.' [3:7]"

Thus the philosophers are advised to say one thing while they understand something else entirely.

The role of the philosophers in society might be clarified by looking, once again, at the parable that Averroes calls a "true analogy" because "the link between the physician and the health of bodies is [the same as] the link between the Lawgiver and the health of souls."[76] Although the Lawgiver aims "solely at the health of souls from which happiness and misery in the future life" follow, the physician is the individual seeking to "preserve" the health of bodies when it exists and to "restore" it when it is lost.[77] Whether or not Averroes here subtly references the philosophers and their role in preserving the "health" of themselves and the community in which they live, the point is clear that the class which has access to the most difficult truths must exercise great caution in the way it presents itself to the masses and political authorities.

Because of this, the philosophers are strongly advised to employ rhetorical and other devices that would help them communicate to those who are unable to grasp philosophic truths. In his *Short Commentary on Aristotle's Poetics*, Averroes mentions that the art of poetics is most properly used to move the souls of the many to believe or do something;[78] it is, therefore, employed by one or only a few people and is intended for the majority of people. This "short" commentary is different than Averroes's other short commentaries in that political uses of the art analyzed

---

76 Ibid., 28.27–28.

77 Ibid., 29.1–15.

78 Averroes, "Short Commentary on Aristotle's *Poetics*," in *Averroes' Three Short Commentaries on Aristotle's Topics, Rhetoric, and Poetics*, ed. Charles E. Butterworth (Albany: SUNY Press, 1977), paras. 1,4.

are emphasized while the technical aspects are not. Because the art of poetics is not primarily intended to portray things as they really are but to move the souls of the listeners in the manner that the poet desires, poetics is then potentially deceptive[79] and thus may, in certain instances, resemble sophistry. This important political role that Averroes ascribes to the poet is more fully presented in the *Middle Commentary on Aristotle's Poetics* where, in the first twelve paragraphs, he presents the poet as encouraging some actions and discouraging others. Indeed, because the poet must set forth the correctness of belief in an effort to compel the people to do or avoid certain actions, he or she must not only explain how something exists but also illustrate the correctness of that thing.[80]

Poetics concerns itself with praise and blame, and Averroes therefore recognizes the special place of the Qur'an in the society and how it may be utilized to effect such significant change in behavior. He claims that, though not itself poetry, the Qur'an does in fact set the goals for imitative speech and that representations of things that are the subject of narrative poetry occur frequently in the Law. Yet not only is the art of poetics (and therefore the poet) capable of such influence, but it may also, if utilized properly, be considered philosophic. Because of its tendency to generalize and to consider only existing things, "the art of poetry is closer to philosophy than the art of inventing parables," and warns that if the poet shuns the description of existing things in favor of inventing parables (which have little to do with reality), then this philosophic level will not be realized. Only if people are persuaded by the poem will their souls be moved.[81] In the end, and throughout his discussion of poetry, Averroes highlights the extremely significant moral and political consequences of poetry. This would also help to explain why he suggests in the *Middle Commentary* that poetry is a kind of rhetoric and therefore somewhat similar to dialectic.

In contradistinction to this, Averroes, in his *Short Commentary on Aristotle's Topics*, emphasizes the technical aspects of the dialectical art. Here, he claims that dialectical art is based on widely accepted opinion;

79   Ibid., paras. 1–3.
80   Ibid., paras. 8, 27, 31, 39.
81   Ibid., paras. 38–39.

it is, therefore, more closely associated with the art of demonstration than both rhetoric or poetics. Dialectic concerns itself with contentious arguments between two interlocutors of fairly equal capabilities; the art, he suggests, should provide the necessary tools with which one may be able to defeat an opponent. Because of this, the learned will have little use for it when trying to communicate with the majority of individuals. The demonstrative class, though, will find both similarities and differences between this art and the art of demonstration. Although dialectical arguments may give the appearance of certainty, Averroes is quick to warn that this should not lead one to confuse it with demonstrative arguments, whose premises are always certain. Dialectical premises may be false because widespread acceptance or renown, not truth, is the primary concern when selecting a dialectical premise. Although there are other differences between the two (such as the fact that the art of dialectic has access to many more classes of syllogisms than demonstration), they are also similar in that, even though a dialectical argument will not attain the level of certainty achieved by a demonstrative argument, dialectic may be used to investigate any subject that can also be investigated by demonstration.

In addition, this art of dialectical analysis resembles the art of rhetoric. Both arts, for example, rely on a certain kind of common opinion and have the same purpose of bringing about assent. And although the primary difference between the two arts has to be the extent to which their respective arguments attain a measure of certainty, the subjects that they investigate are very much alike. Consequently, Averroes insists here and in the *Middle Commentary on Aristotle's Topics* that a fundamental difference between the two involves their relation to sophistry: although rhetoric may, in some instances, resemble sophistry in everything but purpose, dialectic is never to be confused with sophistry because it is never deceptive. Because of this, dialectical arguments may often be extremely difficult and therefore of little or no use when attempting to teach the masses. Averroes clarifies that rhetoric is more suited to this purpose and may even be able to present the crux of a dialectical argument in a manner that is suitable for public consumption.

As he does in his commentary on the *Topics*, Averroes, in the *Short Commentary on Aristotle's Rhetoric*, stresses the technical aspect of the art and as a result does not provide an extensive discussion about how the art might be used; instead, he pays careful attention to the types of arguments which might be employed and how they may be used. While both arts are intended to bring about assent and therefore depend on a kind of common opinion, rhetoric employs persuasive language to a greater extent than dialectic. As a result, rhetorical arguments are less certain than dialectical ones. Averroes explains that rhetoric can either be used by the masses between themselves or by someone well versed in the art when attempting to convey something to the masses. Interestingly, it is in this work on rhetoric, and not in the work devoted to a discussion of dialectic, that Averroes refers to the so-called "dialectical theologians," thereby suggesting that they were either faulty practitioners of their art or actually rhetoricians, or both. Rhetoric is much more suited for instructing the people, as the conclusions that may be derived from it are useful when the individual or individuals are naturally unable to grasp more difficult forms of argumentation like those found in demonstration or even dialectic. Averroes makes it clear that it is best used in interpersonal dealings and political concerns; that he describes it as "this art of public speaking"[82] proves his point. He emphasizes this role of rhetoric when he organizes the types of rhetorical arguments according to which one would have the most persuasive effect on the people;[83] he admits, though, that this means people will be compelled to believe arguments which cannot withstand serious scrutiny.[84] As mentioned earlier, while deception or trickery is not allowed in dialectical arguments, such devices may not only be employed in rhetorical arguments but may, and should, enhance the persuasive effect of such arguments;[85] rhetoric would then begin to resemble sophistry.

Rhetoric employs a variety of other devices intended to enhance the effectiveness of the arguments (such as the "example," "testimony," "reports," "consensus," and "challenging") and which, claims Averroes, have been misused by the theologians and jurists because they failed to recog-

---

82   Ibid., para. 40.
83   Ibid., paras. 2, 3, 6, 8, 12, 13, 18–19, 33.
84   Ibid., paras. 2–4, 12, 29, 31, 36, 38, 40, 42–44.
85   Ibid., para. 17.

nize their rhetorical origins. To correct this misunderstanding, Averroes, in the *Short Commentary on Aristotle's Rhetoric*, defines each of the devices and gives examples of their use and abuse. For instance, "testimony" should be used when trying to communicate with those, like the majority of people, who will be unable to apprehend it.[86] "Consensus" should not be cited to prove the validity of anything[87] and, unless we have seen what has been reported or are able to represent it in some way, "reports" can lead to certainty only if they can be verified by a syllogism,[88] for they are merely persuasive devices and should never be used instead of intellectual understanding. At the very end of the work, Averroes mentions the uses to which rhetoric may be put, and it turns out that, like poetics, this art can be extremely useful in political matters.

Averroes speaks at length, in the *Middle Commentary on Aristotle's Rhetoric*, about the relationship between rhetoric and logic.[89] The primary reason for classifying it among the logical arts has to do with its similarity to dialectic[90] and therefore its ability to approximate the truth.[91] In addition, logic is or should be used to help select the most effective words or phrases when constructing an argument.[92] Because of their ignorance of logic, the theologians failed to appreciate the nature of rhetoric and the other arts and, as a result, used them improperly to confuse the populace. As he suggests in the *Decisive Treatise*, Averroes insists that only those with an understanding of the formal logical arts will be able to best utilize dialectic, rhetoric, or poetics. Indeed, his criticisms of the theologians in the *Short Commentary on Aristotle's Rhetoric* are meant to underscore his view that knowledge of logic is essential to the proper use of rhetoric. To be sure, knowledge of logic is itself not the highest form of knowledge but is, rather, the necessary condition for such knowledge. As he puts it here and in his *Commentary on Plato's*

---

86 Ibid., para. 36.
87 Ibid., para. 42.
88 Ibid., paras. 38–39.
89 Cf. Averroes, *Talkhīṣ al-khaṭābah*, ed. 'Abd al-Raḥmān Badawī (Cairo: Maktabat al-Nahḍah al-Miṣrīyah, 1960).
90 Ibid., 4:3–4, 18:13–16.
91 Ibid., 10:7–13.
92 Ibid., 248:4–9, 249:7–17.

Republic, logic is the propaedeutic art. In the *Middle Commentary on Aristotle's Rhetoric*, Averroes uses this connection between rhetoric and logic to emphasize the moral duty of the rhetorician to instruct the populace.[93]

One consequence of this is that the would-be rhetorician should have a knowledge of the Greek sciences. In the *Short Rhetoric*, Averroes admits that the "ancients" had an intimate knowledge of rhetoric and logic[94] and that their wisdom would be of immense help, even in Islamic matters.[95] Another consequence is that rhetoric can and must have a profound political role.[96] While dialectic is most appropriately used between individuals of fairly equal intellectual capacities, rhetoric can be used to communicate ideas to the vast majority of people who would not be able to grasp more difficult argumentation.[97] Since these people (and indeed the rhetoricians) are members of the political community, the rhetorician would naturally recognize the importance of communicating ideas that are central to the preservation and continued health of the city.[98] Because this responsibility is a political one, it is therefore a moral one as well, and Averroes, in the *Middle Rhetoric*, is quick to point out the immense moral responsibility of the rhetorician. This is evident when he identifies Muhammad as a deliberative rhetorician.[99] This responsibility is always tested because, to repeat, the rhetorician has at his disposal all types of devices that are also used by sophists. The danger might be that the rhetorician, whose art does participate in the truth, would fail to appreciate his art as such and thereby degenerate into a sophist. Averroes clarifies the situation by admonishing the future

---

93 See Charles E. Butterworth, "Rhetoric and Islamic Political Philosophy," *International Journal of Middle Eastern Studies* 3 (1972): 194.

94 Averroes, "Short Commentary on Aristotle's *Rhetoric*," in *Averroes' Three Short Commentaries on Aristotle's Topics, Rhetoric, and Poetics*, ed. Charles E. Butterworth (Albany: SUNY Press, 1977), para. 8.

95 Ibid., para. 44.

96 Butterworth, "Rhetoric and Islamic Political Philosophy," op. cit.

97 Averroes, *Talkhiṣ al-khaṭābah,* op.cit., 20:9–22:1.

98 Ibid., 32:15–39:11; 67:21–71:7.

99 Ibid., 38:2, and passim. See Butterworth, "Rhetoric and Islamic Political Philosophy," op. cit., 195.

rhetorician to keep in mind always the good of the listener that is the final purpose of rhetoric.[100] Only the moral purpose of the rhetorician distinguishes him from the sophist.[101]

Thus, Averroes's insistence that rhetoric be used to communicate matters relevant to political life places a new, and heavier, burden on the rhetorician. To quote Charles Butterworth: "The new rhetoric thus demanded a man who was interested in political life and in the possibility of instructing, as well as exhorting, the citizens."[102] Averroes admits that only a "master of logic" would be able to understand the art thoroughly and use it properly; it is clear from his discussion that the "master of logic" is the philosopher.[103] The responsibility Averroes places on the rhetorician is, then, an aspect of the responsibility he must also place on the philosopher: he must convince the philosopher that he cannot ignore the city but must recognize that he also is a member of that community and therefore has a stake in its survival. As he does in the *Decisive Treatise*, Averroes suggests that the philosopher needs to recognize that to take the city seriously, he must persuade his fellow citizens, in a manner that is pleasing to them, of the appropriateness of philosophic activity in a community defined by a religious Law. He must also take seriously the charge of unbelief that is peculiar to the philosopher, and he must take care to guard himself against it. Thus, Averroes's purpose in the *Decisive Treatise* as well as the *Middle Rhetoric* appears to be two-fold: to recognize a misunderstanding of logic and its parts, and to remedy the situation in a manner that would help to preserve the community. To quote from Charles Butterworth's article cited above:

> The *Talkhīṣ* [or: *Middle Rhetoric*] offered a view of rhetoric which remedied the rhetoric practiced by the theologians and which would help the qualified rhetorician to instruct the populace without endangering the accepted faith or leading to

---

100 Averroes, *Talkhīṣ al-khaṭābah*, op. cit., 13:7–14:21.
101 Butterworth, "Rhetoric and Islamic Political Philosophy," 196.
102 Ibid.
103 Averroes, *Talkhīṣ al-khaṭābah,* op. cit., 9:19–10:8 and Butterworth, "Rhetoric and Islamic Political Philosophy," op. cit., 197.

confusion. To the extent that his new rhetoric was an improvement or remedy for the theologian and jurist to follow, Averroes functioned as a reformer. To the extent that he also provided suggestions about a rhetoric appropriate to the philosophically minded individual and subtly indicated how the philosopher could learn to speak in a manner that would preserve philosophical inquiry from injurious attacks, Averroes acted as a careful Muslim political philosopher.[104]

Such a view may also be applied to the *Decisive Treatise* itself. It may even compel the reader of that book to wonder whether Averroes is not offering an example of the most politic use of a dialectical art so misunderstood (and mishandled) by the theologians. If it is indeed the case, as Averroes asserts towards the end of the book, that al-Ghazali in particular was responsible for subverting both the true meaning of philosophy and its prudential dissemination, then the composition of the *Decisive Treatise* could be viewed as an attempt by the author to reform the political community in a manner that does justice both to philosophy and the Divine Law.

---

104 Butterworth, "Rhetoric and Islamic Political Philosophy," op. cit., 197.

An Unknown Ismāʿīlī Interpretation of Quran 3:7

Carmela Baffioni and Monica Scotti[*]

1. The author and the work

The *Mukhtaṣar al-Uṣūl*—A Compendium of Principles—is an unpublished work by the Ismāʿīlī theologian, and leading figure of the early Ṭayyibī community, ʿAlī ibn Muḥammad ibn al-Walīd (Yemen, d. 1215), who was of Quraysh descent. He had a reputation as a learned and pious member of the *daʿwa*, which earned him the trust of the third *dāʿī* Ḥātim al-Ḥāmidī.[1] He studied under his uncle, ʿAlī ibn al-Ḥusayn (d. 1159),[2] after whose death he became a disciple of Muḥammad ibn

---

[*] Paragraphs 1 and 2 are authored by Monica Scotti, paragraphs 3 and 4 by Carmela Baffioni. Notes belonging to the other author in the paragraphs are marked by the initials [M.S.] or [C.B.]. This article examines a passage of the *Mukhtaṣar al-Uṣūl* by the Ismāʿīlī theologian ʿAlī ibn Muḥammad ibn al-Walīd dealing with the author's interpretation of Quran 3:7. It belongs to chapter 5 of the second Book. The first critical edition of this work has been prepared by Monica Scotti as her 2014 doctoral dissertation at the Università degli Studi di Napoli "L'Orientale"; she was tutored by Carmela Baffioni. This paper is based on manuscripts provided by the Institute of Ismaili Studies in London. The authors thank Dr. Farhad Daftary, co-director and head of the Department of Academic Research and Publications of the Institute of Ismaili Studies in London for authorizing publication of this article; Dr. Wafi Mo'min, head of the Ismaili Special Connection Unit (ISCU) for providing copies of the manuscripts, and the staff of the library of the Institute for their help. The authors alone are, of course, responsible for the opinions expressed in the article [C.B.-M.S.].

1 Cf. Ismail K. Poonawala, "'Alī b. al-Walīd," *Encyclopaedia of Islam*, 3rd ed., accessed on October 13th 2013 http://referenceworks.brillonline.com/ entries/encyclopaedia-of-islam-3/ali-b-al-walid-COM_22932.

2 Cf. Ismail K. Poonawala, "'Alī b. al-Ḥusayn b. al-Ḥusayn b. ʿAlī al-Qurashī," *Encyclopaedia of Islam*, 3rd ed., accessed on October 13th 2013

Ṭāhir al-Ḥārithī (d. 1188),[3] whom he succeeded as *maʾdhūn* (licentiate) of Ṣanʿāʾ for want of the third *dāʿī*. The third *dāʿī* also made him the mentor of his son Alī ibn Ḥātim al-Ḥāmidī, who, on Ibn al-Walīd's recommendation, was designated by his father to succeed him as the fourth *dāʿī*. As it turned out ʿAlī ibn al-Walīd himself became the fifth *dāʿī* of the Ṭayyibī community and next holder of knowledge and authority in the absence of the Imām on Saturday 25th *Dhū ʾl-Qiʿda* 605/31st May 1209.

ʿAlī ibn al-Walīd was a prolific writer, whose works were held in high esteem among the Mustaʿlī-Ṭayyibī community. Most of these works have been preserved either as manuscripts or as published books.[4]

The edition of the *Mukhtaṣar* is based on six manuscripts belonging to the Institute of Ismaili Studies. These copies are relatively recent but represent nonetheless a unique source of information about the literary heritage of the Ṭayyibī community:

- Ms142 (A-): 277 pp., 17.5 x 12.5 /12 x 8 cm, copied in the 18th century.[5] This manuscript was chosen as the basis of the edition because its text is complete and quite clear;
- Ms. 1288 (B): 137 pp., copied 1267/1851;[6]
- Ms. 1204 (C): 51 ff., copied 1280/1863;[7]
- Ms141 (D): 139 pp., 22 x 13.5 / 15.5 x 9 cm, copied in the 19th century;[8]

http://referenceworks.brillonline.com/entries/encyclopaedia-of-islam-3/ali-b-al-husayn-b-al-husayn-b-ali-al-qurashi COM_26325.

3   Cf. Ismail K. Poonawala, "Muḥammad b. Ṭāhir b. Ibrāhīm al-Ḥārithī," *Encyclopaedia of Islam*, 2nd ed., vol. VII [Leiden: Brill, 1990], 410–11.

4   Cf. Farhad Daftary, *Ismaili Literature. A Bibliography of Sources and Studies* [London: I.B. Tauris in Association with the Institute of Ismaili Studies, 2004], 118–19; Ismail K. Poonawala, *Bibliography of Ismāʿīlī Literature* [Malibu: Undena Publications, 1977], 156–61; Poonawala, "ʿAlī b. al-Walīd," *Encyclopaedia of Islam*, 3rd ed.

5   Adam Gacek, *Catalogue of Arabic Manuscripts in the Library of the Institute of Ismaili Studies* [London: Islamic Publications, 1984], 78.

6   Delia Cortese, *The Arabic Ismaili Manuscripts – the Zāhid ʿAlī Collection in the Library of the Institute of the Ismaili Studies* [London: I.B. Tauris in Association with the Institute of Ismaili Studies, 2003], 121.

7   Ibid., 122.

8   Gacek, *Catalogue of Arabic Manuscripts*, 78.

- Ms. 678 (E): 95 ff., copied in 1353/1934;[9]
- Ms. 269 (F): 59 ff., copied in 1359/1940.[10]

The *Mukhtaṣar* is described as a polemical work on the question of the "names of God."[11] As the author himself writes in the introduction, the purpose of the work is to refute the views of: i) the *Ḥashwiyya*, namely the *aṣḥāb al-ḥadīth* (traditionists) whom he identifies with the Shāfiʿīs, Ḥanafīs, Mālikīs and Jabarīs; ii) the *ahl al-ra'y* (partisans of [personal] opinion) - the Muʿtazilīs and Zaydīs; and iii) the philosophers and mis-believers.[12] It consists of four books:

a) Introduction;
b) Refutation[13] of the *Ḥashwiyya*;
c) Refutation of the *ahl al-ra'y*;
d) Confutation of the philosophers.

Contrary to expectations, ʿAlī ibn al-Walīd does not dwell on what exactly the names of God mean, neither does he state what they mean according to his school of thought. He does not list them, nor does he indicate which sources were deemed reliable enough to select them. Indeed, the *Mukhtaṣar* focuses on what the names are not rather than on what they are, and the author seeks to prove that the only way to avoid error and to attain the true knowledge of their meanings is to address the one who truly understands them— that is to say the rightful *imām* descended from the prophet Muḥammad.

Book II in particular refutes the opinions held by the traditionists (*aṣḥāb al-ḥadīth*) identified with the *Ḥashwiyya*. It is divided into seven chapters:

Chapter 1: This group is said to be content with the mere exterior

---

9   Ibid., 79.
10 Ibid., and Poonawala, *Bibliography*, 159–60.
11 However, the expression *al-Asmā' al-Ḥusnā* (for which cf. e.g., Q. 7:179, 20:8, 59:24) never appears in it explicitly.
12 Here the author uses *mulḥidūn* (the misbelievers), *zanādiqa* (the dualists) and *muʿaṭṭilūn* (those who deny [the divine attributes and the Prophecy]).
13 Here the author uses both *radd* and *naqd*.

expressions of the Sacred Book and of religious Law. The author provides some examples of their belief, that he will address more specifically in the next chapters.[14]

Chapter 2: Confutation of the anthropomorphic interpretations of the Quran, and attribution of a meaning different from the literal one to the Holy Book. Such a meaning is said to be "a secret" known by the "men of understanding" (*ūlū 'l-albāb*). The author especially focuses on the refutation of the belief that God may have limbs.

Chapter 3: Negation of the attribution to God of free movement by denying the existence of transient states of pleasure and displeasure that are said to be caused in Him by the actions of men.

Chapter 4: Confutation of predestination, based on the divine attributes attested in the Quran such as power, knowledge, mercy, justice and nobility, which imply the existence of obedient and disobedient people.

Chapter 5: Rejection of the opponents' excuse that the verses implying coercion (*al-ijbār*) are more reliable than those which do not imply it because they are more numerous. The author also introduces the so-called *ḥadīth al-thaqalayn*, in which the Prophet defined his legacy by ordering to hold on two things in order not to go astray: the Quran and his family.

Chapter 6: Confutation of the thesis that the divine reward consists merely in eating, drinking and coupling.

Chapter 7: Negation of the belief that God needs guards and helpers to punish in hell those who deserve to be punished, and that He needs angels who write down the actions of men for judgement.

---

14 God has hands (c.f. Q 5:67; Q 39:67), He possesses a body supported by angels on whom His throne rests (c.f. Q 39:56; Q 89:22; Q 57:4, Q 7:52, Q 10:3; Q 25:60; Q 32:3; Q 69:17), He will be seen by believers on the Day of Judgment (c.f. Q 75:22), He is subject to alternate states of pleasure and displeasure depending on human behavior (c.f. Q 47:28; Q 4:93; Q 5:122; Q 9:101; Q 58:22; Q 98:8), He will reward the believers in the afterlife with pleasures that are similar to those experienced in life (c.f. Q 56:20–22; Q 47:16), He is helped by angels who compute every single action performed by mankind, both the good ones and the bad ones (c.f. Q 82:10).

2. The Text

The passage concerning the interpretation of Q 3:7 is found at pp. 98–113
of Ms 142. It is quoted here in Scotti's edition, with minor changes and—
for the sake of space—without critical apparatus.

فَعَيَّنَ تَعَ عَلَى أَهْلِ الِاسْتِنْبَاطِ [p. 99] أَنَّهُمْ أُولُو الْأَمْرِ وَقَالَ تَعَ: ﴿هُوَ الَّذِي أَنْزَلَ/
عَلَيْكَ الْكِتَابَ مِنْهُ آيَاتٌ مُحْكَمَاتٌ هُنَّ أُمُّ الْكِتَابِ وَأُخَرُ مُتَشَابِهَاتٌ فَأَمَّا الَّذِينَ فِي/ قُلُوبِهِمْ
زَيْغٌ فَيَتَّبِعُونَ مَا تَشَابَهَ مِنْهُ/ ابْتِغَاءَ الْفِتْنَةِ وَابْتِغَاءَ تَأْوِيلِهِ وَمَا يَعْلَمُ تَأْوِيلَهُ إِلَّا اللهُ/
وَالرَّاسِخُونَ فِي الْعِلْمِ يَقُولُونَ آمَنَّا بِهِ كُلٌّ/ مِنْ عِنْدِ رَبِّنَا وَمَا يَذَّكَّرُ إِلَّا أُولُو الْأَلْبَابِ﴾/.
فَعَيَّنَ اللهُ تَعَ وَنَصَّ عَلَى أَنَّ الرَّاسِخِينَ فِي/ الْعِلْمِ هُمْ عُلَمَاءُ التَّأْوِيلِ فَإِنَّ [هَذَا] كَابِرٌ
مُبَاهِتٌ [p. 100] وَقَالَ: ﴿لَا يَعْلَمُ إِلَّا اللهُ﴾ وَقَفَ ﴿وَالرَّاسِخُونَ﴾ فِي الْعِلْمِ﴾ مُبْتَدَأٌ
لَمْ يَعْلَمُوهُ وَلَكِنْ آمَنُوا بِهِ/ قِيلَ: كَيْفَ يَصِحُّ مِنْهُمُ الْإِيمَانُ بِمَا لَمْ يَعْلَمُوا/ وَالِاعْتِرَافُ بِمَا
جَهِلُوا؟ وَقَدْ قَالَ اللهُ تَعَ/ حِكَايَةً عَنْهُمْ: ﴿كُلٌّ مِنْ عِنْدَ رَبِّنَا﴾ فَاعْتَرَفُوا/ بِالتَّنْزِيلِ
وَالتَّأْوِيلِ بَعْدَ مَعْرِفَةٍ/ مِنْهُمْ بِهِمَا. وَالْإِيمَانُ هُوَ التَّصْدِيقُ/ وَشَهَادَتُهُمْ بِكَوْنِهِمَا مِنْ عِنْدِ اللهِ/
لَا يَصِحُّ إِلَّا بَعْدَ الْعِلْمِ بِهِمَا كَمَا حَكَى اللهُ تَعَ [p. 101] عَنْ إِخْوَةِ يُوسُفَ قَوْلَهُمْ: ﴿وَمَا
شَهِدْنَا إِلَّا/ بِمَا عَلِمْنَا﴾، وَقَوْلُهُ تَعَ: ﴿إِلَّا مَنْ شَهِدَ بِالْحَقِّ/ وَهُمْ يَعْلَمُونَ﴾، فَمَتَى لَمْ
يَصِحَّ لَهُمُ الْعِلْمُ بِهِمَا/ لَمْ تَصِحَّ شَهَادَتُهُمْ بِهِمَا/ إِنَّهُمَا مِنْ عِنْدَ/ اللهِ وَلَا إِيمَانُهُمْ بِمَا آمَنُوا
بِهِ إِذِ الْإِيمَانُ/ مَعْنَاهُ التَّصْدِيقُ كَمَا قَالَ اللهُ تَعَ سُبْحَانَهُ/ عَنْ إِخْوَةِ يُوسُفَ ع مَ فِي/ خِطَابِ
أَبِيهِمْ: ﴿وَمَا أَنْتَ بِمُؤْمِنٍ لَنَا وَلَوْ/ كُنَّا صَادِقِينَ﴾ أَيْ بِمُصَدِّقٍ. وَنَقُولُ [p. 102]¹⁵
أَيْضًا: لَا يَخْلُو أَنْ يَكُونَ النَّبِيُّ صلع عَالِمًا بِالتَّأْوِيلِ/ الَّذِي يَعْلَمُهُ اللهُ وَهُوَ تَأْوِيلُ مَا/ أَتَى
بِهِ مِنَ الْكِتَابِ الَّذِي آمَنَ بِهِ الرَّاسِخُونَ/ فِي الْعِلْمِ أَوْ غَيْرَ عَالِمٍ. فَإِنْ قَالُوا إِنَّهُ غَيْرُ/ عَالِمٍ
فَقَدْ عَظُمَتِ الْمُصِيبَةُ وَكَثُرَ الطَّعْنُ/ عَلَيْهِ، وَاتَّجَهَ أَنْ يَرْسَلَ إِلَى قَوْمٍ بِشَيْءٍ/ إِذَا سَأَلُوهُ عَنْ
مَعَانِيهِ الَّتِي هِيَ تَأْوِيلُهُ/ قَالَ: لَا أَعْلَمُ. وَلَوْ كَانَ مَلِكٌ بَشَرِيٌّ أَرْسَلَ/ رَسُولًا إِلَى بَعْضِ
مَمَالِكِهِ بِمَا¹⁶ لَا يَعْلَمُ [p. 103] مَعَانِي مَا أُمِرَ بِهِ لَاسْتَجْهَلَ الرَّسُولَ وَالْمُرْسِلَ/. فَمَا ظَنَنَّا
بِرَبِّ الْعَالَمِينَ وَرَسُولِهِ الَّذِي/ مَا هُوَ عَلَى الْغَيْبِ بِظَنِينٍ. وَإِنْ قَالُوا: بَلْ/ يَعْلَمُ ذَلِكَ لِمَا
رَدَّهُمْ إِلَيْهِ الِاضْطِرَارُ قُلْنَا: فَهُوَ صلع أَوَّلُ الرَّاسِخِينَ فِي الْعِلْمِ وَأَفْضَلُهُمْ/ وَانْتَقَضَ
تَعَلُّقُهُمْ بِالْوُقُوفِ عَلَى اللهِ/ تَعَ فِي عِلْمِ ذَلِكَ، وَانْهَدَمَتْ مَبَانِيهِمْ/. فَإِنْ قَالَ قَائِلُهُمْ إِنَّ أُولِي
الْأَمْرِ الْمَذْكُورِينَ/ فِي الْآيَةِ الْأُولَى وَالرَّاسِخِينَ فِي [p. 104] الْعِلْمِ الْمَذْكُورِينَ فِي هَذِهِ
الْآيَةِ هُمْ عُلَمَاءُ الْمُسْلِمِينَ،/ قُلْنَا لَهُمْ فَهَلْ عُلَمَاءُ أَهْلِ الْبَيْتِ مِمَّنْ/ تَعُمُّهُمُ الْآيَةُ؟ فَإِنْ

15 Unlike Scotti, I accept the reading of B, C, E, F. A has: فنقول [C.B.]
16 I propose to delete the word bi-mā that, according to Scotti's critical apparatus, is missing in F only [C.B.].

قَالُوا: لَيْسُوا مِنْهُمْ أَكْذَبَهُمْ/ كَوْنُ أَهْلِ الْبَيْتِ ع م مِنْ جُمْلَةِ/ الْمُسْلِمِينَ بَلْ أَفْضَلُهُمْ وَصَحَّ لِكُلِّ عَاقِلٍ/ ظُلْمُهُمْ لَهُمْ وَتَعَدِّيهِمْ عَلَيْهِمْ. فَإِنْ قَالُوا: نَعَمْ قُلْنَا: فَقَدْ صَحَّتْ دَعْوَانَا فِيهِمْ أَنَّهُمْ/ أُولِي الْأَمْرِ وَالرَّاسِخُونَ فِي الْعِلْمِ بِإِقْرَارِكُمْ/ لَهُمْ وَاعْتِرَافِكُمْ بِكَوْنِهِمْ أَهْلَ الْاسْتِنْبَاطِ وَالْعَالِمِينَ بِتَأْوِيلِ الْكِتَابِ. [p. 105] وَصَحَّ نَصُّ جَدِّهِمْ/ عَلَيْهِمْ بِالْإِقْرَانِ بِالْكِتَابِ وَبَطَلَتْ دَعْوَاكُمْ/ لِلْغَيْرِ مِنْ عُلَمَاءِ الْمُسْلِمِينَ بِإِنْكَارِنَا أَنْ يَكُونَ لَهُمْ/ مِنْ ذَلِكَ حَظٌّ فَهَاتُوا بُرْهَانَكُمْ إِنْ كُنْتُمْ صَادِقِينَ./ وَسِوَى هَذَا فَلَا يَخْلُو تَعَلُّقُهُمْ بِكَوْنِ أُولِي/ الْأَمْرِ وَالرَّاسِخِينَ فِي الْعِلْمِ هُمْ عُلَمَاءُ الْمُسْلِمِينَ/. إِنَّهُمْ يَعْنُونَ بِذَلِكَ الْخُلَفَاءَ عِنْدَهُمْ مِنَ الصَّحَابَةِ/ وَالْفُقَهَاءَ أَصْحَابَ الْفُتْوَى. فَإِنْ كَانُوا إِنَّمَا يَعْنُونَ/ الصَّحَابَةَ فَقَدْ ظَهَرَ مِنِ اخْتِلَافِهِمْ وَنَقْضِ [p. 106] قَوْلِهِمْ قَوْلَ بَعْضٍ مَا يَدُلُّ عَلَى فَسَادِ مَا فِي/ أَيْدِيهِمْ كَمَا اعْتَرَفَ عُمَرُ بْنُ خَطَّابٍ بِخَطَأِ/ أَبِي بَكْرٍ فِي قَوْلِهِ: «كَانَتْ بَيْعَةُ أَبِي بَكْرٍ فَلْتَةً/ وَقَى اللهُ شَرَّهَا فَمَنْ عَادَ إِلَى مِثْلِهَا فَاقْتُلُوهُ»/ وَقَوْلُ أَبِي بَكْرٍ: «وَلَيْتُكُمْ وَلَسْتُ بِخَيْرِكُمْ»،/ مُعْتَرِفاً بِكَوْنِ غَيْرِهِ أَعْلَمَ مِنْهُ إِذَا لَمْ/ يَتَفَاضَلَ النَّاسُ إِلَّا بِالْعِلْمِ، وَقَوْلُ عُمَرَ:/ «لَوْ لَا عَلِيٌّ لَهَلَكَ عُمَرُ»، اعْتِرَافاً مِنْهُ بِخُلُوِهِ/ مِنَ الْعِلْمِ، وَقَوْلُهُ عَلَى الْمِنْبَرِ: «لَا تَزِيدُوا فِي [p. 107] مُهُورِ النِّسَاءِ عَلَى أَرْبَعِينَ أُوقِيَّةً وَلَوْ إِنَّهَا/ ابْنَةُ ذِي الْفِضَّةِ». وَقَامَتِ امْرَأَةٌ مِنْ صُفُوفِ/ النِّسَاءِ فَقَالَتْ لَهُ: «يَا عُمَرُ تَمْنَعُنَا حَقّاً أَوْجَبَهُ/ اللهُ لَنَا. أَيْنَ أَنْتَ عَنْ قَوْلِ اللهِ تَعَ:/ ﴿وَإِنْ آتَيْتُمْ إِحْدَاهُنَّ قِنْطَاراً فَلَا تَأْخُذُوا/ مِنْهُ شَيْئاً﴾؟». فَقَالَ امْرَأَةٌ: «أَصَابَتْ وَأَخْطَأَ/ عُمَرُ»، وَغَيْرُ ذَلِكَ مِنِ اعْتِرَافِهِ وَإِقْرَارِهِ/ عَلَى نَفْسِهِ بِالْعَجْزِ وَالْجَهْلِ وَقِلَّةِ الْعِلْمِ. وَأَمَّا/ عُثْمَانُ فَكَفَى دَلِيلًا عَلَى جَهْلِهِ مَا حَمَلَ الْأُمَّةَ [p. 108] مِنْ قُبْحِ أَفْعَالِهِ عَلَى قَتْلِهِ. فَبَطَلَ كَوْنُ خُلَفَائِهِمْ/ عُلَمَاءَ. وَإِنْ كَانَ مَرَادُهُمْ بِالْعُلَمَاءِ فُقَهَاءَهُمْ/ فَقَدْ نُقِلَ عَنْهُمْ وَإِلَى الْآنَ مِنَ الْاخْتِلَافِ/ فِي الْقَضَايَا وَالْأَحْكَامِ وَتَفَرُّقِهِمْ فِي فَتَاوِي/ الْحَلَالِ وَالْحَرَامِ وَتَجْوِيزِهِمْ ذَلِكَ حَتَّى أَنَّهُ/ يَقُولُ قَائِلُهُمْ: اخْتِلَافُ الْعُلَمَاءِ رَحْمَةٌ. وَذَلِكَ/ يُنْتَقَضُ عِنْدَ مَنْ أَنْصَفَ نَفْسَهُ وَذَلِكَ أَنَّهُ/ لَا يَجُوزُ أَنْ يَكُونَ الشَّيْءُ الْوَاحِدُ حَلَالًا حَرَاماً فِي/ حَالَةٍ وَاحِدَةٍ عَلَى شَخْصٍ وَاحِدٍ. وَإِذَا [p. 109] أَحَلَّ أَحَدُهُمْ بِفَتْوَاهُ شَيْئاً وَحَرَّمَهُ غَيْرُهُ/ لَمْ يَخْلُ كَوْنُ أَحَدِهِمَا مُحِقّاً وَالْآخَرِ مُبْطِلًا/ لِامْتِنَاعِ كَوْنِ الشَّيْءِ الْوَاحِدِ حَلَالًا حَرَاماً/ فِي حَالَةٍ وَاحِدَةٍ. وَإِذَا ثَبَتَ مِنْهُمُ الْاخْتِلَافُ،/ وَبَطَلَ قَوْلُهُمْ بِاخْتِلَافِهِمْ،/ وَلَمْ يَكُنْ مَا تَنَازَعُوا/ فِيهِ وَأَفْتُوا بِهِ يَكُونُ أَحَدُهُمْ بِالْحَقِّ/ فِي قَوْلِهِ أَوْلَى مِنَ الْآخَرِ،/ بَطَلَ كَوْنُهُمْ عَالِمِينَ بِكَوْنِ عَلَامَةِ الْحَقِّ أَنْ لَا يَخْتَلِفَ فِيهِ/ أَهْلُ مَقَالَةٍ وَاحِدَةٍ. وَإِذَا ثَبَتَ اخْتِلَافُهُمْ [p. 110] بَطَلَ كَوْنُهُمْ عُلَمَاءَ. وَخَلَصَ الْعِلْمُ لِلْعَالِمِ الْأَفْضَلِ/ الَّذِي لَا يَتَنَازَعُ فِي دَعْوَاهُ وَلَا اخْتِلَافَ/ فِي فَتْوَاهُ. فَأَمَّا مَنْ لَا تَنَازُعَ فِي دَعْوَاهُ/ فَلِكَوْنِهِ مَنْصُوصاً عَلَيْهِ مِنْ رَسُولِ اللهِ/ صلع الْمَنْصُوصِ عَلَيْهِ مِنَ اللهِ سُبْحَانَهُ. وَأَمَّا مَنْ/ لَا اخْتِلَافَ فِي فَتْوَاهُ فَلِكَوْنِ مَا جَاءَ بِهِ/ هُوَ مِمَّا عَلَّمَهُ رَسُولُ اللهِ صلع لَا مِنْ آرَاءٍ/ مُبْتَدَعَةٍ وَلَا أَهْوَاءٍ مُتَّبَعَةٍ. وَذَلِكَ أَمِيرُ/ الْمُؤْمِنِينَ عَلِيٍّ ابْنِ أَبِي طَالِبٍ [p. 111] الْقَائِلِ: «عَلَّمَنِي رَسُولُ اللهِ صلع أَلْفَ بَابٍ مِنَ الْعِلْمِ انْفَتَحَ لِي مِنْ كُلِّ/ بَابٍ أَلْفُ بَابٍ». يَشْهَدُ بِذَلِكَ قَوْلُ رَسُولِ/ اللهِ

صلـع: «أنَـا مَدِينَـةُ الْعِلْـمِ وَعَلِـيٌّ/ بَابُهَـا/ فَمَـنْ أَرَادَ الْعِلْمَ فَلْيَـأْتِ الْبَـابَ»،/ وَهُوَ الْمَنْصُوصُ
عَلَيْـهِ بِقَـوْلِ النَّبِـيِّ صلـع: «عَلِـيٌّ أَقْضَاكُمْ وَلَا يَقْضِـي الْقَاضِـي إِلَّا بِالْعِلْـمِ/ وَلَا يَحْكُمُ إِلَّا بِمَـا
أَنْـزَلَ اللهُ». وَإِذَا كَانَ/ أَقْضَـى الْمُسْلِمِينَ ثَبِتَ أَنَّـهُ أَعْلَمُهُمْ. [p. 112] وَإِذَا كَانَ أَعْلَمَهُمْ بَطَـلَ
بِذَلِـكَ دَعْـوَى/ مَنْ ادَّعَى فِـي أُولِـي الْأَمْـرِ وَالرَّاسِـخِينَ/ فِـي الْعِلْـمِ أَنَّهُـمْ عُلَمَـاءُ الْمُسْلِمِينَ.
وَثَبِتَ/ ذَلِـكَ لَـهُ وَلِخُلَفَائِـهِ مِـنْ وَلْـدِهِ الْعِتْـرَةِ/ الْمُقْتَرِنَـةِ بِالْكِتَـابِ الْمُخَاطَبِينَ بِأُولِـي الْأَلْبَـابِ/
صلـع. وَلَـوْ لَا مَخَافَـةَ أَنْ يُقْطَـعَ مَـا/ أُورِدُهُ مَـا نَحَـوْتُ مِـنْ نَقْضِ مَقَالَـةِ الْحَشْـوِيَّةِ/ لَا وَرَدَتْ
مِـنْ إِثْبَـاتِ النَّـصِّ وَالْاحْتِجَـاجِ/ عَلَـى فَضْلِ أَمِيـرِ الْمُؤْمِنِينَ صلـع وَعَلَـى الْأَئِمَّـةِ [p. 113]
مِـنْ وَلْـدِهِ ع م وَكَوْنِهِـمْ الرَّاسِـخِينَ/ فِـي الْعِلْـمِ وَالْفَضْـلِ وَمَقَـرَّ الْإِمَامَـةِ وَوَارِثُ/ عِلْـمِ النُّبُـوَّةِ مَـا
يَدْمُـغُ أَيْسَـرُهُ حُجَّـةَ الْخَصْـمِ الْمُشَـاقِقِ/ وَيَتَّضِـحُ بِـهِ كَوْنُهُـمْ ع م صِفْـوَةَ أَهْـلِ/ الْمَغَـارِبِ
وَالْمَشَـارِقِ وَفِـي بَعْضِ مَـا أُورَدَتْـهُ/ الْحُـدُودُ قَـدَّسَ اللهُ أَرْوَاحَهُمْ/ مِـنْ ذَلِكَ غَنَـاءٌ وَمَقْنَـعٌ لِمَنْ
أَلْقَى السَّمْـعَ/ وَهُوَ شَهِيدٌ.

3. *Translation*

In the translation by Carmela Baffioni, the text is divided into paragraphs for the sake of clarity.

[a.] [God], be He exalted, has defined the people of exegesis [p. 99] as "those charged with authority," and He, may *He be exalted, said, He it is Who has sent down to thee the Book: in it are verses basic or fundamental (of established meaning); they are the foundation of the Book: others are allegorical. But those in whose hearts is perversity follow the part thereof that is allegorical, seeking discord, and searching for its hidden meanings, but no one knows its hidden meanings except Allah. And those who are firmly grounded in knowledge say: "We believe in the Book; the whole of it is from our Lord:" and none will grasp the Message except men of understanding.*[17]

---

17 Q 3:7, translation by Abdullah Yusuf Ali, *The Holy Quran* [Ware: Wordsworth 2000]. The reading, rejected by the majority of commentators, was accepted by Mujāhid ibn Jabr—one of the *tābi'ūn*, d. 722—and others. Cf. note 348 ad loc. [M.S.]. "Radical" interpretations of this verse similar to the one discussed in this article are provided by some modern commentators: Mir Ahmed Ali, for example, counts the Prophet Muḥammad as the first among the *rāsikhūna fī 'l-'ilm*, the others being *ahl al-bayt. The Holy*

Therefore God, be He exalted, defined and determined that *those who are firmly grounded in knowledge* are those who know the interpretation, and that is great and surprising.

[p. 100] [Adversaries claim:] He said, *no one knows except Allah,* full stop; *And those who are firmly grounded in knowledge*—[that is the] subject—do not know it, but believe in it.

[From us] It was asked, "How can faith in what they do not know, and acknowledgement of what they ignore, be right from them?" God, however, be He exalted, reported about them [that they said], "the whole of it is from our Lord," so they acknowledge both Revelation and interpretation after they have known both of them. Faith is trust, and their bearing witness that the two are from God would not be right unless after the knowledge of both, as God, be He exalted, told [p. 101] of Joseph's brothers, that they said, *We bear witness only to what we know,*[18] and [as] His saying, be He exalted, *only he who bears witness to the Truth and they know (him).*[19] So, when the knowledge of the two is not certain for them, their bearing witness of both—that they are from God—would not be right, neither their faith in what they believe [would be right] if the meaning of "faith" is "trusting," as God, be He exalted and praise Him, said of Joseph's brothers, upon them be peace, in the discourse to their father, *but thou wilt never believe us even though we tell the truth*"[20]—namely, [thou wilt never] trust [us as saying the truth].

[b.] And we say, [p. 102] too: either i) the Prophet, God bless him, knows the interpretation that God knows—namely the interpretation of the Book He brought and the well-grounded in knowledge believe in, or ii) he does not know [it].

Qur'an. English translation and commentary [Bahadurabad, Karachi: Peermahomed Ebrahim Trust [1977], 152–53. On the other hand, George Sale considers the *rāsikhūna* to be the *imāms. A comprehensive commentary of the Quran: comprising Sale's translation and preliminary discourse, with additional notes and emendations* [...] by [...] Elwood M. Wherry, 3 vols. [Allahabad India: R.S. Publishing House 20 Mahatma Gandhi Marg., 1979; 1st ed. 1882, repr. 1973], *ad loc.*) [C.B.].

18 Central part of Q 12:81.
19 Final part of Q 43:86.
20 Final part of Q 12:17.

i. If they said that He does not know [it], the disaster would be huge and his defamation great. [In this case, the Prophet] would have been oriented to bring to people something [about which], if they had asked him about its meanings—namely, its interpretation—he would have said, "I do not know." If a human king sent to one of his reigns a messenger, who does not know [p. 103] the meanings of what he was ordered [to bring], the messenger and the one who sent [him] would be deemed ignorant, but we [cannot] refer to the Lord of the worlds and to His Messenger something that is hidden to their views!

ii. If they said, "No, he knows that"—because of what necessity leads them to—we would say, "Then he, God bless him, is the first and the noblest of the well-grounded in knowledge." Their insistence in keeping the full stop at "God," be He exalted, with reference to the knowledge of that [i.e., of the interpretation] would be demolished, and their constructions would be destroyed.

[c.] And if one of them said that "those charged with authority" mentioned in the first verse and "the well-grounded in [p. 104] knowledge" mentioned in this verse are the learned among Muslims, we would ask them: "Are the learned ones of the people of the house among those comprised in the verse?"

[c_1.] If they said, "No," the fact that the people of the house, upon them be peace, are among the Muslims, rather, are the noblest of them, would demonstrate their lie, and their iniquity towards them would be certain for every intelligent person, as well as their attack against them.

If they said "Yes," we would state: "Then our claim about them, that they are 'those charged with authority' and 'the well-grounded in knowledge' is right according to your [own] admission from them, and you have to acknowledge that they are the people of exegesis [p. 105] and those who know the interpretation of the Book."

The determination of them in connection with the Book—from the part of their ancestor—is right, whereas it is false your claim concerning any other learned among the Muslims, beyond our denying that they have part in that, so give your demonstration if you are sincere!

[c_2.] In addition to that, there is their insistence in [maintaining] that "those charged with authority" and "the well-grounded in knowledge" are the learned among Muslims. They mean by that the caliphs—

according to them among the Companions—and the jurists, the authors of the *fatwā*.

If they mean the "Companions," from their discrepancy and the contradiction [p. 106] of their speech it becomes obvious the speech of he who indicates the corruption of what was in front of them [= the Companions]. For instance, 'Umar ibn Khaṭṭāb acknowledged the mistake of [the election of] Abū Bakr in his saying, "the *bay'a* to Abū Bakr was unexpected, may God protect from its injustice, and the one who came back to something like this, kill him!" Abū Bakr's saying "If only you [recognized that] I am not the best among you," recognizing that there was someone else more learned than him, as people did not vie but for knowledge. 'Umar's speech, "If 'Alī had not been there, 'Umar would have been ruined,'" as a recognition from him of his being devoid of knowledge. His speech from the *minbar* "Do not increase [p. 107] the women's dowries over forty ounces, even if they were the daughters of one who owns [lots of] argent." A woman stood up from the women's rows and said to him: "O 'Umar, you hinder from us a right God imposed for us. Where are you in relation to God's speech, be He exalted, *even if ye had given the latter a whole treasure for dower, take not the least bit of it back?*"[21] And [another] woman said: "She is right, and 'Umar is mistaken." And other [tales] about his recognition and his acknowledgment with regard to himself, of imperfection, ignorance and poor science. As to 'Uthmān, it is enough, as an indication of his ignorance, what led the community [p. 108] to kill him for his bad acts. Then, it is false that their caliphs were learned people.

And if their intention were [to claim that] the learned are their jurists, discrepancy in verdicts and judgments has been transmitted about them and up to now, as well as their fragmentation in sentences about [what is] permitted and [what is] prohibited, and their approval of that, at the point that one of them says: "The discrepancy of learned is a mercy."[22] That [hypothesis] collapses in the one who has a right soul, because it is not possible that the same thing is permitted [and] prohibited in the same

21 Central part of Q 4:20.
22 Cf. Jalāl al-Dīn al-Suyūṭī, *Al-Jāmi' al-ṣaghīr*, 3,22; al-Nawāwī, *Fayḍ al-qadīr*, 2,15; al-'Ajlūnī, *Kashf al-khafā'*, 4.5.

condition for the same individual. Since [p. 109] one of them, through his sentence, permits one thing and another one prohibits it, one of them has necessarily to tell the truth and the other the false, as it is impossible that the same thing is [both] permitted [and] prohibited in the same condition. As discrepancy subsists from them and their speech is false because of their discrepancy, and [as] it [cannot] happen—when they contend and sentence about something—that one of them in his affirmation is more probably in truth than the other, it is false that they are learned, since the token of truth is that those who assert the same thing have no discrepancy in it. As their discrepancy subsists, [p. 110] it is false that they are learned.

Science belongs to the noblest scholar who does not contend in his claim and in whose sentence there is no discrepancy. As to he who does not contend in his claim, [he is so] because he was appointed by God's Messenger, God bless him, who [on his turn] was appointed by God, praise Him. As to Him in whose sentence there is no discrepancy, [he is so] because what he brought belongs to what God's Messenger taught, God bless him, not to innovative opinions or later fancies! That is what the Commander of the believers, 'Alī ibn Abī Ṭālib, may God's blessings [p. 111] be upon him, said: "God's Messenger, God bless him, showed me a thousand doors of science, from every one of which a thousand doors were opened for me."[23] The speech of God's Messenger, God bless him, testifies that "I am the city of science and 'Alī is its door, whoever wants science shall he cross the door."[24] He is the appointed by the

---

23 See al-Muttaqī al-Hindī, *Kanz al-'ummāl*, vol. 6, 392 [M.S.].

24 This is the so-called "*ḥadīth* of Medina," which has been narrated in both Shī'ī and Sunnī sources by companions reporting directly from the Prophet Muḥammad, e.g., 'Alī, his eldest son Ḥasan, Jābir ibn 'Abd Allāh al-Anṣārī, 'Abd Allāh ibn 'Abbās and 'Abd Allāh ibn 'Umar ibn al-Khaṭṭāb. See al-Ḥākim al-Nīshābūrī, *Al-Mustadrak 'alā al-ṣaḥīḥayni*, vol. 3, 126–27; al-Khaṭīb al-Baghdādī, *Ta'rīkh Baghdādī*, vol. 2, 377; vol. 4, 348; vol. 7, 172; vol. 11, 48–50; al-Dhahabī, *Tadhkīra al-ḥuffāẓ*, vol. 4, 28; al-Haythamī, *Majma' al-zawā'id*, vol. 9, 114; Ibn Ḥajar Aḥmad al-'Asqalānī, *Tahdhīb al-tahdhīb*, vol. 6, 320; vol. 7, 337; al-Muttaqī al-Hindī, *Kanz al-'ummāl*, vol. 6, 152, 156, 401. This content is similar to another *ḥadīth* in which the Prophet is declared to be "the house of wisdom," whereas 'Alī is "its gate" [M.S.].

Prophet's saying, God bless him, "'Alī is meant to judge you, and a judge does not judge but on the basis of science, and he does not deliver a verdict but through what God revealed."

As he was the one who judged the Muslims, it was established him to be [also] the most learned of them. [p. 112] And as [he] was the most learned of them, for that [reason] the claim of he who claims that "those charged with authority" and "the firmly grounded in knowledge" are the learned among Muslims is false. That was established for him and for his successors from his progeny, [namely,] the family associated with the Book, addressed by [the appellation of] "men of understanding,"[25] God bless them.

If it had not been for the fear of cutting what I am adducing, I would not have ceased to contest the thesis of the *Ḥashwiyya*, who—from the assertion of the text and the objection against the nobility of the Commander of the believers, God bless him, and of the *imām*s [p. 113] from his progeny, upon them be peace, and [against the fact that] they are "the well-grounded in knowledge," the nobility and the abode of the Imāmate, and the heir of the science of prophecy—do not [succeed in] providing that, the smallest part of which marks the proof of the opposing enemy.

It is made clear by that that they are, upon them be peace, the cream of the people of the West and the East. In part of what the [Ismā'īlī] hierarchies, may God sanctify their spirits, have adduced about that [there is] wealth and sufficiency for the one who lent his ear and is a witness.

4. Commentary

Chapter 5 begins with the confutation of the idea that one part of the Holy Book is true and another part is false. This may be linked to the idea, widespread in the various Shī'ī currents, that after the Prophet's death the Quran underwent changes, cuts and perhaps even additions from the part of his enemies, in particular Abū Bakr and 'Umar who

---

25 Cf. Q 2:179, 197, 269; 3:7, 190; 5:100; 12:111; 13:19; 14:52; 38:29 and 43; 39:9, 18, 21; 40:54; 65:10 [M.S.].

aimed at excluding 'Alī from the succession.[26] The author subsequently clarifies the nature of the wisdom to which the Holy Scripture is connected. The explanation is rooted in the inner meaning of the Holy Book: wisdom does not coincide with the *sharī'a* because the exoteric part of the Holy Book implies different opinions and prescriptions that need to be interpreted by those empowered to explain—the people of exegesis—to make sense.

At this point, the author asks who the "people of exegesis" are. The text can be divided into three parts.

In the first, the "people of exegesis" are identified with "those charged with authority" mentioned in Q 4:83. Then, citing Q 3:7, Ibn al-Walīd infers that those who are well grounded in knowledge are those able to find out meaning. We must suppose that the next phrase is pronounced by Ibn al-Walīd's adversaries, who adhered to the "traditional" reading of the verse. If a full stop after "Allah" is postulated, the "well-grounded in knowledge" would not know, but only believe. The author asks how one can believe in and acknowledge something without having known it. Several Quranic verses support the notion that Revelation and interpretation go together: having known them, the *rāsikhūna fī 'l-'ilm* [the "firmly grounded in science"] vest them in God.

The second part establishes that the Prophet knew the interpretation of the Book, and hence is the first of the *rāsikhūna fī 'l-'ilm*. This also contradicts the traditional reading of Q 3:7.

The third part denies that "those charged with authority" and "the well-grounded in knowledge" are the learned Muslims. The first step is to establish that the family of the Prophet is part of the Muslim community. If it is so, they—the noblest—have also to be counted among the learned Muslims. Ibn al-Walīd suggests that they are the only people rightly connected with the Holy Book. The other learned

26 Cf. Mohammad Ali Amir-Moezzi, *The Silent Qur'an and the Speaking Qur'an. Scriptural Sources of Islam Between History and Fervor* [New York: Columbia University Press, 2015]. Original ed.: *Le Coran silencieux, le Coran parlant – Sources scripturaires de l'islam entre histoire et ferveur* [Paris: CNRS Editions, 2011].

men do not deserve these titles: neither caliphs, because they acknowledge their ignorance, nor jurists, because of their mutual contradictions. Science belongs to the man in whom there is no uncertainty or error—the *imām*, appointed by the Prophet, who was in turn appointed by God.

The text quotes Traditions typical of the esoteric theoretical vision of the *Shīʿa*, which have the function of opposing *imām* ʿAlī to *bidʿa* arguments and to personal interpretation.

Later, ʿAlī is identified as "the judge" because legitimate judgement is based on the knowledge revealed by God. The titles "those charged with authority" and "the firmly grounded in knowledge" are accorded only to him and his progeny. ʿAlī kept for his family and intimate followers the true and complete Word of God, which only enables the full comprehension of the Holy Book and the correct behavior according to its proper interpretation.

Quran 3:7 is widely discussed in Islamic literature. It is considered here from the perspective of Islamic philosophy, a field in which the best known "non-canonical reading" of Quran 3:7 is provided by the Andalusian philosopher Averroes (d. 1198) in his *Faṣl al-maqāl—The Decisive Treatise*. His claim that the *rāsikhūna fī ʾl-ʿilm*, like God, knew the inner interpretation of the Holy Book—its hidden meaning—is his way to legitimize *taʾwīl* in the opinion of philosophers, and hence legitimizing philosophy in Islam against Abū Ḥāmid al-Ghazālī's charge of *kufr* ["unbelief"].

This reasoning is weakened by a *petitio principii*: Averroes expounds his theory of philosophical *taʾwīl* on the basis of his philosophical *taʾwīl* of a Quranic verse. Subsequently, he even claims that those who can perform *taʾwīl* have a different kind of faith from those who are unable to do so: this is the meaning of the second part of the verse. On the one hand, his solution clearly contradicts the letter of the Holy Book, which excludes any similarity between God and humankind. On the other hand, his pretensions with regard to the quality of faith appear unfounded in the light of the Quranic text.

I have elsewhere hypothesized that Averroes's source for this interpretation was the Ikhwān al-Ṣafāʾ, whose encyclopaedia was known in

Spain.[27] This is proved by the fact that Averroes and the Ikhwān quote the same *ḥadīths*.[28]

The Ikhwānian argument is stronger than that of Averroes, however, because the *rāsikhūna fī 'l- 'ilm* are for them the *imāms* as a consequence of their Shī'ī/Ismā'īlī perspective, which establishes the existence of a *ẓāhir* (exoteric meaning) and a *bāṭin* (esoteric meaning) in the Holy Book and considers *imāms* to inherit the knowledge of the *bāṭin*.

Ibn al-Walīd's interpretation is also grounded on the existence of an

27 It is not possible to address the question in detail here. Recent studies, however – on the line of the seminal article by Maribel Fierro, "Batinism in al-Andalus. Maslama b. Qāsim al-Qūrṭubī (d. 353/964), author of the Rutbat al-ḥakīm and the Ghāyat al-ḥakīm (Picatrix)", Studia Islamica, 84 (1996): 87–110 – ascertain that the personnage who introduced the encyclopedia in al-Andalus was Maslama al-Qūrṭubī (d. 964), previously confused with the scientist Maslama al-Majrīṭī (d. 1007). Cf. Godefroid de Callataÿ, "Rasā'il Ijwān al-Ṣafā', Rutbat al-ḥakīm y Gāyat al-ḥakīm (Picatrix)", *Al-Qanṭara* 34 (2013): 297–344; Mourad Kacimi, "Estudio de la introducción de la Rubat al-hakín. Análisis de su relación con le Rasa'il de los Ijwan al-Safa", *Revista del Instituto Egipcio de Estudios Islámicos*, 42 (2014): 13–46; Godefroid de Callataÿ - Sébastien Moureau, "Towards the Critical Edition of the Rutbat al-ḥakīm: A Few Preliminary Observations", *Arabica*, 62 (2015): 385–394. This discover anticipates the timing of the Rasā'il several decades at least. The similarities between Maslama al-Qūrṭubī's Rutbat al-ḥakīm and Ghāyat al-ḥakīm – now both reported to the first half of the tenth century – and the encyclopaedia lead to hypothesise Maslama to be one of the authors of the epistles, as firstly demonstrated by Paola Carusi, "Le traité alchimique Rutbat al-Ḥakīm: quelques notes sur son introduction", appendix to "Alchimia islamica e religione: la legittimazione difficile di una scienza della natura", in Carmela Baffioni, ed., *Religion versus Science in Islam: a Medieval and Modern Debate*, monographical issue of *Oriente Moderno*, N.S. 19 (2000): 491–502.

28 Cf. Carmela Baffioni, *Appunti per un'epistemologia profetica. L'Epistola degli Iḥwān al-Ṣafā' "Sulle cause e gli effetti"* [Napoli: Università degli Studi di Napoli "L'Orientale" (Dipartimento di Studi e Ricerche su Africa e Paesi Arabi) and Guida, 2006], 164–65 and "Antecedenti "orientali" per la legittimazione del *ta'wīl* dei filosofi in Averroè?", in Anna Maria Di Tolla, ed., *Studi Berberi e Mediterranei. Miscellanea offerta in onore di Luigi Serra*, monographic issue of *Studi maghrebini*, N.S. 4 (2006): 131–39.

esoteric content of the Holy Book, but he goes further than the Ikhwān al-Ṣafāʾ in that he claims that faith, far from being foreign to knowledge, is brought about by knowledge.

Unlike the Ikhwān, Ibn al-Walīd relies on knowledge that his school considered historical. His pointed opposition even to the well-guided caliphs rests on the most radical Ismāʿīlī tradition.

In the last part of the text ʿAlī is again made both a *dāʿī* and a *qāḍī*, in accordance with the Fāṭimid tradition. Because of the knowledge he displays in both functions, the author infers that knowledge and guide belong to him. On the one hand this implies that only the "people of the house" are entitled to *taʾwīl*; on the other Ibn al-Walīd legitimizes the political role of the Prophet's family, and in doing so he identifies the highest knowledge with practical rather than theoretical science.

Averroes and Medieval Rationalism:
Toward Religious Pluralism of the Modern Era
John R. Pottenger

The evolution toward and solidification of symbiotic church-state relations during the medieval era contributed to the eventual rise of the
Christian commonwealth in Latin Europe. The question of religion's role
in society generally evolved toward a solution consisting of an intricate
relationship between Christianity and diverse political regimes. Toward
the end of the era, at least in some commonwealths, the interests of
church and state were further intertwined in complex arrangements regarding science, philosophy, and religion.

By the late Middle Ages the complex and intricate interplay between
arguments addressing theoretical principles and practical problems of natural philosophy and theology—particularly the descriptive and predictive
anomalies in the former and their implications for philosophical challenges
to the latter—would have unintended but profound consequences for the
emergence of the modern era. Select themes debated in the twelfth-century
Renaissance may be identified as traces of arguments that contributed to
the intellectual support for modern religious pluralism. Crucial among
these themes is the centrality of Averroes's rationalism in debates and disputations regarding the relationship between reason and faith, particularly
when perceived as favoring the prominence of philosophy over religion
in the search for knowledge; the examination of nature to understand revealed truths; and the eminence of final causes once identified.

Renaissance of the Twelfth Century

During the Renaissance of the twelfth century, scientific thinking on the
Iberian Peninsula initiated with the rationalism of Muslim and Jewish

scholars, who wrestled with philosophical questions of such intellectual import that their arguments directly influenced the thinking of Christian theologians in the Latin West. Modern scholars on the philosophy and history of science have often directed attention to the early Renaissance as a pivotal point in the West's evolution from Aristotelian physics to Newtonian mechanics as the epistemological basis of modern science in the seventeenth century. Herbert Butterfield maintains that "a particular development of ideas which was already taking place in the later middle ages has come to stand as the first chapter in the history of the transition to what we call the scientific revolution."[1] Butterfield describes this chapter as focusing on challenges to the "theory of impetus," wherein Aristotle's received beliefs regarding the cause of an object's motion were challenged. An alternative explanation began to take shape that would ultimately shift scientific conjectures away from the view that objects in motion seek their natural state to alternative considerations of motion explained by the interaction of externally applied force and the phenomenon of friction—that is, a shift away from an emphasis on both efficient and final causes to an emphasis on efficient causes alone.

Similarly, Richard Fletcher asserts that Arabic philosophers in Andalusia in southern Spain "played a significant role in the formation of the Old World's civilization," especially with regard to mathematics, navigational devices, and medical science.[2] In fact, says, Fletcher, "the rediscovery of Aristotle's works by this route decisively changed the European mind ... [and contributed to] the shaping of European intellectual culture." He refers to the route of the transmission of Aristotle's translated works and commentaries carried by Arabs in the Middle East, across North Africa to Sicily but primarily across the Strait of Gibraltar to Spain. Arab scholars' adaptation of ancient Greek texts of philosophy and medicine, among others, also contributed to the texts' preservation. The preservation of Aristotle's *Organon* saved his speculations on the

1   Herbert Butterfield, *The Origins of Modern Science: 1300–1800*, rev. ed. (New York: Free Press, 1957), 14.
2   Richard Fletcher, *Moorish Spain* (Berkeley: University of California Press, 1992), 8.

nature of logical argumentation that would later benefit Islamic, as well as Jewish and Christian, theological development. Charles Homer Haskins states, "From Spain came the philosophy and natural science of Aristotle and his Arabic commentators in the form which was to transform European thought in the thirteenth century."[3] Indeed, George Sarton also argues that out of Spain was built "a kind of bridge between East and West."[4] The result of this intellectual bridge was a synthesis of Arabic and Latin ideas in which "the Arabic writers led scientific thought for about three centuries (ninth to eleventh) and remained exceedingly influential for at least two more centuries (twelfth and thirteenth)."

Basit B. Koshul further argues that this bridge between the Arabic world and the Latin West was a necessary condition for the emergence of modern science in the fifteenth century. As a result of the medieval era's influence on modernity, according to Koshul, the "primacy of reason, logic, and the scientific method are the defining characteristics of the western intellectual tradition from the Renaissance to the present."[5] The bridge began to be built in earnest when, shortly after the *reconquista* of southern Spain from the Almoravid dynasty in late eleventh century, Latin scholars, such as Gerard of Cremona, Dominic Gundissalinus, and Michael Scotus, travelled to Spain; discovered Arabic texts of Avicenna, Averroes, and other Arabic thinkers; learned Arabic; and translated these texts for scholars in the West. As a result, according to Susan Wise Bauer, "a wall between the past and the present had been broken down, and more and more thinkers would step over the rubble into a new way of thinking."[6] Thus, to recognize the intellectual

---

3   Charles Homer Haskins, *The Renaissance of the Twelfth Century* (New York: Meridian Books, 1957), 289.

4   George Sarton, *The Appreciation of Ancient and Medieval Science During the Renaissance (1450–1600)* (Philadelphia: University of Pennsylvania Press, 1955), 172.

5   Basit B. Koshul, "The Islamic Impact on Western Civilization Reconsidered," *American Journal of Islamic Social Sciences* 12, no. 1 (Spring 1995): 36.

6   Susan Wise Bauer, *The History of the Renaissance of the World: From the Rediscovery of Aristotle to the Conquest of Constantinople* (New York: W.W. Norton, 2015), 47.

presuppositions of the medieval era's legacy of the new way of thinking, a careful examination of the "organic link" is warranted, says Koshul, between ancient Greek thought and Christian theology: the Islamic intellectual tradition.[7]

The Islamic Intellectual Tradition

Examination of the organic link of the Islamic intellectual tradition that formed the bridge between ancient Greek thought and Christian theology reveals that the link encountered both resistance and acceptance. John Hedley Brooke maintains that "the introduction of the Aristotelian corpus into medieval Christendom" via Muslim commentaries engendered fresh and provocative explanations of Christian beliefs.[8] For many who resisted the influence of the Islamic tradition, the inclusion of Aristotelian natural philosophy appeared to be at odds with generally received Christian teachings, including that of the eternal nature and independence of the universe, which rejected any contingency status with respect to God. According to Brooke, "As interpreted by the twelfth-century Muslim commentator Averroes, it even denied the freedom of the will. It could also be construed as a naturalist rival to supernatural religion, in that it presented the world as a closed system in which the deity was little more than a physical hypothesis to explain motion or change."[9] Nevertheless, for others, the investigation of logical argumentation in the writings of Arabic and Muslim philosopher Averroes of Córdoba occupied the core of the Renaissance's contribution to the primary function of rationalism in the evolution of modern science, especially as it blended with modern political thinking regarding secularism and religion.

Indeed, Kashif S. Ahmed notes that Averroes has often been referred to as "the founding father of secular thought in Western Europe."[10] More

7   Koshul, "Islamic Impact," 37.
8   John Hedley Brooke, *Science and Religion: Some Historical Perspectives* (Cambridge: Cambridge University Press, 1991), 60.
9   Ibid.
10   Kashif S. Ahmed, "Arabic Medicine: Contributions and Influence," in *Proceedings of the 17th Annual History of Medicine Days*, eds. Melanie Sta-

to the point, Fauzi M. Najjar states that Averroes, "the great commentator on, and interpreter of, Aristotelian philosophy, is regarded by liberal-secular Arab intellectuals, as well as by some Europeans, as one of the key figures in the development of the European Enlightenment."[11] According to Najjar, the evidence supporting this claim can be found in select writings of Averroes, where, "As the great commentator on Aristotelianism, he stresses the use of reason and the scientific method."[12]

In fact, during the Enlightenment itself, the impact of Averroes's philosophical thought in the form of Latin Averroism was both energetically promulgated and assailed by intellectual partisans. For example, according to Marco Sgarbi, Averroist tendencies were present in the German Enlightenment of the eighteenth century, although not to the extent as those found in Italy: "Philosophers were strongly influenced by religious topics and, as a result, Aristotle and the Aristotelian tradition (including Averroism) became the favorite targets of philosophical criticism. Aristotelians and Averroists were portrayed as typical products of intellectual hubris, in no need of religious revelation and confident in the power of 'unaided' reason."[13] Johann Gottfried Herder, for one, criticized Immanuel Kant's moral philosophy "as a form of Averroism."[14] With regard to the immortality of the human soul and unicity of the intellect, Herder refused to accept the identity of the passive agent intellect with the external active agent or universal intellect, which he claimed was argued by Kant.

Whether or not the Averroists of later centuries accurately interpreted the arguments of Averroes has itself been actively debated. The

pleton, Jennifer Lewis, and Frank W. Stahnisch (Calgary: Faculty of Medicine, University of Calgary, 2008), 155.

11 Fauzi M. Najjar, "Ibn Rushd (Averroes) and the Egyptian Enlightenment Movement," *British Journal of Middle Eastern Studies* 31, no. 2 (November 2004): 202.

12 Ibid., 206.

13 Marco Sgarbi, "Immanuel Kant, Universal Understanding, and the Meaning of Averroism in the German Enlightenment," in *Renaissance Averroism and Its Aftermath: Arabic Philosophy in Early Modern Europe*, eds. Anna Akasoy and Guido Giglioni (New York: Springer, 2013), 259.

14 Ibid., 256.

diversity of contrary assessments from Aquinas to modern scholars, says Anna Akasoy, "leaves [open] the question whether or not the Averroists interpreted the Arab philosopher correctly and to what extent their thought was independent. Referring to 'Latin Averroism' is a way of alluding to the possibility of an independent Latin development."[15] Indeed, not all scholars and commentators on Averroes' philosophy find a direct and influential link between Averroes's writings and the emergence of the Enlightenment.

The purported intellectual link between Averroes's arguments and the defense of secularism's failure to protect the role of religion in civil society prevents Charles E. Butterworth from endorsing the claims of contemporary thinkers who perceive Averroes as an intellectual precursor to the European Enlightenment. Butterworth's primary concern is that "for the Enlightenment as a whole, religion held no meaning"; and, thus, since Averroes's writings on philosophy and religion in fact affirm the role and importance of religion in society, he ought not to be venerated as a precursor to the Enlightenment with its antagonism toward religion.[16] According to Butterworth, "Averroës strives to defend and clarify the prophetic enterprise while carving out a place for philosophical investigation."[17] And, as Butterworth asserts, "If anything, serious study of Averroës should lead to further probing of how reason and revelation are related and, even more, how that relationship can find expression in political life—expression that preserves freedom while providing for true human happiness."[18]

Scholars have in fact engaged in Butterworth's reference to "the serious study of Averroës … [for] further probing of how reason and revelation are related," including investigation of the impact of that relationship on the modern era. While noting the necessary role played

---

15 Anna Akasoy, "Was Ibn Rushd an Averroist? The Problem, the Debate, and Its Philosophical Implications," in *Renaissance Averroism and Its Aftermath: Arabic Philosophy in Early Modern Europe*, eds. Anna Akasoy and Guido Giglioni (New York: Springer, 2013), 324.

16 Charles E. Butterworth, "Averroës, Precursor of the Enlightenment?," *Alif: Journal of Comparative Poetics*, no. 16 (1996): 7.

17 Ibid., 13.

18 Ibid., 15.

by the rationalism that precipitated the Scientific Revolution of the seventeenth century, Etienne Gilson, for one, asserts, "The fact remains, however, that there has been another rationalism, much older than that of the Renaissance [of the fourteenth century], and wholly unrelated to any scientific discovery. It was a purely philosophical rationalism, born in Spain, in the mind of an Arabian philosopher [Averroës], as a conscious reaction against the theologism of Arabian divines."[19] In effect, Gilson suggests that—out of parameters of ancient Greek natural philosophy—"another rationalism" emerged and left metatheoretical traces that eventually contributed to the development of the modern era and in turn the modern approach to understanding the acceptable place of religion in civil society and its expression in political life.

Averroes's Rationalism and Religion

Gilson maintains that al-Ghazali—"the greatest theologian in Islam"— in his *The Incoherence of the Philosophers* had refuted the claims of Avicenna, whose philosophical arguments, al-Ghazali believed, had diverged from the teachings of the Qur'an. While not in complete agreement with Avicenna's arguments, Gilson explains, Averroes set out in *The Incoherence of the Incoherence* to contest al-Ghazali's denigration of philosophy and adapted arguments from Aristotle's logical reasoning to do so. According to Gilson's celebratory affirmation of Averroes' rationalism, "To Averroës, the absolute truth was not to be found in any sort of Revelation, but in the writings of Aristotle, which he never tired of commenting on and annotating. When Aristotle had said something, reason itself had spoken, and there was nothing more to say about it."[20] Indeed, in the development of his own rationalism, Averroes commented on and often invoked Aristotle's rules of inference for standard form syllogisms. These syllogisms were primarily discussed in Aristotle's *Propositions*, *Prior Analytics*, *Posterior Analytics*, and *Topics* and provided Aristotle with the rational structure for demonstrating knowledge of

19 Etienne Gilson, *Reason and Revelation in the Middle Ages* (New York: Charles Scribner's Sons, 1952), 37.
20 Ibid., 39–40.

something: "By 'a demonstration' I mean a scientific syllogism, and by 'a scientific syllogism' I mean a syllogism in virtue of which, by possessing [principles], we know [something]. . . . Now there may be a syllogism even without these, but such syllogism will not be a demonstration, for it will not produce *knowledge*." (*Prior Analytics*, 71b18–25)[21] Moreover, of the different methods of inferential reasoning, Aristotle preferred as superior the logical validity of demonstrative over dialectical reasoning: "It is also evident that, if the premises from which the [demonstrative] syllogism proceeds are universal, also the conclusion of such a demonstration and, we may add, of an unqualified demonstration is of necessity eternal." (*Prior Analytics*, 75b21–23) In contrast, he maintained that the logical validity of a dialectical syllogism "reasons from generally accepted opinions as premises. ... Generally accepted opinions are opinions which are accepted by all people, or by most, or by the wise, and if by the wise, then by all of them, or by most, or by those who are most known and held in esteem." (*Topics*, 100a30–100b23) The difficulty here, asserts Aristotle, is that the premises of dialectical syllogisms tend to be based on public opinion of uncertain soundness, which are of inferior quality to the veridical quality of the premises of demonstrative syllogisms. Only demonstrative syllogisms yield apodictic conclusions that are derived from the veracity of "each principle in virtue of that principle itself." (*Topics*, 100b21)

Aristotle's understanding of the superior validity and certain soundness of demonstrative logic was employed by Averroes in support of his own development of philosophical rationalism. In the *Decisive Treatise* he too argues that if philosophic understanding is to occur, "dialectical, rhetorical, and sophistical syllogistic reasoning" will not be as useful as "demonstrative syllogistic reasoning."[22] Only the conclusions of demonstrative syllogistic reasoning can precisely infer from received truths, says Averroes. However, dialectical, rhetorical, or sophistical syllogistic

---

21 Quotations (with original emphases) from Aristotle's *Organon* are found in *Aristotle: Selected Works*, trans. Hippocrates G. Apostle and Lloyd P. Gerson (Grinnell, Iowa: The Peripatetic Press, 1983).

22 Averroes, *Decisive Treatise* in *Decisive Treatise and Epistle Dedicatory*, trans. Charles E. Butterworth (Provo, Utah: Brigham Young University Press, 2002), 3.

reasoning relies on claims that are presumed to be authoritatively true, whether about religion or other matters, and then uses specious means to convince others of the veracity of the claims; these specious means may consist of appeals to emotional considerations as well as use subjectively-based, inductive analyses. Alternatively, stipulates Averroes, syllogistic demonstrations rely on initially given premises and then deduce conclusions that logically follow from them. In this way, subjectivity—which limits the flawed approaches to a particular religious or other worldview—is removed, freeing inquirers to use demonstrative reasoning to defend received universal truths. Thus, as with Aristotle, demonstrative syllogistic reasoning "fulfills the conditions for validity," regardless of the provenance of the argument itself.

Averroes refers to demonstrative syllogistic reasoning as a "science of interpretation" and likens it to the methodological rigor of the technique or art employed by mathematics, which builds deductively on the insights of previous arguments and their conclusions: "It is evident, moreover, that this goal is completed for us with respect to existing things only when they are investigated successively by one person after another and when, in doing so, the one coming after makes use of the one having preceded—along the lines of what occurs in the mathematical sciences."[23] Indeed, Averroes further argues that, similar to the logical investigations of the arts of mathematics, geometry, and astronomy, which require individuals to rely on previous conclusions of others to arrive at new insights, no single individual can fully grasp the art of wisdom, which itself fully encompasses all other arts.[24] Thus, he asserts, relying on the insights of demonstrative arguments of predecessors regardless of their "national" origins is not only rationally acceptable but logically necessary. The result of Averroes's "science of interpretation" is that any conclusion of demonstrative syllogistic reasoning "is only of the truth."[25]

While Averroes believed that there was no conflict between the truths of religion and philosophy, the implication of his application of

23 Ibid., 5.
24 Ibid., 6.
25 Ibid., 13.

demonstrative rationalism to religious arguments suggests that if a conflict arises between conclusions of philosophical rationalism and promulgated religious doctrines based on non-demonstrative interpretations of scripture, the outcome would simply but cataclysmically reveal the errant teachings of the latter. In this vein, in his treatise *An Exposition of the Methods of Arguments Concerning the Beliefs of the Faith, and a Determination of Uncertain Doubts and Misleading Innovations in Interpretations,* Averroes challenges the Ashari sect's attempt to use select theological positions to argue about the nature of essences, parts and wholes, and related topics of material existence to prove the existence of God. However, given the diverse hypotheses regarding essences, Averroes states, "it is not in the power of scholastic theology to bring truth out of them. That is the business of philosophers who are very few in number."[26] The logical mistake of the Ashari was their misunderstanding of philosophical categories as well as how to implement methodological approaches to their resolution. Nevertheless, while not necessarily favoring the prominence of philosophy over religion, Averroes suggests that natural philosophy has advantages regarding logical arguments of validity and soundness that may not always pertain to religious disputations.

Similarly, in *The Incoherence of the Incoherence,* Averroes challenges al-Ghazali's understanding of the place of God in the natural movement of the earth as a spherical body within the spherical heavens as well as apparent differences in direction of movement of other spheres and stars.[27] Whereas al-Ghazali relies on dialectical arguments to explain apparent contrary celestial movements, Averroes asserts a preference for demonstrative logic, which results in deductively necessary conclusions: "Thus he who tries to prove the existence of an agent in this way gives only persuasive, dialectical arguments, not apodictic proof."[28]

---

26 Averroes, *An Exposition of the Methods of Arguments Concerning the Beliefs of the Faith, and a Determination of Uncertain Doubts and Misleading Innovations in Interpretations*, in *The Philosophy and Theology of Averroes*, trans. Mohammad Jamil-Ur-Rehman (Baroda: Manibhai Mathurbhal Gupta, 1921), 95–96.

27 Averroes, *Tahafut al-Tahafut (The Incoherence of the Incoherence)*, vol. 1, trans. Simon van den Bergh (London: Messrs Luzac & Co., 1969), 23–33.

28 Ibid., 31.

Consequently, in challenging al-Ghazali's criticisms of philosophy, Averroes relies on Aristotle's demonstrative reasoning and natural philosophy to argue that al-Ghazali misunderstands the logical justification of both demonstrative reasoning and the teachings of the Quran.

While promoting the application of demonstrative reasoning, Averroes also recognizes an important role that dialectical reasoning can offer in the form of inductive logic in understanding and explaining nature. In the *Short Commentary on Aristotle's "Topics,"* he argues that induction may be useful when it reorders the premises and conclusion of a deductive syllogism by replacing the conclusion with the major premise.[29] Given the soundness of the premises with the validity of the conclusion in the deductive syllogism, says Averroes, the interchange of positions of the major premise and conclusion by induction are reasonably acceptable. The value and thus appeal of induction occurs when it is used to reinforce conclusions of previously accepted deductive syllogisms; however, by induction alone, inductive generalizations may hold less validity: "[W]hen the induction is used all by itself to explain an unknown problem, it is not very persuasive."[30] Still, Averroes accepts the value of induction in select situations where demonstrative arguments have yet to occur; in one situation, "induction is needed to reach the essential predicate [of already accepted universal claims]. Now these are known as experiential premises."[31] Yet, he maintains that a universal conclusion by induction may be acceptable to dialecticians simply because "it asserts that a judgment applies to all [of something] because it applies to most of it, for it is generally accepted that the lesser follows the greater." Nevertheless, the uncertain reliability of the premises still allows the possibility that the inductive generalization may be logically invalid or empirically falsified.

Averroes not only maintained the superiority of deductive logic for understanding with greater certainty the dynamics of nature, he also

29 Averroes, *Short Commentary on Aristotle's "Topics,"* in *Averroës' Three Short Commentaries on Aristotle's "Topics," "Rhetoric," and "Poetics,"* trans. Charles E. Butterworth (Albany: State University of New York Press, 1977), 48.
30 Ibid., 49.
31 Ibid., 50.

affirmed the importance of finding causal explanations in the finality of movement. To this end, Averroes asserted a metaphysical equivalence: "He who contemplates a product of art does not perceive its wisdom if he does not perceive the wisdom of the intention embodied in it, and the effect intended. And if he does not understand its wisdom, he may well imagine that this object might have any form, any quantity, any configuration of its parts, and any composition whatever."[32] An inference of Averroes's discussion of dialectical induction suggests the following possibility: Without the guidance of religious doctrines, the identification of an eminent final cause to understand the dynamics and purpose of nature may legitimately adopt inductive arguments based on experiential premises. That is, a generalization inferred through induction from experiential premises can then be stated as a hypothesis to serve as the major premise in a deductive argument regarding universal principles or laws of nature. In fact, adoption of this hypothetico-deductive approach by the seventeenth century would ultimately form the basis of modern science, but only after natural philosophy's dissociation from theology.

Natural Philosophy and Thomistic Theology

During the thirteenth century scholasticism was one of the more prominent intellectual movements of the medieval Schoolmen—including Thomas Aquinas—who attempted to systematize certitudes of theology and philosophy through the integration of ancient Greek rationalism and Christian doctrines via the Islamic intellectual tradition. For Aquinas, the organic link between Arab preservation of ancient Greek thought and European scholasticism consisted of many philosophical writings, including the commentaries, of al-Kindi, Alfarabi, Avicenna, and Averroes, among others.[33] Translations of ancient Greek treatises and Averroes's commentaries were of primary importance for grasping the intent and potential of Aristotle's rationalism and natural philosophy for

---

32 Averroes, *Tahafut al-Tahafut.*, 29.
33 James Waltz, "Muhammad and the Muslims in St. Thomas Aquinas," in *The Muslim World* 66, no. 2 (April 1976): 87–89.

explaining and defending the reach and depth of Christian beliefs and claims.

While adjudging the arguments in Aristotle's *Organon* and other writings as crucial to the development of rational defenses of religious doctrine, Aquinas argued that many of the theological positions of the Latin Averroists ran counter to many of Aristotle's own arguments. In *On There Being Only One Intellect*, he challenges the Averroists in their understanding of the identity of the individual soul or agent intellect with a universal intellect; so that, for the individual who is learning something, "there is a natural principle of knowledge, namely, the agent intellect [or soul]."[34] Aquinas relies on Aristotle's *On the Soul* and its natural philosophy or science (*scientia*) to explain how individuals know anything: "For example, we are said to know both through the soul and through science, but first of all through science rather than through the soul—we know through the soul only insofar as it has science."[35] Aquinas does not reject Aristotle's rationalism, but blames the errant arguments of the Latin Averroists on "Averroes, who was not a Peripatetic but the perverter of Peripatetic philosophy."[36]

While he faulted Averroes for key misunderstandings of Aristotle displayed by the Averroists, Aquinas in fact frequently referred approvingly to Averroes in the *Summa Theologica* as the Commentator *par excellence* on Aristotle's writings in support of his own theological positions. Emblematic of such approval is Aquinas's understanding of the soul and the intellect: "The Commentator (Metaph. xii) says the same thing, namely, that the separated substances are divided into intellect and will. And it is in keeping with the order of the universe for the highest intellectual creature to be entirely intelligent; and not in part, as is our soul."[37] Furthermore, as with light being necessary for human vision

---

34 Thomas Aquinas, *On There Being Only One Intellect* in *Aquinas Against the Averroists*, trans. Ralph McInerny (West Lafayette, Indiana: Purdue University Press, 1993), 135.

35 Ibid., 31.

36 Ibid., 79.

37 Aquinas, *Summa Theologica,* trans. Fathers of the English Dominican Provence, vol. 1 (New York: Benziger Brothers, 1947), pt. 1, q. 54, art. 5, p. 276.

to perceive color as demonstrated by natural philosophical investigations, so, too, says Aquinas, "the active intellect is required for understanding, in like manner and for the same reason as light is required for seeing ... in order that the medium may become actually luminous, as the Commentator says on *De Anima* ii. And according to this, Aristotle's comparison of the active intellect to light is verified in this."[38] Thus, Averroes's commentaries served as a bridge for the transmission of Aristotle's rationalism to Christian apologetics. Still, Aquinas had to reconcile the logical findings of philosophical rationalism with the claims of divinely revealed truths.

Aquinas discusses a question concerning the relationship between the science of theology and the philosophical sciences: "Whether sacred doctrine is nobler than other sciences?"[39] Aquinas denies that sacred doctrine is dependent on philosophy, despite philosophy's ability to reason logically from theological premises. Indeed, from his point of view, "other sciences are called the handmaidens of this one [i.e., the science of theology]." Since the science of theology is both speculative and practical, it surpasses the ability of the science of philosophy, which, he says, is based only on fallible human reason. According to Aquinas, "this science surpasses other speculative sciences; in point of greater certitude, because other sciences derive their certitude from the natural light of human reason, which can err; whereas this derives its certitude from the light of divine knowledge, which cannot be misled. ... But the purpose [final cause] of this science, in so far as it is practical, is eternal bliss."[40]

Nevertheless, in the philosophical sciences, says Aquinas, natural philosophy provides five proofs from nature for the rational defense of the existence of God and the eminence of final causes. By observing nature, the first three proofs focus on cosmological considerations: the origins of motion in nature, the origins of the order of efficient causes found in nature, and the origins of the contingent status of nature; the fourth proof observes that existing beings can be categorized from the highest to the lowest; and the final proof offers a teleological consideration

38 Ibid., pt. 1, q. 79, art. 3, p. 399.
39 Ibid., pt. 1, q. 1, art. 5, p. 3.
40 Ibid.

regarding God's "governance of the world."[41] According to Aquinas, the significance of the character of these proofs is their reliance on natural reason, which he incorporates to develop a natural theology as a precursor to religious faith.[42] Moreover, despite philosophy's love of wisdom in its rational search for knowledge, Aquinas also asserts, "wisdom is said to be the knowledge of divine things. ... Sacred doctrine derives its principles not from any human knowledge, but from the divine knowledge, through which, as through the highest wisdom, all our knowledge is set in order."[43] Consequently, for Aquinas, the final cause of human existence is "eternal bliss," of which "divine knowledge" of this "highest wisdom" can ultimately only be revealed through theological investigation in concert with rational philosophy.

Inductive Logic, Modern Science, and Religious Pluralism

Aquinas's incorporation of Aristotelian natural philosophy and rationalism as promulgated in Averroes's commentaries in the *Summa Theologica* and other treatises prevailed as the preeminent and authoritative theological defense of Christian doctrine during the late medieval era. Alfred North Whitehead praises the medieval scholasticism of Aquinas and others for incorporating ancient Greek philosophy, especially Aristotelian rationalism, whose "habit of definite exact thought was implanted in the European mind by the long dominance of scholastic logic and scholastic divinity."[44] In addition, asserts Whitehead, the importance of induction to support deductive arguments, as advocated by Averroes, provided the epistemological grounding for modern science. Indeed, for the examination of nature to understand revealed truths, the exploratory possibility of inductive logic became "the greatest contribution of medievalism to the formation of the [modern] scientific movement."[45] In its adoption of induction, modern science validated Averroes's recognition of the

41 Ibid., pt. 1, q. 2, art. 3, pp. 13–14.
42 Ibid., pt. 1, q. 2, art. 2, p. 12.
43 Ibid., pt. 1, q. 2, art. 6, p. 4.
44 Alfred North Whitehead, *Science and the Modern World* (New York: Free Press, 1967), 12.
45 Ibid.; cf. 23, 43.

potential contribution of inductive arguments preceding deductive syllogisms, which resulted in the hypothetico-deductive approach of the new scientific method.

One of the earlier and prominent advocates of the hypothetico-deductive approach, Francis Bacon, opposed the deductive methodology and scholastic theorizing of the medieval approach to science because it had yielded no new knowledge of nature. He argued that only inductive reasoning and its continual interaction with concrete problems will lead deductively to new insights about the theoretical structure and laws of nature.[46] Bacon begins with empirical observations derived through perceptions of the senses and then the creation of hypotheses from which axioms may be deduced. In turn, these axioms may suggest more comprehensive theorems.[47] Bacon maintains that this methodological approach will yield more than the simple classification of observations that had been produced by the ancient Greek philosophers: "In establishing axioms, another form of induction must be devised than has hitherto been employed; and it must be used for proving and discovering not first principles (as they are called) only, but also the lesser axioms, and the middle, and indeed all."[48]

Acceptance of Averroes's recognition of the importance of experiential premises and the potential for inductive generalizations to serve as premises for deductive arguments contributed to the emergence of a scientific pluralism of experimental hypotheses free from the constraints of religious doctrines. Furthermore, Bacon's scientific pluralism contributed to the epistemological commitment of the metaphysical foundation of a religious axis that later emerged completely by the eighteenth century.[49] Concomitant with the rise of scientific pluralism, the metaphysical foundation also included religious pluralism and the subjectivity of final causes, whose seeds, perhaps inadvertently, had been planted by Martin Luther.

46 Francis Bacon, *Novum Organum*, in *The English Philosophers from Bacon to Mill*, ed. Edwin A. Burtt (New York: Modern Library, 1939), 30, 33.
47 Ibid., 70.
48 Ibid., 71.
49 John R. Pottenger, "The Religious Axis: Rationality, Conscience, and Liberty," in *Reaping the Whirlwind: Liberal Democracy and the Religious Axis* (Washington, D.C.: Georgetown University Press, 2007), chap. 4.

Luther criticized the Roman Church for its embrace of Aquinas's systematic arguments, which incorporated Aristotelian natural philosophy. In his own biblical commentaries, he frequently mentions Averroes and criticizes Aquinas for his reliance on Aristotelian philosophical rationalism.[50] In a letter to members of the German nobility, Luther maintains that the Church's reliance on Thomistic theology had left the Church in the position of promoting good works over salvation by grace alone, for which promotion he finds no scriptural support: "[Aristotle's] book on *Ethics* is the worst of all books. It flatly opposes divine grace and all Christian virtues, and yet it is considered one of his best works. ... I know my Aristotle as well as you or the likes of you. I have lectured on him and heard lectures on him, and I understand him better than do St. Thomas or Scotus."[51] While Luther approves of Aristotle's books on *Logic*, *Rhetoric*, and *Poetics*—as long as they are read without the assistance of scholarly commentaries—he strongly recommends that Aristotle's *Ethics*, *Physics*, *Metaphysics*, and *On the Soul* be banned from study in the universities: "[Aristotle's] books ... boast of treating the things of nature, although nothing can be learned from them either of the things of nature or the things of the Spirit."[52]

Furthermore, Luther asserts in his *Heidelberg Disputation* that under the influence of Aristotelian natural philosophy, Aquinas had taken Christianity on a fateful and more aggressive turn toward a natural theology, abandoning an even earlier and more promising trajectory that had been set in motion by Platonic essentialism: "Aristotle wrongly finds fault with and derides the ideas of Plato, which actually are better than his own."[53] Indeed, says Luther in his *Disputation Against Scholastic*

50   Adam S. Francisco, *Martin Luther and Islam: A Study in Sixteenth-Century Polemics and Apologetics* (Leiden, The Netherlands: Koninklijke Brill, 2007), 100.

51   Martin Luther, *An Open Letter to the Christian Nobility of the German Nation*, in *Three Treatises*, Martin Luther, trans. Charles M. Jacobs (Philadelphia: Fortress Press, 1960), 94.

52   Ibid., 93–94.

53   Martin Luther, *Heidelberg Disputation*, Philosophical Thesis 36, in *Martin Luther's Basic Theological Writings*, 3rd ed., eds. Timothy F. Lull and William R. Russell (Minneapolis: Fortress Press, 2012), 16.

Theology, "It is truly doubtful whether the Latin-speakers comprehended the correct meaning of Aristotle."[54]

Popular acceptance of Luther's denigration of Christian theological reliance on natural philosophy effectively disassociated investigations of nature—that relied on the new and developing scientific method with its implementation of Averroes's theory of induction—from automatic inclusion in Christian apologetics. In addition to the emancipation of science from the normative constraints of religious final causes, a related consequence of Luther's own theological reconstruction and influence among those disaffected with the Church in Rome was the *de facto* elimination of ecclesiastical jurisdiction over interpretation of Christian doctrines. The removal of ecclesiastical jurisdiction resulted in the exponential growth of diverse personal opinions regarding the correct understanding of final causes and their vigorous propagation by competing religious sects. The increasing democratization of diverse beliefs in final causes and their dissemination contributed to the rapid growth of religious pluralism.

The fruition, then, of the organic link—the Islamic intellectual tradition—between Greek thought and Christian theology predisposed Latin Europe for the emergence and development of a theoretical nexus between Aristotelian analytical philosophy and modern political philosophy. Furthermore, this nexus eventuated in the advent of a religious axial period by the eighteenth century, whose metaphysical foundation included an epistemological commitment rooted in Averroes's commentaries on Aristotelian rationalism and limited justification of inductive logic. This commitment produced an alternative response to the religious question of the medieval era regarding the proper relationship between religious beliefs and practices and the polity, and ultimately between church and state. From this relationship, predicated on the independence of natural philosophy from religious constraints, has flourished subjective reexaminations of—and then ultimately popular rejection of consensus on—the eminence of final causes in the modern era.

---

54 Martin Luther, *Disputation Against Scholastic Theology*, Thesis 51, in *Martin Luther's Basic Theological Writings*, 3rd ed., eds. Timothy F. Lull and William R. Russell (Minneapolis: Fortress Press, 2012), 5.

The Unity of Reason and Revelation: How Faith can lead to Understanding

David Burrell

In an effort to counter the bifurcation between *revelation* and *reason* which tended to characterize modernist portrayal of *falasifa* in Islam, let us propose a fresh review, bringing revelation into conversation with rational strategies inherited from Greeks and Persians. That intentional conversation, I contend, is best called "philosophical theology" and its context, "Islamic." Indeed, part of the fresh story will show how *faith*, which in the Muslim world focuses on *practice*, becomes a path leading to *understanding*, traditionally taken to be the province of *philosophy*. The shifting relations among these axial notions will mark our journey's itinerary, from Ibn Sina to Mulla Sadra, through the good offices of al-Ghazali, Suhrawardi, and Ibn 'Arabi. Let readers decide how much this approach differs from what I call a "modernist" account of Islamic philosophy, very much tailored to a nineteenth-century bifurcation of reason and faith. So that our age demands a fresh account is ever the case in doing philosophy historically.

Phase One: The Standard Story of Islamic Philosophy

The conventional story of Islamic philosophical theology can be depicted in standard categories without impugning any lack of imagination or creativity to individual protagonists, for such stories invariably represent modern Western constructions. It begins with the spectacular overtaking of the hinterlands of the Byzantine empire in the seventh century by disciplined and motivated bands from the Arabian peninsula, who before long sought to assimilate the high culture of that empire. Utilizing the offices of Syriac translators, they made key Hellenic philosophical texts available in Arabic, facilitating the emergence of signal thinkers like al-Kindi, al-Farabi, Ibn Sina [Avicenna], and Ibn Rushd [Averroes].[1] As the equivalent Latin names illustrate, these philosophers—called "*falāsifa*" in Islam—inspired cognate Christian medieval thinkers, with the Latinate equivalent of Ibn Rushd naming an entire way of thinking: "Latin Averroism." The import of this East-West cultural exchange in the eleventh through thirteenth centuries proved especially significant for the West, while the movement in the Islamic world itself was soon to lose its vitality. In the standard story the culprit was another Islamic thinker, al-Ghazali [Algazel], whose trenchant attack on "the philosophers" is said to have sharply curtailed their influence in Islamic culture. That dispute, with Ibn Rushd's stalwart defense, is displayed in two documents: al-Ghazali's "Deconstruction of the Philosophers" and Ibn Rushd's "Deconstruction of the Deconstruction," which itself contains the entire text (of al-Ghazali) it intends to refute.[2] For purposes of this story, Ibn Rushd represents *philosophy* unadulterated by faith, while al-Ghazali's critique based on faith effectively curtails any mediating use of reason to elaborate Islamic tradition. Yet a recent study by Avital Wohlman, hardly favorable to Ghazali as a philosopher, effectively replaces a "rationalist" Ibn Sina with a thoroughly Islamic thinker.[3] The imposing presence of Fakhr ad-Din ar-Razi might also have reminded us how such stories trade in stereotypes, of course, though they have tended to prevail among Western thinkers who prefer their philosophy neat.

In the fresh story I shall propose, al-Ghazali will also function axially, but less as a culprit than as announcing a second phase to be carried on in the heartland of Islamic civilization, as the center returned from Cordoba to Baghdad, turning on such luminaries as Suhrawardi, Ibn al-Arabi, and Mulla Sadra. Al-Ghazali's dramatic role is reflected in the work of Moses ben Maimon [Maimonides], a Jew so thoroughly embedded in

---

1   Richard Walzer, *Al-Farabi on the Perfect State* (Oxford: Clarendon Press, 1985).

2   Abu Hamid al-Ghazali, *The Incoherence of the Philosophers [Tahāfut al-falāsifah]*, trans. Michael E. Marmura (Provo, UT: Brigham Young University Press, 2000); Ibn Rushd, *Tahafut al-Tahafut*, trans. Simon van den Bergh (Cambridge: Cambridge University Press, 1954).

3   Avital Wohlman, *Counterpoint between Common Sense and Philosophy in Islam* (London: Routledge, 2010).

"the Islamicate" that he can be classified an "Islamic philosopher."[4] A sustained inquiry emerged across cultures and generations, including Ibn Sina, al-Ghazali, and Maimonides, as well as Thomas Aquinas, seeking ways to formulate a coherent account of creation which highlighted the creator's freedom, since Jews, Muslims, and Christians each had a crucial stake in the outcome.[5] (By including Maimonides and Aquinas we will see how Islamic philosophical theology resonated beyond the borders of Islam itself.) The issue of the creator's freedom underscores the unique *relation* of creator to creatures in each Abrahamic tradition, though it proved inherently difficult to articulate philosophically. Indeed, the celebrated "emanation scheme," introduced into Islamic philosophy by al-Farabi and elaborated by Ibn Sina, could serve to elide the singularity of this relation by naming the One (adopted from Plotinus) as "the First."[6] Indeed, despite al-Farabi's eloquent delineation of the uniqueness of this *First*, his strategic employment of the scheme of logical deduction to model the way the *One* relates to the ensuing *many* tends to introduce that One as the originating axiomatic principle, differing from subsequent premises only by its functional place in the system. Moreover, the fact that an axiomatic model also introduces logical *necessity* runs counter to the role that the creator's freedom plays, for only a free creator can enjoy the privileges of that *Oneness* which Muslim tradition enshrines in *tawhid,* Jewish thought in God's *unity* (over against *idolatry*), displayed as well in the four-centuries-long Christian path to divine *triunity*.[7] In short, if the origination of the universe is a matter of necessity, its source

4   Oliver Leaman and Sayyed Hossain Nasr, eds. 1996. *History of Islamic Philosophy.* 2 vols. (New York: Routledge, 1996).

5   David Burrell, *Knowing the Unknowable God: Ibn Sina, Maimonides, Aquinas* (Notre Dame, IN: University of Notre Dame Press, 1986); David Burrell, *Freedom and Creation in Three Traditions* (Notre Dame IN: University of Notre Dame Press, 1993); David Burrell, "Aquinas and Islamic and Jewish Thinkers," in *Cambridge Companion to Aquinas*, eds. Norman Kretzmann and Eleonore Stump (Cambridge: Cambridge University Press, 1993), 60-84.

6   Richard Walzer, *Al-Farabi on the Perfect State.*

7   Thomas Weinandy, *Does God change? : the Word' Becoming in the Incarnation* (Still River, Mass.: St. Bede's Publications, 1985).

cannot qualify as a *creator* in the sense demanded by each of the Abrahamic faiths; one of the central complaints al-Ghazali lodged against "the philosophers" in Islam. Indeed, a free creator would have to be distinct from creatures—to be creator—so the uniqueness of the *relation* will emerge forcibly.[8] Let us presume acquaintance with the initial phase of Islamic "philosophical theology," so as to focus on the metaphysical strategies designed to relate creatures to their transcendent origin, as they turn on al-Ghazali, yet are ever beholden to Avicenna's axial distinction between *essence* and *existing* to articulate the *sui generis* character of the relation between a free creator and the universe.

Phase Two: Refining the Creator / Creature Distinction

To help re-cast the constructive role al-Ghazali plays to bridge between earlier and later phases of Islamic philosophy, three figures emerge to mark the second phase: Suhrawardi (1154–91), Ibn al-Arabi (d. 1240), and Sadra al-Din al-Shirazi [Mulla Sadra] (1572–1640). While Ibn al-Arabi actually made the trek from Andalusia to the Levant to carry out his extensive and intensive inquiries in Damascus, each of these thinkers will embody that shift from West to East, or (in ways which need to be nuanced), from a peripatetic, largely Aristotelian philosophical milieu, to one more sympathetically Platonist. Moreover, given the fact that their exposition will attempt to track the ineffable relation of creator to creature, one can expect greater recourse to poetic and allegorical tropes in their writing, though it would be misleading to present their mode of inquiry as attempting to transcend philosophical discourse. Indeed, one may note how Ibn Sina's later allegorical writing presaged this development.[9] Nor can there be any doubt that classical Islamic philosophy explicitly espoused philosophical inquiry, in both phases, as a way to bring inquirers themselves closer to reality; in this case, to the creator of all. Following

8   David Burrell, "The Christian Distinction Celebrated and Expanded," in *The Truthful and the Good*, eds. John Drummond and James Hart (Dordrecht: Kluwer, 1996), 191–206.

9   David Burrell, "Avicenna," in *A Companion to Philosophy in the Middle Ages*, eds. Jorge J. E. Gracia and Timothy B. Noone (Oxford: Blackwell, 2003), 196–208.

Pierre Hadot, we can regard these thinkers as underscoring the existential *telos* endemic to philosophical inquiry among the ancients—a view which has come to prove quite amenable to a postmodern sensibility.[10] And it is precisely this feature which makes al-Ghazali so axial a figure in our story, with a valence quite opposed to that in the standard account.[11]

Al-Ghazali's signal contribution to philosophical theology[12]

We can trace Ghazali's specific contribution by way of a central text: the book of "Faith in Divine Unity and Trust in Divine Providence" [*Kitab al-tawhid wa 'l-tawakkul*] of the *Ihya' 'Ulum al-Din* [*Revivifying Religious Sciences*]. Together with *al-iqtisad al-i 'ttiqad* [*Preserving the Faith*], the effect of these works is to qualify al-Ghazali as a Muslim theologian in the full medieval meaning of that term, and not in the merely descriptive sense extended to include any thinker adept at *kalam*, or the dialectical defense of faith. That is, Ghazali was intent on using human reason, as he found it elaborated in Ibn Sina and others, to lead Muslim faithful to a deeper penetration of the mysteries of their revealed religion, central among them being the free creation of the universe by the one God.[13] The works of the philosophers themselves were not always helpful to him in their native state, so he set out to purify them of their pretensions to offer an access to truth independent of and superior to that of divine revelation-the Qur'an. Hence his need to understand them thoroughly, embodied in the work entitled "The Intentions of the Philosophers [*Maqasid al-falasifa*]," itself conceived as an extended introduction (and hence also published as the *Muqaddima al-Tahafut*) to

10 Pierre Hadot, *Philosophy as a Way of Life*, trans. Arnold Davidson (Chicago: University of Chicago Press, 1995).

11 Hamid Dabashi, "Mīr Dāmād and the founding of the 'School of Iṣfahān'" in *History of Islamic Philosophy*, vol., 1, eds. Sayyed Hossein Nasr and Oliver Leaman (London: Routledge, 1996), 622, 629.

12 This section adapts from the Introduction to Abu Hamid al-Ghazali, *Al-Ghazali on Faith in Divine Unity and Trust in Divine Providence*, trans. David Burrell (Louisville, KY: Fons Vitae, 2000), 2000a, with permission of publisher.

13 David Burrell, *Freedom and Creation in Three Traditions*.

his "Deconstruction of the Philosophers [*Tahafut al-falasifa*]" (Ghazali 2000b).[14] The negative tone of this latter work, together with its detailed refutation by Averroes [Ibn Rushd: *Tahafut al-Tahafut*], has left the impression that Ghazali should never be ranked with "the philosophers" but always left with "the theologians" as a defender of *kalam* orthodoxy in the face of reasonable inquiry. It is precisely that stereotype which is challenged by the *Book of Faith in Divine Unity*, and so can offer Ghazali's own assistance to deconstruct the historical image which he helped to create for himself. It will involve challenging the constructed modernist role of Averroes as the paragon of *philosophy*, to concentrate on Ghazali's intent, leaving an assessment of his success to the reader.

The "Book of Faith in Divine Unity *[tawhid]* and Trust in Divine Providence [*tawakkul*]" is Book 35 in Ghazali's masterwork, the *Ihya' 'Ulum al-Din*, which is intent upon a clear understanding of matters religious, yet one which continues to give primacy to practice: faith is rooted in trust and must needs be expressed in a life of trust.[15] The pretensions of the philosophers to understand the mysteries of *the heavens and the earth and all that is between them* [15:85], proceeding by conceptual argument alone, must be exposed as just that—pretension, in the face of the central assertion that the universe is *freely* created by the one sovereign God. Yet reason, as they are at pains to elaborate, will prove to be an indispensable tool in directing our minds and our hearts to understand how to think and how to live as a consequence of the signal truth of free creation. Such is Ghazali's intent, displayed in the very structure of *Faith in Divine Unity and Trust in Divine Providence* [*Kitab al-Tawhid wa'l-Tawakkul*]. For *tawhid,* or "faith in divine unity," sounds the distinctive note of Islam which grounds everything Muslims believe in the *shahada:* "There is no god but God." Yet what interests Ghazali are the implications of the community's *faith* in divine unity. So what

14   There is no current English (or Western language) translation of the *Magasid,* though one is proposed for the SUNY-Binghamton series under the general editorship of Parviz Morewedge. There are two Arabic versions, neither critical, one published by Muhl. ad-Din Sabri al-Kurdi, Cairo, 1331 A.H.; the other edited by Sulayman Dunya for Dar al-Ma'arif, Cairo, 1961.

15   Ghazali, *Al-Ghazali on Faith in Divine Unity and Trust in Divine Providence.*

is really being asserted? That everything comes from God and that "there is no agent but God." He justifies the two-part structure of the book by way of showing how *tawakkul*—trust in divine providence—is grounded in an articulate *tawhid,* as practice is anchored in faith, or *state* [of being] in *knowledge.* In doing so, he is even more insistent: this first part

> "will consist in showing you that there is no agent but God the Most High: of all that exists in creation: sustenance given or withheld, life or death, riches or poverty, and every-thing else that can be named, the sole one who initiated and originated it all is God Most High. And when this has been made clear to you, you will not see anything else, so that your fear will be of Him, your hope in Him, your trust in Him, and your security with Him, for He is the sole agent without any other. Everything else is in His service, for not even the smallest atom in the worlds of heaven and earth is independ-ent of Him for its movement. If the gates of mystical insight were opened to you, this would be clear to you with a clarity more perfect than ordinary vision" (15–16).

Perhaps enough has been said to begin to make my case for Ghaz-ali as an Islamic theologian, in the normative and not merely descrip-tive sense of that term. If he tends to resolve to "mystical insight" in places where philosophers would prefer conceptual schemes, that is merely to suggest that certain domains quite outstrip human conceptu-alizing. Yet more significant, however, is that everything he says about practice can be carried out quite independently of such "mystical in-sight," as indeed it must be for the vast majority of faithful. In a brief survey of the thinkers who follow, we shall watch them elaborate this goal of integrating theory with practice.

Suhrawardi's "Philosophy of Illumination"

Given the standard story of Islamic philosophy, the bulk of Western crit-ical work has concentrated on protagonists in phase one, yet the quality of available exposition attending both Suhrawardi and Ibn al-Arabi more than compensates for the lack of quantity regarding these phase two thinkers. The inclusion of Suhrawardi, Ibn al-Arabi, and Mulla Sadra can also correct a possible misapprehension of our proposed division of Islamic philosophy into two phases, turning on al-Ghazali. For continuity is invariably present even in the face of a proposed cut, and we shall see how Ibn Sina's presence supplies the continuity between the two phases. Our guides for Suhrawardi will be the commentaries and translations of John Walbridge and Hossein Ziai, while those of William Chittick will move us through Ibn al-Arabi, with Sayyed Hossein Nasr, Sajjad Rizvi, Muhammed Rustom, Hossein Ziai, and Latimah-Parvin Peerwani's translation leading us into Mulla Sadra.

Despite notorious difficulties in presenting and interpreting Suhrawardi's philosophical *opus*, we can plausibly present him as the figure initiating a distinctive phase two, given his critique of Ibn Sina and his novel presentation of knowing as *illumination*. His early and tragic demise at 37, at the behest of Saladin for a complex of strategic political reasons, hardly allowed time for a mature development of his thought, though his *oeuvre* remains considerable. John Walbridge (2005, 203) divides it into four categories: [1] juvenilia, [2] mystical works, notably a number of allegories, [3] works expounding the principles of the Peripatetics according to their methods, and [4] *The Philosophy of Illumination*.[16] The greater part of his extensive work has not been published, and only the last one is translated, but both Walbridge and Ziai are intent on showing him to be a *bona fide* philosopher in the face of Henry Corbin's introducing his thought to the West as "theosophie orientale."[17] I have argued in a similar vein that "philosophical theology" is a more respectable descriptor of the mode of thinking in phase two

---

16   Shihab al-Din Suhrawardi, *The Philosophy of Illumination*, eds. and trans. John Walbridge and Hossein Ziai (Provo, UT: Brigham Young University Press, 1999).

17   John Walbridge, "Suhrawardi and Illuminationism," in *Cambridge Companion to Arabic Philosophy*, eds. Peter Adamson and Richard Taylor (Cambridge: Cambridge University Press, 2005), 204; Hossein Ziai, 1997, "al-Suhrawardi," in *Encyclopedia of Islam* (New Edition) [=EI-2] (Leiden: Brill, 1997), 9:782–84.

than "theosophy," allowing us to recapture the spiritual goals inherent to Islamic philosophy, as well as illuminate why Suhrawardi begins phase two of our story.[18] Yet terminology aside, Corbin's approach does highlight Suhrawardi's intent to acknowledge sources other than the Peripatetics: Egyptian, Indian and Chinese, and ancient Persian. By weaving those sources into Plato Suhrawardi qualifies to initiate of phase two in our story. What will distinguish him from Ibn al-Arabi, and especially from Mulla Sadra, is his absorbing focus on epistemological issues, which can serve us here as a prelude to the metaphysical concerns of Ibn 'Arabi and Mulla Sadra.

Emphasis on *seeing* intimates Suhrawardi's celebrated "knowledge by presence" which attempts to move beyond the *subject/object* structure of knowing endemic to Plato, and led him to reject Peripatetic essential definition to argue that essences could only be known through direct acquaintance. (It is worth mentioning that Aristotle had also evaded the subject/object picture of knowing to propose knowing-by-identity, with the form of the thing known present to the knowing mind. But the "peripatetic philosophy" which Suhrawardi had inherited from Ibn Sina had already been considerably platonized.) But the vision intimated in our key text goes much farther, to introduce an epistemological ascent following metaphysical pathways of reality itself. The pinnacle of this ascent, the "Light of Lights must be infinitely beyond the infinite; for the infinite ... admits of differences" (113). Which will lead him to assert:

> therefore, the Light of lights is the ruling Agent despite all intermediaries, the cause of their activity, the Origin of every emanation, the absolute Creator, without intermediary. There is no effect which does not contain Its effect, although It may allow the relation of activity to be shared with another (114).[19]

18 David Burrell, "Islamic Philosophical Theology," in *Philosophy of Seyyed Hossein Nasr,* eds. Lewis Hahn, Randall Auxier, and Lucian Stone Jr. (Chicago: Open Court, 2001), 644.

19 see Qur'an 55:29.

Given these bold assertions, we would expect Suhrawardi to say that "the Light of Lights is the cause of the existence and the cause of the continuation of all existents" (123). Yet his thoroughly conceptual views on *existence* force him to qualify that statement in anticipation: "since existence is a being of reason, what the thing receives from its emanating cause is its identity" (123). The source of this crucial qualification in his earlier treatment of *existence* indicates why later interpreters will contrast his "primacy of quiddity" with Mulla Sadra's "primacy of existence."

The justification for these assertions can be found in his sustained critique of what he takes to be "the Peripatetic" (that is, Ibn Sina's) view that "existence in concrete things [is] superadded to the substance," for then it would follow that "the existent would be prior to existence" (46). This reflects Ibn Rushd's deconstruction of the obvious sense of the assertion that "existence is an accident," yet Suhrawardi apparently sees no alternative except to make of *existence* a purely conceptual predicate. Yet such severe qualification cannot but jar with the straightforward characterization of "the Light of Lights" as creator of all-that-is, precisely by bestowing *existence*, which in this context can hardly be something "purely intellectual." So Mulla Sadra's apparently contrary insistence on the "primacy of existence" might be seen as offering a way of making his predecessor more consistent!

The metaphor of *light* provides Suhrawardi with a manifestly epistemological tool, yet also helps to express the pervasiveness of the creator's primary causality, for "you will find nothing that has an effect both near and far save light" (130). Drawing from both Plato and Aristotle, created things are ordered by "desire [which] bears the perceptive essences to the Light of Lights; that which is greater in its desire is more attracted and climbs higher toward the world of the All-Highest Light" (145). Indeed, the culminating passages of the book are full of Quranic terminology, showing what can be learned of the mystical quest from the celestial prototype of the Qur'an. So Suhrawardi can hope that his composition will lead readers to the consummation of philosophy, namely "to turn with all your being to God our Lord, the Light of Lights." For "he who studies [this book] will learn that what escaped the Ancients and the Moderns God has entrusted to my tongue. One wondrous day the Holy spirit blew it into my heart in a single instant, though its writing took many months due to the interruption of journeys" (162).

Attaining this goal will mean employing rigorous conceptual argument, of course, yet much more as well: "give it only to one well versed in the methods of the Peripatetics, a lover of the light of God. Let him meditate for forty days, abstaining from meat, taking little food, concentrating upon the contemplation of the light of God, most mighty and glorious, and upon that which he who holds the authority to teach the Book shall command" (162). So with this and other works Suhrawardi was conscious of leading others along a path of argument to a liberating light, as he himself had been illuminated. There is no competition, then, between conceptual methods and intuitive realization, except when such methods refuse to give way to that realization, as it emerges as their transcendent goal.

Ibn al-Arabi: "rationalizing mystic"

If Suhrawardi provides a bridge between phases one and two of our story, Ibn al-Arabi offers the bridge from Suhrawardi to Mulla Sadra, by way of intensifying the "therapeutic" role of philosophy signaled to us by Pierre Hadot, in essays Arnold Davidson introduces with a phrase from Wittgenstein: "philosophy as a way of life."[20] Sajjad Rizvi adopts the descriptor "rationalizing mystic" from Philip Merlan's way of depicting "later Neoplatonists, [to convey] absolute transparency between the knower, the known, and knowledge itself" in its relation to the creator God. Indeed, what specifies this cognitive manner of relating to the creator, as articulated in "illuminationist [ishraqi] philosophy, is its integration of spiritual practice into the pursuit of wisdom."[21] What is sought here is a way of articulating the relation itself between creator and creatures, parallel to that between *existence* and *existents*, a relation

20   Pierre Hadot, *Philosophy as a Way of Life*, trans. Arnold Davidson (Chicago: University of Chicago Press, 1995).
21   Sajjad Rizvi, "Mysticism and philosophy" in *Cambridge Companion to Arabic Philosophy*, 227.

which one knows to be unique, so inassimilable to relations between existents. Here the celebrated "distinction," articulated (albeit differently) in Ibn Sina and in Aquinas, is intensified by insisting that the One alone *exists*. Ibn al-Arabi uses Quranic language to intimate the manner of bestowing a share of that existence on existents: "He originates and brings back" (85:13). While this verse had been understood to refer to "God's bringing people back at the resurrection," Ibn al-Arabi offers a more metaphysical reading linked to the conserving dimension of creating:

> There is no existent thing to which the Real gives existence without finishing with giving it existence. Then that existent thing considers God and sees that He has come back to giving existence to another entity. So it continues perpetually and endlessly.[22]

However difficult it may be for contemporary philosophers to follow such a hybrid inquiry, especially those who cannot avail themselves of a faith tradition of free creation, they could nevertheless be assisted by William Chittick and Salman Bashier to move beyond the stereotype of Ibn al-Arabi as a "monist"—that is, one who elides "the distinction" of creatures from creator.[23] For the precise function of the *barzakh* is to highlight the relation *between* creator and creatures, which, however paradoxical it may be for us to formulate, remains a *relation,* even though comparing it to an ordinary relation between creatures effectively elides creation itself—as Maimonides saw so clearly! On this reading, what makes Ibn al-Arabi so radical is not an heretical denial of "the distinction" between the One and all-that-is, but rather a thoroughgoing attempt to keep that distinction from being so trivialized that the One ceases to be "the One" or "the Real" to become a creature, albeit "the biggest one

22 William Chittick, *Self-Disclosure of God: Principles of Ibn al-Arabi's Cosmology* (Albany: State University of New York Press, 1998), 65–66.

23 William Chittick, *Faith and Practice in Islam* (Albany: State University of New York Press, 1992); William Chittick, *Self-Disclosure of God*; Salman Bashier, *Ibn al-'Arabi's Barzakh: Concept of the Limit and the Relationship between God and the World* (Albany: State University of New York Press, 2004).

around."[24] Yet negotiating such paradoxical articulation will demand the practice of a set of "spiritual exercises," as we have noted to be the hallmark of classical Hellenic philosophy as well as of Islamic philosophical theology, already intimated in the later allegorical writings of Ibn Sina.[25]

Mulla Sadra: the primacy of existing

Ibn Sina's axial distinction between *essence* and *existence* had a manifest influence on Thomas Aquinas, who proceeded to offer a radical adaptation of *existing [esse, wujud]* from *accident* to *act*. That intellectual maneuver succeeded in highlighting the primacy of *esse* as well as the role which creation plays in bringing us to recognize that primacy. Moreover, anyone familiar with Mulla Sadra, notably his summary text *Kitâb al-Mashâ'ir*, will be struck by manifest similarities with Aquinas.[26] Everything turns on the role which *esse* plays as the vehicle, one might say, of God's creating activity. (Aquinas will identify *esse* as the "proper effect of the first and most universal cause, which is God," who needs no intermediaries to bestow it since "God alone is his own existence" [ST 1.45.5].) Moreover, we will find that the mediating notion of *participation*, which Aquinas introduces before long, will play a central role in Mulla Sadra's account of the way in which *wujûd* comes forth from the One to all beings, even though he will not employ a corresponding Arabic term for it.[27] We shall also see how their concerns mirror one another: to find a way to highlight the metaphysical primacy of individual

24 David Burrell, "Creation, Metaphysics, and Ethics," *Faith and Philosophy* 18, 204–21.

25 Henry Corbin. *Avicenna and the Visionary Recital* (New York: Pantheon, 1960); David Burrell, "Avicenna."

26 Paragraph references will be to Corbin's edition and translation of *Kitâb al-Mashâ'ir* (Mulla Sadra), *Le Livre des Pénétrations métaphysiques,* trans. Henry Corbin (Teheran: Institut Franco-Iranien/Paris: Adrien-Maisonneuve, 1964), (English version to appear from Brigham Young University Press.); David Burrell, "Mulla Sadra on 'Substantial Motion': A Clarification and a Comparison with Thomas Aquinas," *Journal of Shi'a Islamic Studies* 2, no. 4 (2009): 369–86.

27 Rudi teVelde, *Participation and Substantiality in Thomas Aquinas* (Leiden: Brill, 1995).

existing things—a goal which Aristotle had set for himself in the face of Plato, but was never able to complete satisfactorily; as well as to find a strategy to capitalize upon Ibn Sina's celebrated distinction of *essence* from *existing* while neutralizing the characterization of *being* as "accidental" to essence.[28]

Yet while it is simple enough to refute the impression with which Ibn Sina left us, it is not so easy to employ the mode of discourse proper to philosophy to articulate what is neither essence nor accident. We could, however, shift to the linguistic mode to put more simply what Mulla Sadra struggles to articulate here, by insisting (with Aquinas) that propositions always refer to the existing individual. Living individuals (which served as Aristotle's paradigms for individual substances) offer the test cases here, for when friends die—be they dogs or persons—we can no longer name what we encounter—the body— with the person's or dog's name, but only refer to the corpse. Anything else sounds strange because it is philosophically incoherent: whatever *kind* of thing something may be figures only obliquely into our references, which are always to this individual; and since the *esse* of living things is to be alive (as Aquinas never tired of quoting Aristotle), when they die we are no longer confronting the same thing. Unlike accidental features, were existence able to be removed, the thing itself could hardly perdure. Mulla Sadra reflects this manner of articulating things when he later expands on the contention that "existing itself is the *quiddity* in its individuality, [to insist] as well that existence itself is the very affirmation of the thing rather than something affirmed of the thing" (par 80). This insistence on *affirmation* reminds us that we can only call attention to the reality of existing by moving from denominating terms (*langue*) to consider how we use them (*parole*) to make assertions, for if we fasten on terms alone, we invariably find ourselves asking what kind of thing it is. Yet that is precisely what both Aquinas and Mulla Sadra deny of *existing*: that it is a *kind* of thing! For a more positive account, then, let us show how the peculiar uses we make of "existing" can lead us to the source of *existing*.

---

28   Edward Booth, *Aristotelian Aporectic Ontology in Islamic and Christian Writers* (Cambridge: Cambridge University Press, 1983).

To move us beyond the abstract analysis which appeared to find two "things" in acknowledging the real distinction between essence and existing, Mulla Sadra shifts our attention to things

"as they obtain outside the mind: the principle of an existing thing is existence, for it properly belongs to existence to emanate from the One who originates, with the quiddity united to it and predicated of it [as statements are made of individuals]. Not, however, as accidents are predicated of what they are joined to; for the quiddity is predicated of existence and united with it in the measure that it is itself the very individuality proper to this existence" (par 77).

So *wujûd* becomes the trace that the cause leaves in the caused, as Mulla Sadra makes clear when responding to one who objects that "we cannot conceive the existence of something caused while neglecting the existence of the cause which necessitates it, for then that cause would cease to be constitutive of the thing caused." Indeed, he retorts, but that is an impertinent objection to our argument "since we say that it is not possible to attain to knowledge of the precise particularity of a mode of existence unless its very individuality be unveiled [*moshâhada*], and that cannot be realized without some kind of unveiling of the cause of its emanation. That is why they say that knowing what possesses a cause is only attained by knowing its cause. Ponder this well!" (par 92). Asking whether there can be any similarity between creatures and the creator— a neuralgic point in Islam—Aquinas responds cagily: "creatures resemble the creator in *existing*" (ST 1.4.3). But if *existence* cannot be a feature [*accident*], then there can be no manifest *similarity* between creator and creatures.

At this point both Muslim and Christian traditions turn to practices which can serve to move the understanding beyond formulations, especially when the very structure of the formulae displays that they will not suffice. And Pierre Hadot reminds us that ancient philosophy did the same. A longtime translator of Plotinus, it appears that the very effort of translating—itself a spiritual exercise!—alerted him to the difference between a modern and a classical conception of the virtues required to "do philosophy." Indeed, modern philosophy seldom alludes to "intellectual virtues," contenting itself rather with "propositional attitudes," yet when one presses the *attitude* part, something like virtue can in fact emerge. That is to say, modernity's *account* of what philosophy is and how one engages in it may well prove inadequate to the activity itself, which could also explain why philosophy continues to criticize itself and not merely its findings. The focus of contemporary philosophers like Stephen Toulmin and Alasdair MacIntyre on practices can help us see how Hadot's presentation of ancient philosophy is far more pertinent than an historical exercise, as his recent summary statement in *What is Ancient Philosophy?* articulates.[29] Mulla Sadra explicitly contends, as we have seen, that we will need some special "illumination" to attain the appropriate metaphysical standpoint. Lacking something of that sort, teVelde intimates, Aquinas's crucial formula—"to be God is to be"—cannot but appear ungrammatical. Yet those who are attuned to what it displays rather than what it (cannot) say, will be able to make connections with Plotinus's pointing to a One "beyond being," to find both Aquinas and Mulla Sadra engaged in a similar struggle to attain the requisite "metaphysical standpoint"—beyond the common conception of being.[30] And it was his own engagement with Plotinus's intellectual journey which taught Hadot the need for spiritual exercises to follow his mentor. Indeed, the master/disciple relationship, and all that it portends, offers a useful way of characterizing the exercises relevant to attaining this metaphysical standpoint. As I have been suggesting throughout, Hadot's suggestions may offer Western philosophers a way to appreciate *ishrâqi* wisdom and the demands it makes on one who would practice it.

While there can be no demonstration of these matters, primarily since *existing* defies definition, we are nonetheless led to realize that we cannot understand created things properly without a sustained attempt to grasp the internal link they have with the creator in their very existing. (It is that "internal link" which al-Ghazali is intimating by insisting that

---

29　Pierre Hadot, *What is Ancient Philosophy?* (Cambridge, MA: Belknap Press of Harvard University, 2002).

30　Lloyd Gerson, *Plotinus* (London: Routledge, 1997).

"there is no agent but God most high").[31] Yet while this mode of inquiry exceeds the bounds of philosophical inquiry as normally practiced by Islamic philosophers in our first stage, like Ibn Sina, it is arguable that they too realized that an authentically philosophical search must move into these more esoteric arenas.[32] Yet Mulla Sadra's inspiration is clearly Ibn al-Farabi, as readers may detect from our all-too-brief treatment of that illustrious sheikh. By using *existing* as the fulcrum, from al-Farabi to Mulla Sadra (with comparative links to Aquinas), one can detect continuity in intent—the goal of wisdom—between what we have marked as "two phases" in Islamic philosophy, as well as a marked shift to incorporate that goal more explicitly, with the practices which allow one to approach it. For that approach is redolent of the Sufi desire to "come near" to the One from whom all-that-is continually derives. So the ineffable relation between that One and all that derives from It becomes an existential journey for the blessed inquirer, since our very inability to articulate the relation invites us rather to traverse it personally—in sh'Allah [as God so wills].[33]

31 David Burrell, *Freedom and Creation in Three Traditions*.
32 David Burrell, "Avicenna."
33 Originally published as "Islamic Philosophical Theology and the West," *Islamochristiana* 33 (2007): 75–90. This version slightly revised, including title.

Interpreting the Interpreter:
Awe and Exceptionalism in the Averroes
of Étienne Gilson
Gary M. Kelly

Those who exemplify tradition are rarely acknowledged by it. Such is the lot of interpreters of significant texts. This is all the more so in the area of French arts and letters, with its deliberate practice of *explication de textes*, intense work that consigns its specialists to relative obscurity while elevating that which is interpreted.

But there are rare exceptions; and Étienne Gilson (1884-1978) lived in an era of large ones. His was a Paris that was the cauldron of that peculiarly post-war French product, the philosopher-celebrity, a mantle that was initially claimed by an interpreter of an interpreter[1] who defied what French tradition demanded: that interpreters shun calling attention to the interpreter.

Accordingly, Gilson plied his trade in reverence and even in awe. Yet, it was awe mixed with exceptionalism. Awe, as Gilson followed hundreds of thousands into mobilization and joined his fellow *poiloux* in the hellhole of Verdun; but exceptionalism also characterizes Gilson. A stalwart graduate of Seminaire Notre-Dame-des-Champs in Paris, he flew in the face of the declericalization of his age, the study of Western reason and revelation being the mainstay of his career. But most importantly for this essay, Gilson famously defied French cultural colonialism by proclaiming works by Averroes to be a "hallmark in the history of

---

1   Allan Bloom notes that Alexandre Kojève is a philosopher for being an interpreter with "a passion for clarity ..." Editor's Introduction, *Introduction to the Reading of Hegel*, edited by Allan Bloom and translated by James H. Nichols (Ithaca, New York: Cornell University Press, 1993).

Western civilization ..." and indeed the "ideal of a purely rational phi-losophy."[2] Placing the Church and a secularizing France in the same cor-ner, Gilson thereby uses an Arab philosopher, and one dealing in the Quran yet, to reclaim the Western tradition of reason.

Gilson holds: "Philosophy is about choice, the will to know" (Pref-ace, *B&SP*, 12). This essay will hold that Averroes' *The Decisive Trea-tise*,[3] a text about which Gilson says nothing, actually exemplifies that balance of awe, of deference, on one hand, and the assertiveness of ex-ceptionalism, on the other, that so characterize Gilson. And in particular it will demonstrate that, in considering Averroes, the concern of Gilson is less the project of interpreting an interpreter than in joining Averroes in engaging in interpretation precisely because of "the will to know" the interpreter in the *Treatise*, an interpreter who, as it turns out, is the di-vine.

To see this, and before exploring Gilson at his most philosophic, we turn to Gilson's understanding of a particular turn in thought in the Mid-dle Ages.

Idea and Society in Coexistence:
Gilson's Argument for the Centrality of Averroes

Rather than making a grand claim for philosophy and history, Gilson ac-tually holds that the key to maintaining reason and revelation in relation, and indeed in actual conversation, is to make the most modest claims for history and philosophy respectively. In his *Reason and Revelation in the Middle Ages*, Gilson runs counter to a monolithic understanding

---

2   *Reason and Revelation in the Middle Ages*, (New York: Charles Scribner's Sons, 1938), 41, 38. Two Gilson works are discussed in the essay: *Reason and Revelation in the Middle Ages*, abbreviated in the text as *R&R*, and *Being and Some Philosophers* (Toronto, Canada: Pontifical Institute for Mediaeval Studies, 1952), abbreviated in the text as *B&SP*.

3   References to *The Decisive Treatise* will generally be to the Charles But-terworth translation found in *Medieval Political Philosophy: A Sourcebook*, 2nd Edition, edited by Joshua Parens and Joseph C Macfarland (Ithaca, New York: Cornell University Press, 2011). References will be directly in the text and simply marked by pagination.

of history, instead implicitly calling on the instrumental use of cultural context. In the shadow of Heidegger, Gilson gives one of his more philosophic works the somewhat cheeky title of *Being and Some Philosophers* (Heidegger not being among them). In the face of a European philosophic tradition that viewed philosophy as the central discipline, Gilson holds that great ideas lie less at a pinnacle and more from a sifting of dialogues that intersect in time and space.

Thus Gilson writes of Averroes: "Averroes had always maintained that philosophical truth was absolute truth, the Koran and its theological implications being nothing more to him than popular approaches to philosophy."[4] Averroes' absolutism need not lead to a confrontation between reason and revelation. Averroes puts the place of determination neither with Western philosophy, nor with the Quran, but instead in society, as reason and revelation flourish among respective social groups. The issue then becomes whether this parallelism brings forth an intermingling of dialogues.

In this sense, *The Decisive Treatise* of Averroes, never explicitly treated by Gilson, would seem to be fertile ground for the contention by Gilson that theology is a "popular" approach to philosophy. Tellingly, in the *Treatise*, Averroes assigns the prescriptive role for a society neither to a religious leader, nor to a philosopher. Instead, Averroes gives this role to a lawgiver. And indeed, the salutation to Averroes at the *Treatise*'s beginning refers to him foremost as "jurist" and only later as an "imam" and "uniquely learned." Similarly, the *Treatise* ends in a salute to the "Law" (124, 139–40). And indeed, an explanation and defense of the Law is central to the *Treatise*, which puts forth the twofold purpose of Law: securing a knowledge or "cognizance" of God and directing the observant through right practice to secure happiness (135). Averroes most certainly allows that philosophy and reason may access the Law, and expresses the firm view that a study of the Law leads to correct concepts and judgments. However, the *Treatise* also holds that everyone must in some manner know the Law, be it through demonstrative, dialectical, or rhetorical means.

Suggestive of Gilson's instrumental use of history to derive

---

4   Gilson, *Reason and Revelation in the Middle Ages*, 53.

philosophic ideas, the *Treatise* discusses these three means or "methods" of accessing the Law in the context of the social problem that history suggests. For Averroes in the *Treatise*, the heart of the problem is how to keep most people in the body politic governed by the Law, the "multitude," observant in the face of false interpretations of the Law. Indeed, in the middle of the argument in the *Treatise*, Averroes seems to address three social "classes," defined in terms of their relation to the Law and the methods of approaching it: (1) a rhetorical class composed of the multitude at least capable of grasping the apparent sense of the Law through imagery and without interpretation; (2) a dialectical class composed of dialectical clerics understanding the Law through mixed appeal to imagery and argument; and (3) a demonstrative class of the "elect" for whom demonstration is interpretation determined through intellectual syllogistic reasoning (125–26, 136–38). Averroes has the most to say about the first and third classes. This is not surprising as talk is as common in the rhetorical class as correct thought is an ideal within the demonstrative elite class.

With these classifications, Averroes turns to political consequences. False demonstration, false interpretation, leads to civil unrest and war, as the multitude are misled. The *Treatise* then turns to more pernicious consequences of the unfortunate encounters between multitude and the Law (compare 138–39). This Averroes terms an additional consequence, one lying neither with the elect and demonstration, nor with the multitude and rhetoric.

In contrast to the transparency of rhetoric, Averroes argues that this neither/nor treatment of the Law can leave matters concealed, unstated, or imagined. It is "obscure" in comparison with the plain-spokenness of rhetoric. Similarly, Averroes suggests that while interpretation—and demonstration—may be rigorously examined within the elect, this neither/nor treatment has no such ready criteria for scrutiny. Instead, this treatment is "sophistical" for its dismissal of basic premises in reasoning (138–39). Averroes makes no frontal assault on dialectic; instead he attempts to undermine the temptation in theology as to dialectic's use.

The key to Averroes' argument, as Averroes emphasizes on multiple occasions as the *Treatise* concludes, is statements on the Law "declared" to or shared by "everyone." Such methods include, but are by no means limited to, the multitude. Averroes here is very much appealing to the common denominator in a society (134–35, 139). The end of the *Treatise* makes this clear in referencing demonstration, that instrument of the elect, as such a common denominator (138–39). The philosophic context for this solution will be discussed in terms articulated by Gilson in a general tribute to Medieval thought, in the section just following.

Averroes' arguments seek to discern a superintending philosophy very much grounded in Islamic jurisprudence and Quranic influence so as to govern a society.[5] First, the argument for a genuinely common solution based on and in favor of social cohesion is an argument for avoiding the problem with corrupted interpretations, those not grounded ultimately on syllogistic reasoning. Averroes' indictment of this practice is less that it leads to misunderstandings of the Law than that it leads to a confusion of the importance of reason and belief, with the distinction too often blurred in dialogue with the multitude (134, 138–39). Again, Averroes sees a truly universally accessible demonstration, presumably through interpretation easily delivered through effective popular rhetoric, as the solution.

Second, Averroes finds that the solution lies in the Law itself. The situs of the Law is both the logical and sentimental choice given the mixed nature of the social political order the *Treatise* addresses. Commonly, the Law is the locus of authority to which rhetoric for the multitude is aimed. However, even the *Treatise* treats the Law as having another side, one that will not accommodate the common denominator of joining the multitude to the elite. Even the conclusion of the *Treatise* acknowledges the continuing importance of mastery of the Law and the unique understanding of certain interpretations by a class "adept in demonstration." At the same time, the *Treatise*'s final salutation to the Law identifies it as having been given "[b]y His Grace ..." (139–40). These are two differing aspects of the Law that demand reconciliation in the form of a boundary between such interpretations of the Law that are universally accessible and those that are the exclusive province of the elect.

---

5   General Introduction, *Medieval Philosophy: A Sourcebook*, 2nd Edition, 2–
     5.

Third, Averroes profiles a solution to the issue of confusion within the social order as singular, what one translator understands as a "middle way of knowing God ..." beyond populistic appeals to authority for authority's sake but without the "turbulence" or confusion of dialectical theology.[6] Underlining either demonstration or interpretation that is accessible through rhetoric as the solution, Averroes summons the multitude to this path, and bids the elect to work to achieve it (139–40). The question then most precisely concerns the content of the accessible demonstration or interpretation.

Averroes indicates that properties of the Law "contain a means of alerting those adept in the truth to the true interpretation" (139). The *Treatise* appears to end in a somewhat conclusory, yet opaque, fashion, with little precise indication as to the identity of the people of truth, or to the exact criteria for a true interpretation.

For Averroes in the *Treatise*, political philosophy is thereby only derivatively a study of man in community and the ideas making community possible, and foremost a running attribution of the sway social context has over ideas, with history and philosophy in mutual indebtedness. With this, we turn to Gilson.

Gilson More Fully Explained: The Philosophical Underpinnings of Averroes' Middle Way

As noted from time to time above, aspects of the *Treatise* lead us to Gilson's position that social conditions influence ideas, a philosophy of history that yields a history of philosophy. This section will explore how Gilson might see this occurring as to the "middle way" of the *Treatise*'s conclusion. It will do so employing principally Gilson's 1938 *Reason and Revelation* and his 1952 *Being and Some Philosophers*.

The middle way for Averroes' multitude at the *Treatise*'s conclusion is fully consonant with Gilson's view of the character of philosophy.

---

6   This reference to the "middle way" occurs in the Hourani translation of *The Decisive Treatise* in *Medieval Political Philosophy: a Sourcebook*, 1st Edition, edited by Ralph Lerner and Mushin Mahdi (Ithaca, New York: Cornell University Press, 1972), 185.

That view borrows the force of rhetoric and piety as to the multitude on one hand, and openness to the force of syllogistic reasoning produced by philosophy on the other. In establishing this middle way, Averroes writes with design and emphasis, especially as to aspects of the Law that are less than fathomable to the multitude. The singular phrase in the *Treatise* that is both repeated and underscored is: "*None knows their interpretation but God*" (133, 137). [7] This is music to the ears of the two sides of Gilson, at once invoking awe of the divine on the one hand, and the exceptionalism of philosophy for the elite exercise of interpretation on the other.

Demonstration, for Averroes ideally supported by interpretation (130, 136), may cure error. But, implies Averroes, demonstration is only for the demonstrative class. However, we must explore a danger to the social order implied by Averroes: the choice between allowing for earthly, human understandings of the Law which are imperfect and therefore corrosive of a societal order, as Averroes' resort to history outlines, and blasphemy, the view that the demonstrative class can access God's interpretation of the Law.

Averroes is willing to risk a bit of both—in order to assert the preeminence of philosophy. First, Averroes calls for silence when the multitude confronts the unfathomable in the Law: rhetoric, the tool of the multitude, should cease, and make way not only for God but for interpretation, the tool of the elite and philosophy.

True to Gilson, but without turning immediately to him, we reference a guiding star in Islamic Medieval thought: that with Law as the center of society, jurisprudential textual interpretation is a philosophic exercise, and philosophy, and not theology, is the superior organizing discipline for providing the interpretation of the Law. The text is the object of access through reasoning, and then becomes the situs of revelation as well.

Gilson's *Reason and Revelation* brings Averroes front and center in the pantheon of thought of the Middle Ages. Averroes is a turning point in the Gilsonian sense. Although Islam differs from Christianity in its

---

7   The Butterworth translation of *The Decisive Treatise* attributes this to the
     Quran 3:7.

emphasis on the Law as center of both reason and revelation, Gilson describes all of the Middle Ages, regardless of the religious tradition, as pre-Averroistic: all three Abrahamic faiths attest to the precedence of revelation over reason in the sense of prescribing philosophy subsequent to revelation *(R&R*, 17–18, 21, 41). Hence, God accompanies interpretation in Averroes' call for a stop, for silence. Awe pervades the silence of all.

But so does the sense of philosophic exceptionalism. Gilson's *Reason and Revelation* boldly proclaims that "Averroes had always maintained that philosophic truth was absolute truth …." (*R&R*, 53). In the context of the way Gilson views the relation of society to idea, it is key to understand what Gilson takes "absolute truth" to mean. It means more than simply a certain truth. Rather, absolute truth implies absolute autonomy in truth-seeking, such that the truth-seeking process is apart from any other discipline outside philosophy.

This autonomy can only be established if revelation's vaunted status as precedent is neutralized relative to philosophy, or at least diminished in comparison to it. We thus look at the place of Averroes in *Reason and Revelation*. Chapter 2 commences with Averroes and the entire book ends with a final two words of introduction: "Thomas Aquinas." In between, Gilson gives considerable play to Latin Averroists, those who not only assert that philosophy is superior to theology, but also demonstrate that superiority, on the same field of endeavor as that for theology.

This latter is no mean trick, for Gilson suggests that the Western Christian tradition is indisputably and critically influenced by Averroes. Indeed, Averroes is both the one figure in *Reason and Revelation* to whom Gilson attributes great transcendent influence across religious traditions and the one figure who carries *Reason and Revelation* from nearly beginning to end. Granted, Averroes is the courier of Gilson's message that ideas emanate from history and society. Thus, in the very same sentence equating philosophic truth to "absolute truth," Gilson concludes with "the Koran and its theological implications being nothing more to [Averroes] than popular approaches to philosophy" *(R&R*, 53). One sees two threads in Gilson's Averroes: one representing a transcendent turn in Medieval thought that has wide implications for Western political philosophy, the other bent on local social cohesion within a community. Again, we see exceptionalism and awe in play.

We return to *"None knows their interpretation but God."* God thereby reflects upon God through the activity of interpretation, God's original handiwork being the Law. Averroes references God's interpretation in the following context: in discussing the multitude, which is particularly susceptible to dialectical and rhetorical approaches, there is a need for a brake on rhetoric imposed by awe as evidenced in silence. The multitude needs to see God's exclusive domain of interpretation in certain cases so as to diminish the possibility for anarchical ambiguity through rhetoric (133, 137). The *Treatise*'s repeated reference to God as initial interpreter is thus instrumental, an idea reflective of the social order and therefore suggestive of Gilson.

However, Averroes leaves us with a challenge. The word of the Law, as an object of interpretation, is a "stop" for the multitude, a brake on rhetoric. This said, it is apparently a "go" for the elite, the demonstrative class. Each time Averroes puts on the brakes for the former group, he does so guardedly and in the context of a larger argument for the demonstrative class to eventually proceed (133, 137). But how to so do in the sacred territory of the divine?

Being and Some Philosophers:
The Intersection of Essence and Existence in the Interpreter

The *Treatise*'s elite interpreters are less formulators, more custodians and administrators of appropriate snippets of interpretation to the multitude. Averroes likens the elite to physicians and holders of a divine deposit (127, 137, 138). In referencing God's interpretation, Averroes actually asks that we interpret a divine interpreter in a properly Gilsonian way: in awe and with a sense of the exceptionalism.

Gilson emphasizes in conclusion: "That, at last, is a Revelation worthy of the name: not as revelation of God to ourselves, but the Revelation of God Himself to us" (*R&R*, 99). As the duty of the multitude is to stop rhetoric, the first duty of the philosopher is to be quiet, to be in awe—so as thereby to be in the realm of the exceptional. The silence of the elite is broken with the realization so emphasized by Averroes that the core of revelation of God Himself is interpretation as *"None knows their interpretation but God."* The interpretation of the elite thus begins by letting God be Himself, by Himself as interpreter. "Cognizance" of such is the core of interpreting the interpreter. Gilson notes in his Preface to *Being* that philosophic choice exemplifies both the reticence that comes with awe—philosophy's sense of reverential modesty accompanying Islamic thought—and the perspective of exceptionalism that comes with philosophy's status as the integrating discipline.

The question is how to retain both Averroes' defense of the immutability of the Law to command the obedience of the multitude, on one hand, and his view of choice of the Law as an object of philosophy, on the other.

Gilson shows that the choice is how to reconcile existence to essence in viewing the Law. Text, as text, contains an apparent sense, as Averroes reminds in the *Treatise*'s many references to "apparent sense" (129, 132–33, 137). Averroes' audience for the apparent sense is almost always the multitude. This is to subordinate the apparent as well as to reassure. Averroes' elite appears equally silent in the face of divine interpretation, but for an entirely different purpose, one the *Treatise* will term "an inner sense" (129). Gilson sees in this sense an emergence of divine essence, from inner divine self-reflection into the textual existence of the Law. As Gilson's conclusion in *Reason and Revelation* signals, "Revelation" is actually philosophic interpretation, in which divine essence is rendered into the lived, the apparent, the practical timeliness of the Law. Or, as Gilson emphasizes, the only "Revelation ... worthy of the name" is that from God, but only after God reflects on Himself. The God of Gilson and of Gilson's Averroes is thus fundamentally philosophical and reflective, before becoming textually juridical[8] and commanding.

Philosophic awe has a very particular profile; its task is to ensure the divine interpretation that the elite will in turn interpret. Thus, philosophic choice entails exercise and practice, but only in the hands of and under the auspices of the learned, the elite, the philosophic. As

---

8   Gilson in *Reason and Revelation* notes that Averroes bequeaths " ... the ideal of a purely rational philosophy ..." in face of revelation to the West, a contribution that Gilson notes is at once a "hallmark" in the history of Western thought, yet one that would imbed " ... in the minds of theologians a growing mistrust of philosophy" (*R&R*, 38, 40, 84).

Butterworth's translation of the *Treatise* illustrates, the Law prescribes the social order, and thereby determines the fashion in which it, the Law, is understood, complete with methods and missteps.

Being specifically holds out much for the philosophy as active and moving quite beyond Averroes' initial injunction to silence. *Being* transcends initial philosophic awe and moves to the ever-present Gilsonian aspect of exceptionalism that characterizes philosophic choice. *Being* treats the relationship between existence and essence from Parmenides to Kierkegaard and Brentano. The second chapter of *Being* presents Averroes as a staunch defender of the classical view that essence is substance, and existence is subordinate, a subsidiary concern associated with his rivals in the pantheon of Islamic thought.[9] From this, however, the *Treatise* seems to elevate existence, yet not employ the term "essence."

The subordination will prove an active one, quite beyond mere and initial philosophic silence in the face of divine interpretation.

For Gilson, the combination of awe in the face of divine interpretation and exceptionalism means that an active philosophic choice is made—but only very carefully. Averroes obliges here:

> It is obligatory for whoever wants to remove the heretical innovation ... to apply himself to the precious Book and pick from it the indications *existing* for every simple thing we are responsible for believing. In his reflection, he is to strive *for this apparent sense* ... without interpreting anything ... (139; emphasis supplied).

Here, Averroes addresses the elite, those adept at demonstration, who might distinguish the apparent from that which is not so (139). As it turns out, the positive action taken by an elite after awe and silence is not creation, but elimination, elimination that targets that "*existing* for every simple thing."

---

9   Averroes seems to hold that Alghazali, an Islamic interpreter of the Quran, blurs the distinction between essence and " ... existent thing that exists from something other than itself" in time (130–31).

The modesty of mere cognizance signals that a Law is not only unto itself, but a divine Law that is largely incomprehensible. By this the *Treatise* means that, to attain the Law that commands both the energy and attention of all in society, as intended by the *Treatise*, the active philosophic choice as to interpretation is simplification.

The simplified, the apparent, has a precedential value, a temporal quality, as Law. As Christianity and John the Evangelist have it in the first sentence of John's Gospel: "In the beginning was the Word ..."[10] The apparent, the temporal and the textual are aligned as they are in the *Treatise*.

But Averroes also has it that the Law has "an inner sense" that is not apparent but that is ripe for interpretation (129). Averroes does not elaborate much here, but Gilson, and the Western tradition to which Averroes belongs, does. Gilson reminds us in *Being* that Averroes subordinates existence to the much superior issue of essence, as he subordinates the business of the multitude to that of the elite (*B&SP*, 56–57). Accordingly, John continues the first sentence of this Gospel: "and the Word was with God, and the Word was God."[11] John proceeds in step, first attesting to the text, then to parallel existence of text and God, and then to the identity of the two. Similarly, as to this last, Averroes again notes: *"None knows their interpretation but God."* Isolated divine interpretation, the Law, is God.

This essay began with remarks as to interpreting the interpreter. This is exactly what Averroes appears to have in mind as to his leaving to the elect, to Gilson's philosophic choice, the interpretation of the interpreter. This need not be as obscure as it might appear. Like John, Averroes works with the intermediate step of the Law and God working in tandem. This implicates agency in the formation of the Law. And so Averroes obliges referencing *"'The spirit is by the command of my Lord; and of knowledge you have been given only a little.'"* (137).[12] Here, Averroes clearly intimates that the spirit is implicated outside the

---

10 John 1:1.
11 John 1:1.
12 The Butterworth translation of *The Decisive Treatise* references the Quran 17:38 as the source here.

realm of the apparent, outside the realm of that which is cognizable by the multitude.

The spirit and God would appear to be eventually indistinguishable. Indeed, in concluding the *Treatise*, Averroes notes the mandate that the elect must secure the "root of the Law" by means of "complete reflection" (140). But this need not mean that the elect immediately reflect. The *Treatise* only holds that they adhere to "the path of reflection" and in fact there may be multiple reflections (127, 140). And the *Treatise* makes it clear that reflection is based on interpretation, but that the interpretation need not be of one's own making. As Averroes notes as the *Treatise* approaches a conclusion: "Sound interpretation is the deposit mankind is charged with holding... God says *'Indeed we offered the deposit to the heavens, to the earth and to the mountains ...'* " (138).[13] And for Averroes, soundness finds its foundation in essence, that which is the cause of the existing thing. Thus, when Averroes emphasizes *"None knows their interpretation but God,"* he is referencing essence as God alone with interpretation, which is to say the perfect interpretation that is Law that is comprehensive and textual. According to the depiction of reflection noted at the commencement of the *Treatise*, a complete reflection is God alone in self-reflection, God alone with "Himself" in the handiwork in the Law, the *essential* cause tied to the then *existing* thing that becomes the text of the Law.

The Law thus becomes the primary philosophic text, and God the indispensable primary philosopher as its author. This gives the jurist cum philosopher a holy responsibility for laboring in the most direct and immediate handiwork of the divine, the text of the Law. But the Law for its momentousness holds the earthly Islamic philosopher at a peculiar distance, a distance measured by awe and reverence and then by a sense of philosophic exceptionalism as the philosopher as interpreter of the divine interpreter begins a careful selective pruning noted above.

Let there be no mistaking—to style the Law as an interpretation is blasphemous—until we realize that we are talking about the Law as God's own interpretation, the product of self-reflection. Here the

---

13   The Butterworth translation of *The Decisive Treatise* references the Quran 33:72 as the source here.

multitude, and the cavalcade of rhetoricians, dialecticians and others taken to task in the *Treatise,* dare not tread. The task of the interpretation of the divine understanding (or interpretation) that is the Law is a job for the elite of the elite.

Entry into the mind of God is a dangerous business, Averroes implies. From the *Treatise,* the exact formula for this needed most masterful of demonstrations is not at the ready. And so it is hard to know where to start.

But Gilson leaves some invaluable clues. In *Being,* Gilson maintains that both essentialists and existentialists make the common mistake of failing to account for eternal essence as the actual existence of essence and a cause of its becoming, of its definition (*B&SP,* 182). The becoming of God as essence thus lies in existence, as that existence is the activity, the becoming of divine essence that is God's self-reflection. This is the possible "inner sense" in the Law in which divine self-reflection lies deep beneath appearances in the text of the Law. As Gilson will acknowledge at this critical turn in modern thought: "God is an essence which possesses in itself sufficient reason for its own existence" (*B&SP,* 123). Gilson extrapolates this point, not to signal the subordination of existence to essence, for existence in being ends up as an activity, the primary activity of being, whereas essence is substance, form. As activity carries form, existence "is both [existence's] own essence and the source of all other essences and existences" *(B&SP,* 124). God's existence, registered through self-reflection, accomplishes nothing less. Whereas existence is an act of being, essence is more akin to what one Butterworth translation of Averroes has termed "quiddity" and its relation to "substance."[14] "Revelation," activity or existence, is that which bears the "Himself" of God, essence, out. Gilson's recast of the relation between existence and essence thus points to a more careful consideration of what the *Treatise* terms the "inner sense" of the Law.

God's self-reflection need not unsettle the Law. To the contrary, Gilson notes: "To be (*esse*) is to act (*agere*) and to act is to tend ... to an

---

14 *Averroes's Middle Commentaries on Aristotle's Categories and De Inter-pretatione,* translated by Charles E. Butterworth (Princeton, New Jersey: Princeton University Press, 1983), 28–29.

end wherein achieved being may ultimately rest" (*B&SP*, 186). Averroes' argument in the *Treatise* carefully maintains that the act of existence that is God's self-reflection incorporates and celebrates divine essence. The middle of the *Treatise* discusses things, and then eternally existing things. Averroes then moves to clarify through the language of levels of existence, speaking of existence in time, and then critically of an "existence before this existence" of being in the world. This is the prior realm of "form," prior to that existence that is worldly appearances (131–32). In the dangerous territory of the mind of God, Averroes is primarily concerned to protect the inner sanctum of the divine, as well as the ability of the elite among the elite to access it. Averroes thus links existence and eternity, which is to say divine essence. Because an interpretation of the Law that undermines eternity and divine essence is inexcusable for Averroes, he implies that the Law is in fact coextensive with, if not identical to, divine interpretation and the product of God's self-reflection.[15] The "inner sense" of the Law means that in the afterlife, one might encounter a realm in which all appearances are discussed, and one might behold God in self-reflection, acting and being, existence and essence.

Gilson's *Being* clearly leads us to understand Averroes in this manner. The Law is a monolith, as only the product of divine self-reflection can be. Averroes terms the Law a deposit bestowed by the divine. It is both existence as self-reflecting act and ethereal essence: *"Then He directed Himself toward the heaven and it was smoke"* (132). And, as Gilson reminds, the philosophic choice is to look behind the din and dust of heavenly smoke, existence and essence in friction, to God alone in self-reflection.[16] As Gilson suggests, it is at that moment that philosophy, and its elite, chooses to behold. And, as for interpreting the

15   Hence, Averroes in the *Treatise* will excuse errors in interpretation among such elite as long as the interpreting elite acknowledges the "existence (of the next life)" and "give a manner of interpretation not leading to the disavowal of its existence" (134).

16   Indeed, Butterworth's work on the *Epistle Dedicatory*, which he sees as a preface to the *Treatise*, promises to go beyond the terms of the *Treatise*. Averroes, *The Book of the Decisive Treatise Determining the Connection Between the Law and Wisdom and the Epistle Dedicatory*, (xxxvii).

interpreter, only heaven knows. Among truly modern men trying to understand Averroes, only a man of awe in Verdun's trenches, and only a man of the seminary's philosophic discernment, could have understood.

American Churches and the Holocaust: The Tragic Struggle Between Revelation and Reason in the 1930s

Melissa M. Matthes

Although Charles Butterworth's most significant contribution to political philosophy has been to the understanding and appreciation of medieval Islamic political thought, his thematic concern with the tensions, contradictions, and overlapping of revelation and reason in political life can help guide understandings of modern contests of revelation and reason. In his translations and commentary on Alfarabi, for example, Dr. Butterworth illuminated how philosophy could help to tell the difference between virtuous religion and ignorant, erroneous, or deceptive religion. Philosophy is a method to secure the truth. Indeed, Alfarabi argued that philosophy could even be employed to confirm the beliefs and opinions of religion. Yet, for Alfarabi religion was more than a mere tool of philosophy. For Alfarabi, as well as for Dr. Butterworth, the relationship between reason and revelation, between philosophy and religion, remained a complicated if contentious one.

These complications and contests have continued through to the modern era. Political philosophers continue to debate and struggle with questions regarding the role of religion in political life. What kind of truth is religious belief? Can religious understandings have political authority? And by what method can a political community arrive at a religious and democratic truth? While the answers to these challenges remain, one of the historical examples that many political philosophers use as a template of tragic failure of reason and revelation to reconcile was the inability of the American Christian Church, writ large, inability to articulate a religious truth in a way which had the political authority to thwart the persecution of Jews in Hitler's Third Reich. Although multiple religious leaders—Protestant, Catholic, and Jewish—knew well the suffering of Germany's Jews, they were unable to craft a political theology sufficiently robust and/or politically effective to engage with and potentially thwart the damage rampant throughout Nazi Germany to all that was holy and truthful by any measure in any tradition, either political, philosophical, or religious.

American religious leaders could not even mobilize the American populace or its government leaders to substantial political action. Part of the failure (and there is a vast literature detailing the multiple failures and the elusive explanations[1]) rests, however, on the neglect of one of Professor Butterworth's signature insights—the necessity of thinking carefully and fully about the historical relation between revelation and reason in political life. American religious leaders and their members tried ineffectually to use Enlightenment reason to achieve what with the benefit of hindsight many now understand might have been more effectively crushed by a public religion fully demanding and practicing its own theological principles rather than accomadate state reason. Here, Dr. Butterworth's attention to the distinctions in political philosophy between various kinds of authority—particularly church versus state, and faith versus reason, is particularly helpful.[2]

Much has been written and debated about what and when American religious leaders knew about Jewish suffering in Germany. There is considerable evidence that they knew quite a bit. As early as March 22, 1933 (a mere three months after the election of Adolf Hitler as Chancellor) American Christian clergy and lay people appealed to the German people to put an end to the persecution of the Jews. They urged preachers

---

1   Among the noteworthy are David S. Wyman, *The Abandonment of the Jews: America and the Holocaust* (New York: New Press, 1984); Henry L. Feingold, *The Politics of Rescue: The Roosevelt Administration and the Holocaust 1938–1945* (New Brunswick: Rutgers University Press, 1970); Robert W. Ross, *So It Was True: The American Protestant Press and the Nazi Persecution of the Jews* (Minneapolis: University of Minnesota Press, 1980); Arthur D. Morse, *While Six Million Died: A Chronicle of American Apathy* (New York: Random House, 1967).

2   See Charles Butterworth, "State and Authority in Arabic Political Thought," in *The Foundations of the Arabic State*, ed. Ghassan Salame (London: Croom Helm, 1987), 91–111.

throughout the United States to rally their congregations on the following Sunday for a united stand against Hitler. The Summons to the Churches was sponsored by the Interfaith Committee and signed by Bishop William T. Manning (Episcopalian), Mr. Alfred E. Smith, the former governor of New York (Roman Catholic), and others of equal prominence. This summons "against intolerance" helped to gather on Sunday, March 27, 1933 a very large collection of the faithful (estimates are that nearly 40, 000 people attended) at Madison Square Garden, New York City. The event was widely reported and there were similar rallies and protests against "the present anti-Jewish policy of the Nazi government" recorded in 65 cities across America.[3]

At the end of May 1933, another "manifesto" was signed by 1200 Protestant ministers from 42 states across America, as well as Canada,

> We Christian ministers are greatly distressed at the situation of our Jewish brethren in Germany. In order to leave no room for doubt as to our feelings on this subject, we consider it an imperative duty to raise our voices in indignant and sorrowful protest against the pitiless persecution to which the Jews are subjected under Hitler's rule.

The statement continued with an acknowledgment of America's own racism and prejudices, but urged Germany not to turn back the hands of its own progress.

The statement acknowledged that the facts were "irrefutable" and the statement even detailed some of the most heinous features of Nazi doctrine. "Nazi doctrine is that Jews are poisonous germs in German blood and must therefore be treated as a scourge. Hitler's followers now apply this doctrine. They systematically pursue a 'Cold Pogrom' of inconceivable cruelty against our Jewish brethren."

---

3   Robert G. Waite, "Raise My Voice Against Intolerance: The Anti-Nazi Rally in Madison Square Garden, March 27, 1933, and the American Public's Outrage over the Nazi Persecution of the Jews" in *The New York History Review*, October 2013. http://nyhrarticles.blogspot.com/2013/10/raise-my-voice-against-intolerance-anti.html. Accessed July 2015.

An additional statement was written by the Executive Committee of the Federal Council of the Churches of Christ in America in November 1935. This statement protested against the treatment inflicted on Jews on two primary counts: first, the treatment was unworthy of a great nation and, second, and more profoundly, "the philosophy on which it is based is a heathen philosophy. Founded on a religious interpretation of race ... it is an attempt of a tribal heathen movement, based on race, blood, and soil to separate Christianity from its historical origin and a Christian nation from its religious past."[4]

These initial statements urged Germany to cease its persecution of the Jews, not primarily because Jews were worthy qua Jews, but because Germany was. Her treatment of the Jews was a taint on *German* greatness and progress. While it may seem a rather odd rhetoric for religious leaders to use, they were apparently trying to appeal to what they imagined to be in Germany's self-interest. Of course, part of why this rhetoric was unsuccessful was because Nazi Germany believed that the persecution (and eventually the elimination) of the Jews was not only a remedy for their post-WWI degradation, but that the contamination of the Jews was also what was continuing to forestall their phoenix-like return to Aryan greatness. So, on the first count—that Germany was interested in retrieving her own greatness, the American clergy were correct; but on the second count, how to achieve it, they were sadly misguided.

While the clerical statements and manifestos seem to have been widely reproduced and reported both in Christian and Jewish publications, as well as in major newspapers, they did not prompt specific political interventions on the part of the clergy (i.e., funding for Jewish refugees). There were two noteworthy exceptions: 1) the Rev. Charles S. Macfarland's personal correspondence and eventual interview with Adolf Hitler, and 2) the attempt by American Catholic, Protestant, and Jewish religious leaders to increase the number of Jewish child refugees admitted to the United States in 1939 and 1940. Both of these examples will be detailed below.

---

4 Quoted from *The Federal Council of Churches Bulletin*, December 1938 in Johan Snoek, *The Grey Book: A Collection of Protests Against Anti-Semitism and the Persecution of the Jews* (New York: Humanities Press, 1969), Part II, Chapter 17.

These early rallies and protests, while potentially a beacon of what might have been possible, simultaneously revealed some of the challenges that would ultimately unwind any meaningful political progress.. First, Cardinal O'Connell of Boston withdrew his participation from the Madison Square Garden event because he had received a telegram from the German Foreign Minister Konstantin von Neurath assuring him that "alleged pogroms against German Jews ... are devoid of all foundation. Hundreds of thousands of Jews carry on their lives throughout Germany as usual ... these stories of discrimination evidently emanate from sources which desire to poison the friendly relations between Germany and the United States and to discredit the new National Government of Germany."[5] While one bishop's withdrawal (even an influential metropolitan one) was not catastrophic, his reasons were foreboding: the protest were not necessary, the problem had already been resolved. The Mayor of New York Patrick O'Brien echoed this belief when he took the stage at the Madison Square Garden rally saying he took comfort from "assurances ... from high German officials that resolute action will be taken in Germany to prevent the possibility of any further persecution of Jews in that country."[6] This was the first wave of the denouement—American officials relying on Nazi war propaganda for information.

The alacrity of the Nazi propaganda machine to reach this granular level of grass-roots religious protestors was a testament to the concern that the Nazi Party had about American protest. Nazi officials called the American rallies part of the "Jewish power struggle against Germany" and a coordinated effort at "atrocity propaganda." Forestalling American religious protests or, indeed, any kind of American protests, was part of the Nazi anti-Semitic agenda. The Nazi press attempted to craft the American protests as part of the continued martyrdom of Germany and its new regime. In fact, as a result of the New York City rallies, Goebbels decided that "we will be effective against this foreign hatred only when we force out its originators or at least the beneficiaries, namely the

---

5   Neurath denies Rumors," *New York Times*, March 27, 1933.

6   "O'Brien Pays Tribute To Jewish Contribution to German Culture," *New York Times*, March 28, 1933.

Jews living in Germany who have remained here untouched." Their response, then, was to call for a major boycott of all Jewish shops in Germany.[7]

The second and concurrent wave of the denouncement crashed with Franklin D. Roosevelt's new Secretary of State, Cordell Hull. After his recent appointment in the spring of 1933, Secretary Hull asked the American Ambassador in Berlin, Frederic M. Sackett, to report on the situation of German Jews; the Ambassador had been reporting for the last several months about the deteriorating situation for the Jews, writing on March 9, "Democracy in Germany has received a blow from which it may never recover."[8] Nonethelss, Hull reported to the press as well as to Jewish leaders, Rabbi Wise and Bernard Deutsch, in a personal telegram that the Ambassador had allegedly reported back "whereas there was for a short time considerable physical mistreatment of Jews this phase may be considered virtually terminated." In fact, Hull gave his press conference *before* Sackett had even responded. Yet, according to Hull, the Ambassador's report concluded that "stabilization appears to have been reached and there are indications that in other phases the situation is improving." This was front-page news in *The New York Times*. Another *New York Times* reporter in Berlin concurred with the assessment, "The German rulers, under the pressure of world opinion, seem to be making a sincere effort to reduce physical persecution and place their regime in a better light before the world."[9]

While not relying on Nazi propaganda, this assessment by the Ambassador as well as by well-known journalists was the result of an overestimation of the reach and power of American political influence. The misunderstanding was also the result of a confluence of personnel limitations—first Secretary Hull was new to his position having been appointed only six weeks earlier (although he will eventually serve with

---

7   Waite, "Raise My Voice Against Intolerance," 8.

8   Arthur Morse, *While Six Million Died: A Chronicle of American Apathy* (New York: Random House, 1967), 105.

9   "Nazis End Attack on Jews in Reich, Our Embassy Finds," *New York Times*, March 27, 1933. Also reported in *The Boston Globe* and *The Chicago Daily Tribune*. See Robert G. Waite, "Raise My Voice Against Intolerance," nn.51–52.

distinction for eleven years as America's longest serving Secretary of State). Second, the Ambassador in Berlin, Frederick Sackett, was a Republican appointed by Herbert Hoover and thus not admitted to the inner circles of Democratic power; Sackett also retired at the end of the month of American protests and rallies in March 1933. His replacement William Dodd, a Democrat, did not arrive in Berlin until July (although he, too, would be largely ineffective).

Within weeks, Americans mistakenly supposed they had rectified German policy regarding the treatment of their Jewish citizens. Apparently, American officials believed that so efficacious was American shaming that the result would be, not a Pharaoh like hardening of hearts, but quick German capitulation. It was a miscalculation without any political or psychological understanding of the forces animating Nazi Germany; it was also an arrogant assessment of the persuasive influence of American political and cultural power in the mid-1930s. Even the progressive magazine, *The Nation*, clucked a mere week after the American protests, "Before the expressed sense of outrage throughout the world, the Nazi head devils have pulled in their horns."[10]

Although ultimately effete, the church declarations are historically important for two reasons: first, they begin to answer the question of when and what American clergy knew about the treatment of Jews in Nazi Germany. The details from both these statements, including that the "facts are irrefutable" and the knowledge that Nazi doctrine "considered Jews poisonous germs" indicate that American clergy were sufficiently (and relatively early) well informed of the travails and discrimination against German Jews. Second, the statements also reveal that while American clergy found the treatment of the Jews largely unjust, they were ill prepared to bring their concerns to the American government and to urge then President Franklin D. Roosevelt to do something dramatic (or even moderate) to ameliorate Jewish suffering. Some of this failure was organizational, some of it was theological and prejudicial, and some of it was the tragic conflation of historical circumstances and personalities.

The organizational limitations were manifest in the approach of Rev.

10 "Nazis Against the World," *The Nation* 136 (April 5, 1933): 360.

Dr. Charles S. Macfarland, then General Secretary of the Federal Council of Churches. MacFarland had studied in Germany, was fluent in German and was engaged in research on church/state relations in Germany. In the early 1930s, he wrote that he had "an enlarged confidence that the Evangelical Church of Germany will, when the confusion of the present hour has passed, be found to be faithful to its trust."[11] As a result, perhaps of this optimism, Macfarland began a well-intentioned (if misguided) correspondence with Adolf Hitler in the autumn of 1933 and eventually had a personal interview with him in 1934. Macfarland wanted it to be plain that he was not to be compromised, so before accepting the invitation for the interview, he insisted that he was coming to discuss his point of view freely. "Well, it must be made clear that I am not going there to discuss Browning or Tennyson and I shall have to be permitted to choose my own subjects."[12] Apparently, Hitler responded that he "desired me to talk freely with him."[13]

During the hour-long meeting, Macfarland told Hitler that the German Evangelical Church "could not and would not yield to his politico-social theory, including his so-called Aryan laws, and that if it did, it would not only cut itself off from the Christian churches of the world, but would cease to be Christian." Hitler repeated often throughout the exchange that he was a "man sent of God" and explained that he was saving Germany from a worse fate: communism/Bolshevism. Hitler, apparently at this point still interested in the good opinion of religious leaders, said that he was willing to meet with any protesting pastors and invited them "to come and I will give them a full hearing."[14]

Macfarland followed up the meeting with additional correspondence, including a letter in which he wrote of the near complete hostility of the American people toward Hitler's policy of dealing with the Jews in Germany. Macfarland also met with Karl Barth while in Germany and consulted with Dietrich Bonhoeffer about what could/should be done.

11 Charles S. Macfarland, *The New Church and the New Germany: A Study of Church and State* (New York: MacMillan, 1934), ix.
12 Charles S. Macfarland, *Across the Years*, (New York: Macmillan Company, 1936), 167.
13 Ibid.
14 Ibid., 166.

Macfarland called for a "constructive measure of justice" although "recognizing the social problem involved." On this count, Macfarland modelled the anti-Semitism of his era. In previous work, Macfarland had acknowledged that German Jews had exhibited undue influence among the professional class in Germany: "It must be admitted that the presence of the Jews, though relatively few in number, did cause a real economic, cultural, social and institutional problem in Germany, as it has to a lesser degree in other nations."[15] While he opposed Hitler's unjust treatment of Jews, he also agreed that there were "issues" that needed to be addressed and "reconciled."

In his correspondence, Macfarland called for Hitler to issue a statement that would establish the freedom of the German Evangelical Church. "It needs to be made clear that the state desires the Church to maintain its own detached life."[16] Hitler apparently valued the influence of the American churches at the time and he replied to Macfarland's letters, stating that he wished "to promote the unity of the Church," and further that he accepted the letter "in the same spirit in which it was written"; Hitler even thanked Rev. Macfarland for his "candid and sympathetic appeal."[17]

Of course, the meeting and correspondence came to naught and on June 2, 1937, Macfarland published an open letter to Hitler in *The New York Times*. The letter began with a reminder of the earlier correspondence and used Hitler's own words regarding responding in a spirit in which the recommendation were given. Macfarland's criticisms were bold and the alarm was clear, "Instead of doing justice to the Jews, you have permitted them to be harassed and despoiled. Your treatment of them has been ruthless, without the slightest appearance of mercy, even reminding one of the infamous edicts of Herod in stretching the hand of violence to the littlest child." The letter continued, "Your attitude toward the little handful of Jews in Germany and your so-called Aryan and

15 Cited in the review, *The New Church and the New Germany*, Dr. Charles S. Macfarland (New York: MacMillan Company, 1934) http://www.jta.org/1934/05/13/archive/the-new-church-marred-by-accepting-of-nazi-facts.
16 Ibid.,168.
17 Ibid.,169.

Nordic ideas have had no little effect ... you undermined the most basic ideal of Christianity, on which unity alone can be secured."[18] Macfarland continued, "You often extol personal courage, but you appear to define it solely in physical and combative terms. If you want to see German value at its best, look at the pastors who are standing for the freedom of the Christian gospel, including those in jails and concentration camps."

The letter ended, "you are leading your adopted nation to an abyss, for you cannot build an enduring nation upon force and hate." This was Machiavellian advice as much as pastoral counseling. MacFarland was telling Hitler how he could hold onto power. Macfarland was NOT preaching to Hitler to be "a good man." Macfarland also took a swipe at Hitler's own genesis story—first, Hitler was himself born across the border from Bavaria in a small village in Austria (hence, "your adopted nation") and Hitler's family tree was complicated and a source of embarrassment to the ethnic cleanser, in part, because the identity of Hitler's maternal grandfather was in doubt. Indeed, there were suspicions that one of Hitler's ancestors might have been Jewish.

Macfarland was a noteworthy American clergyman. He actively tried to understand Hitler's treatment of the Jews, initially defending the revolution in Germany, although not the unjust persecution of religious minorities. When Hitler refused to adjust his treatment, Macfarland publicly renounced him. The renunciation was widely reported across the United States and Germany. What is revelatory about the correspondence and the interview is first, the mere fact that Hitler granted the interview. The interview itself attests to several things: first, Hitler's recognition of the influence of American religious leaders. At this point, at least, Hitler was still actively courting their good will and high opinion or, at least, engaged in the theater of cultivating this good will. Second, the correspondence and interview demonstrated how little political organization and acumen American church leaders had at the time. The idea that a single religious leader could negotiate with Adolf Hitler was quixotic at best, but more likely simply inexperienced. Indeed, even the public renunciation of Hitler revealed that Macfarland took Hitler's duplicity personally, hurling invective at the Nazi that "he had given his word to do otherwise."

18 *The New York Times*, June 9, 1937.

Although the entire episode from start to finish achieved little, the ferocity of the attempt to improve the conditions of Jews in Germany and the confidence with which it was made by Rev. Dr. Charles Mac-farland was nonetheless still admirable in the echo chamber which was American religious leadership throughout the 1930s.

*

Another US religious intervention, again without positive consequence for German Jews, occurred several years later. After Kristallnacht (November 9–10, 1938) the Executive Committee of the Federal Council of Churches in America proposed to set aside November 20, 1938, as "the occasion when prayer will be sought in the United States for refugees, both Christian and Jewish."[19] The officials of both the Roman Catholic Church and various Jewish organizations also designated the same date for a period of prayer and intercession. The governors from a dozen states throughout the United States issued statements and proclamations urging citizens to go to their places of worship on that day for collective prayer for the suffering.

The news of the devastation of Kristallnacht was front-page news in *The New York Times* every day from November 10–24, 1938. On five of the first six days, there were editorials on the tragedy, three of them the lead editorial of the day.[20] The story was national news and the Jewish press responded ferociously.[21] Yet, 77% of Americans polled by Gallup in November 1938 **After** Kristallnacht opposed an increase in the quota of refuges from Germany who would be allowed to come to the United States.[22] And, at a press conference on November 15, when asked whether he was

19 Johan M. Snoek, *The Grey Book: A Collection of Protests Against Anti-Semitism and the Persecution of the Jews Issued by Non-Roman Catholic Churches and Church Leaders During Hitler's Rule* (New York: Humanity Press, 1970), 87.

20 Haskel Lookstein, *Were We Our Brothers' Keepers? The Public Response of American Jews to the Holocaust 1938–1944* (New York: Hartmore House, 1985), 37.

21 Ibid., 45.

22 Ibid., 43.

contemplating a mass transfer of Jews from Germany, President Roosevelt replied, "I have given a great deal of thought to that … the time is not ripe for that." Would he recommend to Congress the relaxation of immigration quotas? "That is not in contemplation; we have a quota system."[23]

Then, after several months of work, on January 9, 1939, a petition on behalf of German refugee children was left for President Roosevelt at the White House by a large group of American clergymen. Leaders of both the Catholic and Protestant churches signed the petition. The petition read in part, "The American people have made clear its reaction to the oppression of all minority groups, religious and racial, throughout Germany. It has been especially moved by the plight of the children." The petition called on "all Americans to join together without regard to race, religion or creed in offering refuge to children as a token of our sympathy and as a symbol of our faith in the ideals of human brotherhood."[24] Senator Robert F. Wagner, a Democrat from New York, attempting to implement the proposal, introduced a resolution to the Senate, known as the Child Refugee Bill. It proposed that a maximum of 10,000 children under the age of fourteen be admitted in 1939 and a similar number in 1940. The clergy's proposal also offered that American families at no cost to the US government would privately house all the children. Initially, the bill proposed that these 20,000 children would be in addition to the yearly German quota.

Then in July, the bill was modified with a compromise that had devastating effects: the 20,000 children's visas would be issued against the German quota. Senator Wagner then withdrew his resolution because he feared that the children's visas would become death warrants for the 20,000 adults they would replace: "One of the chief arguments raised against this bill was that the admittance of 20,000 refugee children to the United States from Germany and the refusal to admit their parents would be against the laws of God, and therefore would be an opening wedge for a later request for the admission of about 40,000 adults, the parents of the children in question."[25] Here the clergy and their allies were undone by

23 Quoted in ibid., 43.
24 Snoek, 89.
25 Ibid., 89 n.4.

their own natural law values—the sanctity and unity of the nuclear family. The clergy did not know how to counter reasons of state; they were unable to make state interests line up with church principles. And, thus, they conceded the issue back to the Roosevelt administration. The magazine, *The New Republic*, chided the ineffective American response: "There is a masochistic type of pity which merely enjoys feeling the woes of the oppressed or the unfortunate but actually is reluctant to do anything effective to ameliorate the plight of the victims since that would end the possibility of luxuriating in the sorrow of others."[26]

In 1939, 61% of Americans opposed the Wagner-Rogers bill.[27] Thus, when ministers urged increasing the number of Jewish refugees they were fighting popular opinion. Many Americans at the time had not recovered financially from the depression and were reluctant to open the ports to those they imagined would be potential competitors. In fact, to soothe such anxieties, Bloomingdale's, the Jewish-owned department store, published their employment figures in order to confirm that of their 2500 employees only eleven were German refugees.[28]

Nonetheless, many Americans did not fully trust the reports of Nazi persecution. Having been deceived during WWI by war-time propaganda, they were suspicious of these stories of systematic destruction. Some contemporary commentators have noted that this pre-Auschwitz generation was the last *innocent* generation of modernity, meaning presumably that after Auschwitz humanity would more readily believe and recognize the barbarism of which human beings were capable of inflicting on one another. The Nazi slaughter was incomprehensible because it was the first systematic modern ethnic annihilation.

Nonetheless, and perhaps most powerfully, many Americans were throughout the 1930s and 1940s still unreconstructed anti-Semites. The most prominent anti-Semitic figure of the era was Father Charles Coughlin, a Canadian-born Catholic priest who had aligned himself with the Christian Front, a US radical pro-Nazi group whose slogan "Buy

26 Editorial, *The New Republic*, Nov. 30, 1938, 87.
27 https://www.mtholyoke.edu/~simon20r/SS%20St.%20Louis/americanforeignpolicy.html.
28 Lookstein, *Were We Our Brothers' Keepers?*, 95.

Christian" was a reminder to Americans to boycott Jewish-owned establishments as well as goods. At the peak of Coughlin's popularity in the 1930s, his weekly radio broadcasts drew an audience of around 3.5 million listeners and his publication, *Social Justice*, had nearly one million subscribers.[29]

While the majority of Americans did not think that Jews deserved annihilation, Jews were still sufficiently "other" to the majority of Americans; polls during the 1930s and 40s reported in the Jewish press that between 25% and 30% of Christian Americans considered their Jewish counterparts "less patriotic" than other Americans.[30] Catholics and Protestants did not fully (or in some instance, even partially) identify with the Jewish plight. And, some still considered Jewish suffering deserved punishment for their imagined ancient complicity in the death of Jesus.

Unfortunately, even those Christians who did recognize Jewish suffering hoped that the suffering would provide opportunities for Christian conversion. Conservative Christians regularly protested the mistreatment of Jews throughout Europe and imagined that the *Shoa* might be part of God's millennial plan for Jewish conversion and salvation. The religious magazine *Presbyterian* contended "the conversion of the Jew to Christianity was ultimately the only solution to the whole Jewish problem."[31] Some feared that without offering solace, Jews would be resistant to Christian conversion. Oddly, much of the initial protest against Nazi treatment was an attempt to recruit Jews to Christianity.

The second prong of the Christian protest addressed the question of refugees. And here, too, the anti-Semitism was explicit. Many denominations focused on "war refugees" rather than Jews, and reminded their congregations repeatedly that many of the refugees were Christians. For example, the Northern Baptist Convention released a statement that deplored racial hatred and discrimination in both the United States and

29 US Holocaust Museum http://www.ushmm.org/wlc/en/article.php?ModuleId=10005516 .
30 Lookstein, *Were We Our Brothers' Keepers?*, 31.
31 Quoted in William Nawyn, *American Protestantism's Response to Germany's Jews and Refugees 1933–1941* (Ann Arbor Michigan: UMI Research Press, 1981), 222 n.28.

Germany, and then channeled most of the money raised to the Baptist Committee for Christian Refugees.[32] The religious periodical *Churchman* complained in 1938 that "It has been a strange but unfortunately indisputable fact that Americans have been slow to realize that the German refugee problem is not solely a Jewish problem."[33]

Nonetheless, the Federal Council of Churches as well as National Council of the Protestant Episcopal Church continued to issue statements and resolutions throughout 1939 urging the US government "to maintain its historic policy of friendliness to refugees. We oppose legislative proposals which would suspend immigration at this time or curtail the established quotas."[34] All of these resolutions were unsuccessful.

Finally, one more element must be considered—the Jewish American response to Kristallnacht. Although the Jewish American response in the press was swift and loud, unfortunately most American Jews misjudged two critical features: first, the political efficacy of the American populace's outrage and second, the commitment of President Franklin Roosevelt to do something in response to Jewish persecution. Throughout the 1930s there was considerable Jewish adoration for Roosevelt. As Lookstein notes, many American Jews "believed in his redemptive power as a savior not only for America but for the rest of the world."[35] So confident were many American Jews in Roosevelt's commitment and power, they were lulled into waiting and believing that he was just about to act.

Further, many American Jews misread American popular outrage to German Jewish suffering. As Rabbi Stephen Wise, then president of the American Jewish Congress[36] asserted, "I led the protest [against Hitler] in 1933 and ever since. I led the protest and I spoke because the world

32 Ibid., 36–38.
33 Quoted in ibid., 56, 223 n.43; "Shall We Help the Persecuted?" *Churchman* 152 (November 1, 1938): 9.
34 Snoek, *The Grey Book*, 90.
35 Lookstein, *Were We Our Brothers' Keepers?*, 31.
36 It is also interesting to note that Rabbi Wise also served on the founding board for the National Association for the Advancement of Colored People (NAACP) in 1914. He was an experienced and dedicated civil rights activist.

was largely silent and the American people seemed to be inert and apathetic to and unconscious of what was happening. At last, at long last, America has spoken and the world has spoken, overwhelmed by the barbarism of the nationwide reprisals in recent weeks."[37] And then again, Rabbi Joseph Konvitz, president of the Agudat Ha-Rabanim (the organization of most European Orthodox rabbis): "The greatest friend we have, who lights up the darkness of the world, is our President, Franklin D. Roosevelt. His words are like balm for the broken Jewish hearts …. Traditional Jewry will engrave, with the blood of our holy martyrs, the names of our President and his people in the annals of Jewish history for generations to come."[38] This belief in Roosevelt's redemptive powers dovetailed with the Jewish American narrative of themselves as Americans first. One of the ways that Jewish Americans had sought to combat the anti-Semitism of the 1930s was by continually asserting how American they were. Even at Jewish conferences after Kristallnacht, Jewish leaders insisted, "This is an American Conference. We are Americans first, last and all the time. Nothing else that we are, whether by faith, or race or fate, qualifies our Americanism. Everything else we are and have deepens, enriches and strengthens, if that can be, our Americanism."[39] This is a chilling echo of the claim that many Japanese Americans would make in 1942 while interned in America's own version of concentration camps.

*

Using some of the sermons that Protestant leaders gave the first Sunday after Kristallnacht, Kyle Jantzen argues in his essay, "The Fatherhood of God and the Brotherhood of Man: Mainline American Protestants and the Kristallnacht Pogrom," that many religious leaders responded from an ideological position concerned with the rights and freedoms of liberal democracy; they argued that liberal democracy is both the pinnacle of

---

37 Lookstein, *Were We Our Brothers' Keepers?*, 61.
38 Lookstein, *Were We Our Brothers' Keepers?*, 70 (from *The Morning Journal*, November 23, 1938).
39 Rabbi Stephen Wise, addressing the American Jewish Conference, August 1943 (!), quoted in Lookstein, *Were We Our Brothers' Keepers?*, 31.

Western civilization as well as the religion of Christ.[40] The accusation against Germany was that it had descended into savagery, thus forsaking its own allegiance to high culture and civilization. While some of the sermons made references to biblical stories, the analytic thrust of the majority of the sermons was that by violating Jewish rights, the German people were putting their entire nation at risk. In his Sunday sermon, Rev. Fosdick, the well-known Riverside Church preacher in New York City, proclaimed, "The appalling persecution of the Jews in Germany is an outrage to the conscience of the civilized world ... decent people of all faiths and races join in protesting the cruel barbarities."[41] Episcopal Bishop William Manning makes a similar claim, "Such barbarous and inhuman acts cannot long continue. Any government guilty of such acts will fall through its own wickedness."[42] The argument was not about implementing theological principles. Rather, it was about the preservation of the nation as founded on and secured by religious tolerance.

This was among the most significant ministerial conceits of church-state relations in America during the 1930s and 1940s: without public religion, the democratic state cannot survive. The ministers argued not so much for the implementation of specific theological principles, but for the necessity of a public religion. Not only does Christianity ensure the maintenance of democratic processes, but the public contest of religious ideas is imperative for preventing tyranny: "Christianity and democracy stand or fall together ... When freedom is destroyed in Germany or Russia, it becomes a world problem."[43]

So, what gave rise to Hitler according to these ministers? The loss of an independent Christian Church. When Hitler attempted to rewrite Christian doctrine in Aryan terms, conscientious German Christians did

---

40   Kyle Jantzen, "The Fatherhood of God and the Brotherhood of Man: Mainline American Protestants and the Kristallnacht Pogrom" in *American Religious Reponses to Kristallnacht,* ed. Maria Mazzenga (New York: Palgrave Macmillan, 2009), 46.

41   Quoted in ibid., Jantzen, 44.

42   Quoted in ibid., Jantzen, 45.

43   Reverend Dr. Ralph W. Sockman of Christ Methodist Episcopal Church, Park Avenue and Sixtieth Street, New York City; sermon reprinted in *The New York Times*, November 21, 1938.

not thwart him because they had become effete. They mistook the nation for the church; they confused the flag for the cross. Reverend J. W. Houck of Pilgrim Congregational Church warned in his sermon of November 21, 1938, "Nations cannot ignore God and expect government to be effective ... it is really not unbelief but inadequate belief ... Belief in God when slackened weakens man's belief in others and himself. This weak faith denounces representative government and endorses the rule of one man."[44] Reverend S. M. Shoemaker of Calvary Episcopal Church made a similar point: "Democracy depends upon men of unselfish character and faith in God ... when democracy strips off the outer controls from human society, it must cultivate inner controls ... and this has been historically inseparable from the presence of the Christian religion."

Nor surprisingly, perhaps, the boldest claims in this regard seem to have come from both Jewish rabbis and Catholic clergy who described the rise of Nazism in Germany and communism in Russia as "wholesale intellectual kidnapping."[45] Rabbi Dr. Jacob Katz insisted, "Nazi excesses are not merely a Jewish problem but a political problem of the first magnitude."[46] Rabbi Hyman J. Schactel echoed the claim, "The religion of irreligion that has taken root in Nazi Germany must be fought by all who believe in democracy and have faith in the omnipotence of God."[47]

Monsignor Joseph M. Corrigan in his sermon at St. Patrick's Cathedral in New York City insisted, "it is the business of the church in America to see to it that our millions of sterling citizens be grounded in the principles of right government and in a knowledge of both their duties and rights in this Republic. The only power that can demand and maintain the democratic formula is one which can create a virtuous people.

---

44 Reverend J. W. Houck, Pilgrim Congregational Church, Grand Concourse and 175th Street, New York City, NY, reprinted in *The New York Times*, November 21, 1938.

45 Monsignor Joseph M. Corrigan, Catholic University, St. Patrick's Cathedral, New York City, reprinted in *The New York Times*, November 21, 1938.

46 Rabbi Dr. Jacob Katz, Montefiore Hebrew Congregation, Hewitt Avenue and Macy Place, Bronx, New York, reprinted in *The New York Times*, November 21, 1938.

47 Rabbi Hyman J. Schactel, West End Synagogue, West 82nd Street, New York City, reprinted in *The New York Times*, November 21, 1938.

That power is the church. It is literally true that the spirit of the American conception of government more closely approaches to that of the church than any other human formula yet evolved."[48]

Cardinal O'Connell made a similar point when he named Nazism as "intellectualism gone mad." He argued that Germany was in a position of "positive slavery": "Where is all their hard-earned reputation for knowledge? They are trying to put God out of His own creation, to take God away from the people and to restore Teutonic mythology. That is like taking away the foundation of this cathedral and expecting it to stand. It is not only a myth—it is insanity!"[49]

This was a political critique as much as a theological proclamation. Ministers, priests and rabbis were arguing in the 1930s against Enlightenment values—reason, science and technology—as sufficient protection against tyranny. As Gary Dorrien notes in his essay on the history of American liberalism, the religious ethos that developed from the Enlightenment sought to be persuasive to unbelievers, to have credibility in the world of science, capitalism, and secularism.[50] In the 1930s and 1940s, however, American religious leaders were not yet willing to relinquish their religious authority completely to the claims of the Enlightenment. As Hitler's rise to power demonstrated to American religious leaders, the claims of reason without the guidance of religion and revelation could lead to tyranny. And what country better demonstrated this than Germany with its high culture of reason, science, and the privileging of knowledge?

The Third Reich became for American religious leaders a vicious reminder of what happens to Enlightenment values when untempered by religious virtues. Because the German Christian Church had become aligned with the German state, it had lost its moral compass. In a radio address, Michael Williams, editor of the Catholic magazine *Commonweal*, called Germany's leaders "high priests of an organized religion which strikes at

48 Monseigneur Joseph M Corrigan, Catholic University, St. Patrick's Cathedral, New York City reprinted in *The New York Times*, Nov. 21, 1938.
49 Cardinal O'Connell, Cathedral of the Holy Cross, Wooster, Massachusetts, quoted in *The New York Times*, Nov 21, 1938.
50 Gary Dorrien, "American Liberal Theology: Crisis, Irony, Decline, Renewal and Ambiguity," *Crosscurrents* 55, no. 4 (Winter 2005-2006).

the very root of the true religion of liberty and love."[51] These "mass gang-sters" of the Enlightenment need religious values as well as religious insti-tutions in order to maintain the democratic foundational principles of human progress. Later, in the late 1940s and 1950s, American ministers would themselves learn to speak the neoliberal language of the state, but in the 1930s and through the early 1940s, their authority was still suffi-ciently robust and their faith sufficiently formidable that their argument re-mained that the government needs the Church considerably more than the Church needs the government. And Hitler's Germany was an ideal but tragic case study that demonstrated what happens when the Church forfeits its independence from the state as well as its prophetic autonomy in a mis-taken bid for political power and cultural accommodation.

While some of the American religious critiques of Nazi Germany, as already indicated, maintained the hollow ring of anti-Semitism, the ministers' insistence that the German church must be released from the clutches of Hitler's regime was an argument grounded in the assessment that the Church cannot be reined in by the needs or requirements of the state. This was an American version of Karl Barth's more radical criti-cism of Nazi Germany: "it is unpardonable arrogance for sinful man to assume that his reason is capable of coming to knowledge of the moral law of God."[52] In other words, only revelation can illuminate God—not culture, not the state, and certainly not the needs of the government to maintain power. While for Barth, embedded in his critique of Nazi Ger-many was a critique both of natural law and the utility of reason for faith, for American religious leaders most of the "Barthian elements" of their critique of Nazi Germany centered on its attempted usurpation of reve-lation for the needs of the state.

In the days immediately following the bombing of Pearl Harbor, however, the narrative would rather dramatically shift.[53] Then, President Roosevelt would use religious freedom as a key feature of the war as

---

51 Rev. Dr. Joseph Sizoo, radio broadcast by the National Conference of Jews and Christians, reprinted in *The New York Times*, November 21, 1938, 6.

52 Karl Barth, "The Theological Declaration of Barmen," 1934. http://www.sacred-texts.com/chr/barmen.htm.

53 See the author's *The Power of the Pulpit: American Political Crises from Pearl Harbor to Ferguson* (forthcoming, Harvard University Press).

well as actively soliciting clerical endorsement of his plans for armed engagement. In December 1941 the state believed it required the endorsement of the Church to authorize its power. The Roosevelt administration wanted the Church to validate the necessity of violence as a religious imperative. But prior to Pearl Harbor the state did not believe needed the Church's permission to continue its resistance to Jewish refugees, and religious leaders did not have a robust way either rhetorically or institutionally to persuade the government otherwise. Citizenship is so firmly and clearly a state privilege that developing theological principles or religious institutions to compel the state to behave otherwise is a challenge that continues to create conflict to this day in American politics. Indeed, as this essay is finished in the summer of 2015, there are graphic and eerie echoes of the Jewish refugee crisis of the 1930s now being repeated as European countries quarrel (and the United States observes) the crisis of Syrian refugees seeking a haven from the genocidal politics of ISIS and the maniacal Assad. How very difficult it remains for revelation to respond to the vicissitudes of historical circumstances. In the twentieth and now twenty-first centuries, it seems that the balance of power continues to favor the reasons of state, which means the faithful must be agile in their thinking about how to make those reasons follow upon and be in service to faith.[54]

---

54 Charles Butterworth, "State and Authority in Arabic Political Thought," in *The Foundations of the Arabic State*, ed. Ghassan Salame (London: Croom Helm, 1987), 91–111.

Montesquieu's Critique of Islam
Joshua Bandoch

Professor Charles Butterworth has been my model teacher-scholar since I took my first class with him in Spring 2003 as an undergraduate at the University of Maryland, College Park. His teaching, like his scholarship, was remarkable for its rigor. In that class, on Jean-Jacques Rousseau's *Émile ou de l'éducation*, Professor Butterworth insisted that we read Rousseau with the same care he did—slowly, no more than five pages per hour, working hard to grasp the deep meaning found in each line. This high standard always pushed his students to reject merely scratching the surface and, instead, to dive deeply into core philosophical texts. I continue to work hard to meet this lofty standard.

Such careful reading has helped Professor Butterworth study, translate, and understand texts in what is arguably the most challenging field in political philosophy—medieval Islamic thought. His research in this field has centered on one of *the* most important questions: what is the relation between reason and revelation? It was Leo Strauss, and then Muhsin Mahdi, who helped spark interest in thinkers like Avicenna, Averroes, and Alfarabi. These medieval thinkers grappled with this challenging relationship, a relationship that goes to the core of human existence. Butterworth has continued the high level of engagement Strauss and Mahdi initiated, becoming the preeminent expert on these texts today by making many laudable contributions to this field. His translations, in particular, are world-renowned for their precision and readability. They have made these texts accessible to future generations. It is with great pleasure that I salute the career of Charles Butterworth as the model teacher-scholar who taught me and countless others about the most important texts, ideas, and questions.

Montesquieu vis-à-vis medieval Islamic philosophy

Averroes, Avicenna, Ibn Tufayl, and, especially, Alfarabi wrote about the deep tension between reason and revelation. If revelation is true, then this truth must shape our societies. But can we rationalize faith?

In stark contrast to the approach of these medieval philosophers, Montesquieu cast aside concerns about this tension entirely. Charles Louis de Secondat, Baron de Montesquieu, one of the most prominent Enlightenment thinkers, shows little if any regard for whether a religion is "true." He concentrates, instead, entirely on the *effects* of a religion. I have argued elsewhere that Montesquieu is a proponent of what I call "selective religious intolerance." "Rather than favoring or opposing re-ligious toleration per se," I contend, "Montesquieu judges a religion in the context of a particular state. Sometimes he views a given religion (e.g., Christianity) favorably, other times unfavorably. He thinks that there are instances when it is appropriate for a state to find non-violent ways to marginalize, weaken or remove a religion from a society." I argue, moreover, that "Montesquieu bases his judgments about the ef-fects of a religion, and how the state ought to relate to it, on a deep con-sideration of how a particular religion fits into a society."[1] Within this framework, there is only one religion that Montesquieu categorically will not tolerate: Islam.

In this essay, I will investigate why Montesquieu judges Islam to be unacceptably bad. This religion cannot fit into a good political order, ac-cording to Montesquieu. In short, he thinks Islam is despotic, is a con-quering religion, enslaves women, and produces bad citizens. By contrast, other religions like Christianity and Judaism do not necessarily have these failings.[2]

---

1   Joshua Bandoch, "Montesquieu's Selective Religious Intolerance in *Of the Spirit of the Laws*," *Political Studies* 62 no. 2 (2016), 351.

2   Some scholars interpret Montesquieu's criticisms of Islam as applying also to Judaism and, especially, Christianity. Diana Schaub argues that he criti-cizes Islam "to gain a hearing that will eventually lead the audience to in-dict its own [Christian] beliefs as much as those of Islam." "Of Believers and Barbarians: Montesquieu's Enlightened Toleration," in *Early Modern Skepticism and the Origins of Toleration*, ed. Alan Levine (Lanham:

My purpose in this essay is to explore Montesquieu's mature critique of Islam. Undoubtedly, a complete consideration of Islam in Montesquieu's thought would consider other texts, above all the *Lettres Persanes*. But others like Diana Schaub already have offered rich commentary of this seminal text.[3] By contrast, there exists comparatively little thorough analysis of Montesquieu's remarks on Islam in *De l'Esprit des lois* (hereafter *EL*). Michael Curtis, in *Orientalism and Islam*, has a chapter entitled "The Oriental Despotic Universe of Montesquieu." But the focus here is on how Montesquieu's analysis of the Orient informs Montesquieu's conception of despotism, rather than Montesquieu's specific critique of Islam. Thomas Pangle, in his recent book on Montesquieu, offers a brief analysis of Montesquieu's concerns about Islam. But Pangle's analysis there is typically ideological and too often is off the mark.[4]

As we proceed, we must be precise about how Montesquieu refers to Islam. Only once in *EL* in any of his mentions of Islam or Muslims does he refer to it or them as such. In Book XXV, Chapter 2, Montesquieu writes: "The Mohammedans would not be such good Muslims, if on the one hand there were not idolatrous peoples who make them think they are the avengers of the unity of God, and on the other

---

Lexington Books, 1999), 238. Sanford Kessler, focusing on the *Lettres Persanes*, writes that "it should be emphasized that he regarded Islam, which has its roots in the Old Testament, as being essentially similar to orthodox Judaism and Christianity" and that Montesquieu views "them as if they were the same" (381–82). "Religion and Liberalism in Montesquieu's Persian Letters," *Polity* 15, no. 3 (1983), 380–96. David Young claims that Montesquieu's "attacks on the social consequences of Mohammedanism, or what he took to be such, often served as a convenient method for condemning the social implications of Christianity" (403). "Montesquieu's View of Despotism and His Use of Travel Literature," *The Review of Politics* 40.3 (1978): 392–405. Consider also Thomas Pangle, *The Theological Basis of Liberal Modernity in Montesquieu's Spirit of the Laws* (Chicago: University of Chicago Press, 2010), 44–46.

3   Diana Schaub, *Erotic Liberalism: Women and Revolution in Montesquieu's Persian Letters* (Lanham, MD: Rowman and Littlefield, 1995).

4   Pangle, *The Theological Basis of Liberal Modernity in Montesquieu's Spirit of the Laws*. Consider for example 44–46.

Christians, for making them believe they are the object of his preferences" (XXV.2.736).[5] Here Montesquieu uses the French word "*musulmans.*" Otherwise, he refers to Muslims as he does at the beginning of the quoted sentence: as Mohammedans. And he speaks not of Islam, but of Mohammedism. As I have noted elsewhere, the terms Mohammedan and Mohammedism "are incorrect and potentially contentious. He seems to suggest that Mohammed is a leader, not a prophet, and that his followers are worshipping a person, not God."[6] And Montesquieu certainly meant the terms to be inflammatory, as part of his sweeping critique of the religion and its founder.

In light of the way he chooses to refer to Islam and its prophet, would it be sensible to conclude that Montesquieu simply was ignorant? Should we just dismiss his analysis? From where did Montesquieu's knowledge of Islam and Islamic countries come? Montesquieu was a voracious reader of travel literature. He examined as much information available to him as possible to learn about these societies. As Young shows, Montesquieu used travel literature to generalize "that there was a close relationship between Islam and despotism."[7] The travelers "provided him with much information about Turkish and Iranian government and society, and even suggested a number of connections among various aspects of despotism." David Young contends, however, that in following the travelers Montesquieu chose to "overlook or to ignore deliberately much of what Chardin, Tournefort, Tavernier, and others had to say."[8] Rather than overlooking or deliberately ignoring these other authors, Montesquieu simply may have found reasons to find the travel literature more compelling. We can be sure that he worked hard to acquire an accurate understanding of Islam and Islamic countries. Accordingly, our focus should be on what his analysis means for his political philosophy.

5   Montesquieu, Charles Louis Secondat, Baron de La Brède et de. *Œuvres Complètes. Tome 2.* (Paris: Bibliothèque de la Pléiade, 1951). I quote from *EL* in the following format: Book, Chapter, page number (e.g., XXV.2.736).
6   Bandoch, "Montesquieu's Selective Religious Intolerance," 365 n.7.
7   David Young, "Montesquieu's View of Despotism and His Use of Travel Literature," *The Review of Politics* 40, no. 3 (1978), 399.
8   Young, "Montesquieu's View of Despotism and His Use of Travel Literature," 405.

And this import is significant. Islam and Mohammed are prominent in Montesquieu's considerations of religion. Montesquieu mentions Mohammed in seven chapters. Jesus Christ, by contrast, appears only in three. Mohammedism appears in twenty chapters, approaching the thirty-plus mentions of Christianity.

Islamic Despotism

We must read Montesquieu's analysis of Islam in light of the first mention he makes of it, in Book V, in the midst of a discussion of despotism. In Chapter 13, entitled "Idea of Despotism," Montesquieu proclaims: "When the savages of Louisiana want fruit, they cut down the tree, and gather the fruit. Voilà despotic government" (V.13.292). Then, in Chapter 14, he explains: "Despotic government has for its principle fear: but for timid, ignorant, beaten down peoples, it is not necessary to have many laws" (V.14.292). Montesquieu elaborates further: "As the principle of despotic government is fear, the goal of it is tranquility; but it is not a peace, it is the silence of the towns that the enemy is ready to occupy" (V.14.294). These snippets help demonstrate the chilling picture Montesquieu paints of despotism. While interpreters disagree about whether Montesquieu had a preferred, best, or ideal regime, and what it might be, no one disagrees that he loathed despotism. Indeed, one might read Montesquieu's entire oeuvre as an attempt to combat despotism.

Enter Islam into Montesquieu's analysis. In despotic states, "religion has more influence than in any other; it is a fear added to fear." This statement is weighty indeed, for it suggests that religion can serve as a kind of double-despotism. His primary target is Islam. He continues: "In Mohammedan empires, it is from religion that the people draw a part of their astonishing respect for their prince" (V.14.296). So Islam promotes the obedience—and awe—the prince needs to continue ruling. That is not all. "It is religion that corrects the Turkish constitution a bit. The subjects, who are not attached to the glory and grandeur of the State by honor, are attached by force and by the principle of their religion." So more than just making citizens obedient, Islam gives them the necessary beliefs and vigor to support their despotic ruler in his imperial endeavors. In "Mohammedan countries, religion regards victory or success as a judgment of God"—so fear and imperialism appear as divinely sanctioned. Sovereignty itself relies on such successes (V.14.296). Were this criticism of Islam not harsh enough, Montesquieu also previews another one of his criticisms of Islam, that it enslaves women: "The princes of despotic States always have abused marriage. They ordinarily take multiple wives, above all in the part of the world where despotism is, so to speak, naturalized, which is in Asia" (V.14.296). But more on this later.

Montesquieu's initial portrayal of Islam is of a religion that is unquestionably despotic. Curtis goes so far as to argue that "Montesquieu's concept of despotism is essentially Oriental in nature."[9] Mixed with the government of one alone, Islam produces a rather vile mixture unsuitable for moderate governments interested in promoting security, liberty, and prosperity.[10]

Montesquieu removes any doubt regarding his judgment of Islam with his first remark about Islam in Part V (Books XXIV–XXVI), dedicated to religion. Chapter 3 of Book XXIV is entitled "That moderate government is more suited to the Christian religion and despotic government to the Mohammedan." Christianity "is remote from pure despotism," in stark contrast to Islam. Whereas the Gospel recommends "gentleness (*douceur*)," Islamic teaching (and the Koran, though he does not mention it explicitly) is infused with "despotic anger with which the prince would do justice and exercise his cruelties." Christianity forbids the plurality of wives, unlike Islam. Christian princes are "less withdrawn, less separated from their subjects, and consequently more human; they are more disposed to make laws themselves, and are more capable of sensing what they cannot do" (XXIV.3.716). Montesquieu continues:

> Whereas Mohammedan princes constantly kill or are killed, among Christians religion makes princes less timid and consequently less cruel. The prince counts on his subjects, and

9   Michael Curtis, *Orientalism and Islam* (New York: Cambridge University Press, 2009), 99.

10 These three goods are central to Montesquieu's political theorizing, which I call the "politics of place." Joshua Bandoch, *The Politics of Place: Montesquieu, Particularism, and the Pursuit of Liberty* (Rochester, NY: University of Rochester Press).

the subjects on the prince. Remarkably, the Christian religion, which seems to have no other object than the felicity of the other life, is also our happiness in this one! (id.)

Unlike Christianity,[11] Islam makes rulers harsher, immoderate, and violent. The harsh conclusion Montesquieu wants his reader to draw is that Islam is destructive to the political and personal goods Montesquieu seeks to promote. Islam is incompatible with a moderate, free political order. Montesquieu criticizes Islam primarily on three fronts: its effects of citizens, its proclivity to promote conquest, and its treatment of women.

Islam vs. Citizenship

Islam produces bad citizens, Montesquieu concludes. And since the purpose of a religion is to "make good *citizens* of *men*" (XXIV.14.724; emphasis added), Islam is problematic. Islam fails on numerous fronts. First, Islam makes people too contemplative. In a chapter entitled "On contemplation," Montesquieu insists that because men are made to conserve, nourish, and provide for themselves, and because men are made to do "all actions *in society*, religion should not give men too contemplative a life" (XXIV.11.722; emphasis added). But Islam does precisely that. "Mohammedans become speculative by habit; they pray five times a day, and each time they must do something that makes them turn their backs on all that belongs to this world: this forms them for speculation" (id.). Islam causes people to withdraw from society and turn their attention, instead, to private religious matters. Such men do not act. They thus are incapable, or at a minimum unlikely, Montesquieu thinks, to be good citizens. Yet, it is not simply that Muslims turn their back on society when they pray. The problem goes further, Montesquieu insists. Muslims' obsession with the afterlife and, in particular, predestination, makes

11 Anne Cohler notes that Christianity's gentleness makes it appropriate for moderate governments, and seems "to offer the possibility that that community is all mankind," and "engenders to find a motive for restraint that is not dehumanizing," *Montesquieu's Comparative Politics and the Spirit of American Constitutionalism* (Lawrence, KS: University of Kansas Press, 1988), 26, 42.

people inactive and unproductive. Montesquieu proclaims: "From the laziness of soul arises the Muslim dogma of predestination; and from the dogma of this predestination, emerges the laziness of soul" (XXIV.14.724). Lazy individuals are less active in society, are uninterested in politics, and are rather unlikely to engage in commerce.

Montesquieu also disapproves of the revered status of the mosque in Islam. Genghis Kahn apparently harbored great "contempt" for mosques. After interrogating "Mohammedans," Kahn "approved of all their dogmas, excepting that which led to the necessity of going to Mecca; he could not understand that one could not worship God everywhere" (XXV.3.737–738). Montesquieu does nothing to suggest that he disagrees with Kahn's criticisms of Islam. Indeed, they align with his concern about Muslims turning their back on the world five times a day, as they turn towards Mecca to pray.

The habits Islam promotes, along with the rigidness with which it insists on adhering to them, cause Muslims to be intolerant of those who do not follow their practices. Montesquieu maintains, in XXIV, 22, that it "is dangerous that religion inspires horror for irrelevant things." To prove this point, he mentions the hate between Muslims and Indians: "the Indians hate the Mohammedans because they eat cows; Mohammedans detest Indians because they eat pork" (XXIV.22.731). Montesquieu considers practices like refraining from eating beef or pork on account of one's religion unnecessary and unhelpful. But he finds the dynamic these practices can create among groups with sharply different practices dangerous. Why would two groups hate each other because of the kinds of meat they eat, or refrain from eating? Montesquieu thinks detesting others on such grounds is indefensible.

Montesquieu does identify two ways in which Islam gives citizens desirable attributes. First, Islam encourages "the propagation of the human species." Both in *EL* and *LP* Montesquieu demonstrates significant concern for depopulation.[12] He fears population decline for many

---

12 For an analysis of Montesquieu's views on depopulation in *LP*, see David Young, "Libertarian Demography: Montesquieu's Essay on Depopulation in the Lettres Persanes," *Journal of the History of Ideas* 36, no. 4 (Oct. – Dec. 1975): 669–82.

reasons. His concerns are more pronounced in Europe, where he sees Christianity as causing population decline. Indeed, right after noting that Islam has encouraged propagation among the Mohammedans, Montesquieu contends that the Roman conversion to Christianity ran counter to propagating the human species (XXIII.21.706). Second, Islam prevents its hateful followers from pursuing a certain kind of injustice. How Montesquieu begins his remark is important: "When there are many subjects of hate in a state ..." The people he is about to discuss—the Arabs—had many reasons for hate. He continues:

> it is necessary that the religion gives many means of reconciliation. The Arabs, bandit people, often did harm and injustices to one another. Mohammed made this law: "If someone pardons the shedding of his brother's blood, he will be able to follow the culprit for damages and interest; but anyone who harms the bad person, after having received satisfaction from him, will suffer painful torments on judgment day" (XXIV.17.727).

In a backhanded way, Montesquieu approves of Mohammed's law. The law essentially says the following: once you have agreed to receive compensation from a perpetrator in lieu of pursuing other punishments against him, you will be punished if you then attempt to pursue the punishments you agreed not to pursue. Apparently among "bandit" peoples such laws represent a kind of progress.

Islam and Conquest

Montesquieu's general views on conquest are somewhat ambiguous.[13] He clearly harbors significant reservations about the use of offensive force. And yet, at the same time he displays a certain admiration both for Alexander's

---

13   For more on Montesquieu's views on commerce, see especially Michael Mosher, "Montesquieu on Empire and Enlightenment," in *Empire and Modern Political Thought*, ed. Sankar Muthu (New York: Cambridge University Press, 2012). Consider also Robert Howse, "Montesquieu on Commerce, Conquest, War and Peace," *Brooklyn Journal of International Law* 31 no. 3 (2006), 693–708.

conquests, and the commercial conquests of England. Still, we can say that Montesquieu is wary of conquests that force other peoples to change. He seems open to the idea only when significant positive changes ensue. When the conquerors bring nothing but ills, though, Montesquieu vehemently rejects such conquests. He deems Islamic conquests to be of this variety.

Islam made the Arabs conquerors. "Nature," Montesquieu contends, "had destined the Arabs to commerce; they had not been destined for war." Montesquieu even identifies the Arabs as "tranquil peoples." What went amiss? They found themselves between the Parthians and Romans, and "they became the auxiliaries of both." Mohammed arrived and "found them warriors; he gave them enthusiasm, and voilà conquerors" (XXI.16.634). How did Mohammed make tranquil peoples conquerors? Montesquieu suggests multiple causes.

Islam makes its followers intolerant and more aggressive towards non-Muslims. Montesquieu contends that a religion attaches its followers more closely to it when there is "a distinction between those who profess it and those who do not" (XXV.2.736). This distinction causes Muslims (as well as followers of other religions that make such a distinction) to view non-Muslims as inferior and wrong about their fundamental convictions. Such sentiments make it significantly easier to attack non-Muslims. On this front, Montesquieu presents Muslims as distinct from all other "peoples of the Orient" who, "excepting the Mohammedans, believe that all religions are indistinguishable from themselves" (XXV.15.749).

The causes of conquest seem to run deep in the veins of Islam. Islam was *established* through force. In a chapter on the Spanish and Portuguese Inquisitions, speaking in the voice of an eighteen-year-old Jewess, Montesquieu notes: "When they flaunt the number of their faithful, you say to them that force has acquired that number for them, and that they have extended their religion by iron" (XXV.13.747). Force, not persuasion, was the principal agent of growth for Islam. Accordingly, Barrera reads Montesquieu as arguing that Islam either is a conquering religion, or a religion of conquerors.[14] A secondary factor that allowed

14   Guillaume Barrera, "Comment certaine religion contredit l'esprit de l'Antiquité et contrarie les temps modernes," *Montesquieu, l'État, et la religion*, ed. Jean Ehrard (Sofia: Éditions Iztok-Zapad, 2007), 116–17.

Mohammed to conquer more effectively was high taxes. In a chapter entitled "On the conquests of the Mohammedans," Montesquieu explains that "excessive taxes ... produced the strange ease the Mohammedans found in their conquests." The people had no desire to suffer from the "continuous humiliations" at the hands of emperors who no longer gave them the benefits of liberty while imposing on them the "horrors of servitude." Instead, many peoples preferred to subject themselves to a "simple tax," even if this meant obeying a "barbarous nation"—the Muslims (XIII.16.469–70). And yet, Montesquieu clearly sees Islam as a threat to freedom generally, and to Europe in particular. "Europe," Montesquieu notes, is "separated from the rest of the world by its religion." But, in a footnote he highlights that "Mohammedan countries almost entirely surround it" (XXIII.25.710). Montesquieu thus seems quite concerned with the threat Islam poses to Europe and its free way of life. Montesquieu's concern about Islam's abridgement of freedom is especially acute in his criticism of its treatment of women.

Islam's Despotism Over Women

Scholars disagree about whether Montesquieu was a kind of feminist,[15] anti-feminist,[16] or something in-between.[17] What is beyond doubt, however, is that he viewed Islam's treatment of women as harsh and wrong. Curtis sums up Montesquieu's views. Montesquieu "connects Oriental despotic power with the servitude of women...Women are at the disposal of the Oriental master and subservient to his pleasure. They are objects of luxury, and generally constitute part of the master's property. Women are confined, spied on, subjected to terror and to

15 Susan Tenenbaum, "Women through the Prism of Political Thought," *Polity* 15 no. 1 (1982): 90–102; Sylvana Tomaselli, "The Enlightenment Debate on Women," *History Workshop* No. 20 (Autumn 1985): 101–24.

16 Robert O'Reilly, "Montesquieu: anti-feminist," *Studies on Voltaire and the 18th Century*, 102 (1973): 143–56.

17 Jane Abray, "Feminism in the French Revolution," *The American Historical Review* 80 no. 1 (1975): 43–62; Katherine Clinton, "Femme et philosophe: Enlightenment Origins of Feminism," *Eighteenth-Century Studies* 8 no. 3 (1975): 283–99.

propaganda."[18] Let us investigate how Montesquieu arrives at such conclusions.

Islam enslaves women domestically. Indeed, many of Montesquieu's criticisms of Islam come in Book XVI, entitled "How the laws of *domestic servitude*[19] have a relation with the nature of the climate." And this enslavement is totalizing:

> In Mohammedan states, one is not only the master of the life and goods of the female slaves, but also of what is called their virtue or their honor ... [in] these countries ... the larger part of the nation exists only in order to serve the voluptuousness of the other. This servitude is rewarded by the laziness that such slaves are given to enjoy, which is yet another misfortune for the state (XV.12.499).[20]

Women exist merely to tend to the needs of their husbands, and these needs include sex and reproduction. To ensure that their women remain "virtuous," Islamic masters enclose their women in the cage that is their house, sometimes in a seraglio. This, of course, is no kind of virtue at all. Women therefore do not have a real opportunity to exercise their moral agency. Muslim men are afraid, Montesquieu alleges, of what will happen if women have the opportunity to do so. Montesquieu interprets the forced enclosure of women as a direct recommendation of Mohammed, with Mohammed's jealousy being a primary cause (XVI.7.518). The tragic result of Mohammed's conquests in Asia, Africa, and Europe was to establish "dependence everywhere" and form

18 Curtis, *Orientalism and Islam*, 84–85.
19 Emphasis added. Montesquieu clarifies his meaning of this term: "Les esclaves sont plutôt établis pour la famille qu'ils ne sont dans la famille. Ainsi, je distinguerai leur servitude de celle où sont les femmes dans quelques pays, et que j'appellerai proprement la servitude domestique" (XVI.1.508).
20 For more on Montesquieu's views of Islam's harshness on women, consider also *LP* XXIV, XXXVIII, LXI-LXIV,LXVII. Schaub notes that "Montesquieu considered Islam to be a religion particularly harsh on women" (*Erotic Liberalism*, 55).

"prisons." "Half of the world was eclipsed. Only the iron gates and the bolts were to be seen. All tended to night in the Universe, and the beautiful sex, buried with its charms, everywhere mourned its liberty."[21] This oppression is felt perhaps nowhere more than in the bedroom.

Islamic men take one, then multiple women as sexual slaves. Or perhaps it is more appropriate to say "girls" rather than "women," because in hot climates, where Islam reigns, girls are taken and given away for marriage at eight, nine, or ten years of age. Montesquieu cites Prideaux to note that Mohammed married Cadhisja when she was five years old, and slept with her when she was eight (XVI.2.509). The effects of this approach are damaging to women. They are "old at twenty: reason never finds itself together with beauty. When beauty demands empire, reason refuses itself; when reason could obtain it, beauty is no more." The consequence is that women stay dependent on men "because reason cannot procure for them in their youth an empire that beauty had not given them in youth itself." A more damaging consequence arises: "It is therefore very simply that a man, when religion does not oppose it, leaves his wife to take another, and polygamy introduces itself" (XVI.2.509). Before considering polygamy, we pause to reflect on Montesquieu's remarks here about how Islam keeps women forever dependent on their husband. It is not simply that women, by being unable to develop their capacities, have no say in their home. Even if they were permitted to engage the world, they would be unable to gain any real power for themselves in the larger world because they would not have developed themselves sufficiently to do so.

Montesquieu finds polygamy problematic on various counts. Women become even more reliant on their husband and his "riches" (XVI.3.510). Polygamy encourages despotism (XVI.9.514–515). Polygamy is bad for everyone involved (XVI.6.512). Besides, many of the justifications for polygamy do not hold up. If the existence of more women than men justifies polygamy in some places, then the presence of more men than women should justify polyandry. But this would shock "Mohammedan ideas" (XVI.4.511). How hypocritical, Montesquieu suggests.

---

21   From *Mes Pensées*, cited in Schaub, *Of Believers and Barbarians*, 55.

Conclusion

Montesquieu's concerns about Islam run deep. He also criticizes how the "law of Mohammed confounds usury with taking interest" (XXII.19.675). And some of its recommendations, like not drinking wine, already were in place in the region (XIV.10.483). Summarizing Montesquieu's views, Curtis explains that Montesquieu is often "caustic about Islam" because he deemed it "a religion characterized by ritualism and taboos, predestination, laziness of the soul, fatalism, apathy, lack of concern for the future, intolerance, economic underdevelopment, polygamy, and demographic depopulation. He constantly links Islam to despotic government, upheavals, and war."[22]

Montesquieu ultimately wants to combat Islam and its ills. He sees no reasons to tolerate, accept, or embrace it. At the same time, in the Preface (and elsewhere) he urges caution when attempting to implement change in society. "One lets an ill remain if one sees the abuses of the correction itself." Given how harshly he judges Islam, though, we can say with certainty that he recommends taking action against it. A full exploration of how he wants to combat Islam is beyond the scope of this query. I explored elsewhere some of the mechanisms he recommends for acting against a religion.[23] They include overt actions like preferring political concerns over religious ones, and more covert ones, especially commerce. The appropriate mechanisms will vary across time and place, but there is no doubt that Montesquieu recommends to legislators that they take whatever measures they can to rid their society of the despotism of what Montesquieu calls "Mohammedism."

22 Curtis, *Orientalism and Islam*, 87–88.
23 Bandoch, "Montesquieu's Selective Religious Intolerance," 363–64.

Transcendence and Society:[1]
On the Critical Understanding of
"Modern" Society

Jürgen Gebhardt

The Principles of Hermeneutic Political Science Reconsidered

"If the human mind be left to follow its own bent, it will regulate the temporal and the spiritual institutions of society in a uniform manner, and man will endeavor, if I may so speak, to harmonize earth with heaven."[2] This statement sums up Tocqueville's view of "religion considered as a political institution." It enunciates the entwining of public order and religio-cultural symbolic forms of order as the central theme of the scholarly discourse on "transcendence and society."

Tocqueville's political science suggests a comprehensive idea of political community. It includes the idea that, even in modern times, the religio-political complex plays a decisive role in the constitution of political society. In 1938 Eric Voegelin restated this notion in theoretical terms in his seminal work on *Political Religions*:

> The life of human beings in political community cannot be defined as a profane realm, in which we are only concerned with questions of law and the organization of power. A community is also a realm of religious orders and the knowledge

---

1   Jürgen Gebhardt, "Das religiös-kulturelle Dispositiv der modernen Politik," in *Demokratie und Transzendenz*, ed. Hans Vorländer (Bielefeld: Transcript Verlag, 2013), 41-79.

2   Alexis de Tocqueville, *Democracy in America, Vol. I*, ed. Phillips Bradley, trans. Henry Reeve (New York: A.A. Knopf, 1945), 310.

of a political condition will be incomplete with respect to a decisive point, first, if it does not take into account the religious forces inherent in a community, and the symbols through which these are expressed, and, second, if it includes the religious forces, but does not recognize them as such and instead translates them into a-religious categories. Humans live in political society with all the traits of their being, from the physical to the spiritual and the religious.[3]

Voegelin developed this empirically grounded concept of political society in the course of his scholarly investigations into the religious make-up of European totalitarianism. Although his studies went unheeded by most of his contemporaries, the fact is that at a very early date Voegelin contested the generally held opinion that views modern ideological mass movements as secular movements, a view that mirrored the all-pervading secularism of the time. As Voegelin remarked: "[A] considerable number of political scientists lack the most elementary knowledge of religious experiences and their expression, they are unable to recognize political-religious phenomena when they see them, and are unaware of their decisive role in the constitution of political society."[4] Voegelin, strongly influenced by the empirical philosophy of the German hermeneutical *Geisteswissenschaft*, reacted critically to the interpretative restrictions of the predominant "scientific" social science model that insisted—and still insists—on the irrelevance of a modern hermeneutical theory and methodology. It denies in principle that hermeneutics can be the chief tool of political science. Voegelin's quest for a hermeneutic understanding of the multifaceted realm of human being in society and history, past and present, resonated with like-minded scholars. But it did not have an impact on the discipline's overall research agenda in the 1960s and 70s. For this reason Voegelin, along with many other learned fellow immigrants, felt closer to the

3   Eric Voegelin, *The Collected Works of Eric Voegelin: Modernity Without Restraint,* ed. Manfred Henningsen, vol. 5 (Columbia, MO: University of Missouri Press, 2000), 70.
4   Eric Voegelin, *Voegelin Papers: The People of God I, MS* (Stanford: Hoover Institution Archives, n.d.), 51.

tradition of interpretive humanities that upheld the hermeneutic principles, an approach that presented a latent challenge to the dominant model of the scientific study of politics. Over time these hermeneutics began to flourish, but they did not succeed in shaking confidence in the prevailing methods of political science. It took the recent shattering experiences of unforeseen political events to change this situation.

In the midst of the fundamental political and cultural upheavals that have engulfed the global ecumene, mainstream political science is now in the throes of a deep crisis. It has called into question the theoretical categories of the scientific belief system that wedded Western political self-interpretation to positivistic scientism, and which indulged in the dream of a universal and unified West on a global scale. This vision, the so-called "modern secular society," is based on an axiomatic faith in the coming of a "modern civilization." The last stage, the "positive" state of humankind, will be shaped by the all-pervading power of "science." This new world view, as it was proclaimed by the godfathers of European positivism, reflected the truly formidable advancement of the natural sciences in the eighteenth and early nineteenth centuries. The positivists believed that their method would result in a cognitive evolution of the natural sciences which would culminate in the new physical science of "social physics." This science was "destined to complete the system of our positive knowledge" and elevate "politics to the rank of the natural sciences" that are based on observation.[5] Such a positive social science was to become the rational basis of a "positive polity"—a novel social system ruled by the new class of savants. In this way society would be liberated from the theological and metaphysical fictions of supernatural ideas. Modern civilization was by definition "secular," i.e., a self-referential natural world. Its scientific hallmark would now be sociology, the guiding science based on direct observation of social phenomena. This science discovers and explicates the fundamental laws of human social existence and formulates the ordering ideas of a natural morality and politics. Such guidelines for human agency reflect the strictly human law revealed by society itself.

---

5   Auguste Comte, *The Crisis of Industrial Civilization: The Early Essays*, ed. Ronald Fletcher (London: Heinemann, 1974), 137.

A vital role in ensuring the long term intellectual success of this sociological imagination was played by the epistemological and methodological precepts of Emile Durkheim's "Les regles de la methode sociologique."[6] Durkheim laid the groundwork for the new science that is modeled on the 'natural' sciences.

'Society' is conceived to be a reality *sui generis*—totally independent of the individuals who, in their entirety, form its substratum. The individual is subjected to the imperative of a rationally structured natural order that is held to be the determining factor of human agency. It is this moment of historical amnesia that paves the way to the unshakable and religiously connoted belief in the axiomatic paradigm of "modern society." It provides the basis for the claim to extend "modern society" world-wide. This is to be done at the expense of demoting the historical manifold of societal forms to the inferior status of "traditional society," i.e., societies that, by definition, must be redeemed by modernity. Epistemologically the experiential world of concrete persons and the meaningful social whole that they create through self-understanding and self-actualization, are reduced to measurable quantifiable data that supposedly reflect the external social forces operating on them. The implication of this positivistic view is that the members of society are unable to acquire authentic knowledge of their own affairs. Such knowledge is disclosed only to those "who by means of professionally acquired and cultivated methods ... [can] elevate themselves over the constraints of social affairs and can work their way to an understanding of what is truly real about social affairs: the sociologist."[7] The international success of the sociological persuasion began with the rise of American social science when Charles Merriam and the Chicago School in the early 1920s developed "a scientific study of politics patterned after the biological and physical sciences."[8]

6   Emile Durkheim, *Les Règles de la méthode sociologique* (Paris: Les Presses Universitaires de France, 1968).
7   Joachim Matthes, "Über die Erfahrung der Erfahrung," in *Enteignen uns die Wissenschaften? Zum Verhältnis zwischen Erfahrung und Empirie*, ed. Hans Schneider and Rüdiger Inhetveen (München: Fink, 1992), 106–07.
8   John Dreijmanis, "Political Science in the United States: The Discipline and the Profession," *Government and Opposition* 18, no. 2 (1983): 198.

The sociological imagination still clings to the monopolistic position of the "social scientific understanding of politics" that is based on the axiomatic assumption of an "observer-independent world" "about which a researcher may systematically discover true facts and reject false ones." Indeed, in an act of disciplinary exorcism, one political scientist declared: "[I]f political theorists believe that social science cannot be done in the mode of natural science ... it is unclear [to me] why they would want to remain in a discipline with so many scholars who believe it can be and who are dedicated to pursuing this claim."[9]

At stake here is the fundamental quest for a scientific understanding of the modern world. In other words: my reference above to Voegelin and to interpretive humanities was not meant to illustrate an outsider's scholarly position, but to introduce the important principle articulated by hermeneutical science: "the self-understanding of man in the modern age of science."[10] This historical challenge to the dominant scientific position needs to be briefly set forth. It emerged in the conception of an interpretative science in nineteenth-century Europe, in particular in Germany. Against the dominant Comtean positivism it insisted on the scientific dignity of all history-based humanistic disciplines (including the traditional moral and political ones). The quest for elaborated rational epistemological and methodological foundations and a common frame of reference for the rapidly developing empirically-oriented historical and philological disciplines arose from the desire to safeguard their theoretical status as sciences (Wissenschaften). This included the rejection of attempts to transform the humanities into so-called hard sciences, analogous to the natural sciences. It is beyond the scope of the present discussion to present the multi-layered—and in many respects contradictory—paradigm of "Geisteswissenschaft," as it was termed by the philosopher Wilhelm Dilthey. The intention of "Geisteswissenschaft" is to reconcile the postulate of objective knowledge with the notion of historical relativity. The latter was the result of the all-pervading

---

9   Andrew Rehfeld, "Offensive Political Theory," *Political Science and Politics* 8, no. 2 (June 2010): 477.

10   Hans-Georg Gadamer, *Wahrheit und Methode* (Tübingen: Mohr Siebeck, 1975), 519.

consciousness of the historicity of human existence—the hallmark of modernity.[11] Within the open horizon of history, human self-reflection discloses the common spiritual ground and the coherence of human life. This is found in an underlying and structurally ordered meaningful whole that comes into view in the range of human experience that unfolds in space and time. This *a priori* of cognition enables the scientifically schooled scholar to understand the manifold manifestations of the historical world that are generated by the interaction of individuals, communities, and cultural systems. It enables the scholar to interpret these manifestations by means of the hermeneutic of exegesis as it was practiced in Dilthey's time in jurisprudence, theology, philosophy, and philology. Dilthey brought this hermeneutic to the study of the historical world which he conceived in the manner of a text to be deciphered: "Life and history have a meaning, as do the letters in a word."[12] The hermeneutic procedure decodes the symbolic fabric of human self-understanding that develops in human experience in the historical process, and brings to it a theoretical interpretation that is grounded in a claim to universal validity.[13] Hermeneutical science thrived in the humanities and modernized their theoretical underpinnings and empirical methods. It established the paramount importance of humanistic research institutions worldwide and fostered their role as stewards of the world's spiritual, intellectual, and cultural legacies. Traditionally, the classical hermeneutics of Geisteswissenschaft had focused on the cultural constitution of the historical world: Only reluctantly did European scholars, under the pressure of the growing European crisis, turn to an explicit interpretive theory of politics that challenged the dominance of positivistic social science and its claim to irreversible ascendancy in a world that was believed to be completely secularized and modern.

Political philosophers like Jouvenel, Ricoeur, Strauss, Arendt, and Voegelin—to name just a few—set the stage for a new hermeneutical

---

11 Jürgen Gebhardt, "Hermeneutics and Political Theory," *Interpretation* 40, no. 2 (2013): 292.

12 Wilhelm Dilthey, *Gesammelte Schriften, vol. 7* (Leipzig: Teubner, 1942), 281.

13 Wilhelm Dilthey, *Gesammelte Schriften, vol. 5* (Stuttgart: Teubner 1957), 319, 331.

approach in the social sciences. In the words of Hannah Arendt: "The historical sciences and the humanities which ... guard over, and interpret factual truth and human documents, are politically of greatest relevance."[14] This call for rethinking the case for a hermeneutic science gained momentum when Paul Rabinow and William L. Sullivan announced the "interpretive turn" in social science that "refocuses attention on the concrete varieties of cultural meaning, in their particularity and complex texture, but without falling into the traps of historicism or cultural relativism."[15] In recent years Charles Taylor made a strong appeal for an interpretive turn in political science. Taylor, a staunch critic of the empiricist's persistent failure to predict or to understand the most important phenomena in a continually changing political world, argued "that mainstream social science is kept within certain limits by its categorical principles which are rooted in the traditional epistemology of empiricism ... and that these restrictions are a severe handicap and prevent us from coming to grips with important problems of our day which should be the object of political science. We need to go beyond the bounds of a science based on verification" to a truly interpretive science of politics that provides us with a hermeneutically undergirded understanding of the meaningful texture of the socio-historical world in general, and the range of human agency in terms of the manifold political orders and attendant symbolic forms of societal self-understanding in particular.[16]

Modern scholarship and the conundrum of religion

Taylor is a prime example of the many voices that have called attention to the unsettling events that have undermined the self-assertive paradigm of modern politics and which have brought about a paradigm shift in the

14 Hannah Arendt, "Truth and Politics" (paper prepared for the Annual Meeting of the American Political Science Association 1966).

15 Paul Rabinow and William M. Sullivan, "The Interpretive Turn," in *Interpretive Social Science: A Second Look*, ed. Paul Rabinow and William M. Sullivan (Berkeley: University of California Press, 1987), 6.

16 Charles Taylor, *Philosophical Papers 2* (Cambridge: Cambridge University Press, 1985), 52 and passim.

socio-historical disciplines. In the final analysis this shift set the stage for a new understanding of the essential traits of humanity's struggle for order that reflects on the permanent issue of the human condition.

And, indeed, a global civilizational ecumene has come into being, but one marked by the strong resurgence of spiritual, cultural, and political forces that challenge the dream of Western globalism. As the late Samuel Huntington stated in "The Clash of Civilizations": "[G]lobal politics is both multipolar and multicivilizational; modernization is distinct from Westernization and is producing neither a universal civilization in any meaningful sense nor the Westernization of non-Western societies."[17] Huntington's cogent interpretive paradigm showed that "the revival of non-Western religions is the most powerful manifestation of anti-Westernism in non-Western societies. That revival is not a rejection of modernity; it is a rejection of the West and the secular, relativistic, degenerate culture associated with the West."[18] Huntington clearly identified the bankruptcy of the secular vision.

The fall of the Shah of Iran and the establishment of an Islamic Republic in 1979 was not just an unpleasant surprise for the USA but for the general public in the West as well. It signaled a radical shift in Muslim societies toward religiously-based revolutionary politics. This shift was further highlighted by the events of September 11 as well as by the earlier rise to power of the Taliban in Afghanistan. Much to the surprise of the experts, the upheaval in the Near East marked a development that extended beyond the Islamic realm and pointed to analogous phenomena in other mainstream religions. In the aftermath of the Iranian revolution, militant and highly focused movements were subsumed under the umbrella term "fundamentalism" and quickly became the object of an intense discussion among political decision-makers and scholars.

An exemplary case is Gabriel A. Almond who, noting "the rise of fundamentalism around the world" bemoaned his own "secular myopia" and admitted: "The denial of the causal significance of religion rests, at least in part, on an inertial persistence of the culture of 'progress'—a

17 Samuel Huntington, *The Clash of Civilizations and the Remaking of World Order* (New York: Simon & Schuster, 1996), 20.
18 Ibid., 101.

survival of Enlightenment expectations of continued secularization, growth of scientific knowledge, technical and institutional creativity, and enhanced welfare, with religion seen only as fading tradition."[19]

At first the Islamist uprising, and the emergence of the parallel religiously-motivated radicalism of Christian or Jewish origin, were viewed as fundamentalist revolts against secular modernity on the part of traditionally theistic religions. But this view did not take into account the secular fundamentalism of earlier totalitarian movements, nor contemporary Islamic totalitarianism. The real quandary of the fundamentalism discourse became evident when the concept of fundamentalism was expanded to the point that any group or movement putting forth a normative claim to ultimate truth, whether religious, political, or moral, was labeled "fundamentalist." Lacking analytical precision, the fundamentalism discourse had reached an intellectual dead end.

However, in the last analysis, it can be noted that the study of global fundamentalism first called for a new look into the historical, cultural, and political implications of the modernization theory, in particular into its secularist underpinnings. It became necessary to reconsider the formative role of religion in modern and modernizing societies. In the light of these questions the fundamentalism discourse turned implicitly and explicitly into a discourse on religion.

Confronted now with the unexpected reassertion of religious traditions secular scientists proclaim the "resurgence" of religion, the "return" of religion, or the "return" of the gods, and postulate the emergence of a "post-secular society." They also call for an update of secularization theory: It "is not a simple-minded theory of inevitable religious decline, but a theory to explain variation."[20] In view of the fact that most of the participants in this religious discourse are themselves secularists, such a turn signifies a dilemma for the intellectual mainstream itself. "The dramatic worldwide return of religions and of their relevance as public power," states Martin Riesebrodt, "has most of us surprised whether we

19 Gabriel L. Almond, et al., *Strong Religion* (Chicago: Chicago University Press, 2003), 4–5.
20 Pippa Norris and Ronald Inglehart, *Sacred and Secular: Religion and Politics Worldwide* (Cambridge: Cambridge University Press, 2004), 13.

are social scientists or not. We all believed more or less to know that a re-strengthening of religions would be impossible." And, Riesebrodt adds: "The various attempts of social scientists to come to grips with their own cognitive dissonance, therefore, have been proven at least as interesting as the surprising return of religion itself."[21] Peter Berger insists that the assumption that we live in a secularized world is false. "The world today, with some exceptions ..., is as furiously religious as it ever was, and in some places more so than ever. This means that a whole body of literature by historians and social scientists loosely labeled 'secularization theory' is essentially mistaken."[22] In view of the resurgence of religion in the present Berger puts the thesis of a de-secularization of the world on the agenda of the ongoing discourse on religion.

It goes beyond the scope of these remarks to sum up and evaluate the still ongoing, highly controversial debate about the meaning of secularization that is essentially bound up with the original Comtean positivism discussed above. Following Berger's convincing argument it may be concluded that, as Huntington maintained, through Western penetration of the global ecumene, non-Western civilizational processes underwent fundamental social, cultural, and political changes. These reshaped the field of religious cultures and the communities of belief in a way that brought forth a far-reaching reconfiguration of the sacred and the secular. Henceforth theoretical reflection as well as political agency will have to reckon with an all-pervasive religiousness and a persistent secularity. These form diversely-patterned constellations that vary in appearance according to their specific historical and cultural settings. As Hans Joas recently stated: Weber had it wrong—the "disenchantment of the world" did not take place.[23]

Once the fundamentalism discourse raised the issue of secularization and religion, the scope of the debate broadened: at stake was the meaning

21 Martin Riesebrodt, *Die Rückkehr der Religionen: Fundamentalismus und der Kampf der Kulturen* (München: C.H. Beck, 2001), 9.
22 Peter L. Berger, "The Desecularization of the World: A global Overview," in *The Desecularization of the World*, ed. Peter L. Berger (Grand Rapids, MI: Eerdmans, 1999), 1–2.
23 Hans Joas, *Die Macht des Heiligen: Eine alternative Geschichte von der Entzauberung* (Frankfurt: Suhrkamp, 2017).

of religion, its defining properties, and the interweaving of religiosity and human agency within societal contexts. Thus, we now observe a scholarly discourse that has begun to reconsider the interweaving of the religious and the political in the formation of political community, which was Voegelin's focus in his seminal study of "political religions." However, in contrast to Voegelin, the current discourse does not extend the analysis of the religio-political symbolic to modern ideological mass movements and therefore does not recognize the universality of the historical phenomenon. But, indeed, this is the very issue that needs to be addressed.

At stake is the fundamental problematic connected with the modern Western generic concept of "religion." Here I can only sum up this concept briefly and apodictically. I begin with the contention that neither the Hellenic world nor Judaism and early Islam nor any of the other great non-Western civilizations developed a generic term 'religion' or a semantic equivalent to it. The term is exclusively of post-reformatory origin.

The Western history of the term "religion" is well documented by Ernst Feil in his four volumes on "religio."[24] It originated with Cicero's coining in order to express the sacred order of the *res publica*. It includes the recognition and cultic worship of the divine based on the virtue of piety. The Christian fathers transmitted the notion of "religio" to Latin Christianity which at the time was considered to be the only true cult of the divine.[25] The Islamic term 'Dīn' seems to be a conceptual analogue. It is a remarkable fact that medieval Christianity marginalized the semantics of "religio" in its theological discourse. This concept of religion as a natural anthropologically-grounded disposition and as the prerequisite for good order and governance survived in the humanistic tradition from Ficino to Machiavelli, Bodin, Montesquieu, and even in the American founders. But it was disregarded in Church-dominated Europe. On the

---

24 Ernst Feil, *Religio I– IV* (Göttingen: Vandenhoeck & Ruprecht, 1986–2007).

25 Jürgen Gebhardt, "Götter, Ritual und sakrale Ordnung der *Res Publica*: Cicero und Varro," in *Staat und Religion*, ed. Oliver Hidalgo and Christian Polke (Wiesbaden: Springer 2017), 49–64.

other hand, the modern generic concept of religion evolved from the post-reformatory denominational struggle within a fragmented Christianity for the right religious-political order. This was characterized by the conflict between state (politics) and church (religion). Modeled upon the central tenets of Church doctrine, the generic concept of religion is burdened with the semantic theological dichotomies that symbolically mirror the chasm between an inner-worldly reality and a world of the imaginary beyond. Thus even the analysts of a resurgence of religion insist on the supernatural, magical, and basically irrational elements of the religiously-defined realm, as distinguished from the supposedly objective rational and natural world of modern scientific civilization. For even the most refined generic concept of religion preserves the contrafactual opposition of "knowledge vs. belief," "reason vs. divine revelation," "rational vs. irrational," and "natural vs. supernatural." Perhaps I over-emphasize this pairing of opposites, but it forces upon the symbolically articulated cosmos of human experience a bifurcation that is empirically unwarranted and destroys the morphological unity of the realm of human-being.

In this way the narrative fiction of "religion" was expelled from the political realm. This was in keeping with the de-spiritualized Weberian concept of exclusively power-related politics. But this ignores the formative role that spiritual experiences play in the mental and symbolical makeup of societal order. But even if, in regard to this question, critical doubts abound in the scholarly community, the professional research culture continues to ensure that the ongoing religion discourse has a secularist bias. Such a biased research design impairs a genuine hermeneutical and trans-cultural understanding of the religio-cultural underpinnings of political community and community formation.

A case in point is the fundamentalism discourse discussed above. The secularist view does not recognize that the nineteenth- and twentieth-century messianic revolutionary movements that tried to create a "new human being" in a realm of inner-worldly perfection are religious-political phenomena. Since the movements' key symbolisms lacked the traditional religious semantics, they were considered to be pseudo-religious rather than authentically religious. The result was that the totalitarian world-view was analytically marginalized—although in most studies of the modern problem of religion this was done with a bad conscience.

A more serious consequence of the secularist's enterprise is the heuristic limitations of the comparative study of non-Western phenomena. According to Fred Dallmayr, it involves "the interpretative creation of a new framework or frame of reference ... that ... explores the explicit self-understanding of a given perspective in the direction of the nonthematized underpinnings or its covert 'otherness.'"[26] His claim is particularly relevant to the controversial subject of "religion." For indeed, most non-Western civilizations do not recognize a religious-theologically defined sphere separate from the symbolic cosmos of the society as a whole. The orders of spiritual life pervade the self-interpretive symbolic forms of the political order. Neither the Hindu, nor the Chinese, nor the Japanese distinguish politics from religion (unless they are Western-trained academics).

The re-conceptionalization of a hermeneutic of the political-religious complex: transcendence, symbol, and society.

A hermeneutical science involves a mode of theorizing that translates the meaning of self-interpretation into the language of rational discourse. A growing number of scholars subscribe to a hermeneutical research program. It aims at a universally valid knowledge of the various modes of political life in its temporal depth and global breadth. The hermeneutic enterprise's claim to universality is based on the heuristic principle of the equivalence of experience and symbolization in history that discovers the "uniformity in diversity."[27] From the awareness of the equivalent representation of humanity emerges the moment of reflexivity that crystallizes in a hermeneutical understanding of the entwining of symbolic form and political order. The proposed comprehensive interpretive political science reflects on the situation of human beings in modernity. In this way, interpretative political science itself represents a self-reflecting modernity. Hermeneutical theory and its conceptual apparatus of analysis is a response to the intellectual challenges of the

---

26 Fred Dallmayr, "Western Thought and Indian Thought: Comments on Ramunujan," *Philosophy East & West* 44 (1994): 531.
27 Bhiku Parekh and R. N. Berki, "The History of Political Ideas: A Critique of Q. Skinner's Methodology," *Journal of the History of Ideas* 34, no. 2 (1973): 178.

present. Its theoretical effort "starts from the concrete, historical situation of the age, taking into account the full amplitude of our empirical knowledge."[28]

From this vantage point the religion discourse brings into focus the religious-political constitution of human existence and its societal modalities. These are evoked by the imaginative power of the human spirit to create community by means of symbolization within an institutional cosmos of meaning. The religious moment that actuates human potential to wrest order from the chaotic powers of disorder has been cogently analyzed by Shmuel N. Eisenstadt. He speaks of the "charismatic vision" that is at the root of any institutionalization of societal order. "This charismatic dimension focuses in the cultural and social realms on the construction of cultural and social order in terms of some combination between primordial and transcendental symbols in terms of relation to some conception of the sacred. This charismatic dimension is manifest in the construction of the boundaries of personal and collective identities, of societal centers, and major symbols of prestige."[29]

This re-conceptualization takes into account the spiritual-religious forms of human self-understanding and self-articulation. The appropriation of the proven concepts of a modern heuristic understanding of transcendence and its symbolization avoids the categorical distinction between religious and secular symbolic forms that impairs a comprehensive historically-oriented and trans-culturally comparative structural analysis of socio-political complexes of order.

Voegelin also offered a critical account of the Roman-Christian template of "religion" and identified its causal role in the theological and ideological wars in modern history. "[R]eligion" he wrote, "is not 'an analytical term of anything.'"[30] "There are no gods," he once quipped, "but we must believe in them." And he hastened to explain: "the gods

28 Eric Voegelin, *The New Science of Politics* (Chicago: University of Chicago Press, 1952), 2–3.
29 S. N. Eisenstadt, *Power, Trust, and Meaning* (Chicago: University of Chicago Press, 1995), 35–36.
30 Eric Voegelin, *The Collected Works of Eric Voegelin: Order and History*, ed. Michael Franz, vol. 17 (Baton Rouge: University of Louisiana Press, 2000), 45.

are symbols by which transcendence is articulated."[31] This passing remark illustrates Voegelin's turn to the theme of transcendence that had evolved as a key concept in German theoretical discourse and removed the "religious and spiritual" dimension of life from its immediate connection with the social form of theologically impregnated religion. Instead it recognized that transcendence is constitutive of human life. As Georg Simmel put it: "transcendence is immanent to life."[32]

The concept of transcendence and the related concept of immanence are decidedly of modern origin, as the lexicographical study of Halfwassen and Enders has proven.[33] The philosophical and theological tradition knew the verbal expression "transcendere," but it was never translated into a verbal noun signifying a concept.

The semantics of transcendence originate with Kant. Without going into the complexities of Kant's philosophy I confine myself to the essentials. Kant limits rational cognition to the purview of the empirical (that is, the phenomenal) world, while the intelligible (that is, the noumenal) world is beyond the experiential realm of rational apprehension and comprises the realm of transcendent rational ideas (*Vernunftideen*) of the absolute. These transcendent, i.e., supernatural ideas (God, immortality, freedom) are regulative principles and postulates of practical reason. As such they are the indispensable precondition for the moral agency of rational human beings.[34]

The universal notion of transcendence connoting the spiritual, religious, and intellectual dimension of humanity became a cognitive concept in the post-Kantian hermeneutical science of Dilthey and his school. Against Kant, Dilthey proclaimed the hermeneutical credo that "the opposition between transcendence and immanence does not mark a

31 Charles R. Embry, ed., *Robert B. Heilmann and Eric Voegelin: A Friendship in Letters 1944 – 1984* (University of Missouri Press, Columbia 2004), 189.

32 Georg Simmel, *Lebensanschauung* (München: Duncker & Humblot, 1918), 14–15.

33 Jens Halfwassen and Markus Enders, "Transzendenz, Transzendieren" in: *Historisches Wörterbuch der Philosophie*, vol. 10, ed. Joachim Ritter and Karlfried Gründer (Darmstadt: Schwabe Verlag, 1998), 1442–55.

34 Ibid., 1447.

border-line of cognition."[35] While the semantic of transcendence gained currency in the emerging hermeneutic discourses it was introduced into the philosophical discourse by Karl Jaspers in his magisterial "Philosophy."[36] The experience of transcendence opens human existence to the unlimited spiritual realm of the comprehensive (*Umgreifenden*) and conveys existential truth to the communicative community of human beings.[37] Following Jaspers the philosophical term "transcendence" began to figure prominently in academic and non-academic discourse. It did not de-legitimate the theistic symbolism of Biblical religion but it explicated a universal modality of human faith that would restore the compatibility of the Biblical and the philosophical against the onslaught of a demonized re-divinized immanence. The most important aspect of Jaspers's idea of transcendence is his concept of the axis-time that grounded the universal experience of transcendence in the authority of the spiritual breakthroughs in the first millennium B.C.

The spiritual outbursts signalled a breakthrough toward a consciousness of the human self, its limitations, and its position in the comprehensive whole of being. It brought forth the "fundamental categories in which we still think today."[38] Jaspers's idea of axial time became the common property of scholarly discourse and so did his language of transcendence. Axial time was called the "age of transcendence" by the sinologist Benjamin Schwartz, and more recently Hans Joas described it as the "age of the emergence of transcendence."[39] Both scholars also resonate with Eisenstadt's ground-breaking theoretical and empirical study of the axial and post-axial age that, following Jaspers and Voegelin, was expanded into a civilizational paradigm with a global perspective.

Historically, the emergence of the ontological difference between

---

35 Wilhelm Dilthey, *Gesammelte Schriften: Weltanschauungslehre - Abhandlungen zur Philosophie der Philosophie* (Leipzig: Teeubner, 1931), 178.
36 Karl Jaspers, *Philosophie* (Berlin: Springer, 1932).
37 Karl Jaspers, *Vernunft und Existenz* (München: Piper, 1973), 73.
38 Karl Jaspers, *Vom Ursprung und Ziel der Geschichte* (Zürich: Fischer, 1949), 15.
39 Hans Joas, "The Axial-Age Debate as Religious Discourse," in *The Axial Age and its Consequences*, ed. Robert N. Bellah and Hans Joas (Cambridge: Cambridge University Press, 2012), 11.

the transcendental order embodying the idea of a higher, or metaphysical, order and the mundane order, led to a far-reaching reordering of societal existence in which the institutional and social structures were attuned to the imperatives of the transcendental vision.[40] The breakthrough toward transcendent visions revolutionized human self-interpretation and brought forth the symbolic and institutional complexes of order that shape global politics to this day: Confucianism, Taoism, Buddhism, Hinduism, Judaism, Christianity, and Islam. Due to the interplay between transcendent ideas and political power, politically organized societies are dependent on a symbolic consensus for their existence which is theoretically articulated at the nexus of transcendence and society.

Voegelin's early hermeneutical attempt at the religio-political analysis of the societal constitution of human-being set the tenor for an interpretive paradigm. In the course of his scholarly work the theoretical framework and its empirical scope underwent considerable revision. I will confine myself here to briefly pointing out the key argument that underlies the conceptualization of transcendence, symbolization, and society as it was formulated by Alfred Schütz and Eric Voegelin and which blended social phenomenology with political theory.

Alfred Schütz, the eminent phenomenological philosopher, agreed with Voegelin on the fundamental problem of philosophical anthropology, "namely, the place of man in a cosmos that transcends his existence, but within which he has to find his bearings. Signs and symbols ... are among the means by which man tries to come to terms with his meaningful experiences of transcendence."[41] Schütz starts from the basic phenomenological observation that, beyond the paramount reality of the everyday world, arise the manifold realms of meaning (science, poetry, myth, etc.) from experiences of transcendence. They break the spell of everyday life and point toward a higher order that is appresented in

---

40 S. N. Eisenstadt, "The Axial Break-throughs – Their Characteristics and Origins," in *The Origins and Diversity of Axial Age Civilizations*, ed. S. N. Eisenstadt (New York: State University of New York Press, 1986), 1.

41 Alfred Schütz, *The Problem of Social Reality: Collected Papers I* (The Hague: M. Nijhoff, 1962), 293.

symbols.[42] In other words: the experience of transcendence is constitutive for all symbolic forms that express communities of meaning. In particular, this means that human beings experience the social and political organization that is society and its order through a specific symbolic self-imagination: "a cosmion illuminated with meaning from within." These were Schütz's words in response to Voegelin's request for a clarification of what Schütz meant by the term "symbolic appresentation of society."

Human society, Voegelin asserted, "is a whole, a little world, a cosmion .... illuminated through an elaborate symbolism ... and this symbolism makes the internal structure of such a cosmion, the relations between its members and groups of members, as well as its existence as a whole, transparent for the mystery of human existence. The self-illumination of society through symbols is an integral part of social reality...."[43] Moreover it conveys the experience of essentiality to human beings in societal existenceas well as the experience of transcending their particular existence by virtue of participation in an overarching whole, a common symbolic universe and normatively coded order. As such, a politically organized society represents itself in terms of a political agency that is capable of sustaining it as a power unit. Beyond that, as Voegelin states, the symbolically articulated societal self-understanding involves a universal claim to represent a trans-historical truth. In this respect "society itself becomes the representative of something beyond itself, of a transcendent reality."[44] As a consequence, each society lays claim to representing a universal truth. Empirical examples abound, past and present: the universal truth of democracy in the Western world, the universal truth of the Koranic order in the Islamic world, or the universal truth of the realm of freedom in the now defunct communist world. Historically, the philosophical quest for universal truth is a response to the challenge of societal claims to truth.

Thomas Luckmann, a student of Schütz, addressed the problem of experiences of transcendence in a series of studies of the religious

---

42   Ibid., 337–55.
43   Voegelin, *The New Science of Politics*, 27.
44   Ibid., 54.

questions involved. Relevant to our discussion is his thesis that "the whole societal structure of meaning (gesammte Sinnstruktur), [and] its historical culture[,] integrates the human being into the individual transcending historico-social world. To Luckmann, the "religious core of this comprehensive figuration of societal meaning" reveals itself in "the construction of 'another' reality."[45] This construction involves first, "the inter-subjective reconstruction of experiences of transcendence." It consists of communicative acts in which subjective experiences of various kinds of this- and other-worldly transcendences are given an elementary social form (mythical narratives, commemorative rituals etc.). And, second, "the social construction of 'another 'reality—the primary inter-subjective reconstructions are interpreted, systematized, reformulated, and canonized—a process that may involve censoring deviant accounts. The reality to which these accounts refer is given firm and usually preeminent ontological status. The relation between ordinary and extraordinary reality is explained, and the norms that guide conduct in everyday life are systematically linked to the ultimate significance of the other reality."[46]

Luckmann's analysis of the sociogenesis of the symbolic order points to the ultimate source of the symbolic construction of societal transcendence: It springs from the personal religiosity or spirituality that Voegelin, in his early exploration of the modalities of religious experience, described in his "Political Religions."

It must be emphasized that the foregoing theoretical analysis takes into account empirical findings in all historical societies, including modern ones. In so far, the charismatic vision functions as a transcendent point of reference that is at one and the same time intangible but not ineffable. It illuminates the meaning of human existence in society by blending the political with the religious. It blends politics with the

---

45 Thomas Luckmann, "Privatisierung und Individualisierung – Zur Sozialform der Religion in spätindustriellen Gesellschaften," in *Religiöse Individualisierung oder Säkularisierung*, ed. Karl Gabriel (Gütersloh: Kaiser/Gütersloher Verlagshaus, 1996), 22.

46 Thomas Luckmann, "The New and Old in Religion," in *Social Theory for a Changing Society*, ed. Pierre Bourdieu and James S. Coleman (Boulder: Routledge, 1991), 170.

numinous, i.e., with a meta-physical absolute that signifies the ultimate ground of societal being in history. On the one hand, this blending is reflected in authoritative symbolic ensembles that articulate—as pointed out above—the idee directrice of public order and the political culture that sustains it. In this sense it may be called the religio-cultural dispositive of any political order and, as such, it is indispensable for keeping a political society in existence. On the other hand, the struggle for the truth of order is beset with elements of power. The ultimate intangibility of the truth of order leads to an ongoing competition and struggle over the meaning of symbols and for control of the institutions that define and articulate the leading values of public order. These provide the public order with its spirit and power even if the spirit is evil and the power corrupt.

The struggle for the truth of order, we should remind ourselves, has often been a question of life and death—it has been so in the past and it is so in the present day.

Publications by Charles E. Butterworth

A. Books

Alfarabi, The Book of Letters, translated and annotated, with an introduction plus a new Arabic text by Muhsin Mahdi (Ithaca: Cornell University Press, forthcoming).

Averroes' Short Commentaries on Aristotle's Organon, edited and translated, with an introduction (Albany: SUNY Press, forthcoming).

Alfarabi, The Political Writings, Volume II: "Political Regime" and "Summary of Plato's Laws," translated and annotated, with introductions (Ithaca: Cornell University Press, 2015).

Jean-Jacques Rousseau, The Death of Lucretia, trans., in The Collected Writings of Rousseau: Letter to D'Alembert and Writings for the Theater, vol. 10, ed. and trans., with Allan Bloom and Christopher Kelly (Hanover, NH: University Press of New England, 2004).

Averroës, The Book of the Decisive Treatise: Determining the Connection Between the Law and Wisdom, and Epistle Dedicatory, translation, with introduction and notes (Provo, UT: Brigham Young University Press, 2001).

Alfarabi, The Political Writings: "Selected Aphorisms" and Other Texts, translated and annotated, with an introduction (Ithaca: Cornell University Press, 2001); paperback edition, 2002; reprinted, with Foreword by S. Nomanul Haq (Studies in Islamic Philosophy, vol. 3; Karachi, Pakistan: Oxford University Press, 2005); Turkish translation (Istanbul: Chiviyazilari Yayinlari, 2008).

Between the State and Islam, with I. William Zartman and others (Cambridge: Cambridge University Press, 2001).

The Introduction of Arabic Philosophy into Europe with Blake A. Kessel and others (Leiden: E. J. Brill, 1994).

The Political Aspects of Islamic Philosophy, Essays in Honor of Muhsin S. Mahdi, with others (Cambridge: Harvard University Press, 1992).

Averroes' Middle Commentary on Aristotle's Poetics, English translation with introduction (Princeton: Princeton University Press, 1986); reprinted, with new preface (South Bend, IN: St. Augustine's Press, 2000); Chinese translation (Beijing: Hermes, 2009).

Averroes' Middle Commentary on Aristotle's Poetics, with Ahmad Haridi, critical edition of Arabic text with introduction and notes (Cairo: General Egyptian Book Organization, 1986).

Averroes' Middle Commentary on Aristotle's Categories and De Interpretatione, English translation with introductions (Princeton: Princeton University Press, 1983); reprinted (South Bend, IN: St. Augustine's Press, 1998).

Averroes' Middle Commentary on Aristotle's Prior Analytics, with Mahmoud Kassem and Ahmad Haridi, critical edition of Arabic text with introduction and notes (Cairo: General Egyptian Book Organization, 1983).

Averroes' Middle Commentary on Aristotle's Posterior Analytics, with Mahmoud Kassem and Ahmad Haridi, critical edition of Arabic text with introduction and notes (Cairo: General Egyptian Book Organization, 1982).

Averroes' Middle Commentary on Aristotle's De Interpretatione, with Mahmoud Kassem and Ahmad Haridi, critical edition of Arabic text with introduction and notes (Cairo: General Egyptian Book Organization, 1981).

Averroes' Middle Commentary on Aristotle's Categories, with Mahmoud Kassem and Ahmad Haridi, critical edition of Arabic text with introduction and notes (Cairo: General Egyptian Book Organization, 1980).

Averroes' Middle Commentary on Aristotle's Topics, with Ahmad Haridi, critical edition of Arabic text with introduction and notes (Cairo: General Egyptian Book Organization, 1979).

Jean-Jacques Rousseau: The Reveries of the Solitary Walker, English translation with Interpretative Essay (New York: NYU Press, 1979);

paperback (New York: Harper and Row, 1982); reprinted paperback (Indianapolis: Hackett, 1992); new edition, in The Collected Writings of Rousseau: The Reveries of the Solitary Walker, Botanical Writings, and Letter to Franquières, vol. 8, trans. and annotated, with Alexandra Cook and Terence E. Marshall; ed. Christopher Kelly (Hanover, NH: University Press of New England, 2000).

Averroes' Three Short Commentaries on Aristotle's "Topics," "Rhetoric," and "Poetics," edited and translated, with an introduction (Albany: SUNY Press, 1977).

Ethical Writings of Maimonides, with Raymond L. Weiss (New York: NYU Press, 1975); paperback (New York: Dover Publications, 1983).

B. Monographs

Political Islam, a special issue of The Annals of the American Academy of Political and Social Science, with I. William Zartman and others, 524 (November, 1992).

Philosophy, Ethics, and Virtuous Rule: A Study of Averroes' Commentary on Plato's "Republic", Cairo Papers in Social Science, Vol. 9, Monograph 1 (Cairo: AUC Press, 1986).

C. Articles

"Medieval Arabic and Islamic Political Philosophy, an Overview," in Sciences et Philosophie Arabes et Islamiques Médiévales, ed. Ahmad Hasnaoui and Abdelwahab Bouhdiba (Tunis: Bayt al-Hikma, forthcoming).

"Alfarabi and the King in Truth: Some Practical Considerations," in Legitimación del Poder Político en el Pensamiento Medieval, XIX Coloquio Internacional de la SIEPM, eds. Pedro Roche, Celia Lopez, and J. Puig Montada (Madrid: forthcoming).

"Which comes First, Theory or Practice? Alfarabi's Political Teaching" in Revue Académique Les Cahiers de l'Islam 3 (2017, forthcoming).

"Reading the Quran," in Revue Académique Les Cahiers de l'Islam 2 (2016, forthcoming).

"Fārābī's *Purposes of Aristotle's Metaphysics* and Avicenna's 'Eastern' Philosophy," in Illuminationist Texts and Textual Studies: Essays in Memory of Hossein Ziai, eds. Ali Gheissari, John Walbridge, and Ahmed Alwishah (Leiden: E.J. Brill, 2018), 257–71.

"Alfarabi's Political Teaching: Theoretical Premisses and Practical Consequences," in Studi Maġrebini, Nuova Serie Vol. XII-XIII, Tomo I, Napoli, 2014–2015: Labor limae, Atti in onore di Carmele Baffioni, eds. Antonella Straface, Carlo De Angelo, and Andrea Manzo (Naples: L'Orientale, 2017), 91–101.

"Constitutionalism and Medieval Arabic/Islamic Political Philosophy," in Strong Democracy in Crisis: Promise or Peril?, ed. Trevor Norris (Lanham, MD: Lexington Books, 2016), 193–218.

"Alfarabi (870–950)," in The Encyclopedia of Political Thought, ed. Michael Gibbons (Cambridge: John Wiley & Sons, 2014), 46–56.

"How Not to Speak Truth to Power: 'Ali 'Abd al-Raziq's Rhetorical Failure in Islam and the Roots of Governance," in Democracy, Culture, and the Grip of Arab History: Essays Honoring the Work of Iliya Harik, eds. Elsa Marston Harik and Denis J. Sullivan (North Charleston, SC: CreateSpace Independent Publishing Platform, 2014), 111–32; revised version of "Law and the Common Good: To Bring about a Virtuous City or Preserve the Old Order?"

"Alfarabi (870–950): Reason, Revelation, and Politics," in Mélanges de l'Université Saint-Joseph 65 (2013), 79–93.

"How to Read Alfarabi," in More modoque, Die Wurzeln der europäischen Kultur und deren Rezeption im Orient und Okzident, Festschrift für Miklós Maróth zum siebzigsten Geburtstag, eds. Pál Fodor, Gyula Mayer, Martina Monostori, Kornél Szovák and László Takács (Budapest: Forschungszentrum für Humanwissenschaften der Ungarischen Akademie der Wissenschaften, 2013), 333–41.

"Law and the Common Good: To Bring about a Virtuous City or Preserve the Old Order?" in Mirror for the Muslim Prince: Islam and the Theory of Statecraft, ed. Mehrzad Boroujerdi (New York: Syracuse University Press, 2013), 218–39.

"Philosophy and Jurisprudence in Islam, A Hermeneutic Perspective" in Existenz 7/1 (Spring, 2012), 65–69.

"Islam as a Civilization," in Academic Questions 25/1 (Spring, 2012), 94–104.

"Alfarabi's Goal: Political Philosophy, not Political Theology," in Islam, the State, and Political Authority: Medieval Issues and Modern Concerns, ed. Asma Afsaruddin (New York: Palgrave-MacMillan, 2011), 53–74.

"Arabic Political Philosophy," in Encyclopedia of Medieval Philosophy: Philosophy Between 500 and 1500, ed. Henrik Lagerlund (Heidelberg: Springer Verlag, 2011), Vol. II, 1047–51.

"The World of Logic and its Detractors," in La lumière de l'intellect: La pensée scientifique et philosophique d'Averroès dans son temps, ed. Ahmad Hasnawi (Leuven: Peeters, 2011), 297–308.

"Arabic Contributions to Medieval Political Theory," in The Oxford Handbook of the History of Political Philosophy, ed. George Klosko (New York: Oxford University Press, 2011), 164–79.

"Early Thought," in A Companion to Muslim Ethics, ed. Amyn Sajoo (Institute of Ismaili Studies Muslim Heritage Series; London: I.B. Tauris, 2010), 31–51; adaptation of "Ethical and Political Philosophy," in The Cambridge Companion to Arabic Philosophy, ed. Richard C. Taylor and Peter A. Adamson (Cambridge: Cambridge University Press, 2005), 266–286.

"Getting Islam Straight," in Political Cultures and the Culture of Politics: A Transatlantic Perspective, ed. Jürgen Gebhardt (Publications of the Bavarian-American Academy, vol. 9; Heidelberg: Universitätsverlag Winter, 2010), 91–107.

"Political Philosophy and Political Thought in the Medieval Arabic-Islamic Tradition of the Middle East," in The Sage Handbook of Islamic Studies, ed. Akbar S. Ahmed and Tamara Sonn (Thousand Oaks, CA: Sage Publications, 2010), 140–59.

"Islamic Political Philosophy," in Encyclopedia of Political Theory, ed.

Mark Bevir (Thousand Oaks, CA: SAGE Publications, 2010), vol. 2, 713–20.

"Blinkered Politics: The US Approach to Arabs and Muslims," in Citizenship, Security and Democracy: Muslim Engagement with the West, ed. Wanda Krause (London & Ankara: AMSS & SETA, 2009), 115–22 and 260–64.

"The Role of Rhetoric in Averroes's Short Commentaries on Aristotle's Logic," in Literary and Philosophical Rhetoric in the Greek, Roman, Syriac and Arabic Worlds, ed. Frédérique Woerther (Hildesheim: Georg Olms, 2009), 185–96.

"What Might We Learn from al-Fārābī about Plato and Aristotle with respect to Law-Giving?" in Mélanges de l'Université St. Joseph, LXI (2008), Actes du Colloque International, Les doctrines de la loi dans la philosophie de langue arabe et leurs contextes grecs et musulmans, ed. Maroun Aouad, pp. 471–89.

"What is (and What is not) Arabic-Islamic Philosophy? A Synopsis of a Thematic Conversation at the MESA Annual Meeting, November 2006," in MESA Bulletin 41/1 (June 2007), 31–32.

"Alfarabi's Introductory Sections to the Virtuous City," in Adaptations and Innovations: Studies on the Interaction between Jewish and Islamic Thought and Literature from the early Middle Ages to the late Twentieth Century, Dedicated to Professor Joel L. Kraemer, ed. Y. Tzvi Langermann and Josef Stern (Paris and Louvain: Peeters, 2007), 27–49.

"Philosophy of Law in Medieval Judaism and Islam," in A Treatise of Legal Philosophy and General Jurisprudence, Volume 6: A History of the Philosophy of Law from the Ancient Greeks to the Scholastics, ed. Fred J. Miller, Jr. and Carrie-Ann Biondi (Dordrecht: Springer, 2007), 219–50.

"Alfarabi's Plato: A Tale of Two Cities," in The Political Identity of the West: Platonism in the Dialogue of Cultures, ed. Marcel van Ackeren and Orrin Finn Summerell (Frankfurt: Peter Lang, 2007), 55–76.

"On Natural Right and Other Un-written Guides to Political Well-Being," in PEGS (Political Economy of the Good Society), 15/2 (2006), 53–55.

"Farabi, al- (Alfarabius or Avennasar)," in The Encyclopedia of Medieval Islamic Civilization, ed. Josef W. Meri et al (London: Routledge, 2006), vol. 1, 247–248.

"Ibn Tufayl," in The Encyclopedia of Medieval Islamic Civilization, ed. Josef W. Meri et al (London: Routledge, 2006), vol. 1, 372–73.

"Averroes on Law and Political Well-Being," in Enlightening Revolutions: Essays in Honor of Ralph Lerner, edited by Svetozar Minkov, with Stéphane Douard (Lanham, MD: Lexington Books, 2006), 23–30. also in Averroes et les Averroïsmes Juif et Latin: Actes du Colloque International (Paris, 16–18 juin 2005), ed. J-B Brenet (Turnhout: Brepols, 2007), 183–91.

"Ethical and Political Philosophy," in The Cambridge Companion to Arabic Philosophy, ed. Richard C. Taylor and Peter A. Adamson (Cambridge: Cambridge University Press, 2005), 266–86; adapted and published as "Early Thought," in A Companion to Muslim Ethics, ed. Amyn Sajoo (Institute of Ismaili Studies Muslim Heritage Series; London: I.B. Tauris, 2010), 31–51.

"Ibn Khaldun on The Essential Accidents of Human Social Organization," in Mélanges de l'Université Saint-Joseph, LVII (2004), The Greek Strand in Islamic Political Thought: Proceedings of the Conference held at the Institute for Advanced Study, Princeton, 16–27 June 2003, eds. Emma Gannagé, Patricia Crone, Maroun Aouad, Dimitri Gutas, and Eckart Schütrumpf, 443–67.

"Finding First Principles, Possibility or Impasse?" in Words, Texts, and Concepts Cruising the Mediterranean Sea: Studies on the Sources, Contents, and Influences of Islamic Civilization and Arabic Philosophy and Science Dedicated to Gerhard Endress on his Sixty-Fifth Birthday, ed. R. Arnzen and J. Thielmann; Orientalia Lovaniensia Analecta; 139 (Leuven: Peeters, 2004), 211–22.

"Conservatism, Society, and Politics," in International Symposium on Conservatism and Democracy: 10–11 January 2004 (Ankara: Ak Parti Yayinlari, 2004), 53–57; Turkish translation, "Muhafazakarlik, Toplum ve Siyaset," in Uluslararasi Muhafazakarlik ve Demokrasi Sempozyumu: 10–11 Ocak 2004 (International Symposium on

Conservatism and Democracy: 10–11 January 2004) (Ankara: Ak Parti Yayinlari, 2004), 61–65.

"Anawati, Georges Chehata," in Encyclopedia of the Modern Middle East & North Africa, Second Edition, ed. Philip Mattar, Charles E. Butterworth, Neil Caplan, Michael R. Fischbach, Eric Hooglund, Laurie King-Irani, Don Peretz, and John Ruedy (New York: Thomson Gale, 2004), vol. 1, pp. 194–95.

"Awad, Louis," in Encyclopedia of the Modern Middle East & North Africa, Second Edition, ed. Philip Mattar, Charles E. Butterworth, Neil Caplan, Michael R. Fischbach, Eric Hooglund, Laurie King-Irani, Don Peretz, and John Ruedy (New York: Thomson Gale, 2004), vol. 1, p. 340.

"Madkour, Ibrahim," in Encyclopedia of the Modern Middle East & North Africa, Second Edition, ed. Philip Mattar, Charles E. Butterworth, Neil Caplan, Michael R. Fischbach, Eric Hooglund, Laurie King-Irani, Don Peretz, and John Ruedy (New York: Thomson Gale, 2004), vol. 3, pp. 1456–57.

"Prisoner of Conscience: The Story of Dr. Sami al-Arian," Preface to Shackled Dreasm, A Palestinian's Struggle for Truth, Justice, and the American Way: The Story of Sami A. al-Arian (Washington, DC: National Liberty Fund, 2004), xv–xx.

"Farabi, Abu Nasr Muhammad Ibn Tarkhan, al-" in The (Oxford) Dictionary of Islam, ed. John L. Esposito (New York: Oxford University Press, 2003), 80–81.

"Aristotle" in The (Oxford) Dictionary of Islam, ed. John L. Esposito (New York: Oxford University Press, 2003), 24.

"Ben Maimon, Moshe (Maimonides)" in The (Oxford) Dictionary of Islam, ed. John L. Esposito (New York: Oxford University Press, 2003), 41.

"Muqaddimah, al-" in The (Oxford) Dictionary of Islam, ed. John L. Esposito (New York: Oxford University Press, 2003), 215.

"Plato" in The (Oxford) Dictionary of Islam, ed. John L. Esposito (New York: Oxford University Press, 2003), 248.

Foreword to Alfarabi's Philosophy of Plato and Aristotle, trans. Muhsin S. Mahdi (Ithaca: Cornell University Press, 2002), with Thomas Pangle, vii–xx.

"Alfarabi" in Encyclopedia of Ethics, Second Edition, ed. Lawrence C. Becker and Charlotte B. Becker (New York: Garland, 2001), vol. 1, 524–26.

"Averroes" in Encyclopedia of Ethics, Second Edition, ed. Lawrence C. Becker and Charlotte B. Becker (New York: Garland, 2001), vol. 2, 825–26.

"Avicenna" in Encyclopedia of Ethics, Second Edition, ed. Lawrence C. Becker and Charlotte B. Becker (New York: Garland, 2001), vol. 1, 115–16.

"Ibn Tufayl" in Encyclopedia of Ethics, Second Edition, ed. Lawrence C. Becker and Charlotte B. Becker (New York: Garland, 2001), vol. 2, 826–27.

Foreword to Muhsin S. Mahdi, Alfarabi and the Foundation of Islamic Political Philosophy: Essays in Interpretation (Chicago: University of Chicago Press, 2001), xi–xvii.

"On What is Between, Even Beyond, the Paradigms," in Between the State and Islam, with I. William Zartman and others (Cambridge: Cambridge University Press, 2001), 14–30.

"Preface to Part I: Nineteenth Century," in Between the State and Islam, with I. William Zartman and others (Cambridge: Cambridge University Press, 2001), 9–13.

"Introduction," with I. William Zartman, in Between the State and Islam, with I. William Zartman and others (Cambridge: Cambridge University Press, 2001), 1–8.

"The Political Teaching of Avicenna," Topoi 19 (2000), 35–44.

"In What Sense is Averroes an Encyclopedist?" in The Medieval Hebrew Encyclopedias of Science and Philosophy: Proceedings of the Bar-Ilan University Conference, ed. Steven Harvey (Dordrecht: Kluwer, 2000), 99–119.

"Georges Chehata Anawati (1905–1994)," with David Burrell, C.S.C.

and Patrick Gaffney, C.S.C., in <u>Medieval Scholarship: Biographical Studies on the Formation of a Discipline, Vol. 3, Philosophy and the Arts</u>, ed. Helen Damico, with Donald Fennema and Karmen Lenz (New York: Garland, 2000), 131–42.

"Ibn Rushd wa al-Ārā' allatī yushtarika fīhā Kull Naz.ar Falsafī" (Averroes and the Opinions common to every Philosophical Investigation) in <u>Ibn Rushd, Faylasūf al-Sharq wa al-Gharb: Fī al-Dhikrā al-Mi'awiyya al-Thāmina li-Wafātih</u> (Averroes, Philosopher of the East and of the West: For the 800th Anniversary of his Death), ed. Miqdād 'Arafa-Mensia (Tunis: ALECSO, 1999), vol.1, 59–74; French summary, "Ibn Rushd et les opinions communes à toute investigation philosophique ou ce que l'on ne peut pas ignorer," in <u>Actualité d'Averroès: Colloque du huitième centenaire</u>, Comptes rendus by Mokdad Arfa-Mensia (Tunis: Académie tunisienne Beït al-Hikma /UNESCO, 2001), 102–06; English version, "Averroes and the Opinions Common to all Philosophical Investigations, or What No One Can Ignore," in <u>The Existential Horizon of Averroes's Thought: Acts of the International Conference Commemorating the Eighth Centenary of Averroes's Death, Marrakesh, 12–15 December, 1998</u>, ed. Muhammad al-Mesbahi (Rabat: Moroccan Academy of Philosophy, 2001), 25–35; also in <u>Averroes and the Aristotelian Heritage</u>, ed. Carmela Baffioni (Naples: Istituto Universitario Orientale, 2004), pp.11–21; also as "Averróis e as opiniões comuns a todas as investigações filosóficas ou o que ninguém pode ignorar," in Rosalie Pereira, ed. <u>Busca do Conhecimento: Ensaios de Filosofia Medieval no Islã</u>, (São Paulo: Editora Paulus, 2007), pp. 179–96.

"A Propos du Traité <u>al-Darūrī fī al-Mantiq</u> d'Averroès et les termes tasdīq et tasawwur qui y sont dévéloppés," in <u>Averroes and the Aristotelian Tradition: Sources, Constitution, and Reception of the Philosophy of Ibn Rushd (1126–1198), Proceedings of the Fourth Symposium Averroicum (Cologne, 1996)</u>, ed. Gerhard Endress and Jan A. Aertsen (Leiden: Brill, 1999), 163–71.

"Averroes, Precursor of the Enlightenment," in <u>Revue Tunisienne des Études Philosophiques</u> 19 (1998), 42–46 (shortened version of the article published in <u>Alif</u>, 1996).

"The Intersection of Islamic Resurgence and Democracy," in Islam and the West: A Dialog, ed. Imad-Ad-Dean Ahmad and Ahmed Yousef (Springfield, VA and Washington, DC: UASR and AMF,1998), 95–114.

"Averroes' Platonization of Aristotle's Art of Rhetoric," in La Rhétorique d'Aristote, traditions et commentaires, de l'Antiquité au XVIIe siècle, ed. G. Dahan and I. Rosier (Paris: Vrin, 1998), 227–40.

"Ibn Khaldūn," in Encyclopedia of the History of Science, Technology and Medicine in Non-Western Cultures, ed. Helaine Selin (Dordrecht: Kluwer Academic Publishers, 1997), 422–23.

"Twelve Treatises in Search of a Title, Averroes' Short Commentaries on Aristotle's Logic," in Langages et Philosophie, Hommages à Jean Jolivet, ed. A. de Libera, A. Elamrani-Jamal, et A. Galonnier (Paris: Vrin, 1997), 99–108.

"Opinion, point de vue, croyance, et supposition," in Perspectives arabes et médiévales sur la tradition scientifique et philosophique, ed. Ahmad Hasnawi, Abdelali Elamrani-Jamal, and Maroun Aouad (Paris/Leuven: Institut du Monde Arabe/Peeters, 1997), 453–64.

"Averroes: Der Beitrag der arabischen Philosophie zur Aufklärung im Mittelalter," in Das Licht der Vernunft: Die Anfänge der Aufklärung im Mittelalter, ed. Kurt Flasch and Udo Reinhold Jeck (Munich: C. H. Beck, 1997), 28–35.

"Paris est et sagesse ouest: du Trivium et Quadrivium dans le monde arabe médiéval," in L'Enseignement des disciplines à la Faculté des Arts (Paris et Oxford, XIIIe-XVe siècles), ed. Olga Weijers and Louis Holtz (Turnhout: Brepols, 1997), 477–93.

"La philosophie morale de l'Islam," in Dictionnaire de philosophie morale, ed. Monique Canto-Sperber et al (Paris: Presses Universitaires de France, 1996), 735–43.

"Alfarabi," in Philosophy of Education: An Encyclopedia, ed. J. J. Chambliss (New York: Garland, 1996), 15–16.

"Avicenna," in Philosophy of Education: An Encyclopedia, ed. J. J. Chambliss (New York: Garland, 1996), 44–46.

"Averroes," in <u>Philosophy of Education: An Encyclopedia</u>, ed. J. J. Chambliss (New York: Garland, 1996), 43–44.

"Averroës, Precursor of the Enlightenment?" in <u>ALIF: Journal of Comparative Poetics</u>, 16 (1996), 6–18.

"On Others as Evil, Towards a Truly Comparative Politics," in <u>The American Journal of Islamic Social Sciences</u> 13/2 (Summer, 1996), 164–72.

"Socrates' Islamic Conversion," in <u>Arab Studies Journal</u> 4/1 (Spring, 1996), 4–11.

"De la traduction philosophique," in <u>Bulletin d'Études Orientales</u> 48 (1996), 77–85.

"The Greek Tradition in Ethics and its Encounter with Moral Wisdom in Islam," in <u>Moral and Political Philosophies in the Middle Ages, Proceedings of the Ninth International Congress of Medieval Philosophy, Ottawa, 17–22 August, 1992</u>, ed. B. Carlos Bazán et al (Ottawa: Legas, 1995), vol. 1, 125–35.

"Islam," in <u>The Encyclopedia of Democracy</u>, ed. Seymour Martin Lipset et al (Washington: Congressional Quarterly, 1995), vol. 2, 638–46.

"Alkindi," in <u>Great Thinkers of the Eastern World: The Major Thinkers and the Philosophical and Religious Classics of China, India, Japan, Korea, and the World of Islam</u>, ed. Ian P. McGreal (New York: Harper Collins, 1995), 439–42.

"Alrazi," in <u>Great Thinkers of the Eastern World: The Major Thinkers and the Philosophical and Religious Classics of China, India, Japan, Korea, and the World of Islam</u>, ed. Ian P. McGreal (New York: Harper Collins, 1995), 443–45.

"Averroes," in <u>Great Thinkers of the Eastern World: The Major Thinkers and the Philosophical and Religious Classics of China, India, Japan, Korea, and the World of Islam</u>, ed. Ian P. McGreal (New York: Harper Collins, 1995), 465–68.

"Democracy and Islam," in <u>Middle East Affairs Journal</u>, 2/2-3 (Winter-Spring, 1995), 56–69.

"The Source that Nourishes: Averroes's Decisive Determination," in Arabic Sciences and Philosophy, 5/1 (March, 1995), 93–119.

"'Ilm," with Sana Abed-Kotob, in The Oxford Encyclopedia of the Modern Islamic World, ed. John L. Esposito (New York: Oxford University Press, 1995), vol. 2, 182.

"Vicegerent," with Sana Abed-Kotob, in The Oxford Encyclopedia of the Modern Islamic World, ed. John L. Esposito (New York: Oxford University Press, 1995), vol. 4, 305.

"Al-Madīnah al-Fadīlah," in The Oxford Encyclopedia of the Modern Islamic World, ed. John L. Esposito (New York: Oxford University Press, 1995), vol. 3, 12–13.

"What is Political Averroism?" in Averroismus im Mittelalter und in der Renaissance, ed. Friedrich Niewöhner and Loris Sturlese (Zurich: Spur, 1994), 239–50.

"Introduction," in The Introduction of Arabic Philosophy into Europe, ed. Charles E. Butterworth and Blake A. Kessel (Leiden: E. J. Brill, 1994), 1–6.

"Translation and Philosophy: The Case of Averroes' Commentaries," in International Journal of Middle East Studies, 26/1 (February, 1994), 19–35.

"Die politischen Lehren von Avicenna und Averroës," in Pipers Handbuch der Politischen Ideen, Band 2: Mittelalter, von den Anfängen des Islams bis zur Reformation, ed. Iring Fetscher and Herfried Münkler (Munich: R. Piper, 1993), 141–73.

"Al-Rāzī: The Book of the Philosophic Life" and "The Origins of Al-Rāzī Political Philosophy," in Interpretation, 20/3 (Spring, 1993), 227–36 and 237–57.

"The Political Teaching of Averroes," in Arabic Sciences and Philosophy, 2/2 (1992), 187–202.

"Political Islam: The Origins," in Political Islam, a special issue of The Annals of the American Academy of Political and Social Science, ed. Charles E. Butterworth and I. William Zartman, 524 (November, 1992), 26–37.

"Preface," with I. William Zartman, in Political Islam, a special issue of The Annals of the American Academy of Political and Social Science, ed. Charles E. Butterworth and I. William Zartman, 524 (November, 1992), 8–12.

"Introduction," in The Political Aspects of Islamic Philosophy, Essays in Honor of Muhsin S. Mahdi, ed. Charles E. Butterworth (Cambridge: Harvard University Press, 1992), 1–9.

"Al-Kindī and the Beginnings of Islamic Political Philosophy," in The Political Aspects of Islamic Philosophy, Essays in Honor of Muhsin S. Mahdi, ed. Charles E. Butterworth (Cambridge: Harvard University Press, 1992), 11–60.

"On Understanding and Preserving Traditional Learning," in College Teaching, 40/3 (Summer, 1992), 102–05.

"L'Education Aristotélicienne des philosophes-rois de Platon dans le Commentaire sur la République d'Averroès," in Internationale de l'Imaginaire, Special Issue, Le Choc Averroès, comment les philosophes arabes ont fait l'Europe, Travaux de l'Université Européenne de la Recherche, Actes du Colloque Averroès, 6–8 février, 1991, 17–18 (Summer-Fall, 1991), 147–52.

"Comment Averroès lit les Topiques d'Aristote," in Penser avec Aristote, Etudes réunies, ed. M. A. Sinaceur (Paris: Erès, 1991), 701–24.

"Al-Fārābī's Statecraft: War and the Well-Ordered Regime," in Cross, Crescent, and Sword: The Justification and Limitation of War in Western and Islamic Tradition, ed. James Turner Johnson and John Kelsay (New York: Greenwood Press, 1990), 79–100.

"The Study of Arabic Philosophy Today," plus "Appendix (1983–87)," in Arabic Philosophy and the West: Continuity and Interaction, ed. Thérèse-Anne Druart (Washington: Center for Contemporary Arab Studies, 1988), 55–140.

"Medieval Islamic Philosophy and the Virtue of Ethics," in Arabica, 34 (1987), 221–50.

"State and Authority in Arabic Political Thought," in The Foundations of the Arab State, ed. Ghassan Salame (London: Croom Helm, 1987), 91–111; Arabic translation in al-Umma wa al-Dawla wa al-Indimaj fi al-Watn al-'Arabi, (Beirut: Markaz Dirasat al-Wahda al-'Arabiyya, 1989), vol. 1, 89–105, and in separate booklet, Al-Dawla wa al-Sulta fi al-Fikr al-Siyasi al-'Arabi, (London: Dar al-Saqi, 1990).

"The Summer of '85: An Egyptian Parliamentary Perspective," in Egypt: Old Realities and New Visions, ed. Edward E. Azar and Abdel R. Omran (College Park: CIDCM, 1987), 66–74.

"Ethics and Classical Islamic Philosophy: A Study of Averroes' Commentary on Plato's Republic," in Ethics in Islam, Ninth Giorgio Levi Della Vida Bienniel Conference, ed. Richard G. Hovannisian (Malibu: Undena, 1985), 17–45.

"The Rhetorician and his Relationship to the Community," in Islamic Theology and Philosophy: Studies in Honor of George F. Hourani, ed. Michael E. Marmura (Albany: SUNY Press, 1983), 111–36 and 297–98.

"Ethics in Medieval Islamic Philosophy," in The Journal of Religious Ethics, 11 (1983), 224–39; reprinted in Islam, vol. 2, Islamic Thought, Law and Ethics, ed. Mona Siddiqui (Benchmarks in Religious Studies; Sage: 2010), 377–92.

"The Study of Arabic Philosophy Today," in Middle East Studies Association Bulletin, 17 (1983), 8–24 and 161–77; Arabic translation in al-Mustaqbal al-'Arabī, 58, no. 12 (1983), 78–112.

"Prudence versus Legitimacy: A Persistent Theme in Contemporary Islamic Political Thought," in Islamic Resurgence in the Arab World, ed. Ali Dessouki (New York: Praeger, 1982), 84–114.

"Averroes' Middle Commentary on Aristotle's Categories and its Importance," in Miscellanea Mediaevalia, Spache und Erkenntnis im Mittelalter, 13/1 (1981), 368–75.

"Frantz Fanon and Human Dignity," in The Political Science Reviewer, 10 (1980), 257–327.

"Philosophy, Stories, and the Study of Elites," in Elites in the Middle East, ed. I. William Zartman (New York: Praeger, 1980), 10–48.

"La valeur philosophique des commentaires d'Averroès sur les oeuvres d'Aristote," in Multiple Averroès (Paris: Les Belles Lettres, 1978), 117–26.

"New Light on the Political Philosophy of Averroes," in <u>Islamic Philosophy and Science</u>, ed. George F. Hourani Albany: SUNY Press, 1975), 118–27.

"Averroes: Politics and Opinion," in <u>The American Political Science Review</u>, 66 (1972), 894–901.

"Rhetoric and Islamic Political Philosophy," in <u>International Journal of Middle East Studies</u>, 3 (1972), 187–98.

"Peer Influences on Levels of Occupational and Educational Aspiration," in <u>Social Forces</u>, with A. O. Haller, 38 (1960), 289–95.

D. Review Essays, Research Notes

"Tahrir Square: Popular Revolution or More of the Same?" in <u>The Faculty Voice, The University of Maryland</u> 25:1 (March, 2012), 3 a-b.

"Questions about Roger Scruton, 'Islam and the West: Lines of Demarcation,'" in <u>American Journal of Islamic Social Sciences</u> 29:1 (Winter, 2012), 143–45.

"Review Essay on Maroun Aouad's <u>Averroès (Ibn Rušd), Commentaire moyen à la Rhétorique d'Aristote: Édition critique du texte arabe et traduction française</u>, 3 vols. (I: Introduction générale et tables; II: Édition et traduction; III: Commentaire du Commentaire)," in <u>Gnomon</u> 82 (2010), 559–62.

"In Memoriam: Muhsin S. Mahdi," in *The Review of Politics* 69 (2007), 511–12.

"Leo Strauss: Philosopher and Neither Straussian nor Imperialist, Reflections on Anne Norton, <u>Leo Strauss and the Politics of American Empire</u>," in <u>Crossing Boundaries, New Perspectives on the Middle East: The MIT Electronic Journal of Middle Eastern Studies</u> 5 (Fall, 2005), 80–83.

María Rosa Menocal, <u>The Ornament of the World: How Muslims, Jews, and Christians Created a Culture of Tolerance in Medieval Spain</u>, in <u>Middle East Policy</u> 11/4 (December, 2004), 148–50.

"To Attend or Not to Attend," in <u>CTE, Teaching & Learning News, Special Issue: Closing the Gap Between Students' and Teachers' Expectations</u>, 13/4 (April/May, 2004), 4.

"Revelation over Rationalism, The Thought of Seyyed Hossein Nasr" Review Essay on The Philosophy of Seyyed Hossein Nasr, edited by Lewis Edwin Hahn, Randall E. Auxier, and Lucian W. Stone, Jr., in Humanitas, XV/2 (2002), 101–04.Interview on Islam Then and Now, in The AMSS Bulletin 3/4 (Fall 2002), 12–13.

Religion and Culture in Medieval Islam, eds. Richard G. Hovannisian and Georges Sabagh, in Middle East Policy, 8/4 (December, 2001), 152–54.

Shams al-Dīn Shahrazūrī, Sharh Hikmat al-Ishrāq, ed. Hossein Ziai, in Journal of Iranian Studies, 32/1 (Winter, 1999), 138–40.

"A Cornucopia of Rousseau Translations," Interpretation 27/1 (Fall, 1999), 71–79.

"Discussion: Two Views of Laurence Lampert's Leo Strauss and Nietzsche, in Interpretation, 25/3 (Spring, 1998), 443–45.

"Review Essay on Salim Kemal's The Poetics of Alfarabi and Avicenna," in College Literature 23/2 (June 1996), 202–06.

"Jerusalem Daze," Amos Oz's Fima and Philip Roth's Operation Shylock, A Confession," in Middle East Policy, 3/3 (1994), 157–63.

"The Political Economy of Liberty in the Arab and Islamic Middle East: A Conservative Perspective on the Israeli-Palestinian Conflict," in Middle East Policy 3/2 (1994), 110–13.

"Revelation and Political Philosophy: What is Islamization of Knowledge?" in The American Journal of Islamic Social Sciences, 10/2 (Summer, 1993), 249–50.

"On Magic and Other Enchantments, Husain Haddawy's New Translation of Alf Layla wa Layla, The Arabian Nights," in Interpretation, 21/1 (1993), 59–66.

Kathryn K. Abdul-Baki, Fields of Fig and Olive: Ameera and Other Stories of the Middle East, in Middle East Policy, 1/4 (1992), 147–51.

"Reply to Harry V. Jaffa," in Academic Questions, 4 (1991), 7–8.

"On Misunderstanding Allan Bloom: The Response to The Closing of the American Mind," in Academic Questions, 2/4 (Fall, 1989), 56–80.

"An Account of Recent Scholarship in Modern Islamic Philosophy," in Interpretation, 16 (1988), 87–97.

"Reply to Harry Neumann," in Independent Journal of Philosophy, 5/6 (1988), 160–61.

"In Memoriam, Robert Henry Horwitz (1923–87)," in The Political Science Reviewer, 17 (1987), vii–x.

"On Scholarship and Scholarly Conventions," in Journal of the American Oriental Society, 106/4 (Oct–Dec1986), 725–32.

"Farabi and Theodorus as Interlopers," in Bulletin de Philosophie Médiévale, 20 (1978), 48–52.

"Religion et philosophie dans la pensée d'Averroès," in Annuaire, Ecole Pratique des Hautes Etudes, V Section—Sciences Religieuses, 86 (1977–1978), 387–89.

"On Paul Sigmund's 'Review of Ralph Lerner's Averroes on Plato's Republic'," in Political Theory, 4 (1976), 505–06.

"Frantz Fanon and the Justice of Violence," in The Middle East Journal, 28 (1974), 451–58.

"On Henry Corbin's Creative Imagination in the Sufism of Ibn Arabi," in The Middle East Journal, 27 (1973), 92–96.

"Thucydides: Human Nature, the Love of Power, and Political Reality," in University of Maryland Graduate School Chronicle, Vol. 4, No. 2, Special Issue, (April, 1971), 9–10.

"The Rhetoric of Philosophy," in Today's Speech, 17 (1969), 43.

E. Book Reviews

Peter Adamson, A History of Philosophy without any Gaps in Journal of Islamic Studies 29/1 (January, 2018), 79–81.

Saud M. S. Al Tamamy, Averroes, Kant, and the Origins of the Enlightenment: Reason and Revelation in Arab Thought in Journal of Islamic Studies 27/2 (May, 2016), 219–222.

Terry K. Aladjem, The Culture of Vengeance and the Fate of American Justice in Choice 45/12 (August, 2008), 7044.

Writing and Representation in Medieval Islam: Muslim Horizons, ed. Julia Bray, in Journal of Islamic Studies 19 (2008), 402–05.

David Lay Williams, Rousseau's Platonic Enlightenment in Choice 45/11 (July, 2008), 6098.

Kelvin Knight, Aristotelian Philosophy: Ethics and Politics from Aristotle to MacIntyre in Choice 45/7 (March, 2008), 4047.

Joshua Parens, An Islamic Philosophy of Virtuous Religions: Introducing Alfarabi in Speculum, 83/1 (January,2008), 231–32.

Mark Philp, Political Conduct in Choice 45/ 3 (November, 2007), 1723.

Akbar Ahmed, Journey into Islam: The Crisis of Globalization in The Middle East Journal 61/3 (Summer, 2007), 554–55.

Pierre Manent, A World Beyond Politics? A Defense of the Nation State in Choice 44/9 (May, 2007), 4302.

Greg Hill, Rousseau's Theory of Human Association: Transparent and Opaque Communities in Choice 44/3 (November 2006), 1788.

Pierre Rosanvallon, Democracy Past and Future, edited by Samuel Moyn, in Choice 44/1 (September 2006), 607.

Jean-Jacques Rousseau, The Plan for Perpetual Peace, On the Government of Poland, and Other Writings on History and Politics: The Collected Writings of Rousseau, vol. 11, ed. by Christopher Kelly with Roger D. Masters; tr. by Christopher Kelly and Judith Bush in Choice 43/ 11 (July 2006), 6833.

Patricia Crone, God's Rule, Government and Islam: Six Centuries of Medieval Islamic Political Thought in The Muslim World 96/3 (July 2006), 523–25.

Jonathan Marks, Perfection and Disharmony in the Thought of Jean-Jacques Rousseau in Choice 43/7 (March 2006), 4307.

Mikael Hörnqvist, Machiavelli and Empire in Choice 43/1 (September 2005), 612.

Ibn Kammuna, Al-Tanqihat fi Sharh al-Talwihat: Refinement and Commentary on Suhrawardi's **Intimations**, A Thirteenth Century Text on Natural Philosophy and Psychology, ed. Hossein Ziai and Ahmed Alwishah, in MESA Bulletin 39/1 (June 2005), 94–95.

David Williams, Condorcet and Modernity in Choice 42/8 (April, 2005), 4905.

Mads Qvortrup, The Political Philosophy of Jean-Jacques Rousseau: The Impossibility of Reason in Choice 42/3 (November, 2004), 1850.

Douglas Moggach, The Philosophy and Politics of Bruno Bauer in Choice 42/3 (November, 2004), 1847.

Islamic Political Ethics: Civil Society, Pluralism, and Conflict, ed. Sohail H. Hashmi, in Islam and Christian-Muslim Relations 15/4 (October 2004), 527–29.

Muhammad ibn Zafar al-Siqilli, The Just Prince, A Manual of Leadership, including an authoritative English translation of the Sulwan al-Muta' fi 'Udwan al-Atba' (Consolation for the Ruler During the Hostility of Subjects), trans. Joseph A. Kechichian and R. Hrair Dekmejian, in The Middle East Journal, 58/2 (Spring, 2004), 323–24.

Sami Zubaida, Law and Power in the Islamic World, in Choice, 41/8 (April, 2004), 4947.

Graham E. Fuller, The Future of Political Islam, in Choice, 41/4 (December, 2003), 2455.

Michael S. Kochin, Gender and Rhetoric in Plato's Political Thought, in Choice, 40/11 (July, 2003), 6693.

Nazik Saba Yared, Secularism and the Arab World (1850–1939), in Choice 40/9 (May, 2003), 5478.

Juan Cole, Sacred Space and Holy War: The Politics, Culture and History of Shi'ite Islam, in e-Extreme, Electronic Newsletter of the European Consortium for Political Research, Standing Group on Extremism & Democracy, 4/1 (Spring 2003).

Aristotle and Modern Politics: The Persistence of Political Philosophy, ed. Aristide Tessitore in Choice 40/7 (March, 2003), 4272.

Cary J. Nederman, Worlds of Difference: European Discourses of Toleration C. 1100-C. 1550, in American Journal of Islamic Social Sciences 20/1 (Winter, 2003), 146–49.

Antony Black, The History of Islamic Political Thought: From the

Prophet to the Present in Islam and Christian-Muslim Relations, 13/4 (2002), 492–93.

An Anthology of Philosophy in Persia, vols. 1-2, ed. Seyyed Hossein Nasr with Mehdi Aminrazavi in The Middle East Journal, 56/4 (Autumn 2002), 735–36.

Martin Kramer, ed., The Jewish Discovery of Islam: Studies in Honor of Bernard Lewis, in Journal of the American Oriental Society, 122/3 (Summer, 2002), 635–37.

Leon Harold Craig, Of Philosophers and Kings: Political Philosophy in Shakespeare's Macbeth and King Lear, in Choice 39/11 (July, 2002), 6707.

Wendy Brown, Politics Out of History, in Choice, 39/9 (May, 2002), 5461.

Iysa A. Bello, The Medieval Islamic Controversy Between Philosophy and Orthodoxy: Ijm_' and Ta'w_l in the Conflict Between Al-Ghaz_l_ and Ibn Rushd in The Muslim World, 92/1-2 (Spring 2002), 209–10.

Christopher Nadon, Xenophon's Prince: Republic and Empire in the Cyropaedia in Choice, 39/6 (February, 2002), 3644.

Jim Colville, al-Jahiz, Avarice & The Avaricious (Kitâb al-Bukhalâ'); Ibn Tufayl and Ibn Rushd (Averroes), Two Andalusian Philosophers, The Story of Hayy Ibn Yaqzan & The Definitive Statement; and al-Nafzawi, The Perfumed Garden of Sensual Delights (ar-Rawd. al-'at. ir f î nuzhati'l khât. ir) in Journal of Semitic Studies 46/2 (Autumn, 2001), 356–59.

Fouad Ajami, Dream Palace of the Arabs: A Generation's Odyssey in The Middle East Journal 55/4 (Autumn, 2001), 702–03.

David W. Carrithers, Michael A. Mosher, and Paul A. Rahe, eds., Montesquieu's Science of Politics: Essays on "The Spirit of Laws" in Choice, 39/2 (October, 2001), 1212.

Patrick J. Deneen, The Odyssey of Political Theory: the Politics of Departure and Return in Choice, 38/10 (June, 2001), 5834.

Noël O'Sullivan, ed., Political Theory in Transition in Choice 38/7 (March, 2001), 4144.

Shaw J. Dallal, Scattered Like Seeds in The Middle East Journal 55/1 (Winter 2001), 150–53.

Wael B. Hallaq, Ibn Taimiyya, Against the Greek Logicians in Journal of the History of Ideas 38/2 (April, 2000), 273–75.

Husain Haddawy, trans., The Arabian Nights II, Sindbad and Other Popular Stories, in The Middle East Journal 54/2 (Spring, 2000), 319–20.

Peter Sacks, Generation X Goes to College, An Eye-Opening Account of Teaching in Postmodern America, in Interpretation, 27/2 (Winter, 1999-2000), 179–82.

Sulayman S. Nyang, Islam in the United States of America, in Middle EastAffairs Journal, 5/3-4 (Summer/Fall, 1999), 319–20.

Maurizio Viroli, Machiavelli, in Choice 37/1 (September, 1999), 612.

John Esposito and John Voll, Islam and Democracy, in Arab Studies Quarterly, 21/2 (Spring, 1999), 100–02.

International Fascism: Theories, Causes, and the New Consensus, ed. Roger Griffin, in Choice 36/10 (June, 1999), 5956.

Brian C. Anderson, Raymond Aron: The Recovery of the Political, in Choice, 36/2 (October, 1998), 1239.

Joshua Parens, Metaphysics as Rhetoric: Alfarabi's Summary of Plato's "Laws", in Speculum 73/3 (July, 1998), 881–83.

Olivier Roy, The Failure of Political Islam, in The Review of Politics, 60/2 (Spring, 1998), 372–74.

Pekka Suvanto, Conservatism from the French Revolution to the 1990s, in Choice, 35/8 (April, 1998), 4777.

Johnson Kent Wright, A Classical Republican in Eighteenth-Century France: The Political Thought of Mably in Choice, 35/5 (January, 1998), 6290.

Mohammed Arkoun, Rethinking Islam: Common Questions, Uncommon Answers, in Middle East Policy, 5/4 (January, 1998), 204–06.

Nicole Fermon, Domesticating Passions: Rousseau, Woman, and Nation in Choice, 34/11–12 (July-August, 1997), 6522.

Peter Levine, Something to Hide in Interpretation 24/2 (Winter, 1997), 239–42.

James V. Schall, At the Limits of Political Philosophy: From "Brilliant Errors" to Things of Uncommon Importance in Choice, 34/6 (February, 1997) 3553.

Akbar S. Ahmed, Living Islam: From Samarkand to Stornoway and Postmodernism and Islam: Predicament and Promise, in The Middle East Journal, 50/4 (Autumn, 1996), 621–23.

David Miller, On Nationality, in Choice, 33/9 (May, 1996), 5371.

Stanley Rosen, Plato's Statesman: The Web of Politics, in Choice, 33/7 (March, 1996), 4190.

New French Thought: Political Philosophy, ed. Mark Lilla, in Choice, 32/9 (May, 1995), 1522.

Virtue, Corruption, and Self-Interest: Political Values in the Eighteenth Century, ed. Richard K. Matthews, in Choice, 32/9 (May, 1995), 1523.

Leon Harold Craig, The War Lover: A Study of Plato's *Republic*, in Choice, 32/8 (April, 1995), 4750.

Athenian Identity and Civic Ideology, ed. Alan L. Boegehold and Adele C. Scafuro, in Choice, 32/1 (September, 1994), 606.

Jean-Jacques Rousseau, Rousseau, Judge of Jean-Jacques: Dialogues, ed. Roger D. Masters and Christopher Kelly; trans. Judith R. Bush, Christopher Kelly, and Roger D. Masters. Jean-Jacques Rousseau, Discourse on the Sciences and Arts (First Discourse) and Polemics, ed. Roger D. Masters and Christopher Kelly; trans. Judith R. Bush, Christopher Kelly, and Roger D. Masters. Jean-Jacques Rousseau, Discourse on the Origins of Inequality (Second Discourse), Polemics, and Political Economy, ed. Roger D. Masters and Christopher Kelly; trans. Judith R. Bush et al., in Choice, 31/10 (June, 1994), 594–97.

Denis Diderot, Political Writings, trans. and ed., John Hope Mason and Robert Wokler, in Ethics 104/4 (July, 1994), 921.

Daniel E. Cullen, Freedom in Rousseau's Political Philosophy, in Choice, 31/5 (January, 1994), 621.

Bonnie Honig, Political Theory and the Displacement of Politics, in Choice, 31/3 (November, 1993), 618.

Dimitri Gutas, Avicenna and the Aristotelian Tradition, Introduction to Reading Avicenna's Philosophical Works, in Journal of Islamic Studies, 4/2 (July, 1993), 250–52.

Donald P. Little, A Catalogue of the Islamic Documents from al-H.aram ash-Sharīf in Jerusalem, in The Muslim World, 83/1 (January, 1993), 91–92.

Maurizio Viroli, From Politics to Reason of State: The Acquisition and Transformation of the Language of Politics, 1250–1600, in Choice, 30/10 (June, 1993), 606.

Yoram Binur, My Enemy, My Self, trans. Uriel Grunfeld, in Terrorism and Political Violence, 5/1 (Spring, 1993), 177–78.

Dominique Urvoy, Ibn Rushd (Averroes), trans. Olivia Stewart, in International Journal of Middle East Studies, 25/2 (May, 1993), 335–38.

Luc Ferry and Alain Renaut, From the Rights of Man to the Republican Idea, in Choice, 30/7 (March, 1993), 619.

James M. Blythe, Ideal Government and the Mixed Constitution in the Middle Ages, in Choice, 30/2 (October, 1992), 688.

Michael Brint, A Genealogy of Political Culture, in Choice, 29/9 (May, 1992), 614.

Jonathan Wolff, Robert Nozick: Property, Justice and the Minimal State, in Choice, 29/6 (February, 1992), 627.

Michael Freeden, Rights, in Choice, 29/1 (September, 1991), 667.

John Evan Seery, Political Returns: Irony in Politics and Theory, from Plato to the Antinuclear Movement, in Choice, 28/8 (April, 1991), 1383.

David L. Stockton, The Classical Athenian Democracy, in Choice, 28/7 (March, 1991), 626.

Andrew Erskine, The Hellenistic Stoa: Political Thought and Action, in Choice, 28/1 (September, 1990), 687.

Antony T. Sullivan, Palestinian Universities Under Occupation, in Modern Age, 33 (1990), 87–88.

David Boucher, The Social and Political Thought of R. G. Collingwood, in Choice, 27/9 (May, 1990), 610.

Jean-Jacques Rousseau, The First and Second Discourses, Together with the Replies to Critics and Essay on the Origin of Languages, trans. Victor Gourevitch; in The Review of Metaphysics, 43 (1989), 181–83.

Maurizio Viroli, Jean-Jacques Rousseau and the "Well-Ordered Society," trans. Derek Hanson; in Choice, 26/8 (April, 1989), 637.

Judith N. Shklar, Montesquieu; in Choice, 26/1 (September, 1988), 672.

Al-Farabi's Commentary and Short Treatise on Aristotle's "De Interpretatione," trans. with intro. and notes, F. W. Zimmermann; in The Muslim World, 78 (1988), 149–50.

Understanding the Political Spirit: Philosophical Investigations from Socrates to Nietzsche, ed. Catherine H. Zuckert; in Choice, June, 1988, 603.

Ralph Ketcham, Individualism and Public Life: A Modern Dilemma; in Choice, April, 1988, 602.

Shi'ism and Social Protest, ed. Juan R. I. Cole and Nikki R. Keddie; in The American Political Science Review, 82 (1988), 269–70.

Ibn Al-Tayyib, Proclus' Commentary on the Pythagorean Golden Verses, ed. and trans. Neil Linley; in Speculum, 63/1 (January, 1988), 174–75.

Michael Joseph Smith, Realist Thought from Weber to Kissinger; in Choice, October, 1987, 649.

W. Montgomery Watt, Islamic Philosophy and Theology: An Extended Survey; in Middle East Studies Association Bulletin, 21 (1987), 253–54.

Barry S. Kogan, Averroes and the Metaphysics of Causation; in The International Journal of Middle East Studies, 19 (1987), 520–21.

Pan-Arabism and Arab Nationalism: The Continuing Debate, ed. by Tawfic E. Farah; in Choice, July-August, 1987, 570.

Haroon Khan Sherwani, Muslim Political Thought and Administration; in The Muslim World, 77 (1987), 137–38.

National and International Politics in the Middle East: Essays in Honour of Elie Kedourie, ed. by Edward Ingram; in Choice, May, 1987, 521.

Fouad Ajami, The Arab Predicament, Arab Political Thought and Practice since 1967; and Israel Gershoni, The Emergence of Pan-Arabism in Egypt; in The Muslim World, 77 (1987), 63–65.

J. Budzisewski, The Resurrection of Nature: Political Theory and the Human Character; in Choice, February, 1987, 527.

Carl Schmitt, Political Theology: Four Chapters on the Concept of Sovereignty; in Choice, September 1986, 729.

Virginia L. Muller, The Idea of Perfectibility; in Choice, June 1986, 550–51.

Robert E. Goodin, Protecting the Vulnerable: A Reanalysis of Our Social Responsibilities; in Choice, March 1986, 488.

Ann Hartle, The Modern Self in Rousseau's Confessions: A Reply to St. Augustine; in Interpretation, 13 (1985), 429–32.

Don Herzog, Without Foundations: Justifications in Political Theory; in Choice, July-August 1985, 592.

George Beam and Dick Simpson, Political Action: The Key to Understanding Politics; in Choice, May 1985, 595.

Ann K.S. Lambton, State and Government in Medieval Islam: An Introduction to the Study of Islamic Political Theory: The Jurists; in Speculum, 60/2 (April,1985), 425–27.

The Muntakhab .Siwān al-.Hikmah of Abū Sulaimān al-Sijistānī, ed. by D.M. Dunlop; in The Muslim World, 74(1984), 225–26.

Hugh Kennedy, The Early Abbasid Caliphate: A Political History, and Jacob Lassner, The Shaping of Abbasid Rule; in The Middle East Journal, 38 (1984), 763–65.

Intellectual Life in the Arab East, ed. by Marwan R. Buheiry; and Paul Khoury, Une lecture de la pensée arabe actuelle and Tradition et modernité: matériaux pour servir à l'étude de la pensée arabe actuelle, I. Instruments d'enquête; in The Middle East Journal, 37 (1983), 696–97.

The Politics of Islamic Reassertion, ed. by Mohammed Ayoob, and Islam and Power, ed. by Alexander S. Cudsi and Ali E. Hillal Dessouki; in The American Political Science Review, 77 (1983), 484–485.

Farooq Hassan, The Concept of State and Law in Islam; in The Journal of Politics, 44 (1982), 1167.

Islamic Philosophical Theology, ed. by Parviz Morewedge; in The Review of Metaphysics, 35 (1981), 404–05.

William Lane Craig, The Kalam Cosmological Argument; in The Review of Metaphysics, 35 (1981), 376–7.

Jean-Jacques Rousseau, Emile, trans. Allan Bloom; in The Review of Metaphysics, 34 (1981), 804–05.

Arab Islamic Bibliography, ed. by Grimwood-Jones, Hopwood, Pearson, et al; in Journal Asiatique, 268 (1980), 179–80.

Angelika Neuwirth 'Abd al-Latīf al-Baghdadī's Bearbeitung von Buch Lambda der aristotelischen Metaphysik; in Journal Asiatique, 268 (1980), 198–99.

Ibn al-Razzāz al-Jazarī, The Book of Knowledge of Ingenious Mechanical Devices, trans. Donald R. Hill; in Journal Asiatique, 268 (1980), 197–98.

Edward W. Said, Orientalism and Bryan S. Turner Marx and the End of Orientalism; in The American Political Science Review, 74 (1980), 174-76.

Walter Ullmann, Law and Politics in the Middle Ages; in The American Political Science Review, 72 (1978), 239–40.

Alfred Ivry, al-Kindī's Metaphysics; in The Middle East Journal, 32 (1978), 364–66.

Fathallah Oualalou, La Pensée Socio-Economique d'El-Makrizī; in The Middle East Journal, 32 (1978), 366–67.

Ismail M. Dahiyat, Avicenna's Commentary on the Poetics of Aristotle; in The Middle East Journal, 30 (l976), 576–77.

Ralph Lerner, trans., Averroes on Plato's Republic; in The Middle East Journal, 30 (1976), 575–76.

Carla L. Klausner, The Seljuk Vezirate; in The Middle East Journal, 30 (1976), 571–72.

François Hotman, Francogallia; in The American Political Science Review, 70 (1976), 613–14.

Robert L. Hoffman, Revolutionary Justice and P.J. Proudhon, General Idea of the Revolution in the 19th Century; in The American Political Science Review, 68 (1974), 1737–38.

Medieval Political Philosophy, edited by Ralph Lerner and Muhsin Mahdi; in The American Political Science Review, 68 (1974), 765–66.

Ibn Tufayl, Hayy Ibn Yaqzān, translated by Lenn Evan Goodman; in The Middle East Journal, 28 (1974), 82–84.

E. A. Belyaev, Arabs, Islam, and the Arab Caliphate in the Early Middle Ages; in Mid- East, 11 (1970), 43–45.

L. J. Crocker, Rousseau's Social Contract: An Interpretative Essay; in The American Political Science Review, 63 (1969), 941–42.

W. Montgomery Watt, What is Islam? in The Middle East Journal, 23 (1969), 40–41.

H. Stuart Hughes, Consciousness and Society; in Michigan State News, 1959.

Walter Adams and John A. Garraty, Is the World Our Campus? in Le Coq Gaulois, 1959.

Walter Adams and John A. Garraty, From Main Street to the Left Bank; in Le Coq Gaulois, 1959.

Festschrift – List of Contributors

Carmela Baffioni, Senior Research Fellow, Institute of Ismaili Studies, London

Joshua Bandoch, PhD in political science from the University of Notre Dame

David B. Burrell, C.S.C., Hesburgh Professor Emeritus of Philosophy and Theology, University of Notre Dame

Christopher A. Colmo, Professor Emeritus of Political Science at Dominican University, River Forest, Illinois

David M. DiPasquale, Assistant Professor of the Practice, Department of Political Science and Islamic Civilization & Societies Program, Boston College, Massachusetts

Steven D. Ealy, Senior Fellow, Liberty Fund, Inc., Carmel, Indiana

Waseem El-Rayes, Associate Professor of Political Theory, Michigan State University, East Lansing, Michigan

Miriam Galston, Associate Professor of Law at the George Washington University, Washington, DC

Jürgen Gebhardt, Professor Emeritus, Universität Erlangen - Nürnberg, presently member of the board of directors, Bavarian-American Academy, Munich, Germany

Steven Harvey, Professor Emeritus in Medieval Islamic and Jewish Philosophy, Bar-Ilan University, Israel

Gary M. Kelly, Lecturer, Hetta Institute for International Development

Terence J. Kleven, Professor of Religious Studies, Central College, Pella, Iowa

Gregory A. McBrayer, Assistant Professor of Political Science, Ashland University, Ohio

Janet Holl Madigan, Lecturer in Politics at Princeton University and Humanities Teacher at The Wilberforce School, Princeton New Jersey

Melissa Matthes, PhD, MDiv, full professor, humanities department, United States Coast Guard Academy, New London, CT

Rene M. Paddags, Associate Professor of Political Science, Ashland University, Ohio

Joshua Parens, Dean of the Braniff Graduate School of Liberal Arts and Professor of Philosophy and Politics at the University of Dallas

John R. Pottenger, Professor of Political Science at the University of Alabama in Huntsville

Monica Scotti, Independent Researcher, PhD from the Università degli Studi di Napoli "L'Orientale", Italy

Shawn Welnak, Associate Professor of Philosophy at Long Island University, New York